W9-CKH-754

Complete Guide to

BUILDING
LOG HOMES

Complete Guide to

BUILDING
LOG HOMES

By
Monte Burch

Drawings by
Richard J. Meyer and Lloyd P. Birmingham

Published by
POPULAR SCIENCE/OUTDOOR LIFE BOOKS, New York

Copyright 1984 by Monte Burch

Published by

Popular Science Books
Grolier Book Clubs Inc.
Sherman Turnpike
Danbury, CT 06816

Book design by Pam Forde Graphics

Brief quotations may be used in critical articles and re-
views. For any other reproduction of the book, however,
including electronic, mechanical, photocopying, record-
ing, or other means, written permission must be obtained
from the publisher.

ISBN: 0–943822–27–0

Library of Congress Cataloging in Publication Data

Burch, Monte.
    Complete guide to building log homes.

    Includes index.
    1. Log cabins—Design and construction.   I. Meyer,
Richard J. (Richard Joseph), 1927–   . II. Birming-
ham, Lloyd.   III. Title.
TH4840.B87   1984   694   84-42694

Manufactured in the United States of America

Fourth Printing, 1989

CONTENTS

(Continued)

(Continued)

PREFACE

Of the many books I've written, this one has been the most fun. I've had a great time meeting and talking with log home builders—individualistic people—gathering what I could from their experiences and pulling all this together in a way I hope will be helpful to anyone who'd like to build a log home.

My research for this project started years ago in my home state of Missouri. During deer and turkey hunting trips in the highlands of the Ozarks, I discovered the remains of many old log cabins. I spent a lot of time poking through the old homes and admiring the craftsmanship. At those times, I felt a sense of loss that mingled with cold wind blowing through the cracks of the old homes. I could almost hear the laughter of the generations of hill people who lived in these secure and secretive hollows.

From those beginnings, my research led me across the country. And I found the log building boom to be everywhere—from Mexico to Maine.

The popularity of log home building stems, too, from the many kit log homes for sale and their practical advantages over building a home from dimensioned lumber.

A project of this size depends on a lot of people. I can't begin to thank all the log home builders, the kit log home manufacturers, and

tool manufacturers who have supplied me with photos, drawings, log home building information, and products. Many of them are listed in the Appendix and will respond to reader inquiries. In addition, I'd like to thank the following companies for their help in producing this book: Armstrong World Industries, Inc.; Beaird-Poulan Co.; Brookstone Co.; Caterpillar Tractor; Collins Axe; Conover Woodcraft Specialties, Inc.; Dow Chemical U.S.A.; Dremel Division of Emerson Electric; Genova Inc.; Granberg Industries, Inc.; Deere and Co.; Echo Inc.; Engineering Products Co.; Homelite Division of Textron; Global Safety Products; La Font Corp.; McCulloch Corp.; Michigan Knife Co.; Oregon Saw Chain; Owens-Corning Fiberglas Corp.; Partner America; Rockwell International; Sears and Roebuck Co.; Snow and Neally Co.; Sotz Corp.; Stihl Inc.; Taos Equipment Manufacturers; Thern Inc.; United States Gypsum Co.

I'd also like to thank log home building experts Dick McAfee of Idaho, Doug Hall and Lane Johnson of Missouri, and Pat Wolfe of Canada for their important contributions.

And a final thanks to my wife Joan, who helps with the research, does the typing, keeps up with the mail, and brings order to my chaos.

Monte Burch

The round-log style (below left) with saddle notch and chinking was widely used, as seen from these old, weathered logs. Chinkless scribed-log construction (below right) has always been a popular style in the North. (Photo, below right, courtesy Pat Wolfe Log Building Courses.)

INTRODUCTION

IS LOG BUILDING FOR YOU?

The log home— a personal statement

A log home building boom has swept across North America. As many as 70,000 Americans build log homes annually. Much of this boom can be attributed to the skyrocketing sales of precut log home kits. Sales of kit log homes have been increasing every year, contrasting sharply with periodic drops in total housing construction. For many, the log home, a venerable symbol of frontier North America, has become a popular means of meeting today's housing requirements.

There are several reasons for the rising popularity of log homes. One of the most important is that a log home can be tailored to fit the owner's needs and resources. It can range from a simple one-room cabin in the wilderness to an elegant multistory mansion in suburbia.

Many of the first American homes were made of logs, including the lodges of the Indians and the log homes of the settlers and trappers. They were energy efficient—warm in winter and cool in summer. Of course, most of them were crude structures, but they remained popular even as the young nation expanded westward. Frontier log cabins dotted the landscape all along the way. Many of these cabins were inventions of necessity, not choice. As the owner's economic status rose, he'd often leave the cabin to some less fortunate family and move into a "real" house in town.

Humble beginnings play a part in the lore, however. Abe Lincoln made the most of his origins in a log cabin. To many folks today, the term "log cabin" brings to mind the image of young Abe Lincoln, his spindly figure huddled inside a primitive log structure, ciphering by the flickering firelight, bundled in rough wool against the chill wind infiltrating the loose, crumbly chinking between the logs.

Styles in log construction vary, depending on the region. Square, hand-hewn logs were often used in much of the South and eastern highlands. (Photo courtesy State Historical Society of Missouri.)

Many who build log homes immerse themselves in the pioneer spirit, as seen here in trappings of earlier times.

This 3,000-square-foot kit log home with a three-car garage fits well in a suburban setting.

The crude structures of Lincoln's day are a thing of the past. If Lincoln, Daniel Boone, and any of the other log cabin folk heroes of a century ago were to return today, they would find structures far removed from those they lived in. They would find log homes, many with full luxury accessories, springing up in the newest and nicest subdivisions, and in urban as well as rural areas. They'd also find that some of today's log homes, which offer the appealing low cost and energy efficiency of frontier homes, are becoming symbols of independence, success, and self-sufficiency rather than poverty.

Today's log homes have a traditional appeal which, coupled with contemporary design, allows them to fit with almost any lifestyle and geographic location. There are several important differences between log homes and conventional homes of dimensioned lumber, and in most instances log construction has the advantage.

Cost

Cost is a prime consideration to anyone considering purchasing or building a home. High mortgage rates, rising building costs, and increasing energy shortages are modern hurdles to anyone wishing to build his own home. A log home is the answer for many. Many do-

it-yourself log home builders have constructed extremely well-crafted and contemporary-looking structures using logs and stones from the builder's own property. The materials cost for some homes can be as low as $1,000. The home builder who is willing to trade time and arduous labor for the high cost of purchased materials can indeed build something for next to nothing.

At the other end of the log-home market lies the purchased, contractor-constructed log home. The price of such a home, even after adding the cost of construction, is usually less than that of a conventional home. And buyers who have the time and skill to do some of the work themselves, can save appreciably more. Depending on how much work you do, you can save from 30 to 50 percent of the construction cost by building your own log home.

There is another advantage to precut kit homes, at least those manufactured by companies with strong engineering and design support: There is almost no waste of building materials. You save because you pay only for what you need. And as the log wall goes up, what you really see is the frame, exterior and interior siding, and insulation going into place all at once.

The return on your investment in a log home is quite good, too. Log homes have been known to double in value in 10 years.

Using log home kits, which consist of precut, pre-numbered pieces, almost anyone can build even an elegant spacious house like this that will look good in any neighborhood. (Photo Real Log Homes, Inc.)

IS LOG BUILDING FOR YOU?

Energy efficiency

Wood is one of nature's best insulators. It is considered four times better insulation than concrete block, six times better than brick, and 15 times better than stone. Wood absorbs warm air from inside the home and releases it slowly at night as the temperature drops. The massive walls of a log structure are also natural passive solar storage systems. If a home is sited properly, that is, with deciduous trees providing shade in summer and allowing full sun in the winter, the home gains energy efficiency.

In addition to the energy savings, log homes help conserve natural resources as well. The United States has 75 percent more forested land than when Columbus discovered America. That's because today's forestry harvesting methods restore forests at a somewhat faster rate than they are cut. In addition, the use of log rather than conventional construction helps conserve wood. That is, it takes considerably less timber to construct a log home than it does a conventional house because there is no waste from having to mill the logs. In addition, smaller, faster-growth trees can be used for log construction, so there is a faster turnover of replenishable resources. In fact, many of the logs used for log construction are the "thinning" trees normally removed to allow better-grade trees to grow to saw-log size. Energy for milling the logs into lumber is saved too.

Many modern kit models take full advantage of the heat-retaining mass of logs and passive solar engineering. (Photos courtesy Justus Log Homes, Inc.)

INTRODUCTION

Maintenance

Because of the durability of logs, the need to paint, if you wish, can be eliminated. It's one of the big advantages in log construction. All of us, from retirees to young families on the go, want to enjoy leisure pursuits without being slaves to our homes. Thus, the ease of maintenance of a log home translates to additional long-term savings.

Trading sweat for dollars

Because of the spiraling cost of home ownership, increasing numbers of people have turned to various do-it-yourself approaches. Log homes are a means to build "sweat equity", which can reduce the mortgage requirement, making it easier to get the money.

Of course, the skills you need depend on how much of the construction you do yourself. One advantage of log homes is that many of the traditional carpentry skills are not needed. This is particularly so for precut log homes. Many of them require nothing more than stacking numbered logs in place following a step-by-step diagram. Log building is much more forgiving than building with dimensioned lumber. With patience and attention to detail, even the beginning log builder can create a solid, sound, and economical home, even if it isn't perfectly crafted. In fact, the files of most precut home manufacturers are full of endorsements from do-it-yourselfers who range from grandmothers to young musicians, all without any previous building experience.

Even a built-from-scratch log home can be erected quickly and easily with today's tools. Hand felling, hauling logs out of the woods with a team of horses, and hewing logs with a broadax are labor-intensive work. Lots of work is needed to acquire a big enough pile of logs for a house. Today's chain saws and power tools make logging and log building much faster, safer, and easier than in early times. In addition, such tools as portable sawmills, radial-arm saws, and planers make finish construction fast, easy, and accurate for almost anyone with basic shop skills.

There are a number of ways of acquiring a log home. One is to build it step by step yourself, hand-hewing. (Photo courtesy Pat Wolfe Log Building Courses.)

If you are interested in log building but fear you don't have the skills you need, you can attend any of several log building schools in the U.S. and Canada (listed in Chapter 27). These schools allow hands-on experience and a dress rehearsal in log home building that can be invaluable. With the blisters to prove your experience you'll be ready to tackle the seemingly monstrous task of log building knowing that it's mostly a series of small steps resulting in a giant achievement.

Log styles

Probably the first choice you have to make is the kind of log you want for your home. Should the logs be round, hewn, or sawn? Round logs are the quickest and easiest to build with, but they don't permit as much precision in construction as squared logs. Logs hewn in the traditional manner take a great deal of time, but they can be milled on a portable or one-man sawmill very quickly, and this method is fast growing in popularity. If you purchase logs rather than fell your own, your choice will

For the hesitant, a course at a log home building school can give hands-on experience, while you build friendships, as well. (Photo courtesy Minnesota Trailbound School of Log Building.)

be restricted to what is available. However, because of the growing popularity of log building, mills around the country are providing a tremendous variety of wall logs. Some home builders purchase logs, then truck them to a mill for sizing and shaping—and still spend a lot less than they'd have to for a home of dimensioned lumber.

Kit homes

Many do-it-yourself log houses are made from precut log kits. The advantages are obvious. Instead of heading into the woods to cut down trees that seem to be the right size and shape, then hauling them out and cutting them to shape, the kit builder has his logs delivered to the site, arriving coded for ease of construction. In recent years, more than 30,000 log home units have been sold each year by over a 100 different firms providing a range of options for potential buyers—from raw logs to ready-to-move-into structures. The log kit home industry continues to boom.

A better life

Increasingly, people are interested in health and natural living. The feeling of independence that comes from building a long-lasting, durable home with your own hands is a welcome change from the wasteful throw-away mentality that seems almost mandated by an industrial society. The past decade has seen many people rush from the cities into the countryside pursuing this better life.

Some of these new rural folks were quickly disillusioned because of the lack of immediate rewards. The hardships of homesteading have sent many back to the urban life, though some surely returned with an enlightened sense of life's basics. Many of these new homesteaders attempted to escape the technology of the cities by substituting the isolation of the rural areas, and, possibly, many abandoned their hope too quickly. We are on the brink of a realistic combination of technologies that can allow rural inhabitants a quality life. Granted, the isolation and independence of country life are important, but very few people truly want to do without indoor plumbing as they scratch sustenance from worn-out, rock-strewn hills.

Technology may give everyone a chance for a better quality life no matter where they live. The advent of computers is probably the best example. Today many people work at home, using a computer for compilation, manipulating, and transmission of data to a company office. By the same token, the advanced technology applied to wood stoves, fireplaces, and solar heating has made these alternate energy sources much more realistic for the future. The phenomenon of a growing number of people who are enamored with the thought of building a home with logs is an example of how combining new technologies with long lasting values can help to reshape American society in terms of its economics and its values.

The information in this book comes from my own experience and the experience of the many log home builders I have interviewed over the past few years. These range from a guide and outfitter in the Idaho wilderness to friends living in the suburbs of Kansas City, as well as the engineers and builders of precut log homes. Aspiring to create your own home is a worthy dream, and I hope the information here helps you realize it.

SAVANNAH

"Picture this beauty on your chos

FIRST FLOOR—1259 SQ. FT.
FOYER: 10'-4" x 4'-6"
LIVING ROOM: 12'-4" x 16'-0"
FAMILY ROOM: 17'-9" x 18'-6"
ENTRY: 4'-0" x 7'-6"
BREAKFAST: 8'-6" x 11'-3"
KITCHEN: 10'-6" x 11'-9"

Sequoia A

Practical . . . Affordable . . . Livable . . . The **SEQUOIA A** combines comfortable family living space with an elegant passive Solar Design. An efficient wood burning system will contribute greatly towards your energy independence.

OVERALL DIMENSIONS: 24'4" x 32'8"

SQUARE FOOTAGE: 1452

FIRST FLOOR   SEQUOIA A
Square Footage 776

SECOND FLOOR   SEQUOIA A
Square Footage 676

PLANNING AND PRELIMINARIES

cascade

CUMBERLAND

"ed log stairway to the loft—a popular option"

FIRST FLOOR—1004 SQ. FT.
COUNTRY LIVING/DINING: 17'-0" x 25'-0"
COUNTRY KITCHEN: 15'-0" x 13'-6"
BATH: 9'-0" x 8'-0"
MASTER BEDROOM: 11'-6" x 14'-0"

LOFT—340 SQ. FT.

ATTIC

LOFT AREA

CATHEDRAL CEILING
OPEN TO LIVING BELOW

ousness of this log
nhanced by a
ceiling and three
ss doors in the
n and dining area.
t a rustic look that
d free—this is the
u.

Chapter 1 **PLANNING**

Dream homes

Imagine spending a winter night curled up on a bear rug in front of a big stone fireplace, surrounded by the natural beauty of wood logs. Add to this the warm satisfaction of knowing that you built the whole house yourself.

Such dreams are not likely to become reality without a lot of hard work, however. A home is probably the most expensive and important investment a family will make. Careful thought and planning are important elements in owning any home, if only to safeguard your family's financial and physical safety. Poor planning may have a detrimental effect on their lives, at best.

After deciding you want to build a log home, the next questions are: What kind, how big? (Photo courtesy Rocky Mountain Log Homes.)

If you're considering log construction, the first question should be: What kind of home do you want? There are endless varieties of floor plans, exterior designs, and interior finishes. For instance, you may want to stick with traditional styling, or you may want an imaginative, modern beam-and-glass design. There's something for everyone in log homes.

Regardless of whether you intend to purchase a precut home or build your own from scratch, start by gathering catalogs and brochures from precut home manufacturers as well as catalogs from distributors of log house plans (see the Appendix for addresses). There

Today's log homes are of endless varieties of shapes and sizes ranging from traditional to ultramodern. (Photo courtesy New England Log Homes, Inc.)

Some log homes are a blend of log and conventional materials that can suit nearly everyone. (Photo courtesy Alta Industries Ltd.)

PART 1. PLANNING AND PRELIMINARIES

are well over a hundred log home manufacturers and many of them offer as many as 50 different floor plans and models to choose from. Cull the most appealing designs, trying to narrow the choices to a manageable number.

It then becomes a matter of sizing up your specific housing needs. This is where you have to be tough on yourself. You should define—on paper—all your family's housing needs and desires. Include the number of bedrooms, the location of baths, the kinds of wood stoves and fireplaces, the need for storage space—anything you think could be significant.

Many conventional home plans can easily be adapted to log home construction, so you might profitably look over a number of conventional house plans as well. Remember, though, plumbing and electrical runs are more easily installed in interior partition walls (not those made of logs), creating a service core in the center of the house.

Ease of heating, too, should be a prime consideration. For instance, a massive fireplace constructed on the inside of a home releases more of the heat it generates to the interior of the home than it would if built on an outside wall.

Outside limitations

On your planning sheet, list any limitations that might have an effect on your home selection. Are there special zoning or building restrictions on building height? Is there a restriction on the maximum dimensions of the home because of lot size, square footage, or lot topography?

Now look over the plans you've culled and eliminate any that don't fit your requirements. Look over the remaining plans and imagine how you would live in each house. Mentally walk through the rooms. In planning your home, you have to consider traffic patterns, family activities, life style, and the placement of furniture. Try to envision the various uses of the house—including entertainment, relaxation, and work.

You can buy a complete turn-key home like this giant from a kit log home builder.

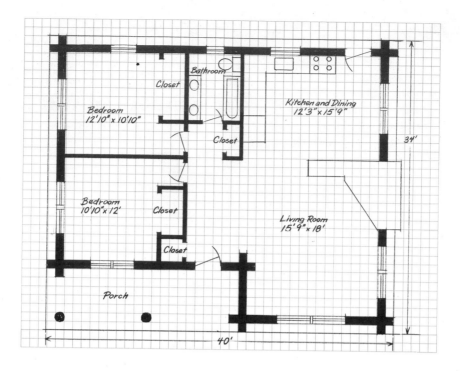

One of the first steps in planning is to make up a floor plan of the house you intend to build.

If you're simply building a one-room log home in the woods, you probably won't need an exhaustive set of plans. However, anything more ambitious probably requires scaled house plans. If you're building a precut kit, these are usually part of the package. If you're building from scratch, rough house plans, even if you must draw them yourself, can be an invaluable aid. You can draw reasonably precise plans using graph paper and a scale rule.

House tour

Start your imaginary house tour through the front door. It should have a foyer or entrance hall for two reasons: It's a place to greet guests, but, just as important, it baffles the cold wind and drafts that come in an opened door. A small closet located near the front door can be handy, and access to a small powder room can be a well-appreciated luxury.

From the main entrance, you should have direct access to the three principal areas of the house—those for sleeping, living, and working. A good example of this is a hallway that leads off to the patio, living room, and kitchen and another that leads to the bedrooms. Whenever possible, the house design should be such that you don't have to walk through a main room to get to another, needlessly concentrating traffic in one particular area.

Study each traffic pattern and the use zones of the house carefully. For instance, the kitchen should connect directly to the dining room, and perhaps a utility room, or basement steps, or to other storage or work areas. You might wish to have an enclosed garage off the kitchen to make it easy access to transfer groceries from the car into the kitchen. Also check to see if the house suits the size of your family. For instance, if there is a breakfast nook, is there room for your entire family to be comfortably seated?

If you want to study floor plans, traffic patterns, and furniture placement in more detail, make an enlarged floor plan using a ¼-inch-to-the-foot scale. Then cut out furniture pieces to scale and arrange them on the floor plan. You can quickly spot potentially troublesome traffic patterns or places where you might want an additional window, or where you wish to close off a wall. You might see the best spot to place that family heirloom too.

16

You can choose among hundreds of elevation sketches and floor plans available from kit manufacturers.

Consider the bedrooms carefully. Depending on the family and life style, you may wish to have the master bedroom near the kids, or if you're older and entertain overnight guests, you might want the bedrooms to be more distant. There should, however, be at least one closet per person in each bedroom or a double closet (or walk-in) for each couple. Bathrooms should be conveniently near the bedrooms. It's best to have separate bathrooms near the bedrooms. You should have bathrooms convenient to other areas of the house as well.

This is the enjoyable, dreaming stage when almost any wish can be included. Eventually, however, you'll have to weed out the things that are impractical and settle on the style and floor plan that best suits your needs.

Estimating precut home construction costs

The following estimating guidelines from Justus Homes are adapted with permission:

Because costs vary from city to city and lot to lot, and because owners do different amounts of work themselves, it's difficult to estimate exactly what your costs will be at the earliest stage. But a good rule of thumb—if you don't do much work yourself—is to double a log home package price. That is, a package that costs $40,000 may cost an additional $40,000 to build and finish to a move-in (turnkey) state. Add to that anywhere from $400 to $3,000 for shipping costs, depending on the size of your house package and how far away you are from the manufacturer. Remember, the "doubling" rule of thumb is only a *rough* guideline.

Following is some more information to help you understand the cost of each component of construction, this will help you deal better with a general (or sub) contractor and figure out where you can save money. These estimates are based on an average 1,600 square-foot log home package built on an easily accessible lot.

Excavation. A bulldozer can cost over $40 an hour. If your home will be built over a crawl space, it might take about six hours to excavate and cost over $250. If you build your home over a basement, the bulldozer work might require 12 hours and cost over $500.

Foundation. This work is critical and should probably be done by a professional. The foundation work for a crawl space can cost from $6 to $8 per lineal foot, or between $1,050 and $1,400 total. The foundation for a basement should cost between $20 and $24 per lineal foot, or from $3,500 to $4,200 total.

A post-and-pier foundation probably will cost somewhat less—and block construction probably a little more—than concrete.

Slab floors. Slab floors for basements and garages can cost between $1.50 and $2.00 per square foot of slab area. With a basement, costs may range from $1,350 to $1,800.

Septic tanks. A septic tank can cost between $1000 or more to buy and have installed.

Rough construction. Rough construction usually includes the basics—installing the floor girders and posts, the joists, the

Some kit manufacturers offer complete sets of blueprints like these.

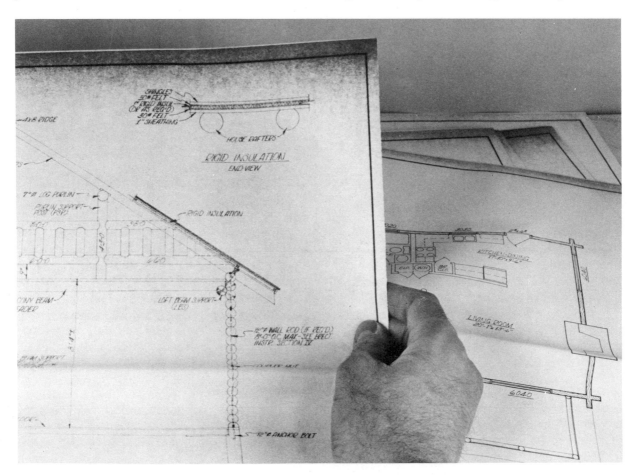

18

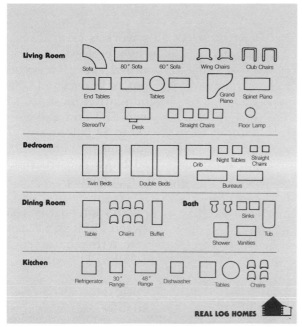

An aid to planning, kits may include scale furniture templates that can be used to plan rooms that will accommodate anticipated traffic patterns. Many such templates are provided in planning kits from manufacturers. (Courtesy Real Log Homes, Inc.)

subfloor, the solid cedar log walls, any interior stud walls, the loft beams and decking, the roof beams and decking, the windows and doors, bare stairs, and the fascia and trim boards.

You can get an idea of what it should cost to have a contractor do rough construction by multiplying the square footage of your house by $3.50 to $5.25. Based on 1,600 square feet, this would equal $5,600 to $8,400, depending on the labor rates in your area and the experience of the workers. Rough construction is one job many owners decide to do themselves.

Finish construction. The cost of installing stair and loft railings, window and door trim molding, and all the other finish construction can be figured at the rate of $1.75 to $2.25 per square foot. Based on a 1,600 square foot package, this phase would cost between $2,800 and $3,600.

Plumbing. One way to estimate plumbing costs is to add up the number of plumbing fixtures (showers, tubs, water heaters, and sinks) you plan to have and multiply by $225 and $275. Plumbing six fixtures would cost between $1,350 and $1,650.

If you have a basement, you may want to add another two fixtures to your plumbing estimate, which would raise it to between $1,800 and $2,200. Custom fixtures may increase these figures.

Electrical. Electrical costs may range from $1.00 to $1.25 per square foot. That's $1,600 to $2,000 to wire the power panel, receptacles, and outlets.

Heating. Although these costs vary greatly from climate to climate, space heating and cooling also can be figured at $1.00 to $1.25 per square foot—for a $1,600 to $2,000 total. Add $1,000 to $3,000 or more for solar heating systems (net cost after tax credits).

Finish roofing. This includes installation of rigid foam insulation and finish roofing material. Roofing materials are measured in 10-by-10 foot units called "squares."

The installation of insulation and nailing strips can cost from $10 to $12 per square. Add to this the $25 to $35 per square it can cost to have the finish roof and flashing installed by a roofer.

Estimate the total by multiplying $35 to $47 per square foot by the 18 squares needed to cover a typical 1,600 square foot home. (These costs are based on a composition shingle roof. Installation of a cedar-shake roof will cost more for materials and labor.)

Cabinets. Estimate the cost of cabinets and counter tops by measuring the lineal feet of the upper and lower kitchen cabinet areas, plus any cabinetry planned for the bathroom. Then multiply by $40 to $50. For example, 55 feet of cabinetry might cost between $2,200 and $2,750. Custom cabinets, islands or special cabinet work would be extra.

Floor coverings. A 1,600-square-foot package requires about 178 yards of floor covering. Multiply this by $18 to $22. The total is $3,200 to $3,916.

Staining and painting. Multiply the square footage of your house by $.80 to $1.00 for an idea of the sanding, filling, staining and painting costs. In our 1,600-square-foot package, this would be between $1,280 and $1,600.

The great bulk of this cost is for labor. So, as with so many other areas of construction, you can do it yourself and save.

Miscellaneous. Allow at least another $1,600 to cover building permits, power hook-ups, surveys, insurance, equipment and tool rentals, and other miscellaneous expenses that can mount up during construction.

Options. Costs for decks, garages, skylights, hot tubs, solar water heating, fireplaces and other "extras" vary from region to region. Consult your dealer to figure the cost of options.

What you can save. Adding up all the estimates, you get a construction cost that could range from $25,000 to $35,000 (or from 63 percent to 87 percent of the package price) for a home built on a crawl space foundation, and construction costs from $34,000 to $40,000 (or 85 percent to 100 percent of the package price) for a home constructed over a full basement.

The main point: You could save between $15,000 and $24,000 by doing much of the work yourself—as the following cost summary shows:

Cost/Savings Summary
Home package: $40,000.
Freight: Low, $400; high, $3,000.
Contractor overhead and profit (10 to 20 percent on materials, labor and subcontracts he administers): Low, $2,500; high, $8,000.

Owner/builder potential savings:
Here are some of the savings possible if you do most of the work yourself. All figures are for labor only, and do not include any amount you may be able to save by purchasing materials yourself:

	Low	High
Contractor overhead	2,500	8,000
Foundation	425	500
Rough const.	5,600	6,500
Finish const.	2,800	3,500
Plumbing labor	675	850
Electrical labor	950	1,100
Installing finish roofing	550	750
Installing cabinets	150	200
Floor covering	350	400
Sand/fill/stain/paint	1,000	1,200
Total	$15,000	$24,000

Subcontracts:	Crawl Space		Basement	
	Low	High	Low	High
Excavation	210	270	420	540
Foundation	1,050	1,400	3,500	4,200
Slab floors	750	1,000	1,350	1,800
Septic tank	900	1,100	900	1,100
Rough const.	5,600	8,400	5,600	8,400
Finish const.	2,800	3,600	2,800	3,600
Plumbing	1,350	1,650	1,800	2,200
Electrical	1,600	2,000	1,600	2,000
Heating	1,600	5,000	1,600	5,000
Roofing	630	850	630	850
Cabinets	2,200	2,750	2,200	2,750
Floor covering	3,200	3,916	3,200	3,916
Stain/paint	1,280	1,600	1,280	1,600
Miscellaneous	1,600	1,600	1,600	1,600
Total	$24,770	$35,146	$34,080	$39,556

Chapter 2 THE LAND

Where to build

Now that you've decided on the style and size of your home and how you're going to build it, the next problem is where to build it. You may already own property with a perfect building site, but most people aren't that lucky. Acquiring land and deciding on a site is an important aspect of building. You can't easily move a log home that's too close to or over a boundary line. Nor can you easily move a log home to improve its solar exposure.

Don't hurry this stage of the planning, there are many factors to be carefully weighed. What

may appear to be a perfect spot could turn out to be full of problems that can cause extra expense.

America's pioneers didn't have the number of problems that modern homesteaders have. Their chief considerations were proximity to water, access to temporary shelter during construction, and availability of logs and stone.

Today, there are more log homes built on suburban lots than in the wilderness, and this complicates siting. Naturally, the building of a log home on a suburban lot or in a small rural town will be governed by more restrictions than in the wilderness. But both have many of the same problems.

The choice of where to build is just as important as the log-home style and the actual construction. A home in the mountains can be terrific. (Photo courtesy Lincoln Logs, Ltd.)

Many of today's log homes are being constructed on suburban lots.

Before we go further, let's define wilderness and rural areas. Rural areas are those that are served by roads and some utilities, and include lakeside as well as hunting and fishing, ski, and other recreational areas. Wilderness means areas devoid of roads or utilities.

Depending on your life style and where you decide to locate, here are some of the more important considerations you face:

1. Finding and buying the land. Determining type of land and price.

2. Availability of timber.

3. Access to utilities.

4. Means of access to the site.

5. Availability of nearby jobs, services, neighbors, and fire and police protection.

6. Local taxes and cost of living.

7. Best siting for view, and the site grades.

8. Topography and ground cover.

9. Drainage.

10. Prevalent weather conditions.

11. Best siting for solar exposure.

12. Access to water.

13. Results of surface and subsurface soil tests.

14. Possible garden locations.

15. Natural hazards.

Choose the land carefully. Consider terrain, remoteness, tillable land—all that you feel is important. (Photo courtesy Air-Lock Log Company, Inc.)

22

16. Titles and deed, entry and mineral rights, riparian (river/lake) rights, necessary permits, and other legal matters.

17. Financing.

18. Site plan.

19. Construction checklist.

If you neglect any of these, you'll be asking for trouble. Don't just buy a piece of land and call in the bulldozer. Take the time to learn about the land. If possible, spend some time camping on it in all seasons. Learn how the frost and fog settle in valleys at night or where the prevailing wind brings cool breezes on a hot July afternoon.

There are several good ways of finding land. First decide upon the general area in which you wish to live. Must it be near good fishing? Skiing? Jobs? Schools? Hospitals? Whatever.

Start watching the real estate ads in the papers of those areas. You can also send for catalogs from the larger real estate companies such as United Farm or Strout. Take heart, because real estate is a booming business and properties are traded and sold every day. Not all land is tied up. Divorces, deaths, job changes, and many other factors are constantly freeing up good land.

Once you have decided to begin your search, go out and hunt in earnest. This can be a pleasant time, and a great way of enjoying the countryside on a weekend—often with realtors doing the driving.

Locating and buying land

If you're planning to locate your home on a city or resort lot, you'll be greatly limited by the lot size. However, if you're planning to build on rural or wilderness property, you'll have more choices for siting. By all means, purchase as much land as you can afford. Often, larger tracts of land can be purchased far more economically per acre than smaller tracts.

Land developers make money by purchasing large tracts and dividing them into smaller lots. Then they increase the price per lot to make a profit. Quite often the price is ten times the original purchase price per acre. You can do this, too, and so in some cases, raise enough money to pay off the land you want to keep.

However, this can be a risky investment unless you understand how to deal in land and are willing to hold the property until you get the desired price. Check with your lawyer. In some states there are laws governing land development or buying large parcels of land and selling it off in small lots or parcels. The law may require a formal development plan, complete surveys, soil tests, and public hearings on proposed dividing plans. On the other hand, even if you don't want to sell lots, just having the extra property can act as money in the bank should you run into financial difficulties. In depressed times, however, land may be hard to sell at a profit.

The scrub-oak timbered hills of the Ozarks, near my home, has become a hot retirement and homesteading area. Here you can pay thousands of dollars for just a small lot. But, nearby, a larger piece of rural property complete with a spring, pond, and even a rundown farmhouse can cost less than $500 an acre.

Another good reason for purchasing larger tracts: You can locate your home near the center of the property and isolate yourself from encroachment.

Even if you can't afford the cost of a larger tract there are ways of achieving the same result. The first and most popular way is to join with a group of friends or relatives to make the purchase. This trend started with communes a few years back and has been a popular means of buying in the Ozarks over the past few years. Each shareholder can then build his own home on the land. Any type of group purchase, however, must be carefully thought out with everything legally committed to paper, so there will be no problems should divorce, death, or disenchantment strike some of the members.

You could also purchase a small piece of property next to a National Forest or other large government land holding. This, in effect, puts thousands of acres in your backyard and can provide plenty of room to roam. Such government land might also offer fishing and hunting. But because the adjoining land is public, you may often be annoyed by trespassers traipsing through your land.

An alternative, especially for those in wilderness areas, is homesteading or a lease arrangement made with the government.

The land

Decide what kind of land that suits your needs and life style. There are many different kinds of land—from a suburban lot to a Maine wilderness lakeside retreat. Perhaps you want to do some homesteading, or simply get back to the simpler way of life. Would you be happy with the complete isolation that the wilderness brings? Do you plan to build your home of logs from your own property, logging them yourself, or do you plan to purchase the logs and have them hauled to the site? Or do you intend to build a kit-log home?

If you're planning a wilderness home, be sure to provide for temporary living accommodations for at least two seasons. That should allow you to properly build and finish a log home of medium size. You may be able to construct a small house in a shorter amount of time, but two seasons will allow you to do a better job on a medium-sized home.

If you plan to homestead and intend to keep a cow or two, chickens, horses, or other livestock, you should buy land that is already cleared. Although you can have a bulldozer clear scrub brush easily, the cost can be quite high. Not only will cleared land allow you to maintain healthy animals, it will also cut down on the work the animals cause you. In most parts of the country it takes at least a couple of acres per cow, although in the South, this may be reduced to an acre on good land with plenty of rainfall. In dry parts of the country you may need 20 acres or more for each cow. Normally, sheep require only about half as much land as cows. A horse requires about the same area as a cow. A pig or two and some chickens or a goat won't require much land. For animals, however, make sure there is plenty of natural water or that you can provide it.

Your own stand of timber

Perhaps you want to purchase woodland so you can build your home from the logs on your land. The forest can provide fuel for heat, too. Careful consideration should be given to the choice. The trees needed for suitable logs should be of the best species and size. If you're not experienced in forestry, contact a forester from your local conservation department to help you determine that you have enough of the proper trees. Chapter 4 on materials gives full information on types of wood, as well as sizes and numbers of trees needed.

If you plan to heat with wood you should estimate how many cords of wood you'll need per month. This may range from one to six cords depending on the severity of your winters, the size and airtightness of your home, and on the type woodburner you select. Normally, five to 10 acres of woodland—properly managed—can be enough to provide a perpetual supply of fuel wood.

Utilities

Depending on your life style, you have many options on power sources. Most of us would be delighted to tell the utility companies where they could put their high-priced bills. However, few of us would be willing to give up the amenities provided by electricity, gas, or oil.

Many folks like the privacy of the rural or timbered areas but don't want to be completely cut off from amenities. This means some sort of utilities. So make sure you know what services are available and where entrances are located on the property for telephone, cable TV, electricity, water, and sewage. You should also determine how much installation of utilities will cost. This can be costly, especially if the service must be brought a considerable distance from an existing utility line.

You should also have a written agreement on maintenance of the utility line area and how maintenance will be performed. For instance, if the right-of-way crosses your garden or new orchard, you wouldn't want it to be sprayed with herbicides to keep it clear, but this may be the way the service company conducts normal maintenance.

Access

If possible buy the land from a public road to your home. If you have isolated property and must go through someone else's property, be sure (consult a lawyer) that you have a right-of-way to your property. If you need to drive to work in winter, you may be dismayed to find your road under six feet of snow and that the county road crews ignore it. Prospective neighbors can answer questions about winter road conditions.

Some land buyers don't realize the value of a good road until winter and their vehicles won't make it up the icy, winding accent—or until they decide to dig a well and the well digger takes one look at the steep, winding road and declines the job. If you purchase a kit log home, you will have to provide access for a flat-bed trailer truck that delivers the kit. And if you plan to use ready-mix concrete, heavy concrete trucks require good roads too.

Clearing wilderness area and building a safe road, especially in mountainous country is an enormous job—and can be quite expensive. If not done properly, the road can be dangerous and might not last through the first spring. Floods often wash out improperly-constructed roadbeds. If there are bridges to build, the cost can go sky high. In building an access road, keep it as simple as possible. A winding path down to a ford over a beautiful creek may seem romantic the first month. It becomes less so when the creek turns into a raging torrent during storms, leaving you stranded.

Building any safe, long-lasting road is not a do-it-yourself job. This requires big equipment and years of experience. First the road has to be cleared and leveled with a bulldozer. Then it has to be topped with gravel that will keep it from rutting. Usually the cost of this type of road can run from $10 to $25 a lineal foot depending on how much clearing and grading is done before the topping is added. This doesn't include the cost of low-water bridges, intersections, or culverts across ditches.

Even if you only have to construct a driveway into your property, take heed of the terrain and weather. A steeply-sloping driveway can be almost impossible to negotiate in icy weather, even if it's only 50 feet long.

Advice from a good road engineer can be a great help. Quite often, roads are designed to follow the contours of the terrain, rather than run in a straight line to the nearest public road.

Access is extremely important. Although a small creek may seem glamorous when it's low and gurgling during the summer months, it may become a raging, dangerous torrent after storms and spring melt-off.

Of course, you may do as some homesteaders have done: Build the garage as close to the public road as possible. As one mountaineer says: "It's a great way of weeding out the unwanted visitors." Those that really want to visit don't mind the mile walk to his house.

Location of nearby jobs and services

If you are of job age, find out the kinds of jobs available in the immediate area.

The next step is to consider the services available. The number of services necessary may vary considerably. If you plan to live entirely off the land, you may feel you don't need any outside services. In that case, what you *do* need is plenty of stamina. Much of the cheap land left won't sustain a field mouse, let alone a young family. The back-to-the-land homesteading movement of a few years ago created a number of disillusioned people who had no idea how much hard work homesteading requires.

Schools. If you have school-age children or expect to, investigate the quality of local schooling as well as school proximity and transportation.

Medical services. If you have to drive 45 miles to a hospital, as is often the case in rural areas, you'd better be well versed in first aid. It's one thing to treat a minor wound, but a badly cut leg requiring stitches or a heart attack far from hospital help can be fatal. This should be of special concern during construction of a from-scratch log home, which requires hazardous tools and strenuous work.

Fire protection. Rural fire protection is almost entirely volunteer. Luckily, some of the best and most conscientious fire fighters are on small-town and rural fire-fighting squads. But check to see if your site is adequately protected and even consider serving as a volunteer.

Taxes and cost of living

In most rural areas, the property taxes are less than those of urban areas. But in some fast-developing resort areas, the taxes may be higher. The reason? The number of new arrivals and the higher cost of servicing those people. You should determine if there are to be new bond issues for community projects such as new schools, road upgrading, or sewage systems because these can mean substantial tax increases. Once you build, your taxes may skyrocket because you've increased the value of your property. This varies in different parts of the country. Land with high productive value, such as good crop land, will be taxed at a higher rate than will scrub timberland.

Note, too, the cost of living of the area. If you are retired with a fixed income and you're planning to move to a heavily-used tourist area, you may find that the cost of living is dishearteningly high.

Siting for the view

No one wants a view onto a hog lot. Your view is vital to enjoying your new home. Give special attention to the site and what your property has to offer. Perhaps you want to have an expansive view of the area behind you. If so, site your home as far forward on the lot as possible so you can enjoy the backyard vista. Not everyone is lucky enough to have a clear view of majestic snow-covered mountains or rolling surf, but often shifting a house site just a little can help take advantage of the best vista your land has to offer. Many landscape architects suggest that a suburban home be built as close to the street as possible to provide a spacious, enjoyable, and private backyard.

Topography and cover

Shade and tree cover can be as important in the winter as in summer. In summer, the shade trees can make your yard and home much cooler and more enjoyable. If at all possible, locate your home so you have deciduous trees on the west and east to shade the house. In the winter, when the leaves are gone the trees won't block the sun. By the same token, the southern exposure should be kept as open as possible. You probably won't be able to find the ideal site, so think about planting such trees. In addition to the location of trees, also consider how much clearing will have to be done and determine beforehand which trees you want to save.

If possible, keep as much older foliage as possible. It'll "soften" the appearance of the house. During excavation earth movers may mistakenly dig through roots and kill some trees. So advise operators to go very carefully.

Drainage and waste disposal

If you're building near an urban area, you'll probably tap into the existing municipal waste and drainage disposal system. In a rural area, however, you will have to provide for your own waste disposal. In most cases, this means a septic tank. To determine whether you'll have a problem with this kind of system, you should have a water percolation test made near the building site. A county agent can suggest a qualified person to perform the "perc" test.

Knowing about local weather conditions helps you choose the correct roof design. Areas that receive heavy snowfall tend to require more steeply pitched roofs than shown here. (Photo courtesy Alta Industries, Ltd.)

Septic tank systems need space. You'll need room for an underground tank *and* a gravel-lined drainage field. If your home is to be constructed on a rocky mountain top, you'll probably have to haul gravel in for the field; the cost can be high. You may also have problems burying the septic tank in this kind of soil.

Steep hillsides can cause storm drainage problems. It's a good idea to examine the building site carefully in several different seasons and weather conditions. In higher sites, you should know where water from rain and melting snow will go. If it runs in sheets over your site, you may have washout problems that can be potentially dangerous. Also potentially dangerous is a dry-wash creek bed that seems safe most of the year but becomes a raging torrent during storms.

If your site is in a lowland, check for history of floods. Even though such an event only hap-

pens every 25 or 30 years, if ever, it only takes one flood to make you sorry.

Weather

If you're moving from one part of the country to another, consider climate. The steady, dry wind of the plains can become maddening to someone not used to it, as can the dampness of the northwest. An example of a poor weather location is the north side of a mountain that is too shady and windy to be comfortable except in hot, arid regions. Find out (from a local airport if necessary) the direction of the prevailing wind in both summer and winter. Then situate your home to take advantage of cooling summer breezes and protection from cold winter winds. Check, too, for the amount of local rainfall. This can determine the kinds of greenery, flowers, or food garden you can grow.

The types of trees and cover surrounding your building site can be extremely important. Rows of evergreens can provide windbreaks, while large deciduous shade trees provide cooling shade in the summer. When deciduous leaves have fallen, the trees to the south allow the low winter sun to provide solar heat.

Siting for solar exposure

Today almost everyone is interested in using solar energy. When building a new home, you have a chance to take *full* advantage of this free energy.

Before deciding on an actual site plan, take the time to study the general path of the sun in summer and winter. (The path of the winter sun is much lower than that of the summer sun.) Take note of nearby obstacles such as trees, existing structures, or possible locations of future structures.

Many of today's log homes are of passive solar design, which requires careful site selection. (Photo courtesy New England Log Homes, Inc.)

In general, at least in northern climes, all windows in daytime living areas—such as kitchen, dining, and living rooms—should face south so they can admit sunshine. To receive less afternoon sun in bedrooms, use northerly or easterly exposures. An easterly bedroom will receive bright, early morning sun, whether you like bright, early mornings or not.

Porches should be located on south, east, and north sides. If the west side is shaded, however, you may want to put a porch on that side for shade in mornings. A garage on the west will serve as a sun shield in summer. On the north side of the house, a garage serves as a wind shield in the winter.

This huge old oak will provide the builder of this home plenty of summer shade and cover, while allowing winter sun to get through.

28

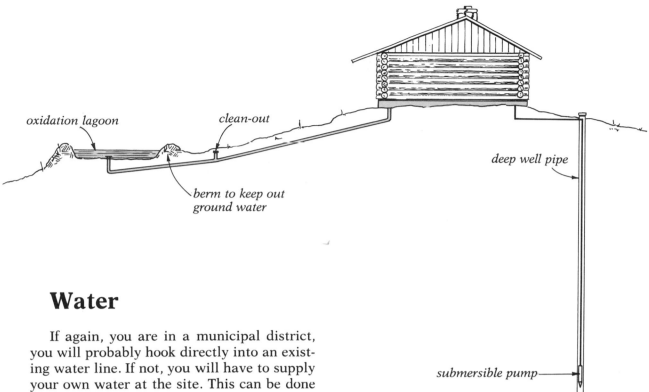

oxidation lagoon

clean-out

deep well pipe

berm to keep out ground water

submersible pump

Of prime importance are both the availability of water and proper sewage disposal. The water source may be a well or spring, and sewage may be disposed into a septic tank or an oxidation lagoon, depending on local conditions.

Water

If again, you are in a municipal district, you will probably hook directly into an existing water line. If not, you will have to supply your own water at the site. This can be done in many different ways.

If you are fortunate enough to have a spring uphill from your planned site, run the water downhill and into your home. If you can't locate the house below the spring, you can pump water from it short distances to the house. In almost all instances, the spring has to be closed or capped off to prevent surface impurities from entering it. More on this in Chapter 21, on plumbing.

In some areas, deeds may stipulate that water rights belong to someone else until you purchase them separately. A real estate agent may gloss over these details. Make sure you understand the fine print.

Have the water tested! You may think that a clear bubbling mountain spring has to be pure and clean. Though it looks pristine, a spring should be considered tainted until proven otherwise. Take a water sample into the nearest extension office. You should also consult with the extension office about the water table in your area. A spring that is running full tilt in May can often be dry in July and August, leaving you without water for a good portion of the year.

Most old farmsteads have wells, but most of these were designed to furnish far less water than is commonly needed today. Old farmsteads usually had a cistern that collected water from roof runoff. You can build your own cistern today. But be sure the soil will support the concrete shell of the cistern once it has been constructed.

You can, of course, get water from a lake or stream, but this requires a purifying unit. Lake and stream water should be a last resort because of the high cost of the purifying unit, chemicals, and electricity needed to power it.

Drilling your own well is another answer, but before you start such a complicated project, check with surrounding homeowners to see if they've had well-drilling problems. Check, too, with the extension office.

Find out how deep typical wells are in your area and the drilling cost per foot. Usually this runs about $10 per foot for drilling plus another $10 per foot for any casing pipe that must be used when the well run is not in solid stone. When you add the cost of piping and a pump, a drilled well can be one of the major costs of your building site.

Locating the well isn't a problem. Most drillers know the normal depth of the water table, then situate the well wherever it is convenient. You should insist that it be as close to the house as possible, to limit the amount of pipe and wiring necessary. But remember, the septic tank must be located at least 100 feet from your water supply and downhill from it.

Subsurface ground conditions

You should obtain a soil and geological report, which may be required in some areas. With it you'll know what size and type of home your ground will support. In earthquake zones, also obtain a seismic report.

The amount and kind of subsoil determine the design and size of foundations. This will be illustrated in Chapter 6. You need to know if the soil is made up of sand, clay, rock, or solid ledge, and how deep each layer is. Watch for any unusual soil conditions. For instance, if solid stone is just a couple of feet deep, you may not be able to dig a basement under your house without blasting—an expensive proposition. If the soil is extremely light and sandy, you may need special building foundations to support your home. On steep hillsides, clay can become a mud slide.

Dig several test holes around the site, through the topsoil and into the subsoil. Then use a thin steel bar to probe deeper to determine the condition of the ground. You should also look for signs of erosion in the area, something you will have to battle for a nice lawn or garden.

Possible garden locations

Although this may not seem important at first, most rural landowners eventually find a garden an ideal addition to their homestead.

It provides healthy food and exercise, and can cut your living costs as well.

A family food garden for four should be no smaller than 25 by 100 feet. French intensive gardening needs less space. The garden spot should be fairly flat, well drained, and on high ground. The site should receive full sun the entire day. Initially, the exact composition of the soil in the garden isn't too important. You can change and build this up as the years pass. Take a soil sample and send it to the county extension office so you'll know the fertilizer and minerals needed to produce the best garden soil.

Hazards

By all means, determine if there is danger from falling rock or danger of mudslides from above the site. Are there large trees with dead branches that could fall on the house? Or could the trees themselves fall? In coastal areas, will high winds or heavy tides be a hazard? In heavily forested areas, would you have plenty of escape routes from forest fires? Is your site subject to severe storms and lightning damage? Find out now, before you buy.

Legalities

Make sure you own all the rights to the land. If you own the land but not the mineral rights, someone could come in and dig up your home and property. And *know* your exact property lines. A survey is the only way you can be certain. A survey can be fairly expensive (depending on the size of the property), but it can save a great many headaches later should your neighbor or the municipality decide you've built too close to the property line. You should also make sure there are no liens (debts) on the property. And find out if there are any easements (rights of others to use the property).

Zoning. Almost all municipalities and counties require building permits before you can build a home. This is for your safety and the safety of the community, and it also assures the quality of the home. Thus there may be zoning and restrictive ordinances that must be met before and during construction. Talk to your real estate agent and your lawyer about the state, county, and municipal requirements. The community and/or development board may have specific laws ranging from trivial to monumental. For instance, the area may be zoned to forbid a home office or parking in the street. Zoning may forbid the parking of recreational vehicles, except if they are kept inside a garage. There may be materials and size limitations on the house you can build. There may also be regulations against tree cutting.

Permits. Most home buyers are unaware of the permits required before a new home is started. Construction drawings or working drawings are needed for a permit application. In cases where a septic system is to be used, the drain field and septic system must be designed for your specific lot and its unique conditions. (Local engineering and surveying firms specialize in design services for their region.)

Your plans will be checked for compliance with local building codes. Depending on locale, you could need permits and/or inspections for various stages of construction. These may include plumbing, foundation, electrical, and energy systems.

The plot plan shows your total site, including where your home and other improvements are to be situated. It also shows the land slope, major trees, and rock formations. A local surveyor usually prepares this plan, but owners often prepare their own.

If you hire a general contractor, all permits are normally his responsibility. If you purchase a kit log home, most companies will help secure all permits.

Hire a lawyer. Just because you see a row of trees meant to define your lot line doesn't necessarily mean you know the real boundaries of your property. Again, *survey* for all property line, utility, and driveway easements. Don't take your neighbor's word on such matters; or you may have to pay for it later. Go directly to the local officials and make sure you understand all rules and regulations.

In municipal areas you must know how far from your property lines you have to locate the house. This may limit the size of house you can build and it may even prevent you from expanding in the future. In some parts of the country, zoning rules may even specify the type of house you can construct. In other words, you may be stopped from building a log home.

Once you have settled on an area and a piece of property, the next step should be to hire a lawyer. If you're unsure of whom to contact, call the local bar association for references of lawyers in the area.

The contract of sale specifies who is doing the buying and selling, the description of the property, as well as the selling price. A title search determines if the seller actually owns the land he is selling. The lawyer can also determine if there are any liens of claims against the property such as might result from unpaid bills by the previous owners. This type of search will also determine any easements (rights-of-use). Quite often there will be utility company easements in rural areas and you should know the exact wording of the easement to ensure your privacy. After a satisfactory check, the lawyer will make up a deed to the property.

Financing

Quite often the cost of financing is so exorbitant that the final cost of the home is shocking.

You may not have as big a problem financing a kit-built log home as you might if you try to finance a log home you plan to build from scratch. In the latter case, you will need a sympathetic banker, one who knows you and has confidence in your ability to build a log home.

The first step: Make up a complete proposal including blueprints of the house as well as site plan. You should also, of course, have a complete cost estimate of the house and land. In most instances, you have to own the land before your house can be mortgaged.

The following financing procedures are used with permission of the Justus Log Homes:

Most of us want (and need) to obtain long-term financing to cover all the costs of building a new home. In many cases, the land for the home qualifies as the necessary equity or down payment on the total real property asset that you're buying and using for collateral to obtain your mortgage loan.

Where can you turn for home financing? Here is a list of sources for you to approach.

• Savings and loan associations are the best place to start because they write well over half the mortgages in the United States on dwellings that house from one to four families. They generally offer favorable interest rates, require lower down payments, and allow more time to pay off loans than do other banks.

• Saving banks, sometimes called mutual savings banks, are your next best bet. Like savings and loan associations, much of their business is concentrated in home mortgages.

• Commercial banks write mortgages as a sideline, and when money is tight many will not write mortgages at all. They hold about 15 percent of the mortgages in the country, however, and when the market is right, they can be very competitive.

• Mortgage banking companies use the money of private investors to write home loans. They do a brisk business in government-backed loans, which other banks are reluctant to handle because of the time and paperwork required.

• Some credit unions are now allowed to grant mortgages. A few insurance companies, pension funds, unions, and fraternal organizations also offer mortgage money to their membership, often at terms more favorable than those available in the commercial marketplace.

The Five C's.

Banks, savings and loans, and other companies have a general set of rules they all abide by. They talk about the five C's of credit: *character, capital, capacity, condition, and collateral.*

Bankers say that *character* should be given half the weight of these five C's. If a person does not seem to be trustworthy or leaves some question in the banker's mind, this can weigh very heavily against the loan. What will the borrower do if he gets into trouble? Is his integrity more important than any legal document or loophole?

Capital refers to the financial statements known as the balance sheet. How much do you have in assets? What is the quality of those assets? How much do you owe and to whom? When are your debts due, and how does that compare with liquidity of your assets (how easily can they be turned into cash)?

Capacity refers to your income. Income that is dependable. With a rising trend, income is the most important factor in determining your ability to pay off your mortgage loan.

Conditions of the economy and local area, and those in the money markets, determine the rates and length of loan but seldom make or break the granting of a loan to qualified borrowers.

A lot of people put a great weight on *collateral*. Banks do not want to foreclose and sell a borrower's home or other collateral. It is *not* the critical thing the lender looks for. What you *earn* is.

You must help the lenders answer the questions about the five C's if you are going to be successful in negotiating a favorable loan.

Timing and preparation.

Most people would not like to make a deposit at a bank where the teller had his hat and coat on. By the same token, bankers do not have much confidence if you come in out of breath, sit down and ask him for $50,000.

In the opinion of experts, the best way to communicate with your banker is to tell him in writing how much you want, how long you want it for, the use of proceeds, the source of repayment, and alternate sources of repayment. This should be done as simply and clearly as possible. Give the lender the overall picture right away. You can then proceed to supplying all the other back-up data that he needs in the form of the five C's in writing.

Types of mortgages.

The types of mortgages available are far more various than most potential home buyers realize.

Traditional loans. Conventional home loans have a fixed interest rate and fixed monthly payments. About 80 percent of the mortgage money in the United States is lent in this manner. Made by private lending institutions, these fixed rate loans are available to anyone whom the bank officials consider a good credit risk. The interest rate depends on the prevailing market for money and is slightly negotiable if you are willing to put down a large down payment. Most down payments range from 15 to 33 percent.

You can borrow as much money as the lender believes you can afford to pay off over the negotiated period of repayment, which is usually 20 to 30 years.

The FHA does not write loans; it insures them against default in order to encourage lenders to write loans for first-time buyers and people with limited incomes. The terms of these loans make them very attractive. The interest rate is fixed by FHA, and you may be allowed to take as long as 35 years to pay it off.

The down payment also is substantially lower with an FHA-backed loan. Recently it was set at three percent of the first $25,000 and five percent of the remainder, up to the $60,000 limit. This means that a loan on a $60,000 house would require a $750 down payment on the first $25,000, plus $1,750 on the remainder, for a total down payment of $2,500. In contrast, the down payment for the same house financed with a conventional loan could run as high as $20,000. Anyone may apply for an FHA-insured loan, but both the borrower *and* the house must qualify.

The VA guarantees loans for eligible veterans, and the husbands and wives of those who died while in the service or from a service-related disability. The VA guarantees up to 60 percent of the loan or $25,000, whichever is less. Like the FHA, the VA determines the appraised value of the house, though with a VA loan, you can borrow any amount up to the appraised value.

The Farmers Home Administration offers the only loans made directly by the government. Families with limited incomes in rural areas can qualify if the house is in a community of less than 20,000 people and is outside of a large metropolitan area; if their income is less than a set minimum; and if they can prove that they do not qualify for a conventional loan.

For more information, write Farmers Home Administration, Department of Agriculture, Washington, D.C. 20250, or contact your local office.

New loan instruments. If you think that the escalating cost of housing has squeezed you out of the market, take a look at the following new types of mortgages.

The graduated payment mortgage features a monthly obligation that gradually increases over a negotiated period of time—usually five to ten years. Though the payments begin lower, they stabilize at a higher monthly rate than a standard fixed-rate mortgage. Little or no equity is built in the first years, a disadvantage if you decide to sell early in the mortgage period.

These loans are aimed at young people who can anticipate income increases that will enable them to meet the escalating payments. The size of the down payment is about the same as or slightly higher than for a conventional loan, but you can qualify with a lower income. The FHA insures different types, including these:

The flexible loan insurance program (FLIP) requires that part of the down payment, which is about the same as a conventional loan, be placed in a pledged savings account. During the first five years of the mortgage, funds are drawn from this account to supplement the lower monthly payments.

The deferred interest mortgage, another graduated program, allows you to pay a lower rate of interest during the first few years and a higher rate in the later years of the mortgage. If the house is sold, the borrower must pay back all the interest, often with a prepayment penalty.

The variable rate mortgage has a growing popularity. This instrument features a fluctuating interest rate that is linked to an economic indicator—usually the lender's cost of obtaining funds for lending. To protect the consumer against a sudden and disastrous increase, regulations limit the amount that the interest rate can increase over a given period of time.

To make these loans attractive, lenders offer them without prepayment penalties and with "assumption" clauses that allow another buyer to assume your mortgage should you sell.

Flexible payment mortgages allow young people who can anticipate rising incomes to enter the housing market sooner. They pay *only* the interest during the first few years; then the mortgage is amortized and the payments go up. This is a valuable option only for those people who intend to keep their home for many years because *no* equity is built in the lower payment period.

The reverse annuity mortgage is targeted for older people who have fixed incomes. This very new loan instrument allows those who qualify to tap into the equity on their houses. The lender pays them each month and collects the loan when the house is sold or the owner dies.

Sample finance kit

The following pages show sample forms used by Justus Log Homes to help buyers of their kit homes obtain a mortgage:

Here is a sample finance kit Justus Log Homes sends to loan authorities on behalf of prospective customers.

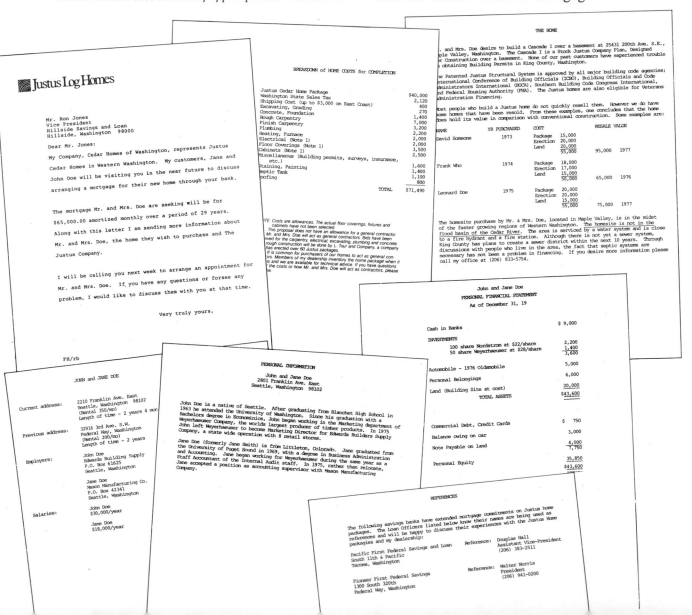

Site plan

At this point it's a good idea to make up a plot plan. The best method is to take stakes and string and actually outline the approximate size and shape of the house on the uncleared land. This is only a rough estimate, but it can give an indication of certain concessions you may have to make on the view or solar exposure. It allows you to see, too, how much clearing and leveling may be necessary.

Then make a scale plot plan showing the size of your site, the home size, and its shape in relation to the property boundaries or building site. Indicate any power lines, driveways, septic systems, wells, sewage lines, and major obstacles. You should also indicate any shrubbery you'd like to retain: Make sure you show the house facing the direction you wish. This can also help your financial proposal.

Make a plan site that shows in scale the property boundaries, locations of sewage or potential sites for septic tank or lagoons, along with water hookups or the well location. Plot too the location for gardens, the sun's path for solar siting, and the location of trees or vegetation you want to leave standing at the site. Make this plot plan as detailed as possible.

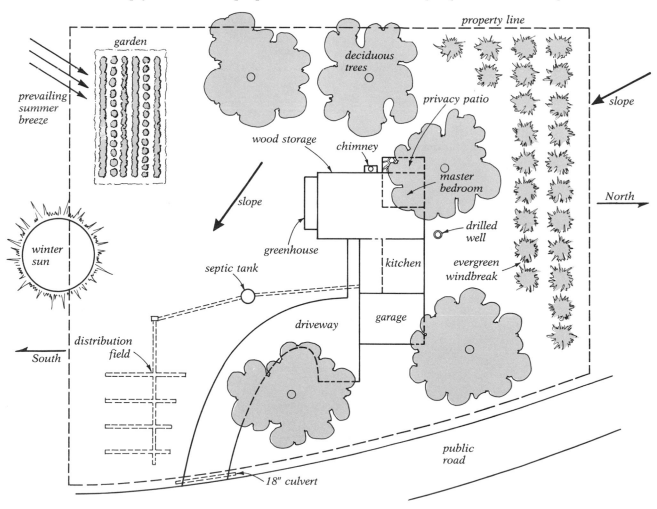

Construction plan

Before you start construction, make up a checklist, like the one following, of the jobs, who is to do what, and the proper sequence. Builders must be furnished with a complete set of blueprints and specifications which spell out exactly what work is to be included. Be sure to delete those items you wish to take on yourself.

Checklist for subcontracting.

What follows is a step-by-step checklist (adapted with permission of Heritage Log Homes) for all major areas where it may be necessary to subcontract the various construction operations for a typical log home. Review the items carefully and then decide how much of this work you wish to take on and how much you wish to delegate to a contractor.

1. Financial arrangements (loan or other arrangement). You'll need blueprints, contractor bids, and proof of net worth.

2. Building permit.

3. Well drilling or city water connection permit.

4. Septic system permit (from health department) or sewage connection permit.

5. Installation of septic system (generally required to be done by professional; may also be installed last).

6. Temporary electric service (by electrician) or portable generator.

7. Job phone (optional).

8. Excavation contractor.

9. Masonry contractor (if you use a masonry foundation).

10. Concrete finisher or rented troweling machine (if you use slab construction).

11. Materials for shell of house.

12. Carpenter/contractor to build shell (includes windows, and exterior doors).

13. Rough wiring.

14. Rough plumbing.

15. Inspection of above work if required by code; notify inspector(s).

16. Roof insulation.

17. Kitchen cabinets.

18. Paneling.

19. Finish electric wiring and plumbing.

20. Inspection for above if necessary; notify inspector(s).

21. Finish carpentry (shelves, hang doors, install trim, finish floors, etc.)

22. Spackle gypsum board and paint interior.

23. Backfill and finish grading (may not be necessary for pole houses).

24. Occupancy permit from building inspector, if necessary.

Chapter 3 **TOOLS AND LABOR**

The right stuff

Having the right tools on hand, knowing how to use them, and keeping them in good shape can mean the difference between pleasant, efficient work and botched, dangerous work. Whether you're buying a hand rule or chain saw, buy only quality name-brand tools. Cheap tools are a waste of time and money and they can be dangerous. This is important whether you build a birdhouse or log home, but quality tools become more critical when building with logs. If a cheap screwdriver bends out of shape, it's usually just a nuisance. But if a winch or come-along breaks at the wrong moment, it can create extreme hazard.

The amount of the work you intend to do yourself determines which tools you'll need on hand. For instance, if you build from a precut log home kit, you won't need as many tools as needed for building from logs you fell yourself.

Many log homes were built with only an axe. However, modern-day tools can make the job easier, faster, and safer. A chain saw is indispensable.

You could build a log home with only an axe, but the right tools can make the job far easier and faster.

The right hand tools can make log home building easy. Quality tools are easier to keep sharp and much safer to use than the bargain-basement variety.

The tools shown here are needed to build a precut log home kit. In addition, you'll need a chain saw, a sledge hammer, a come-along or a ratchet winch, a supply of 2 × 4s and 1 × 4s for bracing and framing, 4 × 4s to support logs off the ground, and a small broom.

A good circular saw is invaluable. You'll need a rugged professional model, at least a 2-horsepower with a 7½ inch blade. A saber saw can also be handy. You might want to have two electric drills: a ½-inch portable for boring pin holes in logs and a smaller, ⅜-inch variable speed drill for finishing chores and smaller boring jobs.

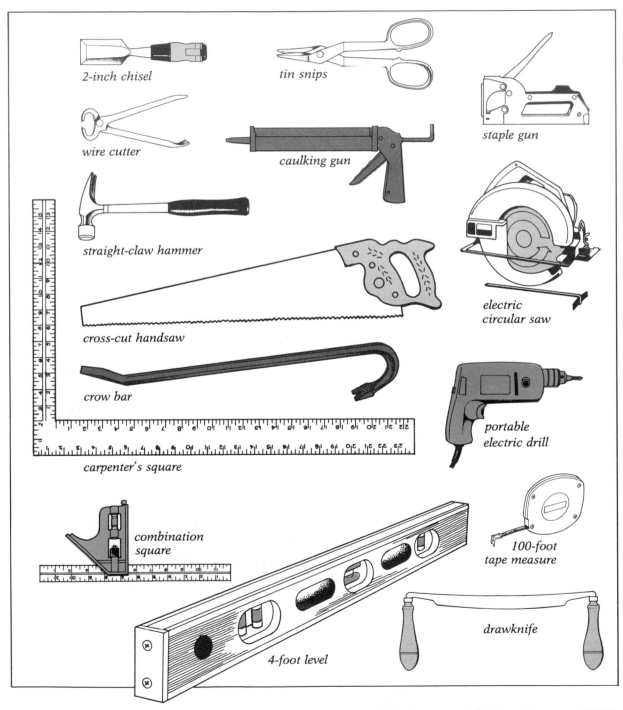

2-inch chisel

tin snips

staple gun

wire cutter

caulking gun

straight-claw hammer

electric circular saw

cross-cut handsaw

crow bar

portable electric drill

carpenter's square

combination square

100-foot tape measure

4-foot level

drawknife

PART 1. PLANNING AND PRELIMINARIES

If you start from scratch you'll need additional tools. You may need digging tools such as a steel bar, pick, mattock, spade, shovel, hoe, posthole digger, and sledges, as well as a wheelbarrow and shovels for concrete work. You'll probably need hatchets and a plumb bob and line, too, as well as hand-boring tools, sharpening tools, sawhorses, ladders, and logging tools shown on upcoming pages.

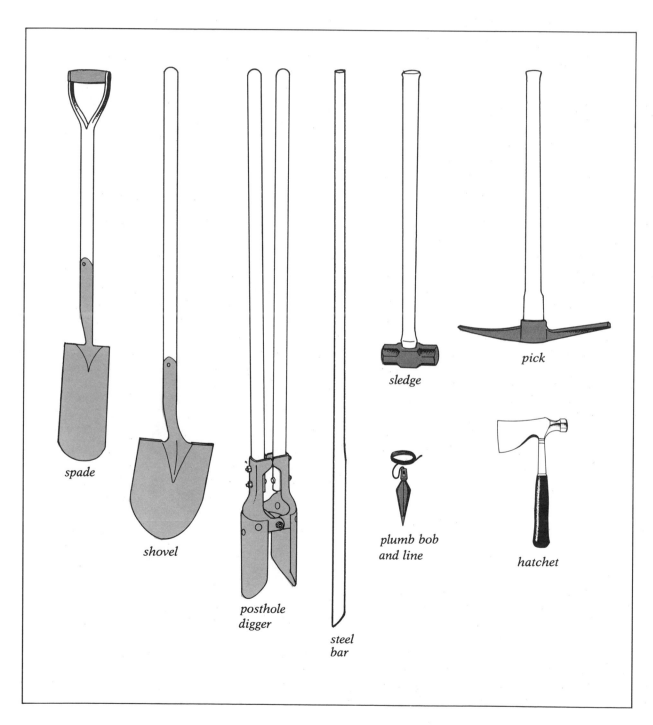

spade

shovel

posthole
digger

steel
bar

sledge

plumb bob
and line

pick

hatchet

Hand-built sawhorses come in handy for a variety of chores. It's simpler though to rig horses from 2 × 4s and metal brackets available at most hardware outlets. Below, for concrete and masonry work you'll need mason's trowels, some mason's line, a line level, string holders, a mortar board, edgers, jointers, and floats. If at all possible you should have a powered cement mixer for concrete work. You may also need a mason's hammer and bolster (brick set).

Below, brace and auger bits can prove invaluable for boring large holes.

PART 1. PLANNING AND PRELIMINARIES

If you plan to dovetail cuts on hewn logs you'll need a bevel gauge, as shown above left. Left, a variety of large chisels are needed for notches and clean-out cuts.

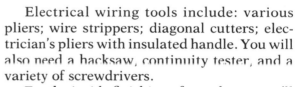

An assortment of planes will come in handy for smoothing joints.

If you plan to do your own plumbing, you'll need specialty plumbing tools, too. These include: pipe wrenches; gas pliers; locking-jaw pliers; crescent wrenches; copper cutting, reaming, and flanging tools; a hacksaw for plastic pipe; propane torch; copper tubing benders. If you plan to install any kind of cast pipe you'll need pipe cutters, a pipe vise, and threaders.

For plumbing chores, you may need a flaring tool, pipe wrenches, a reamer, tube benders, tube cutters and hack saw.

Electrical wiring tools include: various pliers; wire strippers; diagonal cutters; electrician's pliers with insulated handle. You will also need a hacksaw, continuity tester, and a variety of screwdrivers.

For the inside finishing of your home you'll need the above tools plus a coping saw for irregular cuts, a nail set for setting nails, and gypsum board cutting and taping tools.

For electrical work, you may need tools such as a continuity tester, pliers, crimpers, and screwdrivers.

41

Logging tools

Axes. Many pioneer homes were built with only an axe, though saws were often used later. Choosing an axe for logging is a personal choice—everyone has his own opinion on correct size and shape for the handle and head. One point to stress: Though it looks professional, a double-bladed axe is a very dangerous tool, even for a pro. Make yours a single-blade.

The axe handle should be solid and straight. The grain should run parallel with the long axis of the cross-section of the handle, not diagonally as is common with cheap handles. The handle should be about 26- to 30-inches long and made of hickory. There should be no

Logging and building with logs requires a variety of specialized tools, such as a peavey, come-along, loading (skidding) tong, lug hook, chain saw, logger's tape, or any of a variety of calibrated cruising sticks that let you measure tree diameters and gauge the number of logs you'll get before deciding to cut.

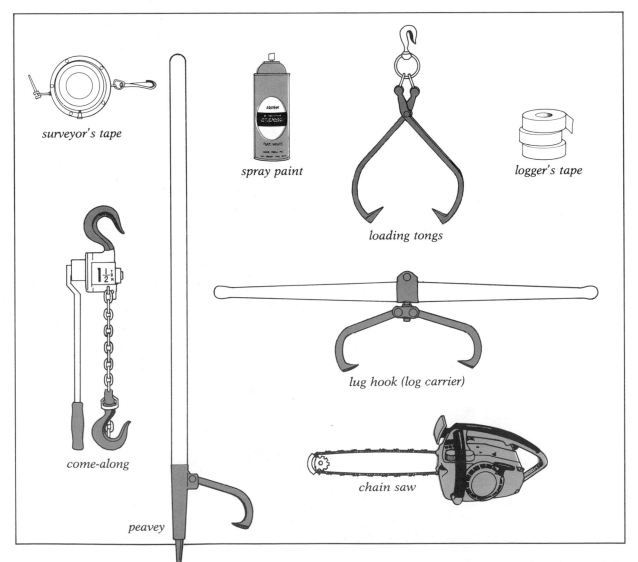

surveyor's tape

spray paint

loading tongs

logger's tape

come-along

lug hook (log carrier)

chain saw

peavey

PART 1. PLANNING AND PRELIMINARIES

evidence of sapwood, knots, or blemishes, and it should not be painted or varnished.

For bucking and limbing you may also want a lightweight three-pound axe. You may also need a felling axe with a four to five pound head.

Log building may require a broad axe, an axe with a broad cutting head. The head usually weighs three to four pounds (for a medium-size axe) and has an offset eye that cocks the handle to the side, allowing you to work close to logs without bruising your knuckles. A broad axe is beveled on only one side, much like a giant chisel and is used like a chisel to cut a smooth, flat log surface. Large broad axes of eight to ten pounds have a 12-inch blade and serve best for major hewing chores.

A log can be completely hand hewn using only a broad axe. But many craftsmen like to do the final finishing with an adz. There are also smaller broad axes called broad hatchets used for work in close quarters and specialty axes, such as the mortise axe, which has a long blade for chopping large mortises or log notches.

Keep all axes sharp. A dull axe can strike a glancing blow, which may injure you or bystanders. To sharpen an axe, first use a 10-inch mill bastard file with a wooden handle and file into the blade edge, stroking at a 45-degree angle. The axe can be held by a vise or by your foot on a stump or log. The main thing to remember: File the axe edge in a convex shape, which helps prevent the wood's binding it. If you thin the edge too much it'll break off with the first stroke.

Safety precautions: Ensure that no one is standing close by before you swing. Make sure there are no overhead obstructions to snag the axe. This is doubly important when removing limbs. An axe blundering into a whippy limb can cause a ghastly accident. Make sure you're well balanced. Space your feet apart in a stable stance. Stand opposite the side of the log you are chopping. Always make your cuts at an angle into the wood. If you try to make a square cut, the axe will only bounce or stick in the wood. Angled cuts are sharp and smooth, allowing you to remove the axe easily after each cut. Keep the handle smooth with a bit of linseed oil, but not slick and dangerous.

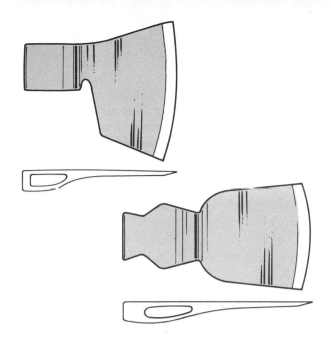

The broad hatchet (top) with seven-inch beveled edge is designed for light trimming and smoothing work. The broad axe (right) is used primarily for hewing from scratch. Both heads should be installed over bent offset handles that allow you to grip close to the head without bruising your knuckles on the log.

An adz can be handy for smoothing surfaces.

Adz. These are available in two head styles: straight and curved, (with about a 3-inch depth of arc). A straight-head adz may be used for smoothing timber after the broad axe has scored the log. The curved or "gutter" adz is used for smoothing inside round surfaces such as log notches.

Peavey and cant hook. These are highly useful tools for logging and for maneuvering logs on the construction site. Moving or rolling a large log without such a tool can be strenuous. The difference between a peavey and a cant hook is that a peavey has a pointed metal end for jabbing into a log while the cant hook has a slight metal hook on the end instead.

Dragging tools. For log dragging or skidding, you'll need a grapple hook or loading tongs. Some builders use large ice tongs for skidding. Smaller logs can be carried around with a lug hook, with a worker on either side of the pole. For lifting and moving logs into place on the walls, you'll need a few hundred feet of ¾-inch polypropylene rope and two sets

A cup adz, with cup-shaped blade, can be used for cutting the grooves on the bottom side of logs for chinkless building and for notch smoothing.

A cant hook, shown, is used for turning, rolling, and moving logs. A peavey looks much like a cant hook except that a peavey has a metal-pointed end.

PART 1. PLANNING AND PRELIMINARIES

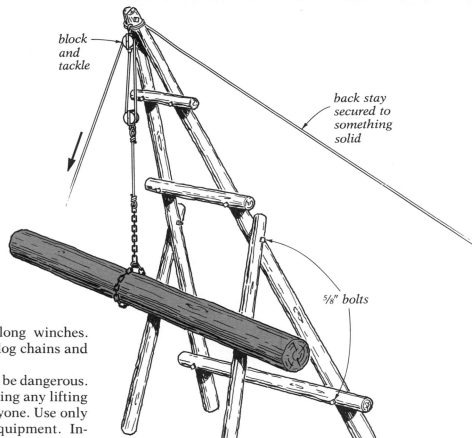

A coffin hoist can be used to lift logs in place.

block and tackle

back stay secured to something solid

⅝" bolts

of block-and-tackle or come-along winches. You will also need a variety of log chains and a hoist.

All log work is heavy and can be dangerous. Take extra precautions when using any lifting setups to ensure safety for everyone. Use only good-quality, well-cared-for equipment. Inspect it daily to ensure that it is not weakened or otherwise damaged.

Loading tongs are used for skidding logs to the site or for grasping them for lifting.

A come-along, like the one below, or block-and-tackle with heavy-duty rope is needed for hoisting and rolling logs into place.

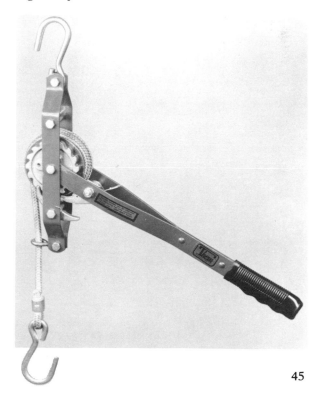

CHAPTER 3. TOOLS AND LABOR

45

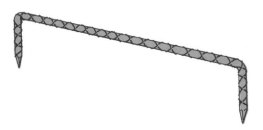

Log dogs can be shop-made. They are used to hold logs in place while you hew or cut notches.

Peeling tools. Bark should be removed before construction. This can be done by means of a number of different tools. Peeling usually takes a couple of tools, the bark peeling spud and a debarking drawknife. You can purchase the drawknife and peeling spud from mail-order sources. Or you can make up your own peeling spud by cutting off the end of an old garden spade. Instead, you could cut off the end of an old car spring and sharpen it. A heavy-duty socket slick can be used to cut and clean up mortises and peel bark.

Froe. If you plan to make your own split shakes, you will need a froe and mallet.

Log dogs. You will need a set of log dogs to hold logs in place for peeling and marking. They can be purchased or homemade.

The bark can be peeled from a log using a variety of tools including a heavy-duty chisel or peeling spud. You can make a home-brew peeling spud from a shovel or from a car leaf spring.

A drawknife works well for bark peeling.

A froe is used to split shakes from short blocks.

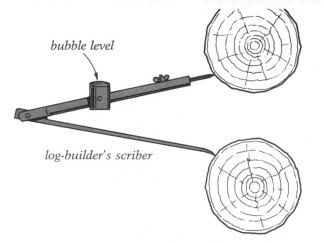

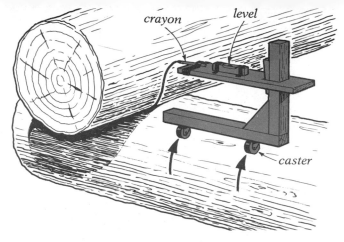

One of the most important tools for log builders, particularly those planning chinkless construction, is a good set of log-building scribers. These have a bubble level on top to keep the scribers vertical during scribing. Better ones have a double bubble.

You can make a log scriber. This one can only be used for scribing the undercut portion of the log.

Scribers. Scribers mark logs before cutting notches. You can purchase a pair or make your own. You can also make your own notching gauge.

Router. A router with a dado cutter can be used to cut insulation channels in logs.

Preservative tank. This can be made from several old steel oil barrels cut in half and welded together to create a long trough.

A heavy-duty router can be used to cut spline grooves.

Handsaws. A large, old-time crosscut saw can be used for tree felling or around the building site if you prefer not to use a chain saw. The saws come in one-man and two-man sizes. Pit saws used to rip logs into boards are used by placing the log horizontally over a pit or on high saw horses. Then a man above and one below operate the saw to cut out the boards.

Hand auger. Hand augers for boring wooden peg holes are another old-time tool that may be of great use in the backwoods.

A bucksaw can be useful around the site.

Chain saws

No other tool has eased the log builder's work as much as the chain saw. With the right chain saw you can fell trees, buck limbs, and shape logs for building in a fraction of the time it took our forebears. That is not to say that a chain saw isn't dangerous and doesn't require skill to operate. It must be maintained faithfully and operated with caution.

For most log home work, even felling trees, you won't need one of the behemoth professional machines. A good, general purpose saw with 3.5 to 4 cubic-inch displacement and fitted with a 19- or 20-inch bar will tackle any log-building task that a larger saw can. The smaller 16-inch bar and chain can be easier to handle, especially when you are working on scaffolding or high on the walls of the building. The shorter bar is also lighter.

Wedges may be of help in felling trees. The aluminum or plastic kind work best. Plastic wedges won't damage saw chains if accidentally nicked. You should also have a safety helmet with goggles or shield to protect your eyes from flying sawdust. The high-decibel sound of some saws can cause hearing problems. So use ear plugs or ear mufflers. A pair of leather gloves helps cushion your hands from saw vibrations and protect them when you wrestle logs.

In addition to the proper chain saw you will need aluminum or plastic wedges to help in felling trees, plus proper safety equipment, including a safety helmet with goggles or else a visor.

Today the single-most important tool (below) in log building is a good chain saw. Although a lightweight model can be used, a medium-sized model of 3.5 to 4.0 cubic-inch engine displacement is better. Such a saw will usually handle the cutting load on the full length of a 20-inch saw bar. Inset photo right: Always wear ear protection. Engine noise and chain clatter create a din higher than 80 decibels, enough racket over lengthy periods to impair hearing.

PART 1. PLANNING AND PRELIMINARIES

As a minimum safety feature, the saw should be equipped with a left-hand guard. A well-maintained automatic chain brake actuated by the left-hand guard can help prevent injury in many instances. Again, as with all tools, buy only name brands. Keep sharpening equipment on hand and know how to use it properly.

Here are a few basic safety rules to help prevent chain-saw accidents:

1. Make sure the chain is sharp. A dull chain causes you to put pressure on the saw, damaging saw chain and bar.

2. Make sure the chain is at the proper tension and that the clutch is properly adjusted. The chain should not turn while the saw is idling. If the chain moves while the saw is idling, you can get a nasty cut should the chain brush against you. This is a simple adjustment that can be done in a moment. Adjust the idler screw according to the saw's instruction booklet.

3. Never try to stop a coasting chain with your hand or allow a coasting chain to contact your clothing.

4. Start your saw on a firm surface—the ground if possible, with one boot inside the back handle. Don't attempt to start a saw while on a ladder or on scaffolding.

5. Turn off the saw before moving with it to a new cutting position.

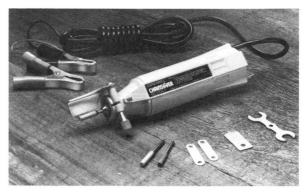

Electric grinders powered by car batteries also can be used to sharpen chain. But they require a skillful hand to avoid nicking cutters and to ensure reasonably accurate grinding of angles.

File guides such as this Oregon model allow precise setting of file angle and height. A small built-in vise prevents the chain from tipping sideways as you stroke the file away from you.

Chain saw models may differ widely in safety features, vibration dampeners, noise levels, durability, and ease of maintenance. As a general rule, you get what you paid for. The fuel cap shown has a label that prescribes gas/oil ratios.

Use the proper fuel mix. Refuel the saw away from the area where you start and use it to avoid possible flare-up of spilled fuel ignited by sparks emitted through the muffler.

6. Keep all debris cleared away from the cutting area. This is especially important when felling a tree.

7. Watch out for falling dead limbs (widowmakers). Wear a hard hat.

8. Make sure before cutting that the tree is not likely to fall on power lines or buildings.

9. Keep children and pets far away from the felling area.

10. Refuel a saw on bare ground if possible. Wipe spilled fuel off the saw case before moving the saw at least 15 feet from the refueling area and starting it.

11. Ensure that there is a clear escape route from a falling tree. Never stand directly behind a tree's direction of fall because the butt of the trunk can jump back at you.

12. Ensure there is no one in the vicinity who might be hurt by a falling tree or a trunk that rolls after it is sectioned.

13. When taking a saw from one place to another, grasp it firmly in one hand and carry it at your side with the cutting bar facing backwards.

14. Be especially alert when the engine is running. The noise can drown out warning voices or sounds.

15. Look out for metal such as nails and wire in logs. Metal can damage chain cutters or cause the chain to break apart and whiplash.

16. When cutting, don't hurry. Plan each cut and stop often for fresh air and rest.

17. Select a saw bar no longer than the diameter of most of the logs you'll be cutting. The occasional oversized tree or log can be notched on the sides to allow through-cuts with the shorter bar.

18. Be especially cautious when footing is treacherous.

19. Try to have someone within calling range should you become injured and need help.

Proper and safe use of a chain saw is extremely important. Follow safety procedures to the letter and wear safety gear, such as steel-toed boots, ballistic-nylon padded leggings, eye protection, ear plugs, and (when felling) a hard hat.

PART 1. PLANNING AND PRELIMINARIES

Make sure you use the proper bar and chain lubricant, and that you refill the chain-oil reservoir each time you refuel.

20. Cover the bar and chain with a specially-fitted guard sleeve when transporting the saw or storing it.

21. Do not run your engine at full throttle unless you are actually cutting wood.

22. Turn off the engine before touching the chain or adjusting chain tension. New chains tend to stretch more than used chains. But all chains stretch when heated by cutting friction and should be checked frequently. A properly-tensioned chain will fit fairly close against the bar's underside.

Chain saw maintenance. Chain saws get rough use by the nature of the work they do. At first thought, saw maintenance might seem complicated. But it is actually quite simple. A bit of time spent on proper care and repair can mean the difference between an easy-to-use and long-lived tool and a prematurely worn-out and wasted one. Chain saw maintenance can be divided into three operations: (1) chain sharpening, (2) guide bar and chain maintenance, and (3) powerhead maintenance.

Chain maintenance. Sharpening a chain is not a mysterious business, nor does it take exotic tools, although some hand and power tools can speed up the job. In fact, a pair of files with file guides plus an understanding of how a saw chain cuts are probably all you need to maintain a chain properly.

The chain must be tightened properly for safe use and to prolong chain life. After loosening bar bolts, adjust the bar position and thus chain tension with the adjusting screw, as shown.

A properly tensioned chain should pull away from the cutter bar about ⅜ inch with a hard pull.

Photo right: This stop-action photo shows full-speed chain cutting wood after the chain has heated up and expanded enough to allow cutters to be lifted off the bar rails as the cutters bite into wood. Here the bite causes a rocking action of each cutter that is limited by the height of the depth gauge. Thus, cutters of a sharp chain will take uniform bites of wood that promote smooth cutting if depth gauges are filed to optimum and uniform depths below cutter heights—usually .025–.035 inch, roughly half the thickness of a dime. (Photo by Neil Soderstrom.)

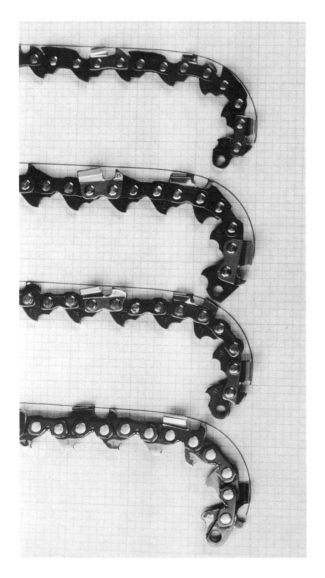

Blunt or irregular cutters mean poor cutting performance and also increase the vibration of the chain, causing premature damage to the saw. Keep the cutters sharp. Make sure both left and right sides are equally sharp and filed back to equal lengths.

The depth gauge controls the cutting depth of the cutter. Reducing the height of the depth gauge makes for a deeper cut as well as larger chips. However, lowering it too much causes excessive wear and tear on your chain.

The bottom tang of the drive link removes the sawdust from the groove in the guide bar. The front of the tang should be filed to its original condition if it shows signs of wear. Also make sure it's not bent or blunted.

Sharpen your chain according to the directions that accompany your saw or chain. Instructions for individual chain models for the same manufacturer may vary quite a bit. Changing the factory angles can cause damage to your saw. Use the recommended file diameter and buy several files when you purchase the chain or chain saw.

Photo left: To reduce kickback tendencies when chain impacts wood as it arcs around the upper quadrant of the bar nose, chain makers have experimented with chain profiles that "smoothen" the arc of chain parts. Note the large kickback-producing-gap between cutters on the old standard chain (bottom). In spite of the dramatic differences in profiles, shown, principles for sharpening the chains are the same. (Photo by Neil Soderstrom.)

bad maintenance of new chain

good maintenance of old, well used chain

In the badly maintained chain (top drawing), peening of the chain tie straps resulted from a worn sprocket. Damage here is so severe that chain parts stick and otherwise move stiffly. Good maintenance is evidenced in the old chain, filed back countless times with no visible wear elsewhere.

This cutter broke for several reasons. This chain, sharpened on a sharpening-shop's disc grinder, has a pronounced and deep hook in each cutter. Then, the chain failed to take adequate bites because high depth gauges prevented it. When even the hook failed, the owner bore down harder when cutting. This caused excessive friction between chain parts and the bar rails, evidenced by wear on the cutter heel. Deep filing of the gullet (between the cutter and the depth gauge) removed supporting sections of the cutters, tie straps, and drive links—weakening the cutters until sawing stresses broke the weakest cutter. (Photo by Neil Soderstrom.)

CHAPTER 3. TOOLS AND LABOR

For field sharpening you'll need a round file, a flat smooth-mill bastard file, and a depth-gauge jointer. Position the chain saw so that you are facing one side of the bar, looking directly down on the cutters and file. Maintain the proper filing angles both vertically and horizontally, as recommended by the chain

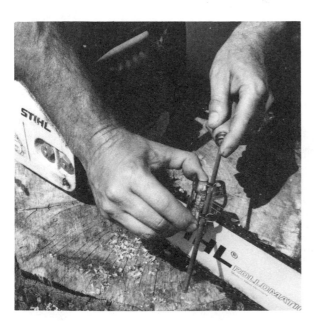

Most files are imprinted with their diameters; some are not. Here files of 5/32, 3/16, and 7/32-inch protrude from the file-measuring section of the plastic Pitch-N-Gauge by Granberg. Note: Some makers recommend that you use a smaller-diameter file than on new chain after you've filed cutters about halfway back. (Photo by Neil Soderstrom.)

Even an unstable file guide like this one can help make filing more accurate than when merely using your eye and feel with only a file.

Bar vises like these can be mounted on stump ends or on horizontal logs to stabilize the saw bar while you are working on the chain. The leftmost vise shown, by Westwood Ventures, screws into a saw kerf. The middle vise, by Windsor, is wedged into a kerf. The Oregon is hammered in. (Photo by Soderstrom.)

After filing all right-hand cutters, as in the photo at left, move to the other side of the bar to file all of the left-hand cutters.

PART 1. PLANNING AND PRELIMINARIES

manufacturer. Stroke away from you and the cutter; that is, from the cutter's inner edge outward. Allow the file to touch only on the push stroke; do not file on the return stroke. Do this several times, counting the strokes, then move on to the next cutter on that side of the chain and continue until you have completed sharpening all left or right cutters. Now turn the saw around or reposition yourself so you can sharpen the cutters on the other side. Use the same pressure and number of strokes on each cutter to assure that you remove a uniform amount of metal from each. This will eliminate any tendency of the chain to pull off center during cutting.

There are several devices that help hold chain vertical as you file, which is not particularly easy to do with fingers. These include simple metal guides that are positioned over the chain and jigs that position the file for the angles needed. A more precise filing guide, or jig, as shown in the accompanying photo can be set to any desired angle. Such a guide takes a bit more time to set up but is then quick to use and very precise.

Regardless of the tool you use, the chain must be fairly tight so it won't rock back and forth or wobble on the chain bar. All sharpening should be done midway along the bar.

Check the cutter in strong light. It should not show any reflection along the edge. If there *is* a shiny portion, it hasn't been filed enough.

For precise sharpening, use an adjustable file guide. It can be set for all chain types and sizes, and can be used to file down depth gauges, too.

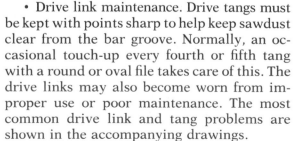

When advancing the chain by hand, pull the chain toward the bar tip. Don't push the chain backwards, toward the saw, because sharp cutters make nasty wounds. Wear sturdy leather gloves for this work, if possible.

Most chain problems derive from incorrect filing, lack of lubrication, and loose chain tension. Here are some of the common chain problems to look for if your chain doesn't cut well. (Adapted from Oregon Saw Chain booklet.)

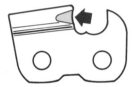

Nick caused by rock or nail.

Heavy damage caused by rock or nail.

File handle held too low, feathering top plate.

File handle held too high, or file was too large.

For safety, wear leather gloves during sharpening because the cutters can easily slice into your fingers. Always pull the chain forward, toward the bar tip rather than pushing it toward the saw.

If the chain doesn't cut properly after filing there can be a number of different causes. One particularly common problem is a *skid-nose* wear pattern. This is caused by cutter damage from metal or rocks, which causes the chain to ride on the wood surface, rather than cutting properly. Also, friction on the edges of the cutters softens them and gradually causes them to become dull. If this looks like your problem, then file all of the softened steel on the front edges of the cutters and set the depth gauge again. Badly damaged cutters require extensive filing, so you may prefer to let your chain saw dealer handle such major sharpening tasks.

• Drive link maintenance. Drive tangs must be kept with points sharp to help keep sawdust clear from the bar groove. Normally, an occasional touch-up every fourth or fifth tang with a round or oval file takes care of this. The drive links may also become worn from improper use or poor maintenance. The most common drive link and tang problems are shown in the accompanying drawings.

• Depth gauges. Depth gauges should be filed about every third or fourth sharpening.

PART 1.   PLANNING AND PRELIMINARIES

Depth gauges should be checked every third sharpening, or so. Check and lower the depth gauges before light sharpening of the cutters. Otherwise, the depth-gauge guide shown would dull sharp cutters.

This is done using a depth gauge tool positioned over the saw chain. Several gauges are available, but choose the one suggested by your saw chain manufacturer. Merely position the tool over the cutters so that a depth gauge projects up through the slot. File off any protruding metal using a small 6-inch flat file. File flush across the slot. Do not exceed the depth-gauge setting recommended by your saw chain manufacturer because this can cause rough, "grabby" cutting. Again, all depth gauges should be filed to the same height, remove the guide and slightly round the forward edge of the depth gauge, taking care not to nick the tooth edge or the tie strap.

To lower depth gauges, place the depth gauge tool on the cutter. If the depth gauge visibly projects, file it level with the top of the tool. Fixed depths of .025 to .035 inch are built into these guides.

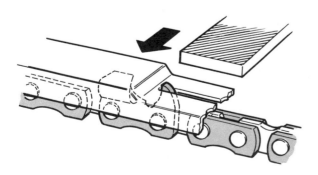

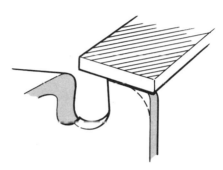

Round off the front corner of the depth gauge to maintain its original shape.

Keep all cutters filed the same length. The cutting edges should be filed so all damage is removed.

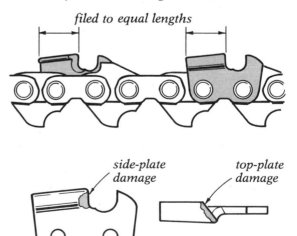

filed to equal lengths

side-plate damage   top-plate damage

Small hand grinders, available with either AC or DC power, can be used in your shop or taken to the field, powered off your vehicle battery. They provide an extremely fast and easy method of chain sharpening. However, they are not as precise as guided files and can remove a lot of metal—possibly too much—in a hurry. For this reason you should practice first.

To operate, first position the saw so that you're looking at the side of the guide bar. Hold the guide flat on the tooth with the proper index aligned for the cutter angle. The grinder must be held at the proper horizontal angle, matching the angles of the chain. Usually only two or three light strokes will restore the cutters. Matching the size of grinding wheel to the cutter is extremely important. As with filing, all cutters must be sharpened to the same depth and angle.

• Chain repair. Repairing a broken chain can be tricky with a punch and anvil because a false hard blow with a hammer can bend chain parts, making them bind. There is a break-and-mend tool, resembling a Visegrip, that allows smooth, even removal and peening of pins. Yet either tool requires that you have spare chain parts. Usually, it's simpler and cheaper to have a repair shop mend your chain.

Guide bar and cutter maintenance. Simple maintenance procedures that can assure a long-lived cutting bar are often neglected.

Clean sawdust from the guide bar using a putty knife or stiff wire. Also clean the mounting pad, clutch area, and the clutch cover at the end of each day. Make sure all sawdust is cleaned from the chain groove in the guide bar, then clean the chain oiler holes.

Each time you remount the bar, reverse its position (top for bottom) to distribute the wear more evenly, unless this is not recommended by the maker, as in the case of an asymmetrical, or banana-nose, bar. Don't use a bent bar guide; replace as necessary.

If you have a sprocket nose on your guide bar, grease it during each day of cutting. This is easiest while the nose is warm and the old grease is soft. Pump the grease into the sprocket nose bearing until the dirty grease oozes out and clean grease appears. Make sure the sprocket nose turns freely without any rough-

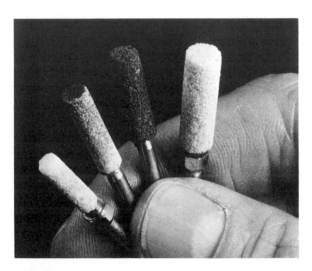

Grinding stones, above, come in all standard chain sharpening diameters and fit chucks of portable electric drills as well as those of electric grinders. The stones tend to cost more than round files and give fewer sharpenings. If you apply a special waxy compound to them, the stones will cut cooler and absorb fewer metal fragments from the chain (below) during sharpening.

PART 1. PLANNING AND PRELIMINARIES

This punch and anvil can be used to break and mend chain but require an expert hand to prevent chain damage and to properly peen rivets.

ness or binding. The bearing should be lubricated at each tank refueling and at the end of the day to prevent moisture from forming.

Clutch, drum, and drive sprockets. Clutch repair is fairly complicated unless you have the proper clutch tools. For this reason, major clutch problems should be handled by your dealer. However, you should clean the clutch drum, sprocket, and surrounding area daily or at the same time you clean, sharpen, and remount the chain and bar. Spin the clutch by hand to see that it runs easily and freely. When you install a new chain, replace the old worn drive sprocket, too, and have the clutch bearing checked. If necessary, replace or repack it (this should be done by a qualified service repairman).

Chain-brake maintenance. The chain-brake mechanism and exterior of the drive clutch should be cleaned daily and inspected before use.

Powerhead maintenance. A chain saw's small two-cycle engine requires proper care to ensure easy-starts and smooth running. Many care and repair steps you can handle yourself.

• Air filter cleaning. The air filter should be cleaned every few tanks of gas. Most saws have a foam filter that can be removed and tapped against a hard surface to loosen caked-on dirt and dust. Rinse the filter in a non-oily petroleum solvent or occasionally blow the dirt from it with an air chuck.

• Carburetor setting and adjustment. A balky, hard-to-start or poorly running chain saw may result from improper carburetor adjustment. The solution is quick and simple. If the engine runs rich, smokes excessively, and

has a lower-than-normal top speed, you may be using a fuel mixture with too much oil. Check the fuel mixture first. Incidentally, using fuel that has been stored for some time can cause the same problem.

If the engine runs too lean and cannot carry a load, again, check the fuel mixture. Then check the carburetor for proper idle and high-speed adjustments. Check the fuel pick-up filter inside the fuel tank for clogging and the fuel line to see if it's kinked or split.

Tuning the carburetor or an engine that will start: If you *can* start the engine, get it warmed up, then make the adjustments. [Note: Be careful, the chain may move if the carburetor adjustment is not properly set.] Make sure the chain is in the clear, then do this:

1. Allow the engine to idle and adjust the idle speed screw to either decrease or increase the idle speed so the engine idles smoothly and the chain does not turn on the bar.

2. Set the LO needle for the highest speed you can get without changing the idle speed screw setting. If the chain rotates, turn the idle speed screw counterclockwise to stop the chain.

3. Accelerate the engine a bit. If the engine quits, turn the LO needle clockwise one-eighth of a turn. Repeat as needed for smooth acceleration.

4. Make test cuts on a log. If the saw quits with a full load adjust the HI needle counterclockwise a bit so the load can be carried. But remember the one main rule of carburetor adjustment: The chain should not rotate during idle with a properly adjusted carburetor.

5. If the saw won't start, make basic carburetor settings according to your saw manufacturer's instructions and try adjustments again. Once the saw is started, adjust and fine-tune as needed.

• Fuel line and fuel pick-up filter. If the saw runs and quits, won't start, or if the engine starves on acceleration, idles too fast, or will not run at full speed, check the fuel line and pick-up filter. Regular maintenance of the fuel filter and fuel line means cleaning and changing the pick-up filters and examining the rubber fuel line for cracks, pinches, or deterioration. The fuel filter can be fished through the fuel filler cap. Clean it in solvent or by using an air chuck.

• Spark plug. Quite often starting problems can be traced to fouling of the spark plug. Periodically replace the old plug with a new one that is properly gapped according to your manufacturer's manual.

Chain saw mills

In addition to crosscutting logs with a chain saw, you can also rip planks for doors, floors, and light framing. There are several different chain-saw mills on the market, ranging from a simple device bolted on the saw to huge contraptions requiring two chain saws.

Chain saw mills are handy for a log home building project. They clamp to the saw and can quickly and easily cut a flat surface such as for a plate log or floor joists. They can be used, too, to plank dimension lumber from logs. For best milling efficiency, use special milling chain or file regular chain at milling angles recommended by the maker.

PART 1. PLANNING AND PRELIMINARIES

Larger sawmills

Some stationary and trailer-mounted mills make worthwhile investments. Probably the most popular is the Belsaw Mill, an old-timer that has been updated for today's power sources. Another type is the bandmill. This is actually a large bandsaw blade on a sliding rail used to slab logs into planks. Either of the two is a large investment, but can be a real help and money saver for heavy-duty sawing in areas where there are no sawmill companies to cut the logs for you.

There are several variations and sizes of mills. Again, rip-cutting chain makes the job easier and less wearing on your saw.

Stationary sawmills with circular saw blades come in several makes. All are small enough to be operated by one man, this one powered by a tractor's power take-off (PTO). By milling your own logs you can construct a house of sawn logs and dimension stock for far less than the cost of purchasing wood milled for you.

Portable sawmills, above, can be transported into deep forest. (Photo: Mobile Dimension Saw.)
Below: Some portable sawmills are large band saws. (Photo: Laskowski Enterprises, Inc.)

Planer

A planer can be used to plane lumber such as flooring and also can be equipped with cutters that create almost any type of molding. If you use sawn planks from your own logs, you can even match up grain in your home's interior.

A planer (below) can more than pay for itself. It's used to trim planks, timbers. Or equipped with special cutters (shown above) it can make all the molding you need for your new home.

Tractor

A tractor can be an invaluable aid for dragging logs. If you can afford a tractor with a front loader you've got many of your log-loading problems solved. The front loader can load logs into a wagon or truck bed and raise logs to position as the walls are going up. There are many small old tractors that can do such work quite nicely. For less than a thousand dollars you can probably purchase an old tractor good enough to do almost any type of homestead work, including grading roads, lifting and pulling logs, and plowing your garden. As a bonus, these old pieces of equipment were made to last. A tractor made in the early '50s can be just as good a workhorse today as when it was new.

A tractor can be great help in logging. If you plan on raising a large garden, an inexpensive older tractor of medium size may be a better choice than an expensive new garden tractor.

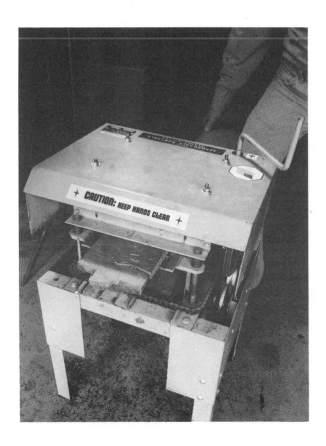

Labor

Once you have decided on the house design and the location, and you have all the tools, the next consideration is labor. Are you planning to do it all alone, with the help of a friend or spouse, or with several neighbors or friends? Do you plan to hire a general contractor or several subcontractors? These are big decisions. Building a log home alone can be an extremely arduous, dangerous, and lonely task. The help of a spouse or friend, even if they don't have the ability to wrestle logs around, can be a great encouragement. Helpers can guide logs into place, run for tools when you can't reach them, and provide moral support when you feel like quitting. The time and effort expended on building a log home can either strengthen a friendship or marriage or break it. This is a time when you have to work together. Naturally, if you can persuade a group of people to lend a hand, so much the better.

There are three ways to build your home whether you utilize a kit home or build one from scratch: (1) You can build it yourself, with help from a spouse, friends, or hired

Although many log homes have been built by a single person, it's easier and much safer if you have some help. Here a family and friends assemble a kit log home. (Photo courtesy of Authentic Log Homes.)

PART 1. PLANNING AND PRELIMINARIES

hands. (2) Or you can act as your own contractor, hiring subcontractors to do the foundation, plumbing, wiring, etc. Here you'd manage the construction and do the finishing chores you choose to do yourself. (3) Or you could have the home constructed entirely by a general contractor so that all you have to do is move in.

Contractors.

Regardless of the degree of independence you choose, make sure you find out about warranties provided by the contractors or subcontractors and then make sure all details are in a contract. Ask for references and talk to those who have had homes built by the contractor before you sign a contract. Make sure the contract states the house size and covers every detail including descriptions of work that you do yourself.

A contract should specify the following:

1. Who pays state sales taxes.
2. Who cleans up after each phase of the work.
3. Who handles change orders. Who authorizes changes and who pays for them (and when?).
4. How any delays will be handled and whether they must be agreed to in writing.
5. The proper conduct of the subcontractor's men on the job.
6. Who has the right to receive materials on the job.
7. Where and how materials will be stored.
8. Who (and when) others can make use of your tools and equipment.
9. Whether you have the right to give working details and instructions to the subcontractor's men.
10. Whether your permission will be required before cutting joists or other components that might result in structural injury to the project.

[The following information is used by permission of Justus Log Homes:] Subcontractors often have their own contract forms, but you can use your own. Though some contractors will adamantly refuse to use any but their own contracts, most will be willing to use yours.

You will, of course, need all kinds of insurance as required by law, including fire,

worker's compensation, public liability, property damage, theft, and malicious mischief insurance. If you are acting as your own general contractor, you should obtain these for yourself.

Subcontractors.

Subcontractors are specialists who handle specific phases of the work and leave you to admire their quality workmanship—providing you select them carefully and protect yourself through a good contract. Here's what to look for in a subcontractor:

Make sure he is a good businessman, as well as a true craftsman. It's extremely expensive to have a subcontractor walk away in the middle of a job. If he hasn't been paying for supplies, wages, or taxes involved in your project, you may have to pay someone else to complete the job. This almost always costs you additional money.

Try to select a subcontractor who has been in business for a few years or more, so you can obtain a credit report on him.

Make sure he does quality work. Look at some of his completed jobs. Drop by a job site, and see him in action.

Make sure he has a record of promptness. If he is late in beginning or completing his project, it could hold up others.

Make sure you deal with a subcontractor, not a person who becomes your direct employee on a piece work or job lot basis. There are important legal differences. For example, if it should be determined that the person is not a subcontractor, the IRS could come after you for unpaid FICA and withholding taxes.

How do you find good subcontractors? General contractors and local building inspectors are usually good sources. But beware of brothers-in-law of the source. Contractors and inspectors are in a position to know the quality of work of most subcontractors in their area. They usually have little sympathy for shoddy subcontractors. Wholesalers, suppliers, and others in the building industry also should be able to suggest names.

Some states require that all subcontractors be licensed, and if you are in such a state, this is probably adequate assurance. If there is doubt, check with your attorney. In the absence of compulsory state licensing laws, building codes and local authorities almost always require licensing of those trades that are connected with health, safety, or general welfare of the people.

Plumbing, electrical, and mechanical subcontractors typically are included in these categories. Some states require that subcontractors be bonded to guarantee performance of minimum standards. A good subcontractor will be happy to provide written information regarding his license and bond so you can verify them.

Generally it is better to have a subcontractor responsible for all labor and material involved in work he is performing. A subcontractor usually has worked in the local area long enough to have found the best and the most economical source of wholesale materials. If you feel for some reason you can save money by furnishing materials yourself, have your prospective subcontractors give you bids both ways—with and without their materials.

You should also stipulate that the subcontractor will be responsible for all labor required to complete his task and for any permits, inspections, and cleanup. The idea is to make him responsible for every aspect of his work so you won't be hit with hidden costs.

Lastly, because you want the best labor and materials at the lowest possible cost, try to get bids from three or more subcontractors for each type of work. Get each bid in writing, so there won't be any disagreements later. This means you'll have to spell out exactly what you want in quality, quantity, size, color, etc. List exact brands and model numbers wherever possible.

Here are some notes about specific types of subcontractors you may find useful:

Septic system designer. If you have a particularly difficult site, you may need to consult an engineer or your local building or health department to design your septic system. The septic installer can usually recommend an engineer, who should be licensed.

Septic system contractor. If you can't tie in with a community sewage system, you'll need a septic tank installer to provide and install the tank and drain field. His bid should include the applicable permits, all trenching, the sep-

tic tank, perforated pipe, washed rock, tight connection to your home, and cost of installation. If you have a site approval from the appropriate health department, make a copy available to the installer. If not, he should obtain it for you. Generally backfilling of the tank and drainfield is the installer's responsibility. He will usually leave his equipment on the job site until the inspection is complete in case he has to make any corrections. The installer usually knows the local inspectors and will arrange for the inspection to coincide with his work schedule. Double-check which of you will schedule the inspection.

You may want to have the installer provide and install the drain tile and rock for the perimeter of the foundation, if required, and the trench for other underground utilities such as the waterlines and underground wiring. These holes usually are filled by whoever does the grading.

Excavation contractor. This person is responsible for clearing the way for the foundation, backfilling, cutting driveways, and other necessary grading. (This may actually entail two separate contractors, who work together.) Don't just look at the price per hour. Consider the kind of equipment to be used and whether it is big enough to do the job. Paying slightly more for a bigger rig might save you a lot of money (look at the total cost, not just an hourly rate). If tree bark or roots are damaged, the trees may die. So ensure that the excavation contractor knows which trees you want to save by tying rags around the trunks. And you should try to be on hand when he works in case he runs into a problem or otherwise has questions. With your consent, he may be able to move a tree instead of spending great amounts of time working around it. Know who is responsible for burning debris and providing permits for burning. Will the contractor remove excess excavation materials from the site? If a drive is included, find out if a permit is required. Is access permissible where desired? Learn what type of gravel will be used for the drive. Will it compact well? Is the culvert included? Again, you should be on the job site during excavation.

Foundation contractor. This subcontractor erects forms for the footings and foundation walls and pours the concrete. A high-quality log home made of cedar will need a high quality, precisely formed foundation to rise from.

Flat work contractor. This one pours the slab, sidewalks, porches, driveway, and curb. Check his jobs for proper preparation, reinforcement, drainage, and finish.

Plumbing contractor. The plumber provides and installs the pipes, fixtures, and hookups for the water system. This should include the water heater, sinks, tubs, toilets, garbage disposal, dishwasher, water softener, and sump pump. Check his reputation for prompt servicing, warranties, and repairs. Be sure he's careful not to cut deeply into structural support members. Plumbing contractors are nearly always licensed, so you can be fairly confident that they are familiar with the local code and that they know how to do the job. Make certain that materials are of the quality specified (for example, plastic, galvanized, or copper pipe). You may want to purchase appliances such as dishwashers ahead of schedule and have the plumber install them.

With daylight or regular basements, it is usually easier and cheaper to have the rough-in plumbing done as soon as the foundation is complete. This makes basement backfilling and slab work easier. You should coordinate work between the septic tank subcontractor and the plumber for the best location of the septic system. You may someday want to finish the basement off. Thus heating runs, plumbing runs, and electrical work shouldn't be exposed. Such work should be drilled through the joists and not just hung from them and in the way of a ceiling you may later want to install.

Well drilling contractor. The well driller drills your well and installs the pump and pressure tank. It's difficult to predict the required depth of a well and time needed to complete the work. So start early to be certain you have water when it is needed.

Landscape contractor. The landscaper provides topsoil, final grading, and fencing, sprinklers, trees and shrubs. You may, in fact, want him to help design your landscape.

Electrical contractor. The electrician usually furnishes the materials, although fixtures may be extra (or provided for in an "allowance" that allows you a set amount of money to pick your own). Electricians are nearly always licensed and may hook up heat and appliances. You may be able to check on the electrician's competence with the local electrical inspector. Ask the electrician to visit the site after the first course of wall logs is in place in case any last-minute adjustments in the plans are necessary. Show him what routes will be available for his wires, and ensure that all work will meet code.

Roofing contractor. The roofer should include installation of flashing, roof vents, and other hardware. The roofer can also bid on charges for installing the insulation before doing the roofing. Because he will have the scaffolding anyway, it may be cheaper for him to install the furring strips and insulation.

Heating and air conditioning contractor. This person provides and installs the heating and air conditioning units, and usually is licensed. Consult this subcontractor early in your planning. If you want a solar system, find a subcontractor who is experienced.

Cabinet contractor. The cabinetmaker does the cabinets, vanities, and other related work. Ensure that he works from actual physical dimensions inside your home, which may vary slightly from plan dimensions.

Painting contractor. The painter does the sanding, the filling of knots and nail holes, painting, and staining. Check his previous jobs for sloppy work, especially inside closets and other semiconcealed areas. See if he has cleaned the windows of paint. Make sure you and he allow time to sand, patch, or clean up raw wood before staining, oiling, or painting.

Carpentry contractor. The carpenter provides basic guidance and labor, helping you install basement framing, joists, subfloor, walls, loft, roof, and finish work. Inspect his work for precise cuts and good nailing.

Part 2

LOGS,
FOUNDATIONS,
AND
BUILDING SITES

Chapter 4 TIMBERS AND MATERIALS

Your logs

If you're not using a kit to build your log house, you will have to take care of getting the logs you need. You should first determine the number, type, and size of logs needed by checking your building plan. You may find it economical to vary the design so that you can use logs available in your area.

Although almost any kind of log could be used, there are a few things to look for in order to make sure your house is solid and long-

You can buy logs or get permits to cut on government land. Regulations vary. The logs for this home came economically: When a state forest commission installed a new fire tower, the owner of this house got the logs in exchange for clearing land for the tower.

lasting. First of all, the logs should be from 8 to 12 inches in diameter and as straight as possible. They should also be fairly uniform in size, or you may have fitting problems—and odd-size logs make the walls look sloppy. Small homes look fine when made of small logs. But larger buildings need larger logs, both for appearance and to span the long walls.

You also have to consider the type of wood. Some woods last longer and are more moisture- and insect-resistant than others; some

Comparative decay resistance of the heartwood of common native tree species
(Chart courtesy U.S. Forest Service.)

Resistant or very resistant	Moderately resistant	Slightly or nonresistant
Bald cypress (old growth)[1]	Bald cypress (young growth)[1]	Alder
Catalpa	Douglas fir	Ashes
Cedars	Honey locust [2]	Aspens
Cherry, black	Larch, western	Basswood
Chestnut	Oak, swamp chestnut	Beech
Cypress, Arizona	Pine, eastern white[1]	Birches
Junipers	Pine, longleaf[1]	Buckeye[2]
Locust, black[3]	Pine, slash[1]	Butternut
Mulberry, red[3]	Tamarack	Cottonwood
Oak, bur		Elms
Oak, chestnut		Hackberry
Oak, Gambel		Hemlocks
Oak, Oregon white		Hickories
Oak, post		Magnolia
Oak, white		Maples
Osage-orange[3]		Oak (red & black species)[2]
Redwood		Pines (most other species)[2]
Sassafras		Poplar
Walnut, black		Spruces
Yew, Pacific[3]		Sweetgum[2]
		Sycamore
		Willows
		Yellow poplar

[1] The southern and eastern pines and bald cypress are now largely second growth, with a large proportion of sapwood. Consequently, these woods are not usually available in the substantial quantities needed for general building purposes.

[2] These species, or certain species within the groups shown, have higher decay resistance than most of the other woods in their respective categories.

[3] These woods have exceptionally high decay resistance.

warp and twist; and some dry with a lot of shrinkage. Among the types of wood grown in the United States, there are also different levels of resistance to decay. For example, the bald cypress is extremely long-lasting, while the willow or aspen are short-lived. Although old-growth bald cypress is the most decay resistant, it isn't practical as a material for log home building.

The accompanying chart provides a general classification of the comparative resistance to decay of the heartwood of most common trees native to the United States.

There are three basic ways to acquire logs: from your own land or by permission from a neighboring wood lot; by special permission from federal or state forests (or in Canada from the Crown Lands); or from a logger. Another alternative is to cannibalize logs from an old log home and use them to build a home on your site.

Photo left: You can buy the logs from the logger. (Photo courtesy Caterpillar Tractor Co.) Below left: If you have enough of the right kind of trees on your own land, you can log and peel your own. Below: Logs may be left in the round or milled at your own sawmill.

Logging your own land

Logging is backbreaking, dangerous work. Unless you have an ideal spot with enough logs in the immediate area of your home site, you'll spend more time logging than you will building.

To the uninitiated, logging may seem like the devastation of a beautiful forest. But it all depends on how you do it. Careful and prudent logging—thinning out the trees—is not detrimental. In fact, it is no different from thinning plants in your garden. It provides more space, more sunlight, and more nutrients for trees that remain.

But you must make an effort to log the area so that there is as little damage as possible to the environment. In some hilly or mountainous country, for instance, logging roads can cause heavy erosion. Carefully choose where the logging road should be so that it results in the least damage. In most cases, this means a road that goes around the side of a hill, not down it.

You'll probably need 50 or more logs for even a small home; so make up a list of the trees you need for each purpose. For instance, you'll need logs for short sections between windows, as well as long logs for full wall sections (though you may prefer to build solid walls, and then cut away for windows). In any case, once you have in hand a close estimate of the size and number of logs you need, then take a timber inventory. In many states, state foresters will help you with the inventory. At any rate you want to determine how many trees there are on the land, what kind are available, and what the environment will be like after logging. If you plan to take 75 to 100 trees, you will need quite a bit of property to avoid over cutting or outright clearcutting. And remember: an area that at first glance seems to have enough trees to build a fort may only provide a handful of usable trees. The rest may be the wrong species or size, may have too many limbs, or may be crooked, twisted.

If after a preliminary check it appears that you have enough trees to do the job, then purchase a roll of survey marking ribbon. Locate a usable tree, stand back about 100 feet from it and, with a three-foot ruler (or timber cruis-

To find out if you have a sufficient number of logs, take timber survey using a logger's cruising stick, which come in various designs. This stick is held against the butt of the tree about six inches above the flare height. There calibrations tell you the diameter of the tree.

PART 2. LOGS, FOUNDATIONS, AND BUILDING SITES

ing stick) held up at arm's length, determine how straight the tree is. Do this from two or three different vantage points. Crooked trees can be used, but of course they require more skill to prepare than straight, evenly-formed trees.

After selecting a tree that appears usable, measure about six inches above the stump height to determine the diameter. Although the cruising stick can be used for this, a special diameter tape that can be wrapped around the tree trunk is more accurate. Use spray paint to mark the stump height.

Now measure the height of the tree using the cruising stick. Use the part of the stick that is marked "number of 16-foot logs." This is a standard log size that yields the least amount of waste. Start with your heel at the base of the tree and pace off approximately 50 feet. Try to stay at the same elevation as the tree, if possible, so that you can measure its entire

usable length. Estimate about where the last, top cut can be made, usually where the tree is eight inches in diameter. Then, holding the stick 25 inches from your eye (which is normally an arm's length and in a vertical position, shift it up or down until the lower end is even with your line of sight on the stump height marker. Then shift your eyes (but not your head) upward to read the number of 16-foot logs between the stump height and the cutoff height.

Once you have determined the number of logs, mark the tree with paint, and note it on your list. If it's for a special use, make a note and tie it to the ribbon on the tree. After the tree has been felled and bucked, this note will remind you not to use the tree for general building. In fact, you should try to keep together all logs used for specific purposes. It's a good idea to batch logs of the same size and general appearance as well.

To determine the number of 16-foot logs in a tree, hold the cruising stick at arms length and, standing about 50 feet from the tree, read the appropriate scale. The straight edges of the stick also allow you to determine how straight the tree is. Sight the tree from several directions.

If the tree is sound and the correct species and size, mark it for cutting with bright surveyor's ribbon or spray paint. If the tree is selected for a special purpose, such as a central overhead girder or beam for an exposed ceiling, fasten a note. Record measurements of each tree to help you determine when you've marked enough timber.

Tree felling can be dangerous work. Wear eye and ear protection, gloves, and a hardhat to help ward off falling limbs.

Your hunt for usable trees should begin in fairly dense stands of trees. Trees in deep woods are straighter and have fewer low limbs than trees in more open areas. Ideal logs are up to 20 feet in length, are without limbs, and measure from 8 to 14 inches in diameter, tapering from the butt to the tip.

You may also want to cut lumber from the trees for flooring and finishing stock. You can mill logs yourself with a chain saw attachment or a portable sawmill.

Felling. Felling is an extremely dangerous job, even under the best of circumstances. You can easily be killed or seriously maimed. Here are some hazards to watch out for:

1. The tree could fall backwards on you and your saw.

2. The butt of the tree could kick up (and back) at you.

3. Limbs could be thrown back at you as they break off in the fall.

4. The tree could hang up in surrounding trees.

5. The tree could twist and fall sideways.

6. You could slip on the ground as you try to get away from the falling tree.

7. You could fall into your chain saw or have it knocked into you by the action of the falling tree.

Felling a tree is fairly simple—if the tree is straight and not leaning too much, or is leaning in the direction you want it to fall. First, determine the lean of a tree by using a plumb bob (a string with almost any kind of weight tied to the end of it). Hold the line and weight out at arm's length and sight the tree against it. The difference between the line of the tree and the vertical line of the string indicates the lean of the tree. Sightings should be made from several places to determine the exact amount and direction of lean.

If at all possible, the tree should be felled in the direction of it's natural lean, but make sure there's nothing that can be damaged in the path of the fall. You should also check for wind—felling trees on windy, gusty days is dangerous.

Before felling the tree, make sure you have a clear line of escape to one side and a bit behind the area where you expect the tree to fall. You should also have plenty of room to get away from the butt of the tree, should it kick back and up. Clear out brush or other obstacles that could cause you to trip. If possible, find another tree to stand behind for cover. Check the tree you are about to fell for any dead, loose, or broken branches or bark that could fall as you work; knock them loose with a long pole.

It's a good idea, if you've never felled a tree, to practice on some small trees. You can use them for firewood and the practice will give you a good idea of what to expect when you get to larger trees.

You can use an axe, chain saw, or one-man or two-man crosscut saw to fell trees, but always cut as close to the ground as possible. You'll get a longer log and won't leave a stump. After the log has been skidded to your home site, saw off the large butt ends to create an evenly dimensioned log. The butt ends can be split into firewood.

Before felling a tree, use a weighted line or else your cruising stick to determine its lean. Try to let the tree fall toward its natural lean if possible. Only skilled fallers can make a tree fall away from its lean.

CHAPTER 4. TIMBERS AND MATERIALS

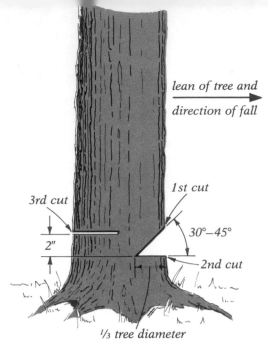

lean of tree and

direction of fall

3rd cut

1st cut

30°–45°

2"

2nd cut

¹/₃ tree diameter

These are the three typical cuts you must make to fell a tree toward its lean. Make the third cut (back cut) about two inches higher than the notch.

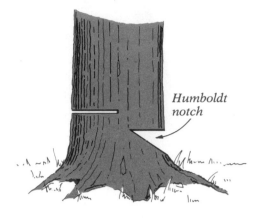

Humboldt notch

Some loggers make a Humboldt wedge cut in order to increase the amount of usable log.

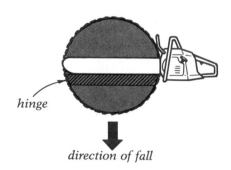

hinge

direction of fall

Above and below are cross-sectional views of typical cuts on small and large trees, showing the parallel edges of the hingewood that serve to guide the tree as it begins to fall.

To begin felling a tree, first cut out a notch on the side of the tree facing the direction you want it to fall. Make the notch by cutting in horizontally and following with an undercut sloping up to the horizontal cut. The notch should be about one-third of the diameter of the tree. (You can make the notch with the top slanting, instead of the bottom, but there is more waste when the log is trimmed.) After the undercut is started, swing the saw around and cut a short distance into two sides of the tree. This is called "cornering" and prevents the bark and the sides from tearing when the tree falls.

The notch section should be wide enough to permit the tree to lean 30 degrees from upright before the two faces close together. After the undercut has been made, remove the resulting wooden wedge.

Now move behind the tree and make the back cut about an inch or two above the notch. If the back cut is not aligned with the notch, the tree will twist and fall in an unplanned direction. Be sure to leave a "hinge" on the tree during cutting. The hinge is usually about 1½ inches thick on most moderate to medium-sized trees. This hinge is what holds the tree in place until it hits the ground and helps prevent it from kicking back or jumping off the stump as it falls.

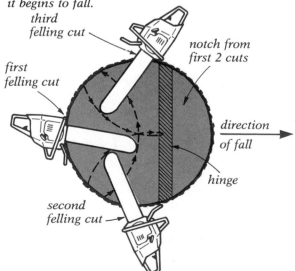

third felling cut

notch from first 2 cuts

first felling cut

direction of fall

hinge

second felling cut

retreat at 45° angle

The tree will gradually start to tip toward the notch, which you'll notice because the backcut begins opening. Immediately shut off the saw and set it down. And move quickly, though sure-footedly, back at a 45° angle from the axis of fall. This angle helps keep you out of the path of the butt should it jump backward off the stump.

If the tree is too wide for the cutter bar to reach across, cut notches in the sides of the tree.

To avoid an early topple of a large excessively leaning tree, make shallow cuts on each side and then make the wedge cut shallower than normal. Make the back cut at an angle. Then, if necessary, drive wedges.

Drive wooden, rubber, or aluminum wedges into the back cut, if the tree tends to lean back and bind on the cutting bar. Stop the engine when the wedges are being hammered in place. The wedges should not touch the chain or cutter bar.

If the tree settles back onto the chain, free the chain by driving plastic or soft aluminum wedges into the backcut. These wedges will often lift the tree enough to make it fall in the direction of your wedge cuts.

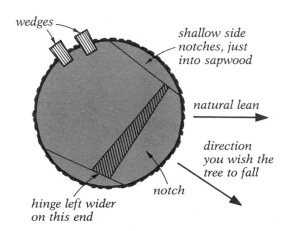

wedges

shallow side notches, just into sapwood

natural lean

direction you wish the tree to fall

notch

hinge left wider on this end

CHAPTER 4. TIMBERS AND MATERIALS

The back cut must not go through into the undercut. The goal is to leave a strip of "hinge-wood." If the back cut goes completely through, the tree may swivel on the stump, slide off erratically, or bind on the bar and chain.

As soon as the tree starts to fall, call out a warning, stop the saw and set it on the ground quickly, and move away immediately on your predetermined path of retreat. If your saw binds just as the tree starts to fall, leave it, and get out of the way! It probably won't be damaged, but if it is you can always replace it. Also, watch out for flying bark and tree limbs as the tree falls. Whipping tree limbs act like deadly catapults.

A tree that falls partway and then hangs up on other trees is called, aptly, a hanger; it is an extremely dangerous problem. It may fall over at the slightest touch or may be so tightly wedged that you'll have to cut down the supporting trees, a very dangerous chore. Stop and examine the situation carefully before deciding on what to do.

The best time for cutting trees is in the winter. The next best choice is late fall. There are several good reasons for winter logging. Tree sap is not running, and logs are less susceptible to sap stains, insects, fungi, and checking and splitting. In addition, logging is

If you must cut a tree near a house, use a rope anchor and have a helper pull the rope as you make the back cut. Be sure people and pets stay away.

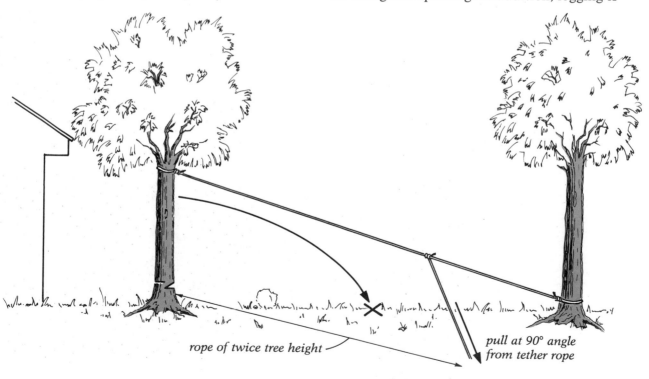

rope of twice tree height

pull at 90° angle from tether rope

PART 2. LOGS, FOUNDATIONS, AND BUILDING SITES

just plain more comfortable during winter. (You'll find that out if you try logging on a 100-degree day in July, with mosquitoes and flies buzzing about your face.) And in winter the leaves are off, so you can see better in the woods and get around more easily. It's also easier to skid logs over frozen ground and snow, rather than through the muck of a spring thaw. The logs have a chance to cure properly, too, when they're cut in winter and used in the spring or summer.

Limbing and bucking. With the tree on the ground, you've gotten to the hard part. The next step is limbing, which is removing the limbs and top of the fallen tree. Start at the butt of the tree and work toward the top, cutting only limbs on the upper side. Cut from the crotch side of the limb and as close to the tree as possible. Watch that limbs don't fall, catch, or buck back at you as they're being cut.

Avoid hangers, or trees that hang up in the limbs of nearby trees, because they are especially dangerous to bring down. The safest method is usually to pull the butt end with a come-along or a vehicle.

Conifers have symmetrically arranged small branches that are best limbed by starting at the butt and working towards the top. Move the saw from side to side as you go up the trunk. Cut supporting branches underneath last. Unless your saw bar has an anti-kickback noseguard, be very careful not to let a revved or coasting chain inadvertently strike a limb and thus cause the bar to kick back at you. Among professional loggers, limbing accidents are the most common kind.

start

Once the tree is on the ground, the limbing process begins. On deciduous trees with a large spreading crown, start at the outer tips of the branches. Start on the highest branches but avoid reaching higher than shown at right. Otherwise tree-limb vibration and muscle strain can conspire to result in injury.

After all nonsupporting limbs have been removed, the supporting limbs are next. To avoid excessive tension on supporting limbs, force a support log under the trunk to receive the weight as the limbs are cut.

crotch cuts →

With the limbs cut away, buck the log into the lengths you need. If only a long butt section is to be used, the upper end can be cut into firewood. Here cuts through crotch sections, later allow you to split wood that would be troublesome otherwise.

If the log or limbs are under a sagging stress, the stress will cause a lone topside saw kerf to pinch the saw bar. To avoid pinching, force a large support log underneath and make an initial overbuck as shown. The angled underbuck allows the stump here to fall away from the saw bar.

1. overbuck

stress

2. angled underbuck   support log

Once all the upper limbs have been sawed away, cut the underside limbs. First make a top cut about halfway through, or until you notice just a bit of pressure, then complete the cut from the underside. Watch out that the tree doesn't roll over on you as you cut. Don't bind your saw in these limbs. You may need to go to the outer end of a limb, cut from the underside, and allow the tree to settle a little at a time to get it safely on the ground.

Never cut on the downhill side of a tree because the tree can roll on top of you when supporting branches are cut away. Watch, too,

that a log doesn't roll and catch you from behind with a branch. (If you are going to use the limbs for firewood, cut from the crown towards the butt as shown.)

You may want to cut the tip of the tree off, before limbing the lower branches. Not only does this take some of the weight off the holding branches, it's easier to do when the log is not lying directly on the ground. The larger limbs can be bucked or cut into firewood-size lengths and stacked. The smaller limbs (or slash) should be piled in big brushpiles to provide cover for small animals.

Once the branches have been cut away, you're ready to "buck the log" (cut it into proper lengths). In some cases you may have to move or roll a log to complete a cut, especially if it rests directly on the ground. Cutting completely through it would bring the tip of your chain in contact with the ground, one of the quickest ways to ruin a sharp chain. Use a peavey to roll the log in the direction you want, again making sure you work from the uphill side of the log.

Skidding. With the logs limbed, the next step is to skid them from the woods. The old-fashioned method was to use a horse to pull individual logs by means of a harness and big grappling hooks. This is still common practice in some parts of the country; it's one of the best methods of extracting logs from heavily wooded areas. The horse can go into places you wouldn't think of taking a vehicle and, if you work in the winter, there will be little damage to either the woods or the logs.

Few of us today have access to a trained workhorse, though, and the next best bet is a tractor. Even a small tractor can be used to snake individual logs out, without the need for expensive haul roads. Use a skidding pan, which can be made as shown. Place the end of the log on this and chain it. It makes sliding the log over the snow and frozen ground much easier.

A small- to medium-size tractor can be used for skidding. Smaller logs can be skidded out with a four-wheel-drive vehicle. Below: Once your logs are cut to length, you must skid them out. Commerical loggers use heavy equipment. You may want to hire a logger to do the job. (Photo courtesy Caterpillar Tractor Co.)

Old-timers skidded logs with horses and a homemade sheet metal skidding pan that supported the end of the log and kept it from digging into the ground.

Skidding tongs grip the log so you can pull it out.

Two logs can be used to create a culvert over small creeks or gullies.

The alternative to skidding is hauling the logs. This may be necessary if you cut the logs some distance from your building site, but it takes a lot of heavy equipment. Even the best old farm truck strains under the load of a full-sized log and it is better to hire a custom hauler. Many of them use a gigantic machine that has a lift with a huge claw. With this equipment, haulers can load and transport your logs to the building site, and stack them neatly.

You'll have to provide a haul road for the trucks; so it may be prudent to skid the logs to a central loading area first. This will cut down on the cost, time, and damage to your property. Haulers with their big trucks often don't watch for prize trees, and they can tear up a lot of property quickly.

Flatbed trucks and wagons can be loaded by means of plank ramps and heavy rope or cable.

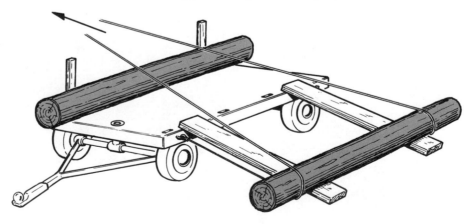

PART 2.   LOGS, FOUNDATIONS, AND BUILDING SITES

Once the trees are down, a cruising stick will help you determine the board feet of lumber in the log. This information is useful should you cut and mill your own planks and framing materials.

Cribbing and curing. Logs may be either cured or green. There are advantages and disadvantages to both. Logs to be cured are first cribbed (stored in stacks) on supports off the ground.

Without the bark, they can be left for six months to a year. If the bark is left on, the logs can be left for a couple of years for slow curing (peel the bark off just before the logs are used). The problem with curing unpeeled logs is that they become more discolored and insect infested than peeled logs. However, insect infestation is eliminated once the logs are peeled (markings left by the insects can even add charm and individuality to the logs). A more serious problem with curing logs is that they may twist, sag and warp, taking on an awkward set as they dry. This makes them harder to work.

To crib logs properly, place skids four to five inches apart on a flat, smooth, level area that is free of brush. Then lay the logs on the skids. Stack the first layer six inches above ground for full air circulation and make sure the skid pans are short. Place spacers on the logs and place another layer on top. Cover with a layer of branches and a tarp or plastic to keep out rain and weather. If you have the time, you can lay all the logs flat on the skids and turn them all 90 degrees every week. This prevents warping and sagging, but it requires more space and labor.

Depending on climate and humidity, the logs will lose all free water in the cell cavities of the wood and start to shrink in five to six months. Continued curing (for about three months) will bring the moisture content down to about 15 percent depending, again, on climate, time of year, and type of wood. So, if the logs are cured for nine months before being used, most of the shrinkage will already have taken place. Probably the best curing takes from two to three years, but this is ordinarily too long to wait.

The logs should be cribbed, or stacked, for curing.

Building with green logs eliminates both the problems of curing and the wait involved. (But even logs that are to be used immediately should be cribbed off the ground.) One advantage of building with green logs is that they're somewhat limber before they dry and take a set; they'll bend and sag somewhat to fit a wall. The disadvantage with green logs is that you have to compensate for the shrinkage that occurs when the logs dry.

The best way to build with green logs is to construct the walls and framing members, and then leave the entire structure (without floors, roof, windows or doors) to cure for about a year. You could start on the building within six months but you'll have to live with much more shrinkage. Make allowances for shrinkage by providing extra room in all header spaces (over doors, windows, and partitions, etc).

Peeling. Though some log homes have been built with unpeeled logs, it's best to use logs that have been peeled of bark. Bark left on will harbor insects and prevent the logs from curing properly. The bark will fall off eventually anyway, creating a mess inside your home. It can also promote fungus and a musty smell.

Peeling logs is easiest in early spring when the sap is up, but this is the worst time for logging. Try to fell and crib the logs in winter, allow them to cure until spring, and then peel their bark just before using them. This schedule can also help prevent checking of the logs before they're to be used.

All kit-built log homes are made with peeled logs. Most of them also use milled logs, so they'll be of uniform size and shape. Peeled logs are also easy to finish on the inside of the home. If you prefer, you can mill the logs on three sides, leaving the bark on the exterior side for a rustic appearance. (Incidentally, if you're building a hewed-log house, you won't need to peel the logs first.)

You can buy special peeling spuds for peeling logs or make them up yourself. To make a spud, you can use a section cut from a car spring or just an old spade. You will also need a heavy-duty drawknife for smoothing and cleaning the logs.

The logs should be peeled. This is best done after they have been hauled to the building site. During hauling the bark will protect the surface of the log from hauling damage. Peel with a peeling spud.

To peel a log, place one end in a notch cut in a smaller (holder) log and secure it with log dogs. Then, using the peeling spud, strip off large sections of the bark. Use the drawknife to remove the last slivers of bark, to smooth the log, and to remove burrs or ragged cuts left from trimming off limbs. This is hard work and takes time, but it will be worth the effort. Make sure you keep your peeling tools sharp. Once you have the log peeled, carefully stack it, keeping it up out of the dirt.

Preservatives

Using proper preservatives can add years to the life of your home by protecting it from insect infestation, fungi, and decay. But you have to take into account the health risk from chemical treatments. In many cases, proper design and construction of the home can help alleviate moisture and insect problems. Dry wood will not decay—keep this in mind when designing and building your log home. To prevent your home from deteriorating, use construction methods that reduce water collection and keep the wood as dry as possible.

Provide good drainage around the foundations of the home, too. This means grading the area immediately around the foundation so water runs off quickly. Gutters and down-spouts also direct rainwater away.

Untreated wood should not be used for any part of the foundation, or where it will be in contact with the soil. The bottom (or sill) logs should be placed 18 inches above soil level on concrete, brick, or stone foundations.

Proper ventilation is also important. A home built on piers ordinarily has adequate ventilation under the floors. You can add a wooden latticework to prevent small animals from getting under the house. If you do, use treated wood. If the foundation is continuous, provide plenty of opening spaces, screened to keep pests out. In areas with extremely cold winters you can close these vents to help keep the floor warmer. If the ground stays damp under the house in your location, you may find it necessary to place a vapor barrier of polyethylene sheeting on the ground in the crawl space.

Fit the wall joints carefully. Storm water that quickly runs off log surfaces won't harm anything, but cracks and crevices where the water can collect may become points of decay. Some kinds of log joints are particularly susceptible to this. Chapter 7 illustrates the various kinds of log joints and their moisture resistant qualities. In every case, make sure joints between the logs are as tight as possible and completely sealed with caulking or sealant. Cupped log undersides help too.

The roof overhang should be wide enough to prevent rainwater from blowing into and around the house. A steep roof pitch that causes the rainwater to shoot faster (and farther) from the house also helps. The roof overhang projection should be at least 18 inches for single-story homes and at least 24 inches for two-story homes. A 36-inch projection is best.

Interior preservatives. The inside of a home can be preserved with a good non-yellowing alkyd varnish or penetrating oil sealer. Window sills and lower rails may need extra protection.

Exterior preservatives. Water-repellent penetrating preservatives contain fungicide which stops the growth of fungus and mildew. These finishes allow the wood to weather naturally to a mellow tan or brown color, without the graying and streaking that occur when wood is not given any protective coating at all. This preservative is simply brushed on the exterior walls of the house after it's built. Pay particular attention to areas between log joints, exposed end grain, or water-trapping areas. Several coats, particularly on end-grain spots are needed for good protection. This kind of finish usually prevents mold and mildew problems for a couple of years.

Pigmented penetrating stains provide the same basic protection, but they change the color of the wood and hide the beauty of the grain. But the color is even, and this kind of appearance may be desired. Also, these types of finishes don't blister or peel, a problem with varnish or paint; they're a better choice for exterior log finishes. Varnishes are not recommended for log home exteriors.

Finish preservatives are available through most building supply yards. The accompanying chart illustrates some of the commercial water-repellent preservatives available.

Commercial water-repellent preservatives available for exterior wood use (following manufacturer's directions and cautions).

Note: In no case should these preservatives be used for interior use.

Preservative—water repellant (for exterior use only)

Ingredients	For 1 gallon	For 5 gallons
40 % pentachlorophenol (10:1)	1 ¾ cups	2 quarts
Boiled linseed oil	1 ½ cups	1 ¾ cups
Paraffin wax	1 ounce	4–5 ounces
Solvent (mineral spirits, turpentine, or paint thinner)	Add to make 1 gal.	Add to make 5 gal.

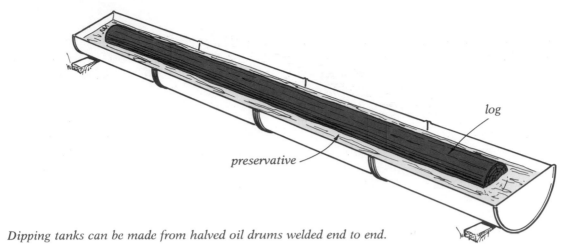

Dipping tanks can be made from halved oil drums welded end to end.

The following is suggested by R. A. Link, Information Officer of the United States Department of Agriculture: "Logs treated with creosote or pentachlorophenol should never be used inside a structure because of the concerns about their effect on human health. Logs pressure treated with waterborne preservatives provide a clean and paintable wood surface, free from objectionable odor. Two such chemicals are ammoniacal copper arsenate (ACA) and chromated copper arsenate (CCA)."

If you want more information on the use of pentachlorophenol, write to the manufacturers of Penta, The Dow Chemical Company, Designed Products Department, Midland, Michigan 48640 and ask for their bulletin, "Pentachlorophenol, A Statement Concerning Its Use and Exposure in Log Home Construction."

In addition to preservatives applied after the log home is built, some builders dip the logs in a preservative prior to construction. This you can do in a number of ways, but remembering that penta or creosote chemicals must not be used because dipping would be a whole-log treatment. Anytime the log is cut, the cut areas have to be treated again.

Most logs in log house kits are dipped in a preservative before shipment. This protects against mold and stain until the house is erected. Then a final coat of preservatives for exterior protection is applied. Sill logs or those meeting the foundation can be given an additional treatment at a commercial treating plant.

Builders using their own logs can use the same treatment to protect logs until they're used in construction. You'll need a homemade vat (as shown) for soaking the logs. Freshly-peeled logs do the best; preservatives prevent the staining that can happen soon after logs are peeled.

The following methods are suggested by the USDA Forest Service, Forest Products Lab in their General Technical Report, FPL-11, 1977: *Protecting Log Cabins from Decay:*

Preservative—simple diffusion.

Preservative protection is especially desirable for the lowest two or three logs of a cabin. Logs can be treated when they are freshly peeled or after they have been air-dried for some months. The "simple diffusion" process is relatively easy to use.

Many different compounds can be used for a simple diffusion preservative; a 10 percent solution is recommended. Mix 10 pounds of zinc chloride with 12 gallons (approximately 100 lb.) water.

Whole logs should soak in the solution for one to two weeks. Any small parts such as steps, rails, or window sills can be soaked for half that time. Treated logs should be allowed to dry for one to two weeks after the soaking process and before construction begins.

Preservative—double diffusion.

"Double-diffusion" treatment requires more time but provides greater protection. The double-diffusion process involves soaking wood first in one chemical solution and then in a second. The two chemicals combine to form a compound that cannot be leached out.

The process described here uses two solutions made up with water at air temperature.

This should be done outdoors when the temperature is not below 60 degrees Fahrenheit. For the first solution mix 16 pounds of commercial grade copper sulfate with 10 gallons (84 lbs.) water.

Because copper sulfate dissolves slowly, the solution should be mixed a day or two in advance, using warm water. The solution should be stirred very thoroughly to make sure all the salt is dissolved. Logs should soak for two to three days in this first solution.

An iron tank cannot be used for the copper sulfate solution.

To make the second solution first mix 7 pounds of commercial grade 70 percent arsenic acid solution with 11 gallons (93 lbs.) water. Then, in a separate container, mix 21 pounds of commercial grade sodium chromate with 9½ gallons (79 lbs.) of water.

When these two separate solutions are completely dissolved, mix them together to form the second solution.

Soak the freshly peeled logs two to three days in the copper sulfate solution and then transfer them for soaking for two to three days in the second solution. The treated logs should be piled to dry for several days. When the cabin is to be constructed, wash off any residual chemicals on the surface of the dry logs.

The amount of solution required for each of the diffusion treatments depends on log size and tank size. To determine the amount of liquid (gallons) required, the length of the tank should be multiplied times the depth and the width, all in either feet or inches:

1 cubic foot = 7.5 gallons.
1 cubic inch = 0.0043 gallons.

For example, if the solution tank is 20 feet long, 2 feet wide, and the largest log is 8 inches in diameter, the volume is:

$20 \times 2 \times \frac{2}{3}$ feet = 26.4 cubic feet.

Then, the amount of liquid preservative required is:

26.4 cubic feet × 7.5 gallon/cubic feet = 198 gallons.

Or, if tank volume is:

(20 ft. × 12 in./ft. =) × (2 ft. × 12 in./ft. =)
240 × 24 × 8 inches = 46,080 cubic inches.

Then the amount of liquid preservative required is:

46,080 cubic in. × 0.0043 gallon/cubic in. = 198 gallons.

No more solution than is necessary should be prepared at one time. Too little mixture can be supplemented. Too much mixture has to be disposed of.

Melt the paraffin in a container heated with hot water. Be sure the solvent is at room temperature. Slowly pour the hot paraffin into the solvent, mixing the new combination vigorously to keep the wax from solidifying at the bottom of the container. When the wax has been added, add the linseed oil and then the penta. Stir until the mixture is uniform.

Brush the mixture into cracks or joints.

If the solution is held at low or freezing temperatures, the ingredients may separate. Should this happen, the solution can be reheated to room temperature and stirred to a uniform mixture once again.

Preservative—pigmented. Stains are the most durable when applied to rough or weathered surfaces. When two coats are applied to a rough surface, the second coat should be applied before the first has dried, so that both coats can penetrate. Stain that remains on the surface after three or four hours should be wiped up or rubbed in to provide a uniform, flat appearance. To avoid lap marks in the application of penetrating stain, the full length of a log should be finished without stopping for more than five minutes. The preservative should also be stirred frequently to maintain uniform suspension of the pigments.

Caution: Wood preservatives can be injurious to man, animals, and plants. Therefore, for safe and effective usage, it is essential to follow the directions and heed all precautions on the labels. The wood preservative pentachlorophenol, for example, is toxic to animals and humans and is a strong root poison and defoliant. It is, therefore, advisable to wear rubber gloves and protective masks and to cover nearby plant life when using any material containing pentachlorophenol. Pentachlorophenol and creosote-containing preservative solutions should never be applied to the inside of a cabin.

Store preservatives in original containers under lock and key—out of reach of children and pets—and away from foodstuff. Use all preservatives selectively and carefully. Follow recommended practices for the disposal of surplus preservatives and preservative containers.

Note: Registrations of preservatives are under constant review by the Environmental Protection Agency and the Department of Agriculture. Use only preservatives that bear a federal registration number and carry directions for home and garden use. Since the registration of preservatives is also under constant review by State and Federal authorities, a responsible State agency should be consulted as to the current status of any preservative.

Health and environmental concerns of wood preservative. Again, careful consideration must be given to the use of any chemicals used as preservatives. Wood preservatives are fungicides and when applied on site have much the same health problems as pesticides. Even if used properly, they can be a hazard. Make absolutely sure you read all directions for their use and follow all safety precautions.

Chapter 5

THE NEW HOMESTEAD

Starting work

Now that you have your materials and tools on hand, you're ready to begin actual work on your new homestead. Take your time and carefully think through the beginning steps. It can save you a lot of headaches later.

Clearing the site

This is one area that you definitely shouldn't rush into. You have to decide just how much clearing and excavation must be done. At the very least, the immediate area of the house should be graded flat and cleared of all brush and trees. Trenches for the foundation have to be dug, and excavation is also required for sewer lines, laterals (off main outlets), and septic tank. If the home is to have a basement, that section of the site will have to be excavated. Build any needed access roads at this time so that delivery trucks can get to your site with materials.

Hiring an excavation contractor is the easiest way to do all of this. You could do the work yourself if you're strong and willing to put in days of back-breaking work. Or you could do many of the initial chores, and then hire an operator to finish the heavy digging

jobs. This gives you more control over the clearing, but it takes time. If you do hire an excavation contractor to do all the work, be on the site whenever he is working. Make sure the operator understands what you intend to keep and what you need to remove. It takes only a moment for heavy equipment to undo something it took nature 100 years to produce.

With all the planning materials on hand, including the site plan and house building plans, you're ready for action.

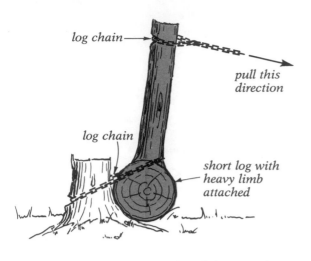

log chain

pull this direction

log chain

short log with heavy limb attached

You can use an old fashioned settler's stump lever to remove stumps from the area.

To clear the building site, do as much of this as you can, using your chain saw or axe. Clear out small brush, cut down trees that will be in the way, and grub out rocks and stumps.

If you want to do some or all of the clearing yourself, the first step is to clear away all the brush and trees. Small tree stumps can be removed by grubbing out, but larger stumps pose a real problem. Old-timers removed them with a log lever, as shown in the drawing, but they are best removed with power equipment.

Incidentally, if you want to use the bulldozer to clear large trees by pushing them over, leave the trees whole. Cutting a tree off several feet above ground makes it almost impossible for a bulldozer operator to grub out the stump without tearing up a lot of ground in the area—the height and weight of the standing tree is what gives the operator leverage for pushing it over. Remember, though, when large trees are pushed over, they can damage other trees and surrounding shrubs.

All brush should be piled away from the building site so it can be burned later (if allowed) as it dries. Make sure it's piled far enough away for safe burning. And remember, a brush pile can create a hot fire that can destroy surrounding trees.

Regardless of the method you use for clearing, be sure to save the topsoil by pushing or carrying it aside. You can spread it back later over the areas you want to replant.

The main thing to remember is that excavation and clearing can become destructive very fast. Save every tree, shrub, and patch of wildflowers you can, because it makes landscaping your home much easier: the natural look of the area helps your new log home blend in with the surroundings and you don't have to put in large numbers of domestic plants.

Make sure the immediate area of your driveway is cleaned, too. This is the best location for storing materials—including your logs. Soil removed from the excavation must be put somewhere; just piling it out back leaves a chore that you will later regret. If you can't find a low spot to fill, have it trucked away from the site.

If topsoil on your site is thin and rocky, you must not disturb it any more than necessary. Extensive disruption of this type of topsoil leads to erosion that can wreak havoc on your site and possibly endanger the house itself. Also, improper excavation in extremely dry climates can take many years to correct.

At the excavation stage, everything looks a mess. It's tempting to drive around the site, taking materials to a particular spot the easiest way. But a set of deep ruts cut in soft, springtime mud may stay for a long time and be extremely hard to remove unless you have the area regraded. This is something you will probably want to avoid if the rest of the area is to be left as natural as possible.

Follow your site plan carefully. To help keep the area clear during excavation, stand by with your chain saw and, as trees are pushed over by the bulldozer, buck off the stumps and tops. Then have the equipment operator push the stumps into a pile.

Trees that are close to the immediate site can be damaged by heavy equipment operators during the excavation. If there are valuable trees near the area, wrap them with discarded furniture boxes or lean boards against the tree and tie them in place with

You can make many of the small excavations yourself, such as those needed for piers.

Use a compass to ensure that the house will be sited in the most advantageous direction.

Once your site is leveled and cleared you can temporarily stake out the rough outlines of your home.

Small foundations, even water or sewer lines, may be dug by hand, soil and locality permitting.

binder twine or heavy cord. Even a small gash on a tree can cause it to become infected with pests and die. Watch, too, for low overhanging limbs; prune them back to allow room for the equipment to work in the area.

If the house is to be built against a hillside, you'll need a diversion terrace to run water around and away from the house. If you alter

Grade and provide terraces or water diversions to control water around the building. This is far easier during initial excavation than after the house is built.

the ground level, make sure you protect trees in the area; you can't fill around a tree without suffocating it. Build a masonry retaining wall around the tree before the fill is placed. The retaining wall must extend out from the tree for at least a foot on all sides. If you remove soil from around a tree you must shore up around its root system.

If you have to change the grades around trees, be careful not to cut into roots. If you're building up around a tree, build a circular wall to prevent smothering the tree.

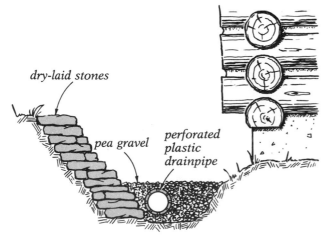

dry-laid stones

pea gravel

perforated plastic drainpipe

Temporary electricity

It takes time to get power into a new home site, often weeks—so apply early for an electrical hookup. Make sure you comply with local requirements and all code rulings concerning temporary power connections. In some locales you can hang a temporary power box (usually two 20-amp circuit breakers) to a tree or pole. In other areas you aren't allowed to run wiring above ground even temporarily. You should, of course, install a ground fault interrupter in the temporary power box.

Once you determine how and what you can do, install your temporary box and run cable to the meter pole, or meter location designated by the power company. Ordinarily they'll install the meter box. The temporary line is then connected into the meter box. Note: in some instances you may be prohibited from doing this feed yourself. Make sure you understand from the power company what you can and what you can't do.

At the same time you're getting your electricity, you should also arrange for a telephone hookup, one you can unplug and take home at night during construction. It will give you an immediate link to suppliers, subcontractors, and others.

Install the septic tank and laterals at this time. See Chapter 21. It may be a good idea to have the water supply installed—have at least one temporary aboveground faucet put in.

Taking delivery of a kit

Knowing how to take delivery and properly stack and store materials for a kit log home is important. The following is adapted from a Justus Homes, Inc., publication and gives a number of helpful tips on what to do when a log house kit arrives.

Okay, you've got your permits, hooked up temporary power, installed your septic tank, and completed and backfilled your foundation. Now it's time to take delivery of your package.

Temporary utilities, as on the pole at right, will give you power during construction. Any electrical supply must follow local codes. For temporary power, be sure your outlet is in a weatherproof box and is protected by a GFCI (ground-fault circuit interrupter).

On the big day, it would be a good idea to invite your most industrious family members and friends to a "cedar picnic" (they bring the food and drink, you provide the cedar!). Actually, you can buy the fried chicken and other fixings yourself with all the money the extra helpers will save you by unloading the truck. Because, although the first hour the truck is at your site is free, many trucking firms charge a fee of $40 an hour or more after that.

Unloading. Give thought to the truck or piggyback van that will be bringing in your package, because it will be a big one—usually with a 40-foot flatbed trailer.

Walk down your access road or driveway and determine just how much truck you can get on your land. If your land is relatively flat, you may be able to bring the truck as close as you want to. But, on steeper or heavily wooded lots, you sometimes have difficulty just getting the trailer off the road.

Renting a forklift is a good idea if delivery is by flatbed truck, especially if you are going to have to carry the materials any distance from the truck to your building site. A forklift can save enough time to eliminate waiting fees for the truck and it can help prevent damage, as there is less handling of the materials.

If you rent a forklift, make sure it has large pneumatic tires (not the small hard ones used

Upon arrival of precut kit logs, a forklift speeds and eases unloading.

PART 2.   LOGS, FOUNDATIONS, AND BUILDING SITES

in warehouses) so it can more around easily on your property.

A 6,000-pound forklift should be sufficient. But if you have to go to a 10,000-pounder to get the off-road pneumatic tires, by all means do it. Standard four-foot forks are fine. Hydraulic lateral adjustments are great (because you won't have to repeatedly move the entire forklift around), but they're not essential. The main thing is to make sure the forks are clean, and that you don't stick them too far into the load or slide them around beneath it unless you are certain that you aren't damaging the materials.

Some long-distance shipments come in enclosed trailers. This means using hand unloading procedures and six to eight persons will be needed.

If your site has a limited turning area, you may want to use a truck with two smaller trailers, called a set of doubles. In some cases, you can even have the load delivered by a truck with a boom attached.

Stacking materials.
Store materials in 30, 40, 50, or more separate stacks, according to the function, dimension, and length of the materials—and do a complete inventory immediately. With a logical and orderly beginning, every step that follows will be that much more certain and efficient.

Guide to site storage plans.
What follows is a good storing/stacking plan if space isn't a problem. This plan can also be used when space is a problem.

It doesn't really matter where you put your materials, as long as they're in stacks separated according to function, dimension, and length of the wood. For instance, you'll want your 14-foot lengths of 2 × 10 utility wood for joist blocking to be in a pile separate from your 14-foot lengths of higher grade 2 × 10 floor joists. Obviously, it is important to be aware of the different grades of woods and the different functions they have. That way, for example, you won't use pieces with a beautiful, clear grain for hidden structural pieces.

Place materials needed earliest in the construction (like the girders and joists) closest to the foundation. This is so you will spend only a minimum amount of time handling and re-

stacking them during construction. Think of the procedures you will go through with the different materials and come up with a good plan *before* the truck arrives.

Tarps and dunnage.
Before the truck arrives also have on hand plenty of dunnage and plastic to protect your materials. Stacks of material should be at least four inches off the ground; higher, if the ground is spongy or if they're going to be sitting there for more than three months.

Utility grade 4 × 4 is inexpensive dunnage, and you will always be able to find a use for it later. You'll need perhaps 100 or 200 linear feet. Extra height can be gained by adding utility 2 × 4s. You might even lay the dunnage out according to your site storage plan before the truck arrives and use a grease pen to tell your helpers what gets stacked on each space. Make sure the dunnage is laid out as level as possible so it doesn't distort the wall timbers.

A 20-foot-wide by 100-foot-long roll of either four-mil or six-mil plastic will cost perhaps $40 and will be very important in protecting your materials. Make sure it isn't clear plastic. That way the sun won't discolor the finish lumber before it has been stained or painted. (Hint: This plastic can also be used as your vapor barrier later on when you pour your basement floor.)

Provide a safe, dry storage space for materials, especially your logs.

The arrival. With these preparations, you will be in good shape when the truck pulls into position with your new home.

Start by unloading the truck. Everything but the wall timbers goes directly to its proper pile. The timbers can be put together in temporary stacks (so you can do a piece-by-piece inventory as each is carried to its pile.)

The windows and sliding glass doors should be checked immediately—even before the truck departs. Completely unwrap all glass and check carefully for any small cracks or broken glass. Rewrap them if they are not going to be installed or finished right away. Note any such damage directly on the bill of lading so a damage claim against the carrier can be processed.

After you have checked the windows, make sure that they are stored upright in a secure fashion (store doors this way too). Cover them with plastic as well.

Items such as doors, windows, and framed glass must be handled with care to prevent damage. Do not try to unload these alone, especially the heavier items because you risk both serious personal injury and damage to the materials. Framed-in glass can crack under its own weight; therefore, handle carefully and carry it *vertically*.

Ideally, a storage rack is the best way to keep your stopped-in glass until it is needed. This eliminates dangerous, uneven concentrations of pressure that can break the glass. If you decide not to build a storage rack, do what you can to store glass in a position as close to that of a rack as possible. Please also keep in mind the following:

• Handle stopped-in glass twice: from truck to storage, storage to rough opening.

• The larger the glass and gable angle, the greater the chance the glass will crack.

• Any pressure against the tips of gable glass will cause uneven loading and result in cracking at the gable angle.

• Store gable glass with the larger units at the back.

• Same size units should be stored together, back to back.

• Never store more than six units together. Sills are wider than frames which creates an increasing angle as each piece of glass is laid against the next. Cardboard packaging, folded up and placed between the units, will equalize the pressure.

• Secure your stopped-in glass! A gust of wind can "blow you away".

The inventory. As soon as the last piece has been unloaded and you've made a quick check of the windows for damage, you can send the truck on its way and begin your inventory. Unless it is absolutely pouring down rain, this inventory should be done immediately.

Begin with the items covered by the shipping list. Just go up to your stack of 12-foot floor joists and count them against what is listed on the shipping list. Then go to your pile of 16-foot floor joists and so on. Because you've already stacked each length in a separate pile, the inventory will be easy—and the entire construction process will be simplified because you'll always be able to walk right up to whatever you need. And because your stacks are well separated, there will be little chance of your using materials incorrectly.

Continue this process as you work your way through the entire shipping list, checking everything from the mudsill to the insulation, nails to caulking. When you check your beams, make sure they are well dunnaged with supporting pieces every four feet or so to protect them from sagging. These beams are heavy so you will want to make sure you have enough dunnage to keep them off the ground. You may want to use 2×4s on top of your 4×4s here. You also will want to leave them in their protective coverings until you are ready to use them.

Make sure no one has placed plastic beneath the piles because that will just block the natural absorption of the soil.

Chapter 6 BUILDING THE FOUNDATION

A solid support

House construction progresses through a series of stages, and laying the foundation is the second stage. Up to this point the work has been preparatory but now actual construction of the house begins. Make no mistake, this part is slow, hard work, especially if you do it all yourself. But before you charge ahead, make sure you understand the building techniques.

Many old cabins were built on nothing more than piles of flat stones or "piers" along the outside edges of the building. As these stones sank into the ground, they gave the structure a characteristic sag and tilt. Dry-laid stone foundations of flat rocks can still be used, particularly if you want to cut cost. However, most of today's log homes are set on solid foundations.

You could pour a concrete footing, then use flat stone piers on top of the footing if you want to cut costs, but the results may not be worth the effort.

If you are not building out in the wilderness, you will probably be restricted to some sort of conventional foundation by local building codes. And because of the weight of logs, the walls need a good solid footing.

Foundation types

On hard ground, where bedrock is close to the surface, buildings usually require only a minimum foundation.

There are four kinds of foundations: The simplest and least expensive is a pier. This can be made of concrete, concrete blocks, or (for simple buildings) flat stones that are either mortared or laid dry. In some areas, treated wood can be used.

Many old-time log homes merely rested on piles of dry-laid stone.

Building the foundation of your log home is one of the most important aspects of the job. This is hard, heavy work and some types of foundations require expensive equipment. Thus, most log home builders choose to let a subcontractor do all or a portion.

Your decision to do some or all of the work yourself may depend largely on the type foundation you choose, the masonry experience you have, and the tools you have or can rent.

The next least expensive and probably one of the simplest kinds of foundation is the concrete slab on grade. Sewer, water, heating, air conditioning, and electrical outlets must be installed before the slab is poured.

Another kind of foundation is the continuous foundation with a crawl space. This is also sometimes called a perimeter foundation. It may be of concrete, concrete block, or in some cases, stone.

The most complicated form of foundation is the full basement. It may be made of poured, reinforced concrete or concrete block.

Regardless of the type of foundation you choose, it must rest on proper footings, which must be laid at a depth that is slightly below the frost line for your locale. If the foundation wall is concrete or block, it's generally 8 inches thick. However, 12 inches may be required by some local codes, especially if the foundation has been excavated several feet below grade. You may also be required to make the foundation wider because of the extra width and weight of the logs.

Subcontracting the foundation

If you decide to subcontract your foundation, the following information, used by permission of Justus Homes, Inc. may be of value:

We strongly recommend that the foundation be poured *before* you take delivery of the log home kit package for two reasons. You won't have to move stacks of materials to make room for the excavation equipment. And your package won't sit around waiting for concrete work to be completed.

Another recommendation is that if you subcontract the foundation work, make sure you get a real pro to do the job. Because kit timbers are precision cut, the diagonal, horizontal, perimeter, and elevation dimensions of your foundation should be square and level within one-eighth inch.

Exact positioning of the piers and girder pockets is also required. Write into the contract the requirement that your subcontractor is to pay for and make any corrections that are needed.

Mainly, you want a professional job—so that your wall timbers will pound together as true and as snug as possible. Ask a potential subcontractor how he gets a foundation to grade. If he says that he can eyeball it, or tells you he pours the concrete soupy enough to seek its own level, or if he says he makes his own forms, get someone else. Good subcontractors use a transit to level your grade and use commercial forms. Also, ask him if he pours the footings and walls at the same time. The conscientious subcontractor will do this separately, so adjustments can be made before the walls are poured.

When you get down to the actual pouring, make sure that your subcontractor places all pier blocks, footings, and girder pockets according to the foundation plan and that they are of the right dimensions. For plumbing and utility access, make sure your subcontractor checks with the other appropriate subcontractors to determine proper placement. Have him use solid wood blocks (that can later be drilled out) or plastic pipes. This way you won't have to chisel out the concrete later.

Need for steel.
Because the cost of rebar is negligible and its tensile strength is good insurance, always have your subcontractor put steel reinforcing bars in the concrete footings (even if code doesn't require it). Should a corner of your foundation be undercut by unusual settling, flood, or earthquake, the bars will hold it together.

These reinforcing bars usually are ½ inch in diameter and run parallel along the length of the footing. Some concrete subcontractors come in and just drop the rebars on the ground before pouring. That doesn't do much good. The bars should be suspended by wires so they will become an integral part of the concrete.

Inside the post footings, two or three bars should run each way to form a grid that can be encased by the concrete.

For basement walls, vertical bars should be placed approximately every 32 inches, with horizontal bars wired to them a minimum of every 32 inches. Always check local codes and take into account special conditions before deciding on steel work design. If one wall faces an uphill slope and has a retaining function, place the bars approximately 16 inches apart. (Some counties require an engineer-certified wall for bulkheading and retaining—a good concrete subcontractor will know this.)

For the actual pouring, make sure your subcontractor has enough concrete to pour all the walls at one time. After pouring, he should tap the forms with a hammer to prevent exposed rock pockets—and to create smooth walls. You could ask your subcontractor to add a substance called Darex to the concrete before it is poured.

Anchor bolts.
Also check the placement of the anchor bolts that your foundation man provides. These are usually 10 inches long, with an umbrella-handle at the bottom end to keep them anchored in the concrete. The bolts in turn anchor the wood structure of your house to the foundation.

Anchors should be set 4 feet apart—but within 8 inches of each corner and within 12 inches of all door openings. Having too many bolts can be a luxury. Having too few can be a real headache.

Make sure they're straight up and down (so you don't have to drill angled holes in your mudsill), and that they protrude at least 2½ inches (so they can go through a mudsill 1½ inches thick and still have room for the washer and nut).

Also make sure post footings have a vertical steel rod in the center, protruding from the top, so that you can later drill a matching hole in the base of each post for lateral support. Or have your subcontractor use a manufactured post bracket.

Concrete floors.
A few days after pouring the walls, the basement floor can be poured. Make sure you have provided for any rough-in plumbing or electrical needs first.

The garage floor could be poured at the same time. Make sure your subcontractor first lays down a mesh wire grating to give the slab the extra strength it will need to support your car or truck. It is a good idea to pour the garage slab with a gentle slope toward the door, about 1 inch for every 10 feet.

If the house is to be built square, the foundation must first be laid out and constructed square. Establish a right triangle with two adjoining walls. The rest of the walls can be measured to fit. Tie the string to the stakes you have temporarily driven (pull it tight but not enough to move the stakes), then measure nine feet and mark the string for one wall. Measure 12 feet and mark that location on the adjoining string. The distance between the two marks should be 15 feet. If it is not, you can square the corner by shifting one or both strings until you achieve the 15-foot diagonal measurement. Then measure from the square corner to accurately locate the other three corners.

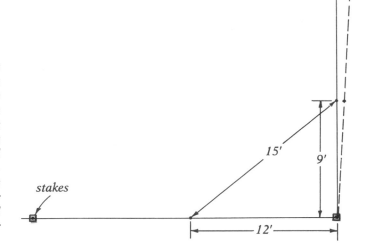

A compass helps establish the house's relation to the sun. Then drive tentative corner stakes and measure for equal wall lengths.

Staking out the house

If you don't plan to subcontract the foundation, here's how to do the job: First establish the exact outside boundaries of your home. At first this task might seem complicated, but actually it's quite simple. It must, however, be done as accurately as possible. A small error in a dimension or an out-of-square foundation will multiply when you start building walls.

Establish a level starting line. This will be the top of the foundation receiving the sill logs.

Drive a temporary stake for each corner of the building. This includes inside and outside corners for L-shape or T-shape buildings as well. Use 2 × 2s for these stakes—sharpen the ends so they can be driven into the ground easily. Drive a copper or aluminum nail into the upper center of each stake. To position accurately, locate one corner of the proposed building in your cleared area and drive the stake into place, making sure it's driven as solidly as possible so that it can't be accidently knocked out. Using a 100- or 50-foot tape (depending on the length of your house), measure one long wall of the building to the approximate location of the second stake. Use a compass to situate this wall exactly where you want it, according to its location on your site plan. Have someone hold the tape on the exact center of the tack in the first stake. Now drive the second stake.

To lay out the second (adjoining) wall, move the end of the tape to the second stake and measure for the second wall. Drive the third stake in the approximate location of the end

PART 2.   LOGS, FOUNDATIONS, AND BUILDING SITES

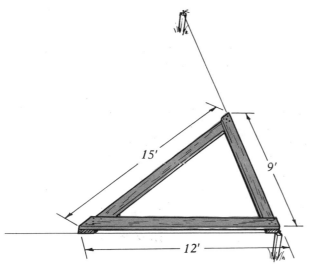

Make up a large wooden triangle of 1 × 4s to help speed the squaring.

of that wall, outlining an approximate 90 degree L-shape.

Now you have to establish a perfect 90-degree angle between the two walls. This can be done in one of two ways. The simplest: Use a triangle with proportions of 3:4:5. Tie builder's line to the nail at the first stake, run it around the nail at the second stake and over to the third stake. Tie it there. Starting at the second stake, measure off 9 feet on one side and mark this measurement on the line with chalk or a carpenter's pencil. Then measure 12 feet on the adjoining line and mark it. If the angle of the two lines is 90 degrees, the measurement between the two points (the hypotenuse of the triangle) will be 15 feet. If it's not, move the third stake in or out to achieve the exact measurement.

The other method is to make up a giant measuring triangle of 1 × 4s. Then merely lay it along the lines and move the lines in or out as needed to line up with the triangle.

To position the fourth stake, merely measure each side to get the exact measurement and drive the stake at that location. It helps to have a couple of tapes on hand. It also helps to have a person holding the tapes at each corner stake. Do this for each corner of the building—including any additional rooms.

Make a final check to ensure that the building is perfectly square by measuring diagonally from corner to corner. Then switch and measure diagonally between the opposite two corners. If the measurements are not exactly the same, either move the corner stakes or the nails in the top of them in or out until both diagonal measurements are the same.

After driving the stakes for all four corners, measure diagonally between the stakes. The diagonal measurements should be the same for a square building. If they are not, shift the stakes until they are.

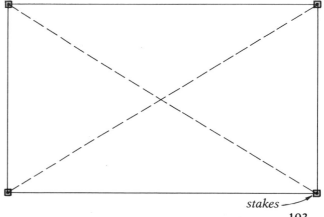

stakes

CHAPTER 6. BUILDING THE FOUNDATION

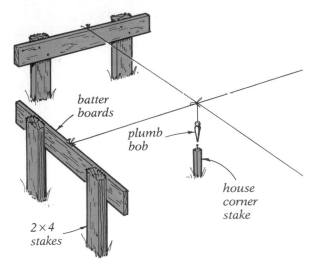

batter boards

plumb bob

house corner stake

2×4 stakes

Once batter boards are erected, they stay in place until the foundation job is completed. They must be at least six feet outside the footing and foundation boundary. Make them with 2 × 4 stakes, which you will drive solidly in the ground. A 1 × 4 is nailed over the top of the stakes.

The tops of the batter boards must be horizontal and absolutely level with each other. Establish whether they are with a transit (if you have one) or by using a water hose with a glass tube in one end.

Batter boards

Now you should have the entire house outlined with builder's string. The next step is to erect batter boards. The outlining stakes will be removed, but the batter boards stay in place until the entire foundation, footing, or basement has been constructed. Batter boards are held by 2×4 stakes driven solidly into the ground in a triangle or L-shape around the corner. Then nail 1×4 or 1×6 batter boards to the stakes to create a right angle. Note that the batter boards must be set back at least 4 feet from the building outline or outline stakes. The tops of the batter boards must be the same height as the tops of foundation corners.

To locate these properly, start at the most elevated part of your proposed foundation and measure straight up to the height of the foundation (make sure this height is no less than 18 inches to prevent damage from termites). Nail the batter boards in place at the proper height. Now determine the height of the next corner board, which must be level with the first. This can be done using mason's string line and a string level, or if the building is small enough, a long board with a level on it.

A more accurate method, however, is to use a hose level. Place a funnel in a hose and put the funnel end at the first established height. Take the opposite end of the hose to the next corner. Hold the top of the hose exactly flush with the top of the first batter board and slowly pour water into the funnel. The opposite end of the hose should be held in place near the location of the second set of batter boards.

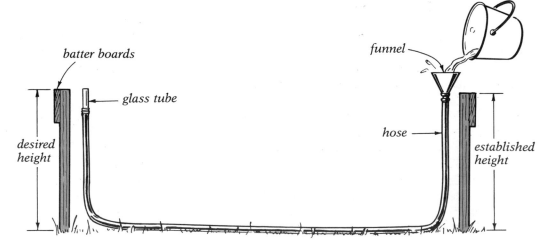

batter boards

glass tube

funnel

hose

desired height

established height

When the water is level with the top of both ends of the hose, it indicates a level line, establishing the height of the second set of batter boards. If you use a pair of glass or clear-plastic tubes in the ends of the hose, you can see the water height better. Establish the height of all the batter boards in this manner. A transit is the best tool for establishing a level height.

Once all batter boards have been installed on all corners at the correct height, mark the building outline. To do this, tie weights to builder's string and drop them over the tops of the batter boards as shown. Drop a plumb bob where the two strings cross at each corner and shift the strings until the plumb bob falls exactly on the nail head or tack in the corner stakes. Drive a nail at the exact location of the string lines on all batter boards. This locates the outside boundary of your foundation.

To mark the inside boundary, measure the width of the proposed foundation and drive another nail at each batter board for each corner. Now, to establish the footing width, measure past the foundation marks on both sides to the width you want your footings to be and drive marker nails. Any time you need to re-establish any of these reference points, merely refer to these positions and hang the string again.

Excavating footings and foundation

Use builder's lime to mark the outlines of the footing excavation. Then remove the strings and dig the footing: Usually, if you plan a basement, the general area is excavated first, making the excavation at least four feet larger on all sides than the proposed building. Then batter boards are installed in the excavation for reference to the footings and foundation walls.

If you're going to use piers instead of a foundation, you should still erect batter boards for reference and correct installation of the piers. If you want to install piers under the center portion of the house, a single batter board can be used at each end of the foundation to locate them. But again, make sure the tops of the piers are level with one another.

Once the batter boards are installed, run string lines and drop a plumb bob to establish the exact location of the outside edge of the foundation. Measure the thickness of the footing and foundation and drive nails on each batter board to establish these points. By tying string between the nails on opposite batter boards, you can see the outline of the footing.

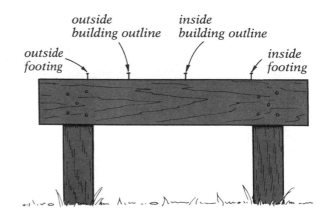

outside building outline   inside building outline

outside footing   inside footing

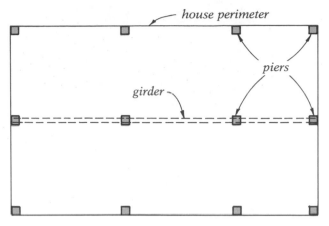

Piers are needed for girder support on larger buildings.

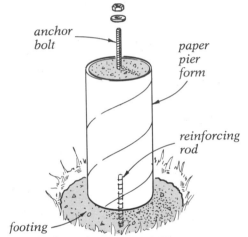

Piers can be formed in several different ways. For this you can use disposable fiberboard pier forms available from building suppliers.

Building foundations

Here's how to construct various kinds of foundations:

Piers. Piers may be made of various materials. Some woods such as redwood, cedar, cypress, or locust may be used for piers, since they are resistant to insects and decay. However, they're not nearly as durable as masonry or stone piers.

The best pier is made of concrete. Concrete piers must be sunk below the frost line or they'll heave in winter. The average size should be 2 feet square.

Normally the size of the footing is twice the width of the wall, but never less than 8 inches wide. It's as thick as the wall is wide. The wall foundation should be centered on the footing. Pier footings are usually a bit deeper and larger because the load is concentrated on them. Codes say that the footing must run to 12 inches below the frost line, which can be up to 6 feet deep.

Check with local building suppliers or your county extension agent to determine the exact depth of the frost line in your area.

Make the pier tops extend at least 18 inches above ground level to provide a well-ventilated crawl space. Piers can be poured in one piece (for low piers) or in two pieces (first a pier footing and then the pier itself).

You can create your own forms quite easily. The piers shown here were made in two ways. The small doubled forms were made using sections of stove pipe material tied tightly with wire. The larger corner pier was made by inverting a metal garbage can on a heavy footing, then cutting out the bottom and filling it with concrete.

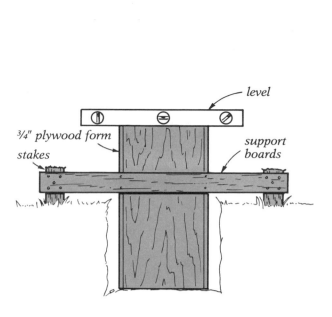

Reusable pier forms can be made of wood. This pier and footing form allows a one-piece, one-time pour, and is quite often used for short piers.

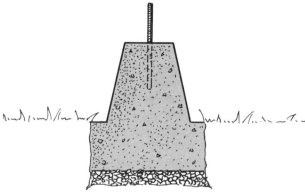

A two-piece pier has a wider footing, shown, which is poured first, after which the pier form is built.

Use 1 × 12s or exterior plywood to make the forms. Make sure the forms extend into the ground a bit so that none of the concrete is forced out as it's being poured. Install ⅜-inch vertical reinforcing rod in the excavation, driving each until it is just below the top of the pier. Tie cross braces of reinforcing rod in place, using tie wire.

To make a two-part pier, excavate as before and install the reinforcing rods, including two

that will extend up into the second pour. Make the first pour, tamping it in place. Rough the surface so the second pour will adhere, and then allow it to cure. After it has cured, build a form for the upper pier around the reinforcing rod and pour. Make sure that the concrete is well-tamped.

Even if you plan a perimeter foundation, you may need cast-concrete footings on the inside to support concrete girders.

These are form boards for pouring the footing.

A precast concrete footing and pier can be used for short piers or where a wooden pier will be placed on top of the precast pier.

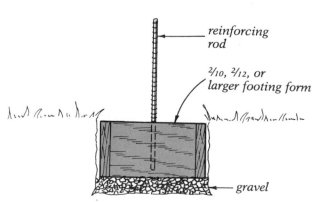

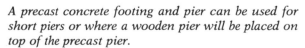

A concrete-block pier can also be used. Set the block on a layer of tamped gravel (with mortar on top) or pour a concrete footing pad. Then double the blocks, mortaring them crosswise to each other. You can also fill the centers of the blocks and insert reinforcing rods.

You can use stones and mortar for piers, but you need an adequate number and a variety of shapes of stones.

Note: a metal termite shield should be placed over the top of the pier to prevent termite infestation. Also anchor bolts must be installed while the concrete or mortar is still soft.

Slab foundations. A slab on grade is considered by some to be the easiest to build. It costs more for materials than piers, but because you eliminate floor joists, the final cost is usually less than a foundation and crawl space. It's also a lot less expensive than a full basement. The only requirement for a slab foundation is that the site be graded to a flat, level surface. This usually means filling in certain areas with stones, then fill dirt, and tamping solidly.

There are three kinds of slab foundations. In hot, dry climates where there is hard or dry ground, slab foundations can be nothing more than a slab of concrete with the edge thickened. In other places, the slab may have a perimeter footing poured at the same time as the slab (all in one piece). Or a perimeter footing may be poured first, then the slab poured within its boundaries. The latter two types would be the best choice for log homes because

A slab foundation consists of a combination one-piece wall support and concrete floor. The edges of the slab should be strengthened with a footing that extends below frostline.

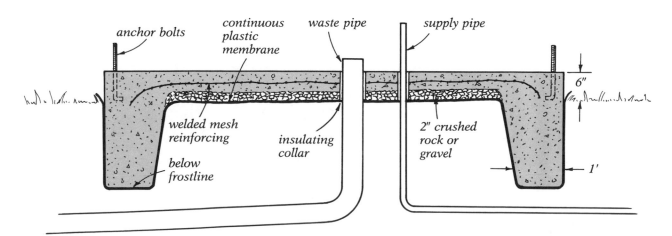

     PART 2. LOGS, FOUNDATIONS, AND BUILDING SITES

of the weight of the walls. Local codes regulate foundations, footings, and slab requirements.

The first step in creating the monolithic, or one-piece slab-with-footing foundation, is to lay out the building outlines with a batter board. Then remove all turf and topsoil within the boundaries of the building and a few feet past the building outline. Now dig the footing trenches. The outside edges of the footing must be directly under the edges of the building slab.

If the soil is loose, compact it solidly using a hand tamper. Next you install the form boards for the outside of the slab and footing edge. On hard dry ground, the slab can be poured directly on the ground as shown. Normally, however, you will need to add a layer of gravel covered with a moisture barrier.

Insulate the slab if your area has heavy frost. Before pouring, all services that run through or under the slab, such as sewer, water, gas, and electrical lines, should be installed. All of these must be insulated with tar paper or thin plastic foam if the runs are to be buried in concrete or protrude from the slab. Make sure pipes protrude well above the surface of the slab.

Materials and tools

It's almost impossible to mix enough concrete, even with a power mixer, to fill the slab and footing without some of the concrete hardening before the pour is completed. Call a ready-mix company. Have the entire form in place when the truck arrives. Also have rein-

forcing rods positioned as outlined by your local codes. In most cases, you need two reinforcing bars running horizontally through the footing, about halfway up from the bottom. These can be held up on stones placed in the bottom of the trench.

The slab itself also has to be reinforced. Code rulings on this may vary. Welded wire mesh placed in the concrete at the center of the pour (on stones) should suffice. You could add reinforcing bars running in both directions through the slab, about four to six feet apart. This is prudent in areas subject to earthquakes.

Before you order the concrete from a ready-mix company, make sure you have on hand some shovels, a rake, and an old hoe for pushing and pulling the concrete around in the forms. You'll also need a screeding board for leveling the concrete off with the tops of the forms. You should have some old rubber boots to wade in the concrete and a bull float for the final dragging off of the concrete. Steel trowels are used for final troweling. If the slab is large, you may want to rent a power concrete finisher. It can help you do a better job.

Large slab foundations are poured in two or more sections. Pour one section, screed it off, and bull float it smooth. Then (on a three-pour job) pour the middle section when you can safely walk on the two previously-poured sections.

The slab foundation is simple to form. All waste and supply piping as well as conduit for electrical runs should be installed before pouring the floor.

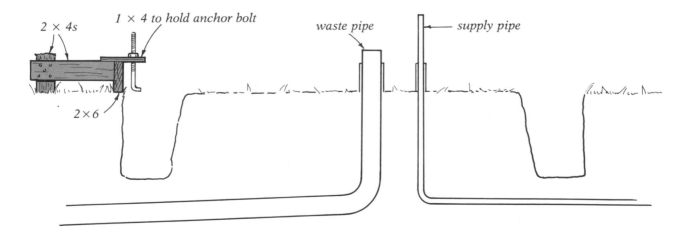

Concrete for basement floors (as shown) and for concrete slabs is usually delivered by a large ready-mix truck, which backs as close to the site as possible and pours ready-mix through sloping shoots into waiting wheelbarrows. The mix is then wheelbarrowed to the far end of the floor and spread with shovels and rakes before being screeded (as shown) by skimming a straight long 2 × 4 with forth-and-back motion, along the tops of the forms.

Making the pour

With form ready, the truck on hand, and all tools nearby, you're ready to make the pour. Start pouring in the far back corner, pushing and pulling the concrete around with the rake and shovel until the footing and slab areas are full, working toward the front as you go. Avoid overworking the concrete or moving it around too much as this only makes it soupy and weak. Jab the rake up and down in the concrete to settle it well in the form and around all the reinforcing bars. Strive to remove all air pockets or voids. Occasionally bang on the outside edge of the form to knock away any air pockets that may have formed there.

Make sure the form is completely full. If you have any concrete left over, dump it in a wheelbarrow until you've finished screeding.

Screeding. Next step is to remove the excess concrete from the form. This is done by dragging a screeding board—usually a 2 × 4—across the tops of the form boards at the same time you push it back and forth with a jiggling motion. This will settle and force the concrete down, bring water to the top of the concrete and remove any excess, leveling the concrete with the form sides. It takes two people to do this on a wide pour—it can be heavy work. As the concrete builds up ahead of the screeding board, rake it out of the way. Fill in any low spots with more concrete and go back over it with the screeding board. You have to start at the end each time you screed, and level to the other end. It normally takes at least a couple of passes before the concrete is leveled. On large pours you can make the pour in several sections by using temporary 2 × 4s in place (as

Next a jitterbug tamper (above left) with open metal grate at the bottom is plunged repeatedly into the pour to help release air bubbles. After the floor is screeded again with the 2 × 4, a bull float (as shown right) is used to smooth the surface further. Later, the concrete will set hard enough to support small sections of plywood laid over the surface like islands to distribute your weight enough to allow you to move out on them to finish with a hand trowel. Last, edging trowels are used to cut smooth edges along the forms.

shown), screeding to level out the concrete. Then remove the 2 × 4s and fill in with extra concrete.

It's a good idea to pour alternate sections as shown, then fill in the center afterwards, screeding as you go. You can walk in the concrete during screeding so long as you keep filling in your foot holes and screeding over them.

Finishing. A bull float smooths and levels the slab. This evens out the ridges left from screeding and removes excess water from the surface. Make sure you keep strokes parallel to the bull float, lifting at the end of each pull. Start as far onto the slab as you can reach. Always keep the float tilted so the edge doesn't dig in.

The final finish is done with a metal trowel—smooth as desired. Sprinkling a bit

of water over the surface before using the trowel gives a slicker surface. Use small sections of plywood to kneel on, working backwards. Pick up the plywood as you go, smoothing the area after each piece has been removed. Because the job of troweling takes quite a bit of time, you'll probably need some help on this portion, although a power trowel can make the job fast even for one man.

Curing. The concrete should cure at least three days before you remove the form boards. After the concrete has set up for about four to five hours, spray it with a fine mist to dampen, but not soak, its surface. Then cover it with burlap, old newspapers, or plastic and keep the surface damp for four or more days. Curing should continue for at least a week before you walk on the surface.

Perimeter footings and foundations

Foundations for log homes should be built with the ends of the foundation wall half a log higher than the side walls to accommodate the starting logs. Perimeter footings and foundations can be made of concrete, concrete block, or concrete faced with stone. If made of concrete, they can be one piece or two (footing and foundation).

Single-pour footing/foundation.

This design isn't used quite as much as separately poured footings and foundations, but it does simplify the task and cuts down on time. Lay out the outside dimensions of the footings, the wall thickness, and the outside boundary of the wall on the batter boards. Then position builder's or mason's string to show the dimensions. Excavate the footing and construct the forms. Bring all service pipes in below the footing and frost line before pouring the footing. Make sure any low spots under the edge of the footing are filled with stone.

Two-piece footing/foundation.

Usually, the footing is poured separately from the foundation and, if the soil is stable, the footing is poured directly in a trench dug without forms. However, with less-stable soils you'll have to construct forms to hold the concrete in place. The forms must be leveled using a carpenter's level. Fill in holes under the form with stones to keep the concrete from running out.

If you're pouring without forms, drive small wooden stakes into the soil at the bottom of the trench. Their tops should be level with the height of the footing. Pour the concrete and smooth more or less to the height of the stakes—then pull them out and fill the holes with concrete and smooth over.

Form a key in the footing to help hold the concrete foundation in place when it's poured on top of the footing. Form the key by using a beveled 2 × 4 (coated with used crankcase oil) set flush in the freshly poured concrete of the footing.

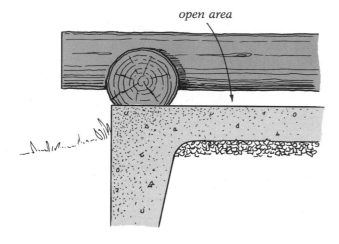

open area

The ends of the walls on a slab in most cases will be open unless special forming is used to raise the height of the concrete there.

A single, one-piece, one-pour foundation can be used in some localities.

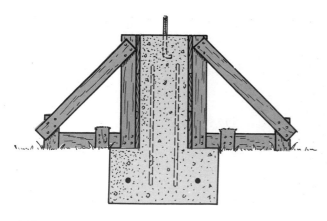

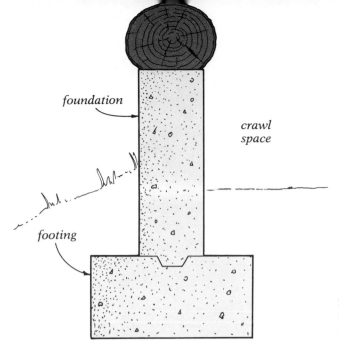

foundation

crawl space

footing

A two-piece (footing and foundation) pour is the most commonly used continuous foundation.

The first step in pouring a two-piece foundation is to form and pour the footing. Note the 2 × 4 key installed in the top of the footing form. When the wood key is later removed, it leaves a groove that will interlock with the foundation that follows.

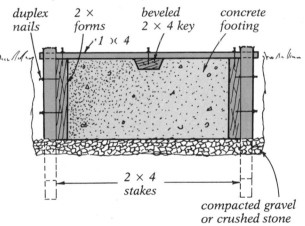

duplex nails   2 × forms   beveled 2 × 4 key   concrete footing

1 × 4

2 × 4 stakes

compacted gravel or crushed stone

If a footing must be poured on a slope, make stepped footing forms.

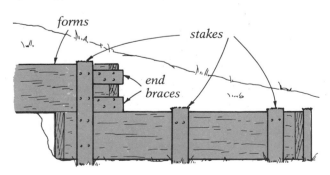

forms

stakes

end braces

Reinforce the footings with two to three reinforcing bars spaced about 3 to 4 inches off the bottom of the trench, held in place on stones. Bend them to fit around corners. Make sure they run the entire perimeter of the footing.

You may be required to have an inspection after the forms for the footing are completed, but before the concrete is poured, to determine that you have the proper size footing and the correct amount of reinforcement.

If you're building on a steep hill you may want to make use of stepped footings. These are nothing more than a series of steps to avoid ending up with a high, unsightly, and expensive foundation at the low end of the hill. Pour the bottom portion first and allow it to set up, then pour the upper portions. Reinforcing rod must run from the upper into the lower parts.

Normally, you don't have to wet down footing concrete. However, it's a good idea to wet the soil in the trench before the pour. Remove forms within a couple of days or they will become hard to remove.

This is a typical perimeter foundation for a crawl space. (Photo courtesy Authentic Log Homes Corp.)

CHAPTER 6. BUILDING THE FOUNDATION

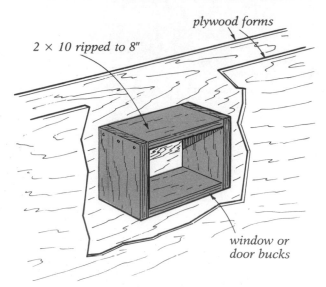

2 × 10 ripped to 8"

plywood forms

window or door bucks

Any opening you want in the wall must be provided for with bucks enclosed in the formwork.

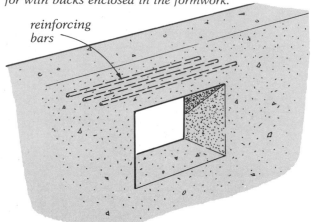

reinforcing bars

The area over openings, if any, must be reinforced with steel bars.

Girders should be set in girder pockets preformed with wooden bucks in the concrete.

The biggest problem in providing a full basement is the large excavation needed. For this, allow two or three feet of perimeter clearance.

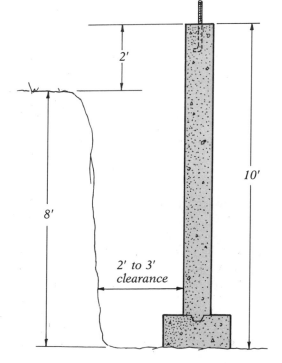

2'

10'

8'

2' to 3' clearance

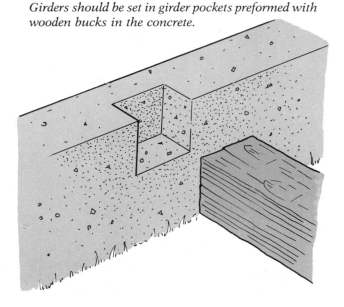

PART 2.   LOGS, FOUNDATIONS, AND BUILDING SITES

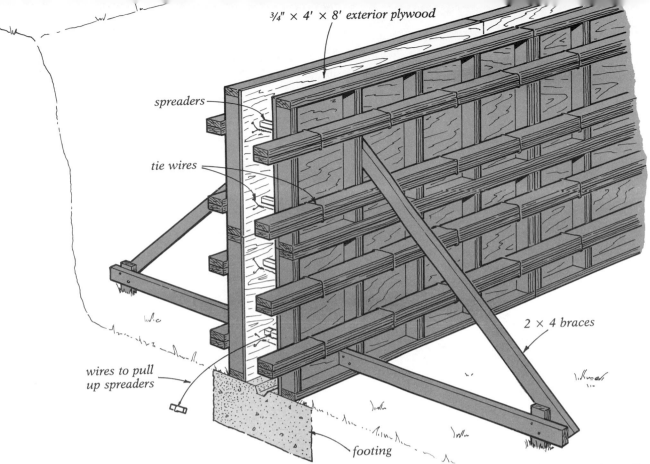

3/4" × 4' × 8' exterior plywood

spreaders

tie wires

wires to pull up spreaders

footing

2 × 4 braces

Once the basement excavation is made, the footing is poured the same way a shorter foundation is. The walls are formed and poured, making a continuous concrete wall for the basement. You can rent special forms for basement work or build your own using dimension lumber and oiled or exterior plywood, which later can be used for subflooring.

Pouring the foundation

After the footing has cured for about five to six days you're ready to form the foundation. Remove the form boards and wooden keys and construct the form for the foundation as shown. You can make it of either plywood reinforced with studs on the back or of 2-inch-thick boards. Forms for foundations have to be constructed properly; seeing a yard or two of concrete pouring through a broken form is enough to make a grown man cry. There is no remedy! Everything must be correct before the pour.

Individual sections of forms should be nailed together from the outside using duplex nails (nails that have a double head so they can be pulled out easily). Set up the outside form boards first, then use a carpenter's level to establish the correct height of the ones on the inside. Set them level with the outside ones; use ties and spreaders.

A foundation wall may be only a couple of feet high for a crawl space wall, or 8 feet high for a basement foundation wall. The basic principles are the same, but the form requirements for a full-height basement wall are more stringent. The weight of the poured concrete can cause problems. Constructing a proper form for a basement takes a great deal of work, material, and some knowledge of working concrete. Any openings in the wall of the foundation must be boxed in with wooden forms called a buck.

Making the pour. Higher, larger foundation walls should be poured slowly to allow the concrete enough time to set up and hold it's own weight. Start the pour at the back corner of the foundation, if possible. You can't push a large amount of concrete around the deep forms as easily as you can in shallow ones. Make sure the concrete is settled well down.

The proportion of water, cement, and sand should be such that a fairly soupy mix results. It will level itself out without a lot of pushing and shoveling. Once the concrete pour reaches a spacer, pull the spacer out.

When the concrete reaches the top of the forms, screed it off and set the sill anchor bolts in place. Use a wooden float to smooth down the top surface of the foundation wall. Make sure you get the areas around the sill bolts smooth and flush.

Allow about a day for the concrete to set up, then remove the forms by cutting away the form-holding wires or snapping off the special form-holding bolts. Later on you can cut back the wires or snap ends and patch up the holes in the concrete. Any opening in the wall that will have concrete above it must be supported with reinforcing bars.

Stone-faced concrete foundations

An easily adaptable variation of the concrete foundation is a combined stone-and-concrete foundation. First build a standard concrete form on the back side. Brace it well

A concrete block or poured concrete foundation can be made more attractive by veneering the surface with stones. (Photo courtesy Boyne Falls Log Homes.)

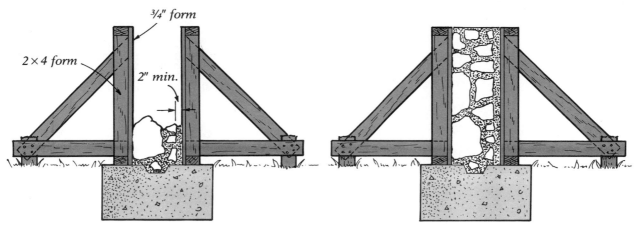

Here's an alternative way to erect a stone foundation, especially for the inexperienced stone mason: Build a combined poured concrete and stone foundation. This typically is used on many timber-frame or beam houses. You would pour the materials between the beams. It's sometimes called slip forming; entire houses can be built this way.

from the back, then set stones in mortar on the front and pour concrete. Set stones in this, then pour concrete behind and between the stones to the form back. This can be done a little at a time—as you get time to work on the project—and is an excellent method of achieving a good solid foundation economically, if you have the stones on hand.

A similar slip-forming method may also be used to create an economical foundation. Place

When building with slip forming, typically a footing is poured first; then a shallow form is erected. Concrete is poured over the footing and stones placed against the outside surface of the form. Then more concrete is poured, and the job is continued until the foundation is completed.

movable forms in position as shown. Pour a layer of concrete on the bottom, then place a layer of stones against the outside of the form. Now pour concrete in around them. Another layer of stones can be positioned and more concrete poured. Pour until you reach the top of the form. If you're pouring a large, high wall such as a basement foundation, pour only about two feet, allow the concrete to set up, then raise the form and pour another couple of feet.

Clean the mortar from between the stones with a hand broom to finish off the job.

A strong veneer goes over metal wall anchors installed in the block-wall joints during construction. The stones are mortared in place. A string line can be used as a guide to ensure a parallel surface of the stones. Note the extended edge of the footing for the concrete blocks below the stones.

CHAPTER 6.   BUILDING THE FOUNDATION

Concrete blocks can be used in foundations. They're fairly easy for do-it-yourselfers to lay. As a bonus, they can be laid gradually over a long period as you have the time. The skills you need are easily learned. (Photo courtesy Alta Industries Ltd.)

Concrete block foundations

Log home foundations can also be made of concrete block. This is a method that has several advantages for the do-it-yourselfer, one of which is that the foundation can be done a little at a time. For instance, you can mix a batch of mortar, lay a row or two of blocks in a few hours, and then come back to the job later. You can build the foundation during your spare time or on weekends.

One of the biggest advantages of constructing a concrete block foundation is the ease with which it can be done. This is not to say it is not backbreaking work, especially when you get to the upper courses of blocks on high basement foundation walls. But learning to lay concrete blocks is easy and, because you can work at your own pace, it can be fun.

There are several kinds of concrete blocks. Blocks may weigh anywhere from 25 to 50 pounds depending on what they're made of. There are also many different shapes and each is used for a different job. Check with local suppliers to see what is available in your area. You may have to use the blocks specified by your local building code.

You need heavyweight blocks to support the weight of the log home, especially if you plan a basement foundation.

Concrete block walls must be laid on a footing. First construct the forms and pour the footing. Keep the top of the footing level, flat, and smooth.

Laying concrete blocks. Blocks are laid by starting at the corners of the structure, building up a pyramid of courses, and then laying blocks between the corners, using a string line as a guide.

The bottom course must be laid out with corners square to the outline of your building foundation outline. Using string guides from the batter boards, locate the outside foundation corners and scratch these positions in the concrete footing. With the locations of the corners established, snap a chalk line between any two. Then lay a course of blocks dry to determine the course layout. Leave a ⅜- to ½-inch space between the blocks.

If possible, the first course should consist of full blocks only. If this is not possible, make the wall end on a half block. Most concrete blocks are made to be cut in half, but cutting them any place else can be almost impossible. If a half block won't work, you may wish to resize your house slightly. Otherwise, you'll have a hard job of fitting blocks into the alternating courses.

When you're satisfied with the layout of the blocks, remove them from the footing and stand them on end—out of the way, but close to the footing on the inside. Mix a batch of mortar in a wheelbarrow, mortar tube, or portable cement mixer. On the footing, drop a layer of mortar about 1½ inches thick and at least 2 inches wider than the block. Use the tip of the trowel to flatten it out. Position the first corner block on this mortar bed and drop a plumb bob from the outside foundation string lines of the batter boards to ensure you have the outside corner of the block located exactly. Make sure the block is level in both directions, tapping it gently with the handle of the trowel to seat it.

Now go to the opposite corner of the wall and do the same thing. Place a string holder on each corner block and run a mason's line between the two, using a string level to see if the blocks are level with each other. If one of the blocks is higher than the other, tap it down into place.

1. *Use a mortar board to hold mortar during the job. The board can be simply a piece of plywood supported on a couple of blocks.*

2. *Apply mortar to the footing, and then butter the ends of the blocks.*

3. *Grasp the block and carefully, but fairly quickly, set it in place.*

4. *The top edge should almost, but not quite, touch the string line. Level it both ways.*

This is the start of a typical corner. All unlaid blocks should be stacked close at hand.

A jointer tool (below left) is used to force the mortar into the joints. Then excess mortar is removed with the edge of a trowel.

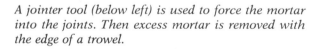

CHAPTER 6. BUILDING THE FOUNDATION

Use a corner block (it doesn't have the open web) for corners, positioned with the thicker side up. With corners in place, lay a half dozen blocks, working from each end toward the middle along the string line to establish the first course. To lay a second block against the first, stand it on end and butter the two webs, then lightly set it into place. Make sure the block almost, but not quite, touches the line strung between the two corner blocks.

Repeat these steps for all corners of the building. When you get all corners established, mortar corner blocks on the top of the bottom courses. The mortar should be about 1 to 1½ inches thick. Be sure the block is level in both directions.

Lay several blocks at each corner until all corners are as high as you can take them without extending the bottom course. Then position the string lines and string level from corner to corner. Lay succeeding courses so that the blocks are the same height as the string level at their outside upper edges. Don't let them touch the string line. They must be level crosswise as well as lengthwise: check with a small carpenter's level after laying each block.

Lay a closure block to finish off a course. Butter one end of the laid block, then butter the opposite end on the closure block. Care-

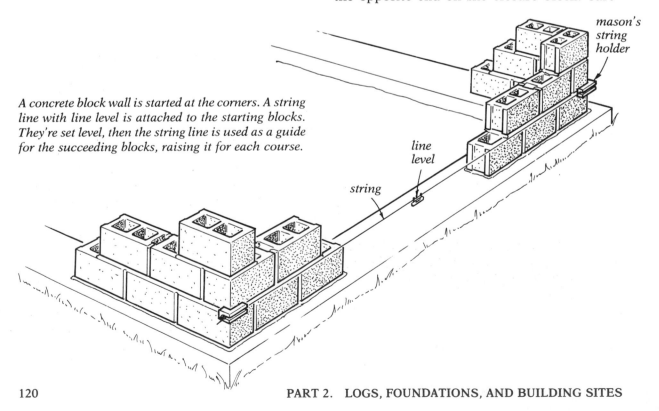

A concrete block wall is started at the corners. A string line with line level is attached to the starting blocks. They're set level, then the string line is used as a guide for the succeeding blocks, raising it for each course.

mason's string holder

line level

string

PART 2. LOGS, FOUNDATIONS, AND BUILDING SITES

fully slide the closure block in place. Try to keep as much mortar in place as possible. If you knock it off, just force mortar around the blocks and smooth it out with a trowel.

You'll have to cut a block to complete the alternate courses. To do this, lay the block down on its side on a smooth, flat surface. Use a stone hammer and chisel to tap along the centerline. Don't attempt to break it now, just score the side of the block. Then turn the block over and do the same on the opposite side. It will probably break in half as you tap the score line. (This may take practice.)

The courses should be reinforced as per your local code. This usually means girder reinforcing placed between block courses. When two walls meet at right angles, the girder material ties the two walls together.

To finish the wall joints after the blocks have been laid, first use the side of a trowel to knock off excess mortar. Scoop it off the wall and flip it back into the mortar bed. Use a jointing tool to compress the mortar between the blocks. Then cut off the excess mortar with the edge of the trowel. Add sill anchor bolts in the upper rows of blocks.

Areas over doors and windows must be supported with a steel lintel bar or a one-piece reinforced lintel block.

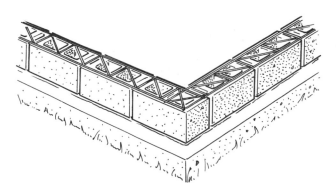

Anchor bolts (photo) are installed in the tops of the blocks. A large threaded rod (with the bottom end bent) makes an excellent anchor rod.

Local requirements vary as to means of reinforcing joints. Shown below are welded 1/4-inch rods. Screening may be required instead.

CHAPTER 6. BUILDING THE FOUNDATION

Waterproofing the wall

A concrete block foundation wall must be waterproofed. This is done by applying 1½ to 2½ inches of mortar, then asphalt, to the outside of the finished wall. Do it in two coats. First, moisten the wall with a fine mist of water. Use a trowel to apply the first coat of mortar about ¼-inch thick. Let this become somewhat hardened, then scratch the surface with the edge of the trowel or stiff bristle broom. Allow this coat to set for about 24 hours, keeping it moist with an occasional fine mist of water. Now apply a second, thicker, coat, rounding it outward at the bottom to form a water-runoff slope. Keep this coat moist for another 24 hours. The coating should run up at least 6 inches above grade, but you'll probably want to extend it to the top of the foundation for the sake of appearances.

Once the mortar coat has dried thoroughly (a couple of days), use asphalt waterproofing to cover the entire foundation. Make sure the coating is smooth and even. Use an old steel

Many old homes used mortared stone foundations. This is still a good alternative, if you pay as much attention to workmanship and materials as you would with concrete and block foundations. The key factor is an economical supply of stones.

Stone foundations are normally set on a concrete footing to ward against settling.

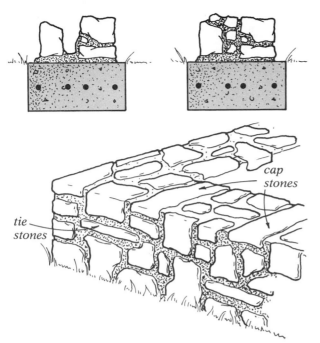

tie stones

cap stones

To lay a stone foundation, first place the inside and outside stones. Fill between the outside stones with mortar and rubble. Place tie stones regularly throughout the walls. Finish the top with cap stones and install anchor bolts.

trowel. For building sites that are extremely wet, add a layer of 30-pound felt to the wet asphalt before it sets up. Whether the basement is block or poured concrete, it should have a parge coat (waterproofing plaster) followed by a coating asphalt.

Foundation drains

A drain should be placed around the foundation to help carry off excess water that collects at its base. Put a 2-inch layer of gravel around the outside of the bottom edge of the footing, as shown. Then put clay drainage tile or perforated plastic on top of this, around the outside of the footing. Throw from 2 to 6 inches of gravel over this, extending up over the top edge of the footing by at least 2 inches. If perforated pipe is used, first cover it with 30-pound felt paper to prevent gravel and dirt from getting down in the perforations.

Insulating the basement

If you need insulation for the basement, install 4-inch-thick batts of rigid foam with a moisture barrier below the concrete floor and on the gravel. You can install insulation on the outside of the foundation wall in the same manner.

Insulated slabs are often made in three different pours: (1) a footing, (2) the perimeter foundation to slab height, then, with solid rigid insulation added, (3) the concrete slab between the foundation walls.

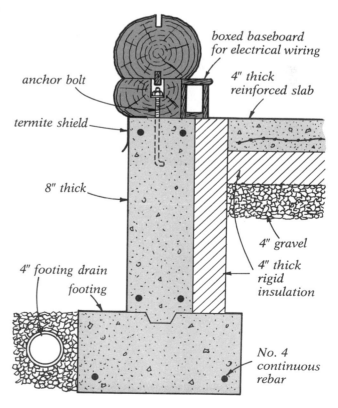

boxed baseboard for electrical wiring

anchor bolt

termite shield

4" thick reinforced slab

8" thick

4" gravel

4" thick rigid insulation

4" footing drain footing

No. 4 continuous rebar

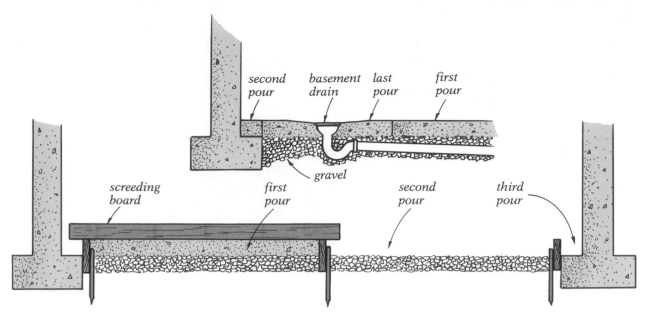

After the walls are poured and cured, the floor of the basement is poured. This can be done in two or three pours, as illustrated, rather than in one large one. Make provisions for the basement drain as shown at top. This drain area is poured last.

Pouring basement floors

Usually the basement floor is poured after the forms have been removed from the foundation. In some cases, though, the building may be erected first, before the floor is poured. If so, you must make sure to leave an opening through which to pour the concrete.

To pour the floor, first position the floor drain as needed. This may be in a corner or the center of the room. (The drainpipe should already have been installed before the footing and foundation.) The floor drain should be about ½ inch below the surface of the finished concrete floor. The floor should slope gradually and evenly toward the drain at a pitch of about ⅛ inch per foot. Place a small form around the location of the floor drain and at the exact height necessary. Position form guides from the sides of the building to the edges of the floor drain.

There are several different methods for pouring the floor. Most are similar to pouring slab sections. The first step: Make a concrete pour in the back, in the corner farthest from the door. Screed this off using a screed on the outside guide and center guide. When the first section is finished and somewhat set up, remove the center guide and pour the next sec-

tion. Allow this to set up enough to work on, then remove the outside wall guides and fill the gap with concrete, screeding with a short board. If you leave any holes in the concrete while working, fill them, tamp, and screed. Be careful not to slop concrete against the poured wall—it'll be difficult to remove later on.

You can also pour half of the wall length at a time, allowing it to cure completely before pouring the second half. This is a bit more difficult to screed because you must not allow the end of the screeding board to protrude past the center form guide. If it does, it will dig into the previously poured concrete. After the second half has been poured, remove the center guide, fill in with concrete, and screed with a short board as before.

Once the floor has been poured, tamped, screeded, and then bullfloated, the floor is finished off the same way you would a slab pour, troweling it to a slick, smooth finish. If you're pouring basement steps, form them and then pour after the floor has cured sufficiently. Remove the form around the floor drain after the floor has set up.

You can also make the pour in three sections, as shown, by pouring the two outside sections first and allowing them to set up. Then make the center pour, removing the forms and filling in the channels, screeding, and then finishing the surface.

PART 2. LOGS, FOUNDATIONS, AND BUILDING SITES

Pouring a basement floor is hard work and must be done at a fast pace to prevent the concrete from setting up before you can get it all finished. It takes three or four experienced people to do a good job—make sure you have plenty of help on hand.

You may have to add lally columns if they are required by your local building codes. The footings for these must be located under the floor. Pour these before the floor is poured. They should be poured to the same depth and width as the rest of the foundation.

Sill anchors

Almost all building codes call for some sort of sill anchor. Many kit log homes come with counterbored holes for sill anchors.

Sill anchors are typically ½ by 12-inch anchor bolts set in the wet concrete of a poured foundation wall or in the mortar-filled pockets of concrete block walls. The area around these must be smoothed down so there will be no humps or ridges to prevent the logs from sitting flat on the foundation top. Anchor bolts may also be installed in the poured footing and floor for any lally columns used to support the center portion of the house.

Chimney footings

Because of their weight, chimneys must have adequate footings. This is one place where you don't want to skimp on materials. A small, inadequate chimney foundation is nothing but trouble. The foundation must extend well below frost line, and the footing should be at least 2-feet thick, more if the chimney is to be a two-story affair. The footing must be well reinforced with mesh and rod.

After the footing has cured, pour a foundation or construct one of concrete block. Be sure to form a hollow box for a cleanout. You can fill the excavation with gravel, stone, and tamped soil if you don't want a cleanout. Pour a reinforced concrete slab over this to support the hearth and fireplace itself. This should rise to just below the floor level and allow for the thickness of the mortar and stone, or brick, etc. which will cover the fireplace and hearth.

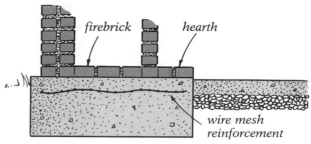

Fireplace footings are poured at the same time the house foundation is poured. The simplest fireplace footing is a slab, shown above. Below, a fireplace in a house with a crawl space can have a clean-out area. This is created by pouring the footing and then providing for the clean-out area when you build with block or when you build your concrete forms.

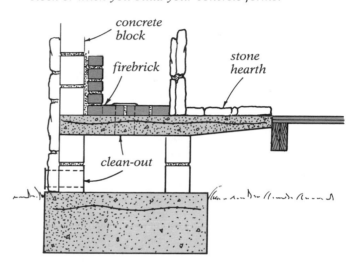

A full-basement house may have a fireplace only on the upper floor or it may have one in the basement, too. The footing must be strong enough to support the masonry of a two-story fireplace.

Part 3

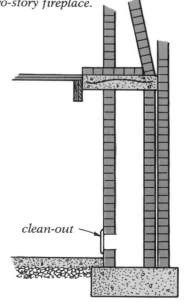

HOUSE RAISING AND FINISH WORK

Chapter 7 HOUSE RAISING: FIRST LOGS

A good start

With the foundation completed, it's time to begin work on the upper, log structure. Here, the first step is to fashion and install the sill logs—the logs that rest directly on top of the foundation and are fastened to it by means of anchor bolts. This is an important part of the job because, if the sills are not laid in squarely and securely, the entire structure may be affected.

The various steps for selecting, hewing, notching, and installing sill logs are covered in detail in the following sections of this chapter. There are also sections on installing the flooring, which is put in along with the sills before the walls are erected—if you use cured logs to build your house. Among other things, putting in the floor joists and frame before going ahead with the rest of the wall logs gives you something solid to stand on.

Almost all kit log houses require complete floor framing before the wall logs are placed. In most cases this consists of framed floor joists such as those used on standard lumber homes. A skirt board attached to the sill and joists covers them and ties the wall logs into the foundation.

When you use your own logs, there are a number of joist variations you can choose from—dimension, full log, and so forth—depending on the availability of materials and your own skill. But no matter which scheme you choose, be sure that any area that has to carry extra weight, such as a pool table, is reinforced with additional bridging, or even supporting piers.

Log walls start with the sill logs (bottom logs). If these are correctly installed and securely anchored, the rest of the logs should follow according to plan.

Hand hewing, as shown, is one means of creating flat surfaces on a round log.

If you are using green logs for your house and plan to leave it standing to cure, there are two different approaches to laying the logs on the foundation. For one, you could put up the walls without cutting in the floor joists, while making provisions to put them in later after the wall logs have cured. Or you could install the floor joists and lay no flooring. If you lay dry material, it may become damaged during the curing year.

The most practical timetable is to cut the logs in early winter, peel them in early spring, and then start construction. With luck you can build through the summer, fall, and into winter—in time to get the roof on before the snow flies.

Sill logs

Choose the straightest, largest, and most uniform logs for the sills. If you don't have full-length logs you can join them using a half-lap splice, spiked or held together with lag screws. Splices can be almost anywhere on continuous foundations, but they must be directly over a pier on pier foundations.

Sill logs must have a flattened bottom so they sit squarely on the foundation. Hew the log bottom with a broadaxe, an adz, or a chain saw accessory.

Hewing. Hewing logs to flatten the sides was until recently almost a lost art. Years ago, loggers made their living hewing railroad ties. These fellows were called tie hackers and they made an art of the chore. Now there has been a revival of this old-time skill.

Although hewing appears complicated, it isn't. All it takes is careful attention to detail and plenty of practice. If at all possible, hew logs while they are still green. Hewing a seasoned log, especially a hardwood such as oak or walnut, is very difficult.

The first step in hewing is to get the log off the ground and onto short sections of wood. Then fasten it securely so it won't roll. Use log dogs. Drive nails in the ends of the log where you want the hewn side to be. Using these nails as a guide, snap a chalk line along the log. Some experienced hackers never use a chalk guideline; they merely eyeball the job as they go. For the first-timer a chalk line is a great help, especially on crooked logs.

Stand on top of the log with your legs spread apart and score the side of the log using a scoring axe. These are single-bitted axes usually weighing five to seven pounds (almost any heavy axe, though, will do in a pinch). Make the scoring cuts every 6 to 8 inches and as deep as the chalk line mark for the entire length of the log. (You can also make notches instead of the scoring marks.)

PART 3.   HOUSE RAISING AND FINISH WORK

To begin hewing a flat surface, first snap a chalk line to mark the outside edges of the surface to be squared.

Use a heavy axe to score into the log surface to the depth indicated by each chalk line. If you stand on the log for this chore, be sure of your footing, axe control, and the stability of the log.

An easier way to cut into the log is to position the log on short blocks; dog it down with log dogs; and, standing well away, make downward chopping strokes.

You can make wedge cuts to each side of the straight cuts to create V grooves.

The hard work of hewing comes in removing the wood between the scored lines. Some hewers prefer to stand on the opposite side of the hewed line (photo above), behind the log to protect their legs. Others (middle photo) stand on the same side. Straddling the log (bottom) is especially dangerous. Work with safety in mind and use slow, controlled chopping strokes.

The next step is the hardest—it requires the use of a broad axe. Standing on the hewing side of the log, work from the trunk backwards to the head, using the axe to cut away the slabs between the scored marks. Depending on whether you are right- or left-handed, you need a handle that is offset so you don't bang your fingers on the bark side of the log as you make the cuts. You should also watch out for your toes (wear steel-toed shoes) as you cut. Make small, controlled swings. Place some old slabs or planks under the log to prevent the tip of the axe from digging into the ground.

When the bottom of the sill logs has been hewed flat, bore holes in it for the anchor bolts. You should counterbore the tops of the holes for the anchor bolt nuts. If the bolts stick up above the sill logs, you'll have to bore holes in the second course for them to fit into. This actually is the best design because it doesn't leave a pocket for rainwater to collect.

Old-timers used to place a bed of mortar on the foundation for the sill log. Today you can use sill seal on top of the foundation. This is a 6-inch-wide strip of fiberglass; you can make up your own by cutting strips from a roll of batting with a sharp knife or shears.

PART 3. HOUSE RAISING AND FINISH WORK

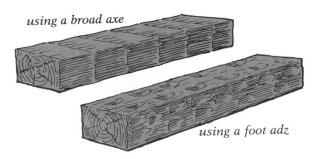

using a broad axe

using a foot adz

Adz-hewed logs generally have a smoother surface, compared to a log hewed with a broad axe.

Photos at left: You can quickly and safely score the log to the chalk lines with a chain saw. Then tilt the log with the hewn line at an angle from you and dog the log down securely. Use a hewing axe to knock out chunks between scored cuts before smoothing.

Hewing with an adz is slower than with an axe.

CHAPTER 7. HOUSE RAISING: FIRST LOGS

Above: To cut a slab from a log with a chain-saw mill, first fasten a guide board to the log. Right: Slide the sawmilling assembly along the board. Below: The result is a clean, smooth log surface.

Above left is another kind of chain-saw mill for cutting a flat surface. The entire log is being cut to a square timber for use as a girder.

Above right, a small tractor-powered sawmill can also be used to mill flat surfaces, or you can have a local sawmill do the work.

Bore holes at the exact locations of the foundation anchor bolts. The nuts and washers are installed on the anchor bolts and tightened into place.

CHAPTER 7. HOUSE RAISING: FIRST LOGS

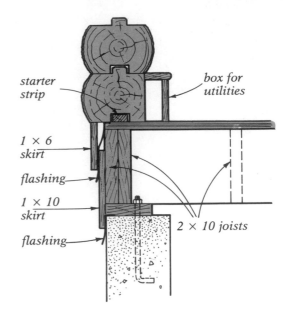

You can also install the logs on top of the flooring frame and subflooring, covering the joint edge with a skirt board. (Design by Vermont Log Buildings Inc.)

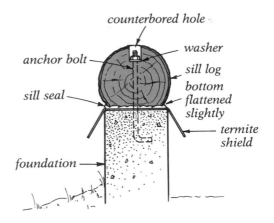

The sill log may rest directly on the foundation. A layer of sill seal and termite shield are sandwiched between the log and the foundation. Anchor bolts from the foundation hold the sill logs securely.

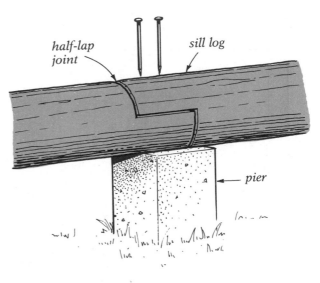

Sill logs should be the straightest, largest logs you have. And they should be joined with a half-lap and spiked joint at any splice. The splice must be directly over a pier or supporting foundation.

In areas where termites may be a problem, now is the time to install termite shields. You can buy shields or make them from aluminum or copper flashing, cut as shown. Bond and rivet them together, then seal with silicone at the joints and place them under the sill seal.

After putting the termite shields and sill seal in place, position the first two long-wall sills. Lay the large butt ends facing opposite directions. Secure with anchor bolts. The corners of the sills should protrude over the foundation if you plan an overlapping corner notch. If you're going to use another style of notch, cut the sill logs to suit.

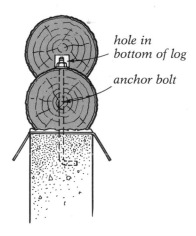

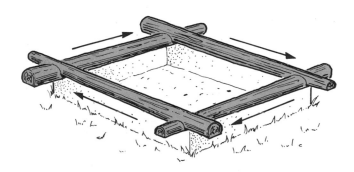

Place the sill logs so the large butt ends at diagonally opposite corners face opposite directions.

You can extend the anchor bolt and nut up into the underside of the second log, which provides a fairly weatherproof surface, leaving no large hole for water to drain into.

With most notches it's best to build up foundation ends (short walls) a half log higher than the long walls. This is particularly true with a saddle notch as shown. Otherwise you'd have to caulk and chink the area.

Install the short wall sills next. If you are using a saddle joint with protruding corners, build the foundation so that the short walls start exactly ½ log higher than the long walls. Scribe and cut a saddle notch so the short sill logs fit down over the long logs. The bottom of the short logs must rest firmly on the raised foundation ends, as shown. This may take quite a bit of fiddling, cutting, and recutting for an accurate, pest- and moisture-free joint between the two end logs and foundation.

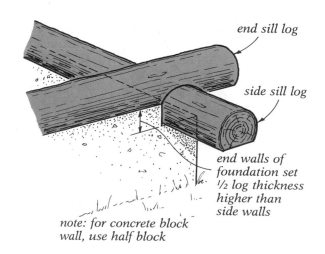

note: for concrete block wall, use half block

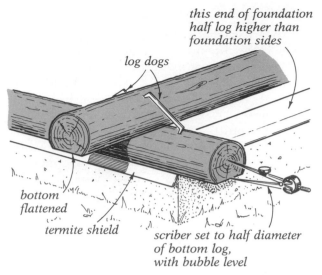

this end of foundation
half log higher than
foundation sides

log dogs

bottom
flattened

termite shield

scriber set to half diameter
of bottom log,
with bubble level

Saddle notches like these old axe-hewed notches are strong and fairly easy to make.

Step 1. *To cut a saddle notch, roll the short-wall sill log into place over the previously anchored long-wall logs and hold it in place with log dogs. Use a scriber to determine half the diameter of the long sill log.*

Corner joints

Saddle notch. Also called a common joint, this is the simplest joint and the most frequently used. Spiking is not necessary for the saddle notch.

Position the short-wall sill log on the long-wall sill logs, again using one of your largest,

straightest logs. The butt end of the log should be opposite the long-wall log butt. Position the log, making sure it produces the straightest possible wall, with the best side of the log facing inside. The crown of the log should be up. Dog it down so it won't roll and, using scribers, mark the log for a notch on the bottom, as shown.

Step 4. *Using a chain saw, cut saw kerfs to within ⅛ inch of the scribed line. Leave material enough for finish-fitting of the joint. Use an axe or your chain saw to remove the material between the scored lines.*

Step 5. *Rough trim the area with a chain saw.*

PART 3.   HOUSE RAISING AND FINISH WORK

start scribing on bottom
of top log—bubble level

contour of bottom log
is marked on top log—
bubble level

Step 2. *Starting at the bottom of the short (upper) sill logs, scribe the shape of the lower log onto the top log. Keep the scribe level at all times.*

Step 3. *The contour of the bottom log is marked on the bottom side of the upper log. Do this on each end of the short, sill log.*

Roll the log over on its top side, dog it, and cut the notches with either an axe or a chain saw. The first cut should be straight down to the scribed line. Then cut a notch to the first cut. Finally, clean out the notch to the boundaries of the scribe. Now cut the notch on the other end of the log. Remove the log dogs and roll the log down into position. The notch should be cut to one-half the thickness of the log. The log should rest equally on the notches and the sill sealer. It should make firm contact with the foundation for the full length.

Again, it may require a bit of hewing and notching to make a solid, tight fit. When you're satisfied, lock the log down with the anchor bolts.

Steps 6 & 7. *Roll the log in place, trial fit, and remove any bumps or irregularities. Then smooth the notch with a chisel and mallet, as shown in the photo. The log should then fit snugly over the log beneath it.*

log is notched
on bottom side
following
scribed line

CHAPTER 7. HOUSE RAISING: FIRST LOGS

Gallery of corner notches

As mentioned earlier, there are many corner notch variations. Some of the joints have the logs extended past the corners and others have the log ends cut flush with the corners. The illustration shows the other most common corners, how they are constructed, and their advantages or disadvantages.

Butt corner. This joint is not as strong as the saddle notch. One log extends past the corner while the next log is butted up against it, scribed to fit, and fastened in place with spikes. The next course of logs has the extending log going the opposite way. Spiking is necessary throughout.

Double notch. A notch is cut one-fourth the way through each log, both on top and bottom. This is one of the strongest notches, but takes more fitting time. Moisture can collect in the notch. It doesn't need to be spiked.

A and V notch. This is one of the simplest notches to make and can be easily hand-hewed. This notch is used on small logs because very little material is taken out to form the notch. It also sheds water well. Spiking, though usually done, is not necessary.

Sharp notch. A variation of the A and V notch, except the entire end of the log is beveled rather than cut as a notch. This notch needs spiking and, while not necessarily strong, is quite easy to make.

Tenon joint. This is similar to the double round, except it has flat joining faces instead of round. It's easy to make and is very sturdy. First cut down into the log with a saw for each side of the flat. Then use a chisel or axe to cut the flat area. The notches are cut to one-fourth of the log thickness on top and bottom. It sheds water quite well and doesn't need spiking.

V-joint. This joint is similar to the butt joint, except a V-notch is cut in the extending log. A point to match is cut in the butting log. It must be spiked.

Dovetail. This is one of the hardest notches to make but is also one of the strongest. The simple dovetail, which only has the joint angled on one face, needs to be spiked. The compound dovetail, which has angled joint lines on both faces, doesn't require spiking. This is a flush joint and is rarely used on round logs but is common on hewed square logs.

Half-cut notch. This is considered one of the easiest joints to make. But it is not a very strong joint and can cause a real water-trapping problem. It's primarily used on barns and other rougher outbuildings, where speed and ease of building are more important than strength and water resistance. It has to be spiked together. To fashion this joint, saw the log halfway through and then split or saw away the end.

Saddle-end notch. This is almost like the half-cut notch, but a bit better. The only difference is that the underside of the notch is scribed to fit down over the log below so it sheds water better. It doesn't lock; so it should be well spiked.

Corner post. This is very easy to make. It utilizes a dado cut into two sides with tenons cut to fit in each log. You must make sure you choose a solid straight post for the corner. It must be spiked and waterproofed with caulking.

Quarter corner post. This is made by cutting corner ends of the logs flush and adding in a quarter section of a post. Is not particularly strong or waterproof, but is easy to do.

Plank corner post. This is made by using an L-shaped wooden plank nailed to the corner ends of the logs. A quarter log is nailed in place over that. It's stronger and more watertight than the quarter log construction, but not much. When the house dries and settles there will be some opening of the joints and consequent moisture problems.

The joints are described for round logs. Square or hewn logs require somewhat different corners. Kit log home builders make use of many of the different joints shown, as well as some unusual factory-milled ones.

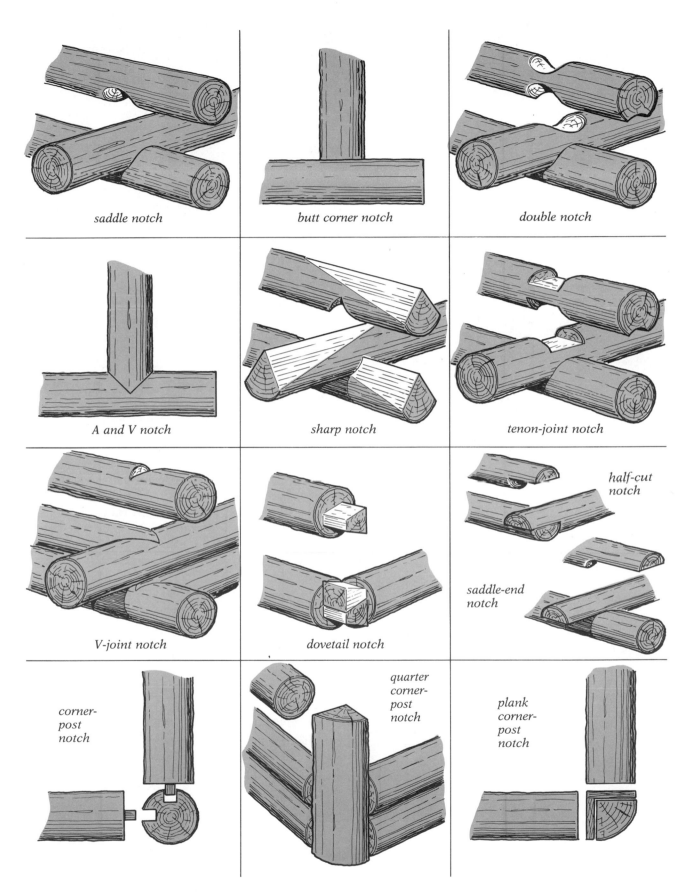

saddle notch

butt corner notch

double notch

A and V notch

sharp notch

tenon-joint notch

V-joint notch

dovetail notch

half-cut notch

saddle-end notch

corner-post notch

quarter corner-post notch

plank corner-post notch

Joists

Joists must be strong and well supported or they can cause such problems as weak, sagging, and rubbery feeling floors. There are almost as many different ways of framing floor joists as there are corner joists. You can make the joists of logs, or of dimension lumber. The choice is purely personal, depending on what materials you have on hand and how much hewing you want to do. Log joists aren't as exacting as dimension lumber, but it takes skill to make the floor flat.

Continuous foundations require one type of joists, piers another. For continuous foundations you can use log joists 6 to 8 inches in diameter, spaced 18 inches apart. Sawed or dimension joists must be 2 × 6s for 8-foot spans and 2 × 8s for anything longer. Spans of over 16 feet may require a supporting girder. Sawed joists should be spaced no farther apart than 16 inches. Joists may be set in notches cut in the sill logs, or they may be fastened to sill plates, as is common with dimension lumber.

Log joists. Joists are most commonly supported by a mortise-and-tenon joint. They fit into the long-wall sill. The notches are in the sill logs and the tenons are on each end of the joists. Cut the mortise using a chain saw and chisel. You can also cut it with a large chisel alone. The joist logs are cut to fit exactly between the notches. Their tops are hewn with a minimum of 2 inches flat to support the floor. Measure the depth of the notches from this top flat area. Hew the end of the log to fit the notches in the sill logs.

Note: If the depth of all the notches is identical, and if the depths of the hewed ends of the log are identical, the floor will come out level and even. You must make absolutely sure the bottoms of the notches are level or you'll have problems later on. Remember, the level line may not be the same distance from the top and bottom of the sill logs. You can be sure of the level by using the water-and-hose method (described in the chapter on foundations) to establish level points at all four corners. Then use a chalk line to mark the locations of the bottom of the notches.

After trial fitting the joists, lay a straight

Floor joists may be constructed of logs with their top surface flattened. Tenons cut on joist ends fit into notches cut in the sill logs.

The notches may be cut with a chain saw or large chisel before installation of the sill. The upper surface of the log joists must be flat, and they must be level with each other to provide level support surfaces for the floor. Measure from the bottom of the sill to the bottom of the joists. Snap a chalk line and cut joist notches to this line.

edge across them and use a four-foot carpenter's level to determine if the floor is going to be level. If not, shim or trim the tenons. Spike the joist tenons to the sill logs. If you're using oak, which will split easily, you may want to predrill the holes.

In some cases, joists are cut as saddle notches over sills. These are extremely strong joists but may allow some moisture to get into the house.

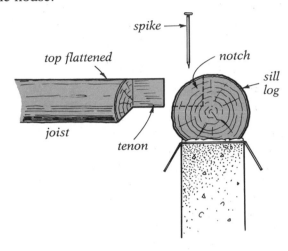

Install the sill log and cut the floor joists to shape. There should be a flattened tenon surface on the end tenons so all upper surfaces of the joists and lower surfaces of the tenons will be flat and parallel. All joist tenons should be the same size.

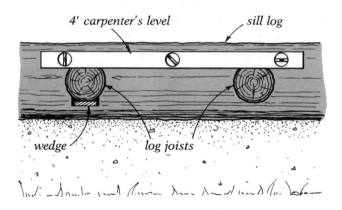

Position the joists. Then using a long level, shim or trim to ensure that the top surfaces of the joists are level in all directions.

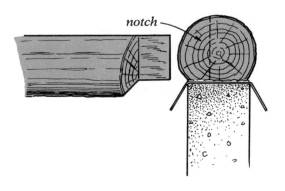

You can notch completely to the bottom of the sill log so that the joist tenons rest on the foundation.

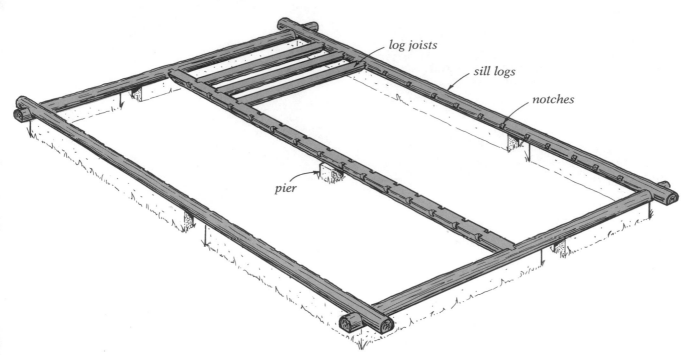

log joists

sill logs

notches

pier

You may have to provide a girder to shorten the floor joists and provide a stable, strong floor. The girders must rest on piers or metal columns over footings.

Girders are notched into the sill logs. The floor joists are notched into the girders. Maintain a perfectly flat and level surface to attach the subfloor. You can create the girder pocket when pouring foundation.

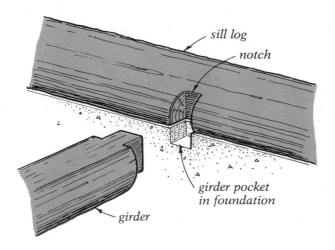

sill log

notch

girder pocket
in foundation

girder

Girders.

You may need girders, or "sleepers," as support beams are sometimes called. Provisions should be made for them in the foundation, as shown. You'll need a pier for center support, too. Flatten the girder on the ends and over each pier. Make sure it's level. The underside of each joist is flattened in the area of the girder and set in place over it, notched into the sill walls and spiked solidly to the girders.

If a span is so long that you must use a girder down the center, then fit the ends of the joists into the girder center using mortises and tenons.

Dimension joists.

You may also use dimension lumber for the joists. Cut notches in the logs and set the lumber in the notches, then spike in place. The upper, or second, log will probably have to be notched to fit over the upper portion of the joists. The upper corner of the joists may be notched instead to allow for this. A notch on the lower side of the joists will weaken them.

Probably the simplest method of installing dimension floor joists is to use headers nailed to the sill logs. The header should not extend above the top of the sill log and should not be below the edge of the foundation on continuous foundations. On piers, it goes directly on top.

PART 3. HOUSE RAISING AND FINISH WORK

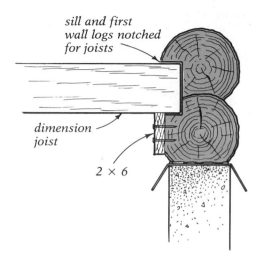

sill and first wall logs notched for joists

dimension joist

2 × 6

You could nail on a header and then notch the logs to accommodate a lumber joist, but this is pretty tricky notch work.

To install the headers, find the floor height. Mark this on one corner, establish a level line on both long walls, and level the line with the other walls. Nail the headers to the long-wall sill logs. You may have to shim headers with chunks of wood if the sill log protrudes over the foundation. Spike an edge joist to each short-wall sill log, between the long-wall headers. Mark the joist centers on the long-wall headers and the girder (if any). Floor joists are most commonly spaced on 16-inch centers. Two-foot centers can be used but the floor will not be as strong.

For strength, the joists should be fastened to the headers using joist hangers, which are metal straps shaped to fit around the joists to make for solid nailing and support. Do not toenail joists to headers; this will not provide enough support. If the joists join on the girder, offset them. The spaces between the joists should be bridged with solid bridging or X-bracing.

On small buildings you can sometimes assemble a complete floor and, with help, lift and fasten it in place. The job, however, requires careful measuring and fitting.

An alternative to using the headers: Place a ledger plate under the floor joists on the first sill log, then install the second log course. Cut a flat for the joists and then toenail them into the log.

Most kit homes use a standard floor frame, as shown on page 136, and then the log walls are assembled on top. This type of frame can also be used on a pier foundation.

Floor openings

You may have to provide openings in the floor for such things as a chimney or staircase. These openings must be framed properly or they will not support the floor. Depending on whether you use log joists or dimension lumber, there are several ways of framing floor openings. If you use logs and the opening is smaller than the distance between the joists, just use 2 × 4s for framing and nail it in place. This provides a nailing edge for the flooring. In most instances, however, the openings are larger than the distance between two joists. In this case, an opening should be framed with logs. Mortise and tenon joints hold the logs together.

The same technique can be used to create a floor opening of dimension lumber. All headers must be doubled. The joists and headers should be fastened together with joist hangers to ensure that you construct a solid supporting framework.

Termite control

If your house is being built where termites are a problem, you should plan measures to control termites now. Later, after the home is built, it's more trouble. You can prevent many termite problems by using continuous wall foundations of poured concrete to support sill logs the proper height above the ground. Concrete block foundations are not quite as good because termites can enter through the hollow portions of the blocks. A minimum height for crawl spaces is 18 inches on the outside. The foundation must be at least eight inches above grade level. Termite shields should be placed over the tops of the foundation.

You can treat the soil in the crawl space, the backfill soil, and the foundation itself with special chemicals before backfilling the foundation wall. Make sure you read the safety rules governing the application of the chemicals.

Pick up all wood and paper debris from around the building site. Don't allow wood chunks to be pushed into the backfill. Termites thrive on cellulose buried underground. Make sure stacks of lumber kept at the site are off the ground on skids or concrete blocks.

Any wood that runs from the house to the ground (such as wooden piers) can cause problems. You can use wood, such as redwood, that is insect resistant, but not insect-proof.

The most common subflooring is plywood or flakeboard. Remember to brace between joists with crossbridging, as shown. (Photo courtesy of Authentic Log Homes Corp.)

Flooring

Don't bother to finish the floor until the roof is on, though it's a good idea to install some sort of solid sheathing over the floor joists so you can walk around inside the house. You could recycle the plywood sheathing that was used to make forms for the foundation walls. The sheathing can be nailed in place temporarily or installed permanently as an underlayment for the finished floor. In any case, it's a good idea to cover it each night with sheets of black plastic.

Chapter 8 WALLS

The new walls

When the sill logs are laid and anchored, you're ready to raise the walls of your house. You'll probably find this job easier than the preparation. There are several ways of installing wall logs, including round logs laid with chinking, round logs without chinking, or logs flattened on two sides or more. Splines can be used with most of these methods.

Round logs with chinking

This is probably the simplest to construct, but it requires the most maintenance and the wall is not as moisture resistant nor as strong as walls made with other log shapes. Chinked joints were typically used by early settlers when they had only an axe and little time to build a shelter before winter. The technique is still used today for some backwoods hunting camps, but not as much as in the past.

One of the problems is that as logs cure, they shrink. This can continue for several years. As a result, the chinking material pulls away from the logs and falls out (unless it's constantly maintained). In the old days, mud,

When the sill logs are anchored and the first corner notch is fitted, the rest of the walls become a routine of cutting and stacking logs.

moss, or a combination of them was used between logs. In addition, the joints were often filled with a sawed slab or a sapling jammed between logs. Mud mortar was then applied around the fill. In fact, almost everything imaginable was used to fill cracks.

If you are redoing an old cabin, you may be stuck with this kind of joint. The most common repair method is to fill the joints with a standard mortar mix, smoothing the surface as much as possible. This provides a gray look to the chinking. If you want white, use white mortar or stucco mix. You can also use this same technique on a log home that has been erected and allowed to cure for a year or so.

Careful cutting and fitting of the joints are important not only to provide a safe, sturdy, and weatherproof house, but because this is where good workmanship really shows.

There are several ways to lay wall logs. Round logs with chinking has traditionally been the most popular, particularly in the eastern and southern U.S.

PART 3.   HOUSE RAISING AND FINISH WORK

Chinkless round logs— without splines

This is a popular style in the north, and particularly Canada. It's an extremely tight, waterproof, and strong design if crafted carefully. It takes practice, but it can be done entirely with hand tools; so it works well in bush country. However, even chinkless joints are normally chinked with a bead of caulking along the inside edge. In some cases the joint may be mortared over, although the flexible sealers are better. In the far north, some of these joints are also packed with sphagnum moss.

Careful chinking can result in workmanship that enhances the appearance of the home's exterior.

The "chinkless style" is popular in the northern U.S. Here the logs are scribed, and then the underside is cut with a cup or V-notch so a log fits tightly over the log below it.

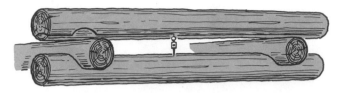

Step 1. *To create a tight fit with the chinkless method, position each log over the log it must fit over. Then scribe the top log at the saddle notch and along the underside for the cup or V cut. Use a log scriber with a double bubble level, which indicates when the points are directly horizontal.*

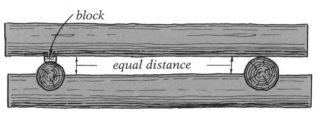

block

equal distance

Step 2. *Before starting the scribe, raise the end of the upper log with small wedges of wood to create an equal gap all along the logs.*

Step 3. *Below, set the scribers by measuring the distance at the largest gap and adding about a half inch. This will create a lengthwise groove three inches deep in the log.*

Step 4. *Drawing at right: Scribe lengthwise. (Include the saddle notch of the log that is to fit over the lower log.) This may take practice. You should try for near perfect-fit logs without gaping holes or cracks.*

To create a tight, waterproof horizontal joining of the logs, each log is scribed and cut to fit over the log below it. There are two different ways to create this joint. For the first, you create a rounded trough with a cup adz on the underside of the log. This is done by scribing a notch—usually a saddle notch on the end only—and then cutting it. You scribe the side of the log and mark the notches half the thickness of the upper log. It takes a lot of hard work, cutting, rolling over, and trial fitting, but this is one of the handsomest styles in log home building.

You can also cut the area of the log between the cross logs with a chain saw in a flat V-shape, as shown, and then scribe and cut the ends protruding over the cross logs to create much the same appearance. The edges must be well sealed with flexible silicone sealer. In some instances, the hollow, cut portion of the log can be stuffed with fiberglass insulation or sphagnum moss and the edges coated with silicone before the log is put in place.

An alternative to this is to cut a V-groove in the bottom of the upper log and a matching wedge on the top of the lower logs. These cuts can be made using a circular saw or chain saw with the shop-made adapter. This type of log joint is not as popular as the others because it takes a lot of work. Also the cut edge of the log is exposed below the upper log and this detracts from the appearance.

set dividers for space between logs; scribe for notch

PART 3. HOUSE RAISING AND FINISH WORK

Step 5. *The underside of the log can be cupped by first making a rough trough with the tip of a chain saw.*

Step 6. *Using a cup adz, complete the groove, and smooth it to fit properly. You can leave the V shape cut made by the chain saw if you don't want to go to the trouble of hand-fitting the logs.*

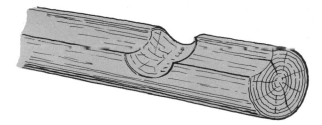

This is the ideal appearance of the underside of a typical chinkless round log cut to fit.

Step 7. *This is how the logs should look after they're rolled into position.*

CHAPTER 8. WALLS

Round log with spline

Round-log walls can be strengthened by the addition of splines. The grooves for the splines can be cut with a heavy duty router, a circular saw and dado blade, or with a chain saw.

Rip the spline from solid stock to the size of the slot cut in the logs. If the logs are cured, the splines should fit snugly. If the logs are green, the spline should be loose to allow for shrinkage. Getting the spline to fit properly can be a problem but, once in position, it helps hold the logs along their entire length. The best method is to seat the spline in a bed of caulking in the lower log. You then apply a bead of caulking or flexible sealer along the top face of the spline before lowering the next log into place. For the sake of appearances, you can stop the spline run before getting to the end of the log.

An alternative to the chinkless scheme, but one that provides a fair amount of weatherproofing, is to fit round logs with splines. The spline is cut from dimension stock and tapped in place with fiberglass insulation around it. A spline fits into a stopped groove cut in the under and upper sides of each log. Make sure the grooves are directly over each other by marking their positions on the log ends.

Logs with flat surfaces

The spline can be fitted into round logs, but flattening the logs makes a better-fitting joint for the spline. A two-surfaced log can be made using a chain saw and special attachment, with a broadaxe or adz, or with a small sawmill.

Logs can also be flattened on three sides, then grooved for the spline, as shown. This is typical of kit homes. It provides a smooth interior surface and leaves the rough shape of the logs for an exterior surface. The technique takes work, but it makes for a solid, moisture-resistant wall.

The inside joint can also be finished with a batten if preferred. These help level the wall and provide nailers for paneling or drywall. You could also taper the joints and fit shaped molding in place. For an even stronger joint, if the logs are wide enough, you can use two splines with beads of caulking applied between the splines and on all faces.

Spline grooves can be cut with the tip of a chain saw, a heavy-duty router, or a dado blade in a portable circular saw.

Handling logs

Ideally, you should distribute logs around the four sides of the building, so that they are ready to use. But you can place them on two

PART 3. HOUSE RAISING AND FINISH WORK

You can also use logs with flat surfaces on two or three sides.

adjacent sides, or even on one side, and raise them all from those locations by turning and rolling each into place. Raising logs is hard work and can be dangerous if you don't use the proper tools, follow all safety rules, and watch carefully what you're doing. It's hard for one person to do the job, so a helper or two would be a great asset.

Adding a spline or splines and insulation (plus caulking) between logs adds to the weather resistance.

Most kit log homes use a log that is milled so that it includes a mortise-and-tenon groove.

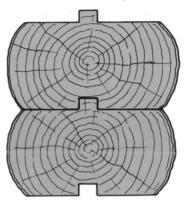

Before you start, make sure you have all logs peeled, cured, and ready for use. Put them close to the wall so there'll be less handling once you start.

The biggest problem is getting the logs up onto the walls. Just starting the sill logs can be a problem if they're large. The higher you go, the harder and more dangerous the job can be. A 20-foot wall log can weigh more than 600 pounds. If it breaks loose and rolls down a steep hillside, it'll crush anything in its way. Logs can usually be rolled into position at the sides of the building using a peavey, but in some instances, they may have to be hoisted.

You could hire a crane for the lifting job. A crane, though, usually tears up the property and is very expensive. Small logs can sometimes be lifted a short distance using a bucket on a large tractor, but the bucket should be fitted with back braces to prevent the log from rolling onto the tractor as it is lifted in the air.

The two most popular tools are old-fashioned and, some feel, still the best. They are: a log ramp; and gin-pole, tip-up hoist with block and tackle. One of the newer cable come-alongs can be useful, too. In fact, one of these on a handmade gin-pole fitted to the back of a truck can do a lot of work.

The simplest method is a log ramp. This

Small logs can be hoisted with home-made log booms and hoists. (Photo courtesy Arkansas Log Homes, Inc.)

Moving heavy logs can be dangerous. There are several ways to get them up on the walls. One requires overhead cable run between trees on either side of the construction. (Photo courtesy Minnesota Trailbound School of Log Building.)

154   PART 3.   HOUSE RAISING AND FINISH WORK

can be used to load logs or roll them up onto walls. Always place the ramp on the uphill side of the construction if possible, and stack logs where they can be rolled into place with the least effort. Once on the wall, logs can be turned and rolled as needed. Short logs that won't reach across long walls have to be rolled up from the short side; so you may need to install two ramps—one for the long wall and one for the short wall.

To ensure that logs don't roll off the wall on the inside of the house, check to see they are at least two or three feet longer than the wall. Stop blocks, temporarily nailed in position can help prevent the logs from rolling too far once you have them off the ramp and on the wall.

The log ramps should be at about a 30-degree angle. Cut a small notch in the upper ends of the ramp logs to prevent them from rolling off the wall. Cut the tops of the ramp at a taper to allow the loaded log to drop over the ends quickly. Stake the lower end of the logs as shown to prevent them from sliding around or slipping off the wall.

To pull wall logs up, tie off the ends of the rope and loop them over the log as shown, and roll them up. You may need a block and tackle to pull large logs. Make sure everyone stays clear of the log. A couple of people to guide the log ends can be a help. Use 1-inch nylon or polypropylene rope. A log rolls faster on the butt end, so place the smaller end farther up the ramp before starting the roll.

Logs for both sides of a building can be pulled up in sequence. Start with the long back-wall log. Pull it into place, roll it over the end wall and scribe, then fit and anchor it in place. Now roll the long front-wall log in the same manner. Go to the short walls and roll up the first short-wall log, fit and secure it, and then roll up its opposite.

As the walls become higher, a rented steel scaffolding placed inside the building puts you in a better position to work. You could build your own scaffolding.

The rope-and-ramp method only works for round logs, and you'll need a hoist for flattened logs. Two hoists, one on each log end, tend to work even better.

The safest and simplest method for raising logs is with a log ramp. Pull the logs up the ramp with ropes looped over each end and fastened solidly and roll them to back walls. Or the ramps can be moved. Or you can have a set of ramps for all four walls.

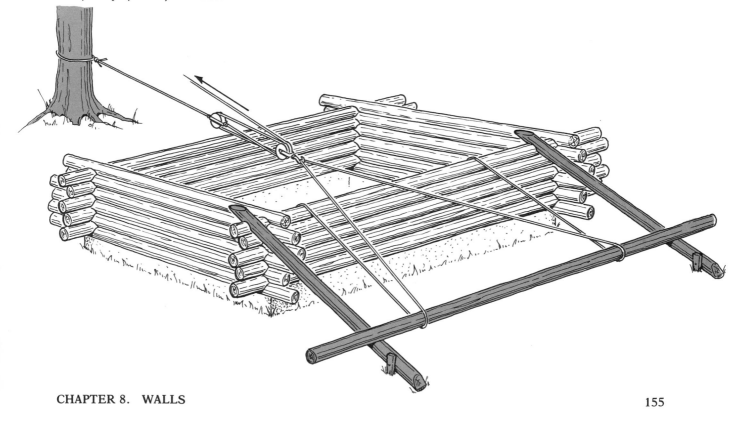

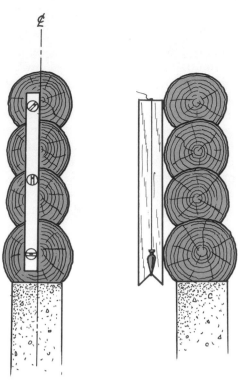

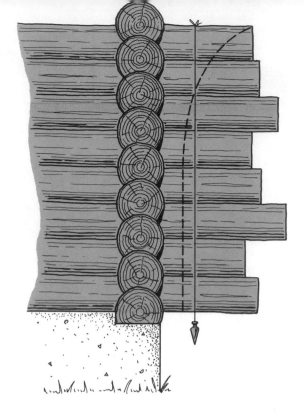

The walls must be plumb. Above left, you can plumb the log centers using a plumb line or long level. If you plumb from the inside, you need a plumb bob and board positioned as shown, above right.

With a saddle joint, the log ends usually are uneven. Leave these ends uncut until you assemble the entire wall. For a vertical end use a plumb bob and chalk line to snap a plumb line before cutting the ends off square with a chain saw. For a decorative outward sweeping arch, cut along dotted lines shown.

Plumbing walls

You can make the inside or the outside of the wall flush, or the logs centered directly over each other. A wall of centered logs is the most stable.

Round logs may vary in size. This doesn't make much difference except that, unless laid properly, they look awkward. Naturally, the largest logs should be on the bottom, proceeding to the smallest diameter logs for the top. To make the log wall flush on the inside, roll the log into place and use a plumb-bob board, as shown. Dog the log securely with log dogs when you get it flush. Then scribe it for the cut needed.

To make a wall with centered logs, use a level turned on edge to mark a plumb centerline on the wall log ends. Shift logs back and forth to get the best fit. Let the log ends protrude until you get all the walls up. Then mark a plumb line and cut the logs off flush, or taper them from the bottom up. (You could use any

of a number of decorative cuts to give your home a customized look. An outward sweeping arch, as shown above, is popular.)

Try to get as tight a fit as possible between the logs. If a knot prevents a log from going into place, trim the protrusion with a chain saw or hewing hatchet. Always cut the upper log to fit logs together. This puts the cut area on the underside, where it won't collect rainwater. If you're not using cupped or V-cut logs you can fit them together by clamping them solidly and then running a chain saw between them.

The logs are likely to be tapered; some will have a more pronounced taper than others. Oak trees, for instance, are usually more tapered than softwood trees such as pine. Therefore, you must alternate butt and tip ends to produce a level wall. Some builders create a level wall by always placing the butts the same way, while others reverse them with each course. The difference is just a matter of personal choice.

Get as tight a fit as possible. Cut away protruding knots before lifting the log up into place. Any small bumps can be cut away with a sharp broad-hatchet.

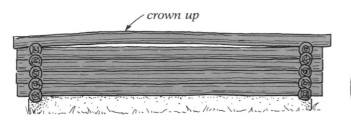

Position logs with the crown up whenever possible, and alternate butt ends around the perimeter.

Use sight poles with string lines tied to them to line up logs as you build.

Lining up logs

You'll find that few logs are perfectly straight, except for those milled for kit log homes. To make an unbowed wall, you'll have to work the logs around, preferably placed with the crown up. You can line logs up with each other by positioning four poles, one at each corner, then tying a string line to each pole. With the string laid over the top of a log as it's put into position, you can determine just how far out of line each log is. You'll have to make concessions as you turn logs to get the best results. But wall strength, no matter how crooked the logs, will not be affected.

If allowed to get too far out of line, a wall can be hard to get back on center. The problem tends to compound itself with each succeeding log. One common problem is a wall that flares out at the top. This can be avoided by carefully lining up each log. You should also check corners to see that the building is being erected square.

To ensure that the building is going up straight, continually check diagonally (center-to-center of the logs) to ensure that diagonal measures are equal.

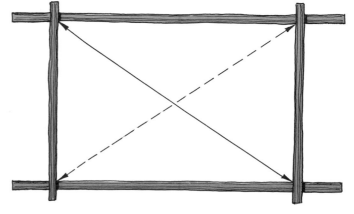

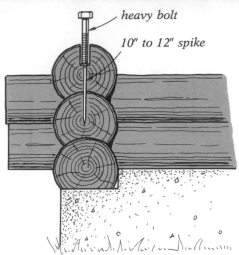

heavy bolt

10" to 12" spike

In most instances, a 10- to 12-inch spike driven in place holds the logs together. If you're using hardwood logs you will have to drill the holes. A counterbored hole at the top allows you to set the spike below the log surface using a large bolt as a driving pin under a small sledge. Spikes should be spaced about three feet apart. Put one over each log joint and stagger the remainder.

spikes staggered   lap

Securing the logs

Fasten new logs to the previous course with spikes that are long enough to go halfway through one log and halfway into the log below it. You counterbore the nail holes in the top log and, using a large steel bolt or rod, sink the nails into place as shown. This normally means a spike from 10 to 12 inches long. Place spikes every 3 feet along the log, at each end joint, and at each door and window opening. The nails are usually driven straight down through the logs or, with splined logs, slightly to one side of the splines. The spike may be common or spiraled. A spiraled spike holds better and is easier to drive. You can use wooden dowels in predrilled holes in the logs, but they won't hold as well as spikes.

Photos below: Once the logs are in position, anchor them with steel spikes or a through-bolt, which is a long threaded rod, shown, running the depth of the walls. Wedges, below, space the logs until a window buck can be installed.

In softwoods, the spike holes need not be predrilled, except for the counterbored portion. Stagger the spikes so you won't run into those previously driven in lower logs.

You will need a five- to six-pound sledge for driving spikes. A carpenter's hammer won't be up to this task.

All electrical and plumbing holes should be bored and aligned as you install the logs. Most log home wiring, however, is run in floor boxes or ceilings. But you may have to run wire for switches. Cut openings in the wall logs for these, as shown. This is done by boring the hole to depth. Use a large chisel to clean it out for the wiring or box, and then bore from the underside of the log into the opening. It's easier to do this before the log has been fastened in place on the wall.

Cavities for electrical wiring such as switch boxes and wire runs must be cut before the logs are installed.

The easiest way to cut switch box openings is to first mark around the box, then bore a series of holes with a brace and bit.

Clean out the corners of a mortise with a large chisel.

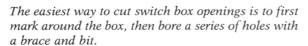

Door and window openings

Many builders try to place bad spots on the logs where there is to be a window or door opening. Then, after the wall has been erected, the openings for the doors and windows are cut with a chain saw. Keep these areas marked with chalk so that you will know where they are as you lay the logs. You could make a starting cut in the logs with the point of the chain saw, but this is dangerous. Instead, notch the logs in these locations as you go.

For a window opening, first shape the window sill log, as shown. Then, when you reach the log that will create the window top, notch it and lay it in place. Use a long carpenter's level or a plumb board to determine the upper plumb location. Mark this on each end notch. Continue with the walls or cut out the upper log, as shown.

To cut an opening, put a 2 × 4 guide board in place, temporarily nailing it to the inside of the wall. Starting at the notch, use the chain saw to cut out the opening, following the guide board with the saw bar. Remember, the door or window opening must be the opening width *plus* the width of both jambs and a bit more added for settling. The window sill log should

This is a typical door and window framed-in with rough bucks.

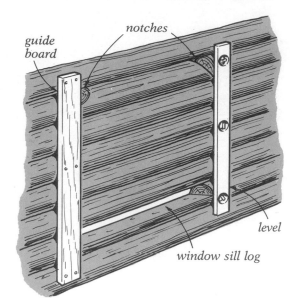

One way to provide door and window openings is to lay logs full length for the entire wall, up to the top of the intended window. Then cut the wall for windows and doors with a chain saw using guide boards nailed in place. You can make the job easier and safer by cutting notches, as shown, before installing the logs.

be cut on a downward slope to prevent water from running back into the building.

Doors are framed the same as windows, except the notches are cut in the door sill log at the same level as the floor joists.

Once the logs have been cut, the openings should be rough framed with jambs. You can

To accommodate settling of the logs, the window buck usually isn't fastened directly to the log. Instead, a spline and dado are used to anchor the buck. Then the log over the window or door opening is laid.

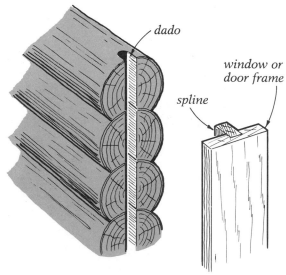

PART 3. HOUSE RAISING AND FINISH WORK

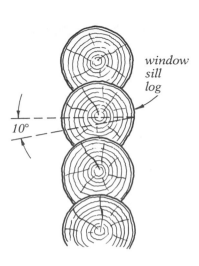

window sill log

10°

Cuts made for window sills must be at an angle that will run off water.

Once the openings have been cut, frame them in with rough jambs. Use fairly heavy stock that complements the appearance of thick log walls.

make the jambs the same width as the average log diameter or cut the jambs down and taper log ends to match. Apply preservatives to the cut ends of the logs and thoroughly caulk the entire assembly.

A stronger joint between the jamb and log ends can be made by cutting a dado into the

log ends and fastening a spline to the jamb. Use a router or circular saw with a dado blade. You could also bore 2-inch holes down through each log at the appropriate points before each is installed. Then when you cut the opening you create the slot. You'll have to do some chisel work to smooth the slot.

Step 1. *A buck spline is cut by first boring down through the log with a large bit.*

Steps 2 & 3. *Saw off the waste end of the log and chisel the slot square.*

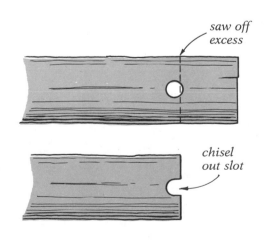

saw off excess

chisel out slot

You have to allow for settling between wall logs when installing the top jamb piece. Leave an open area of at least 2 or 3 inches between the header log and the top jamb. Fill in the space with insulation material that compresses. Cover the outside with a caulked, decorative board. Fasten it only to the header, not the jamb. You can also use a metal drip cap nailed to the underside of the header, as shown.

The settling allowance must be ¾ inch per foot of wall height and must be made for green or dry wood. For dry logs, though, you can safely reduce the amount to ⅜ inch per foot. The tops of doors and windows are normally about 7 feet high. All work should be done on them when you reach that height.

Here, cured logs were used and the bucks were nailed directly to the log ends (note window bracing).

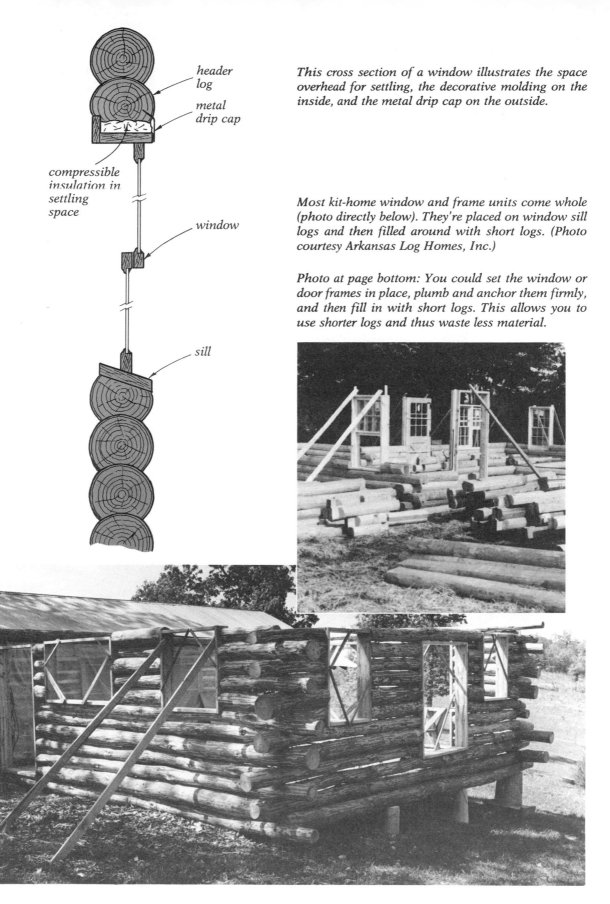

header log

metal drip cap

compressible insulation in settling space

window

sill

This cross section of a window illustrates the space overhead for settling, the decorative molding on the inside, and the metal drip cap on the outside.

Most kit-home window and frame units come whole (photo directly below). They're placed on window sill logs and then filled around with short logs. (Photo courtesy Arkansas Log Homes, Inc.)

Photo at page bottom: You could set the window or door frames in place, plumb and anchor them firmly, and then fill in with short logs. This allows you to use shorter logs and thus waste less material.

You can use shorter logs to fill in between window and door openings. Cut the logs long, put them in position, and nail an upright support across the inside or outside of the log surface (depending on whether the logs are flush inside or outside). Cut ends off after construction is finished. You can also install window and door bucks or frames and fit logs between. In any case, the window or door frames must be installed before additional wall logs are to be placed above them.

In this unusual approach, the window and door openings were created during wall construction by using short logs. Through-bolts and wedges hold the logs in position until they can be anchored.

SECOND STORIES

A floor above

If your log house is to have only one floor, you'll have to decide whether to create a cathedral ceiling or build a ceiling (and attic). You can use open, exposed beams or dimension lumber. With dimension lumber, ceiling joists must be covered with ceiling tile or wallboard. You can also create a second story. This could be a full-size upper floor or a partial second floor with the rest of the ceiling open to the roof beams. The latter gives you a combination of cathedral and upper balcony or loft.

Open cathedral framing

If you decide on a cathedral style for any portion of the house, you'll have to use tie beams across the long walls to prevent the walls from spreading apart.

If you want a ceiling, you can either create a storage area above the ceiling or build the walls higher after installing the ceiling joists, creating an upper story. You can have full-height walls on the sides of the second floor or knee walls, which are shorter walls providing a partial second story (page 167). Again,

the matter is a personal choice and depends on the amount of material you want to use, as well as the amount of space you need. The design of the upper floor also depends on the number and location of partition walls. Interior walls may be framed after the exterior walls have been erected (but before construction of the ceiling); or you can wait and do all interior work after the house is enclosed. The latter method allows you to get the house enclosed quicker. Because all partition walls must

Traditional log homes were mostly single-story, but today people are building many two-story log homes. This kit home is a good example. (Photo courtesy Boyne Falls Log Homes.)

be made with an allowance for settling, constructing these walls in sections and swinging them upright into position is no problem.

Ceiling joists can be designed to use partitions as partial support. But the partitions are not load bearing, so the upper floor joists should not be dependent upon them. Again, provisions must be made for settling. The upper floor must be just as sturdy as the main floor. Normally, 7 ½ feet is considered the minimum height for a ceiling. On small cabins the ceiling is usually no higher than one or two logs above the window and door height.

Log floor joists

This is a traditional design for an upper floor in a log home. Before erecting the logs, make sure that all bark and loose material is removed.

Although simple log joists spaced 24 inches apart have been used on some small homes (under 12 to 14 feet in width), on larger spans you should use girders fitted with joists. The girders should be a minimum of 10 inches in diameter for a 24-foot span and should be supported by partitions. The girders are then fitted with 6-inch diameter (or larger) joists spaced on 24-inch centers. Notch them into the girders with tenons. Larger spans may require narrower joist spacing.

The girders should be arranged to run parallel to and on top of partitions if possible, or to cross them for added support. Pier foundations or lally columns should be placed under partitions that are below girders, for extra support.

The girders should be notched into the wall logs as shown and their tops flattened to create a smooth support surface. Cut the wall sill notches before installing the logs, otherwise you'll have to work from scaffolding or a ladder.

Wall logs that have flattened tops and bottoms make this chore easier. Cut the notch to the full depth of the log, allowing the joists to rest on the flattened surface of the wall log beneath. Again shimming or trimming levels the top surfaces of the joists.

If the bottoms of the girders and joists are to be left exposed, there is no need to flatten

This popular design shows off the beauty and massiveness of the log beams. (Photo courtesy New England Log Homes, Inc.)

Tie beams are used in open areas, and normal ceiling joists are used in the enclosed upper story. (Photo courtesy Eureka Log Homes, Inc.)

PART 3. HOUSE RAISING AND FINISH WORK

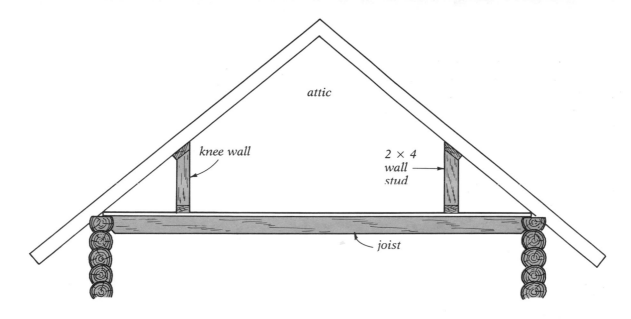

attic

knee wall

2 × 4 wall stud

joist

You can build a full-height second story which adds the height to the walls, or an attic with knee walls to provide a smaller upper story. A combination upper story adds short stub walls to gain a bit more height.

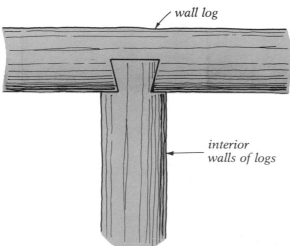

wall log

interior walls of logs

If you want interior and partition walls to be of logs, install them before proceeding with the upper floor joists. Dovetail keys can be cut in their ends so you can fasten them securely to the wall logs.

Notch log joists into the wall logs. Cut a beveled edge on the bottom side for a more finished appearance.

Wall logs with flattened tops and bottoms make notching far easier than for round logs.

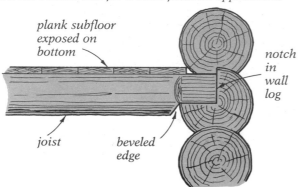

plank subfloor exposed on bottom

notch in wall log

joist

beveled edge

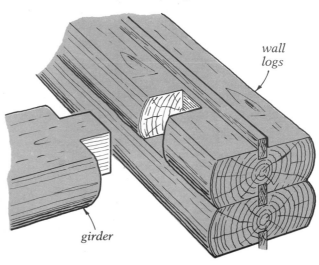

wall logs

girder

CHAPTER 9. SECOND STORIES

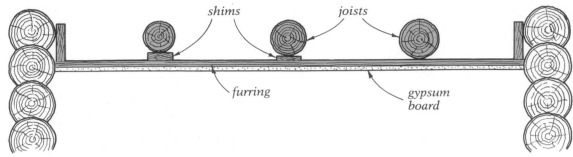

For a finished ceiling, furring strips must be nailed to the underside of the logs. Shim the space between the furring strips and logs to provide a level surface to which you can attach gypsum board or ceiling tile.

Use dovetail mortise and tenons on the girder or joists to solidly tie walls together. This was a common technique in European log buildings.

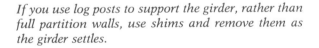

If you use log posts to support the girder, rather than full partition walls, use shims and remove them as the girder settles.

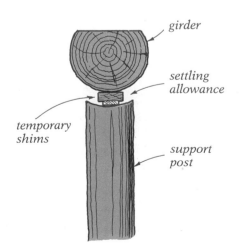

Temporary shims at the top of partition walls prevent the girder from sagging while it settles.

them. If you plan a ceiling, the bottom edges will have to be flattened to allow for furring strips. Creating a covered ceiling usually takes a lot of effort and most builders don't want to cover up the beauty of the overhead log beams.

If the bottom of the beam is to be exposed, beveling it on the bottom can improve its appearance and ease the fitting of joists against the rounded surfaces of the wall.

Joists must be securely fastened with spikes to prevent slipping and to keep the walls tied securely. Using a dovetail mortise and tenon (page 168) helps create an even stronger tie girder, as shown. To prevent the girder from sagging as the house settles, use shims between it and the supporting wall. Gradually remove the shims as the building shrinks and settles. With a porch or balcony at the second floor, the joists often go through the wall, providing a cantilevered balcony.

PART 3. HOUSE RAISING AND FINISH WORK

Dimension floor and ceiling joists

Ceiling joists can be made of dimension stock. In most instances, dimension-stock second floor joists are put up the same way they are in a traditional wood-frame house. One problem: proper attachment of the joists to the upper logs, which varies depending on the layout of the house. If the house is small, with no partitions, nail headers in place to the upper wall logs, and fasten joists to the header with joist hangers.

For larger houses, there are a number of different ways to arrange the joists. A center girder, running the full length of the house, may be needed to support joists. It, in turn, may need support posts at the center and other locations, depending on its length. The joists are fastened to the girder using metal joist hangers. At the other end, they're notched into the upper wall logs or fastened to a header. In any type of joist framing that supports weight, run the joists to make them as short as possible. Joists may also run from girder to girder, if there is need for more than one girder.

The upper-floor joists of dimension lumber are installed the same way as the first-floor joists. One effective method: Notch floor joists into wall logs.

With notched joists, the finish ceiling is fastened directly to the underside.

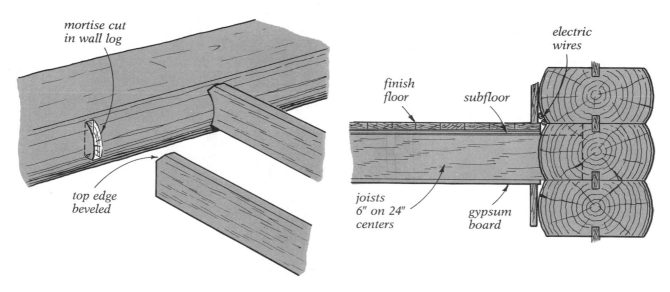

The upper floor is supported by the outer wall logs. Where the joists or girders cross partitions they must be higher to allow for settling. The allowance for this is normally, again, ¾ inch per each foot of wall height for green logs and ⅜ inch for cured logs. Add several shims and remove a few each week. You must allow enough space for a few shims to be left permanently. Wide trim, anchored to the ceiling but not the wall, covers the gap.

You could also conceal steel support posts (with screw tops) in the partitions and other areas and adjust them to allow for settling. All supports have to be directly supported by piers or a sleeper girder under the lower floor.

Install floor underlayment to walk on, covering it each night with black plastic until the job is finished and the roof is on.

Upper story walls

Full wall or stub walls: A shortened upper story (for a story and a half) uses stub walls. It can be used along with knee walls on the interior to form a partial upper floor in the center part of the house. Stub walls may vary from a couple of feet to about 4 to 6 feet, anything higher is considered a full wall. The roof joins at the stub wall height.

Any location where girders or joists cross a partition, a settling space must be provided.

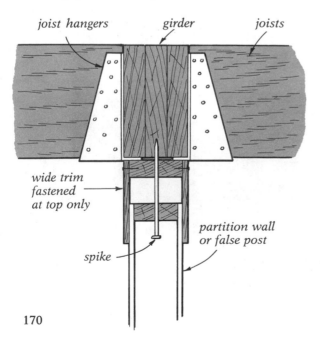

An adjustable steel support post can be concealed in a wall or false support beam.

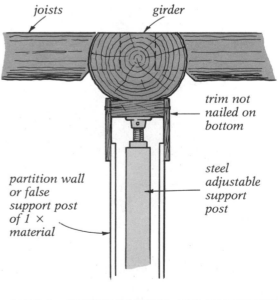

PART 3. HOUSE RAISING AND FINISH WORK

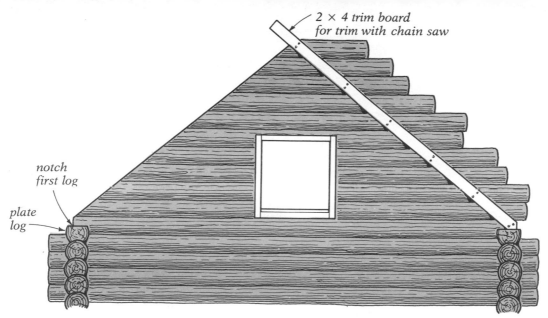

2 × 4 trim board
for trim with chain saw

notch
first log

plate
log

The gable ends can be finished in one of several ways. One method is to continue adding logs up the gable end. Plumb and brace the end thoroughly—from the inside and outside—as you go up to keep it plumb. Spike each log. Use a 2×4 guide to trim the end with a chain saw.

Whether stub or full height, upper floor walls are constructed the same way lower floor walls are; you merely continue higher with the logs.

Plate logs. Once the side wall height has been reached, the plate log is installed. This is the last log on each side of the building. This log is where the rafters and tie beams or upper ceiling joists are to be fastened. Plate logs are no different from the rest of the wall logs, except they must be shaped to suit your rafter style. This may mean notching, or flattening the top surface, depending on the kind of rafter you choose. The top surface of the plate logs or notches for the rafters must be absolutely straight and flat because the roof line follows it.

Windows or doors that lead out to a balcony or porch are installed in the same manner as those on the lower floor.

Gable ends. The upper part of the end walls of the house (the gable ends), continuing up from long wall height to the peak of the roof, can be finished in various ways depending on whether you use logs or dimension lumber. If gable ends are to be constructed of logs, you merely continue with logs. Dimension gable ends, however, are normally constructed after the roof framing has been erected.

The top plate log of the long wall must have a perfectly flat, level surface onto which rafters fasten.

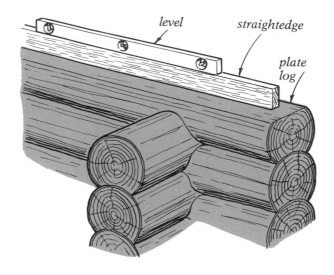

level

straightedge

plate
log

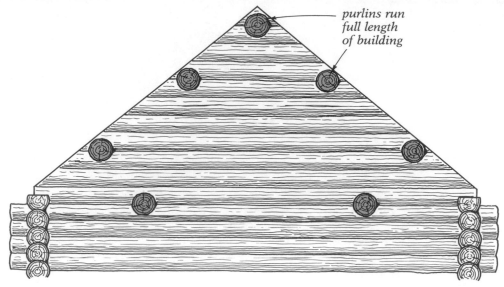

purlins run full length of building

Supporting full-length log purlins make the building of gable ends easier and they provide added stability.

Purlins help hold the gable end logs in place. (Photo by Minnesota Trailbound School of Log Building.)

Log gable ends. If you plan to make the gable ends with logs, the rafters are usually also logs. The gable logs are held in place with log purlins that reach the entire length of the building, and extend the length necessary for the roof overhang. These are fastened to the gable end logs using double notches, as shown.

Purlins must be placed at a distance equal to the depth of the rafter *below* the desired roof line. The purlins must also line up properly with the rafter roof line. After determining the roof pitch, locate purlins as shown. The roof planks should extend out over the gable ends and be fastened to them to help hold the gables securely.

Lofts

A loft is actually a partial second floor. It is installed in much the same way a full floor is. The outer edge, which does not end at a wall for support, must be supported by a girder notched into the wall logs. Long spans should have support posts. A loft can be made of either logs or dimension framing concealed behind a ceiling.

Gable ends on traditional log homes were often framed with dimension lumber and covered with shingles or sawn planks. This is still popular, as shown, but builders like board-and-batten shown, or plywood siding.

Chapter 10 ROOF FRAMING

Logs or lumber?

There are many different roof styles and methods of construction. Some are quite simple, some not. With log framing your choice of roof designs is limited. With dimension framing you can use almost any type of framing you desire. Naturally, if you build the roof framing from your own logs, you'll save money. But you can save money on dimension framing by milling the material yourself.

The most common roof styles used in log homes are the gable, the L-shaped gable, hip roof, L-shaped hip roof, and gambrel. A gable roof may have dormers in it to add light and extra space to an attic or loft.

In addition to styles, there are various methods of constructing roofs: these use trusses, rafters with a ridge-pole, rafters without a ridge-pole, and purlins and rafters. Except for purlins and rafters, the basic principles of framing are similar, whether logs or dimension stock is used. Because of the weight involved, log-framed roofs are not normally designed as trusses.

The most common method of log-roof framing in the United States is rafter framing. Purlins-with-rafters are common in Canada. Again, the choice is yours, depending on the style of house and availability of materials.

Purlin logs must be long and straight to run the full length of the roof and extend past the gable ends. With purlin-and-rafter framing, the entire gable-end wall is normally made of logs.

Log framing is attractive where exposed beams are a part of the decor, such as with cathedral ceilings. (Photo courtesy New England Log Homes, Inc.)

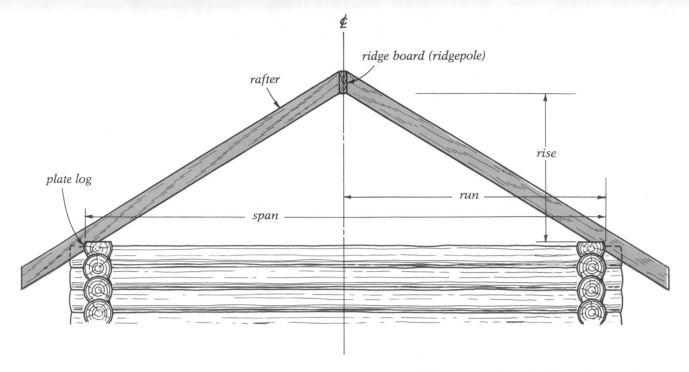

This typical dimension gable-rafter framing has a ridge board. Note the triangular formation of the rafter framing pieces.

Dimension stock framing

Dimension framing is used because it's quick, easy, and requires less fitting than log framing. It is also usually the choice where enclosed ceilings are used, and for special areas such as gable ends and dormers.

Because of the ease of construction, this is more popular, although the cost may be greater. Techniques for laying out and cutting rafters are the same for both log and lumber.

Gable roof. A roof must have a slope (or pitch) to allow water and snow melt to run off. The choice of pitch should be influenced by climate and weather conditions in your area. Homes in areas of low rainfall and warm climates can have lower-pitched roofs. Homes in areas of high rainfall must have steeper-pitched roofs. Homes in heavy snowfall country need steeper pitches yet.

There are a number of standardized roof pitches that are used in the construction industry—you must take into consideration not only climate, but ease of construction and maintenance. The materials to be used to cover the roof is also a factor in determining the roof pitch. Also, you should choose a roof pitch that complements the design of your house.

The elements of roof framing are simple triangles and the pitch is just the ratio of the

PART 3. HOUSE RAISING AND FINISH WORK

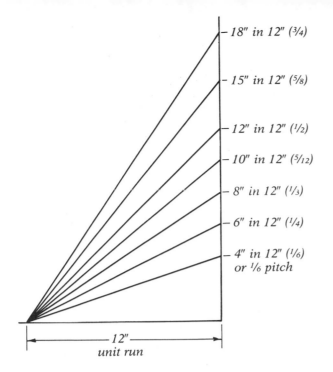

- 18" in 12" (¾)
- 15" in 12" (⅝)
- 12" in 12" (½)
- 10" in 12" (5/12)
- 8" in 12" (⅓)
- 6" in 12" (¼)
- 4" in 12" (⅙) or ⅙ pitch

12"
unit run

A variety of roof pitches can be used depending on the location or design of the house.

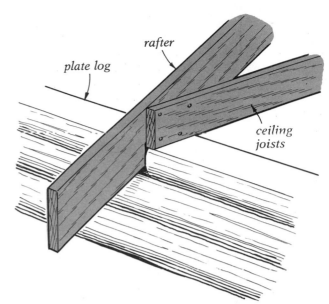

Spacing of the rafters is important. With overhead ceiling joists, the rafters are often spaced to fit against them. The two can then be nailed together for extra strength.

rise to the span. You can determine the most popular roof pitch for your areas by asking at local building-supply dealers or at county extension offices. Check local building codes, too, for suggested roof pitches. Pitch may be expressed in two different ways. For example, "8 in 12" means the roof rises 8 inches for each 12 inches of run. This could also be expressed as a ⅓-pitch roof.

In addition to the correct pitch, the spacing, number, and size of rafters must also be correct for the load the roof is to carry. (Rafter spacings run from 16 to 24 inches, with 20 inches the most common measurement.)

There are two items to be considered when figuring what load the roof is to carry: dead load, which is the weight of the roof framing and covering; and live load which is snow, wind, workmen, etc.

If you intend to finish off the underside of the rafters with a ceiling in the attic, you should space rafters the same distance apart as the floor joists. This enables you to fasten the rafters to the sides of the joists. The narrower spacing provides a stronger structure, though it is more costly and creates a greater dead load. Spacing on all rafters should be calculated for spacing to make application of the sheathing easier.

This shows the parts of a common rafter. The notch is called a bird's mouth.

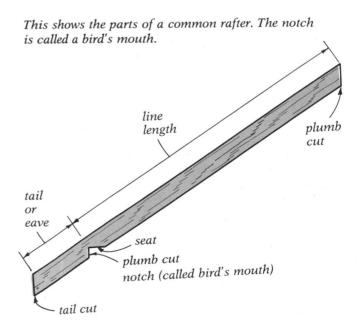

By knowing the rise per foot of run and line length of the rafter, you can lay it out using a carpenter's square.

Step 1. *If you're using an 8-in-12 pitch, locate the eight-inch mark on the tongue and the 12-inch mark on the blade. Mark these on the board. Then, as shown, measure the distance between. This should measure 14⁷⁄₁₆ inch. Multiply the 14⁷⁄₁₆ figure by the run to determine the line length of the rafter, not counting the length for overhang.*

Step 2. *To lay out the rafter, position the square so the tongue is facing to your left and on the 8 and 12 marks. Measure from the top of this point the length of the rafter.*

Laying out common rafters. If you know the rise per foot or run, it's easy to lay out a common rafter. Use a carpenter's framing or rafter square. Hold the square so that the manufacturer's name is on the side facing you. This is the face of the square, the opposite side is the back. The long arm is called the blade; the short arm is called the tongue.

Say you are going to use a ⅓ pitch (8 in 12 pitch) roof. The first step is to locate 8 on the tongue (which represents the rise), and 12 on the blade (which represents the unit of run). Now measure from the point on the blade to the point on the tongue. It should measure

14 ⁷⁄₁₆. Multiply this figure by the run. This gives the actual rafter length, not counting the overhang. For instance, with a run of 10 feet, the rafter length would be 144 ⅜. To this we add the overhang. If the overhang was to be 1 foot, the final rafter length would be 156 ⅜.

After determining the necessary length, lay a rafter board on a pair of saw horses with the crown facing away from you. Position the square so that the tongue is facing to your left. Lay the square so that the 8-inch mark on the outside edge of the tongue and the 12-inch mark on the blade fall on the upper edge of the board. Mark along the side of the tongue. This gives

PART 3. HOUSE RAISING AND FINISH WORK

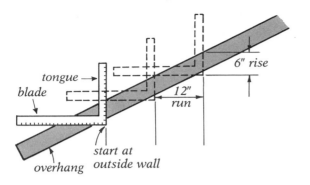

You can simply step off the rafter, moving the framing square up as shown for each step until you reach the correct rafter length.

Step 3. *Mark these locations and use the 8 and 12 measurement to mark the notch and the top plumb cut. Add the overhang length and mark this as the plumb cut.*

Step 4. *Cut a couple of rafters and trial-fit them. Then use one of the rafters as a pattern to cut all others.*

you the desired plumb cut at the ridge.

Next measure from the top of this point to the length of the rafter (excluding the overhang) and make a mark. If you're planning to use a ridge pole, you must subtract one-half its thickness from the run dimension to get the true dimension of the rafter length (without overhang). Position the square as before and mark the line. This indicates the plumb cut for the seat. Measure perpendicularly from this line to the length of the overhang and mark this line. The square should be in the same position. Cut the rafter on this and the ridge line.

Now measure the width of the plate log and, holding the square in the same position on the board, mark perpendicularly from the plumb cut to the edge of the board. Mark along the underside of the square to make the tail cut mark. Cut out this notch (the bird's mouth) and the rafter is completed.

You can also use the 'step off' method, laying out rafters as shown.

After cutting a couple of rafters it's a good idea to temporarily fasten them together to insure that you have the proper measurements. You can then use these patterns to cut the remaining rafters.

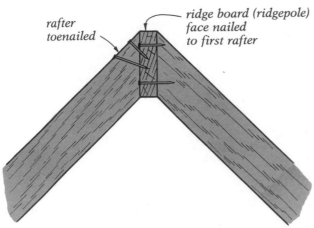

rafter toenailed

ridge board (ridgepole) face nailed to first rafter

In most instances, rafters are erected with a ridge board or ridge pole between them. You can make up a temporary ridge board, erect the rafters, brace them, and then add the ridge board after you get enough rafters installed to hold it.

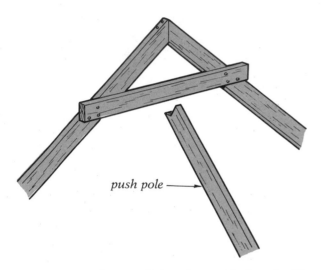

push pole

Rafters may be installed without ridgeboards. The rafters are nailed together and a temporary brace is nailed over them. You can also nail a permanent collar beam in place. Use a pole to push the rafter pairs into place until they can be secured.

Regardless of the type rafters used, a collar beam should be solidly nailed up to prevent the rafters from pushing outward on the building.

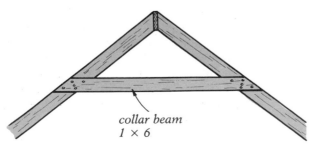

collar beam 1 × 6

Rafters with ridge boards.

Stand one gable-end rafter in position flush with the outside of the wall so the bird's mouth is positioned correctly over the top of the plate log. With someone holding up the opposite end of the rafter, nail it securely to the plate. Fasten the opposite rafter in place on the opposite side of the gable. Put a scrap of stock (the same thickness as the ridge board) temporarily between them. Brace securely. Go to the opposite end of the building and repeat these steps.

If the ridge board must be joined along the roofline, locate rafters at these joints and install. With these rafters securely fastened in place, just slide out the temporary blocks, place the ridge board in position (make sure it is level and straight), and nail the rafters securely to it. Be sure the rafters are spaced properly. The ridge board must run past the gable rafters for the distance of the extended rake. Now, mark the locations of additional rafters on the plate and ridge board, and nail them in place.

An easier method—erecting the rafters in pairs—is also shown.

Rafters without ridge board.
Rafters can also be installed without a ridge board, but if the roof is to have valleys, it must have a ridge board.

You need two workers for this method. One nails a rafter in place to the plate log while the other holds the end of the rafter up. Then the opposite rafter is positioned and nailed at its plate log. The two rafters are then nailed together at the roof peak.

An easier method, one that can be performed by one person, is to lay both the rafters together, as shown. Nail their upper ends together, and then place a temporary cross brace on them. You then swing them up into position with a push pole and brace them, until you can nail them solidly in place. Single rafter sections must be braced solidly until the roof sheathing has been installed. This is a disadvantage of not using a ridge board. However, even with a ridge board, the rafters should be temporarily braced with end to end diagonal bracing, at least until the sheathing has been installed.

Because of the weight of the roof, rafters

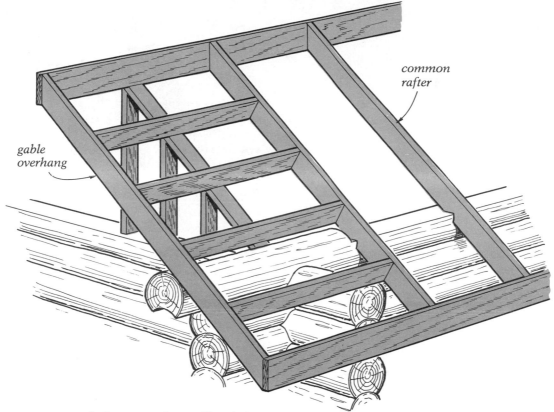

common rafter

gable overhang

deliver an outward thrust to the walls of the house. Adding collar beams as shown provides additional strength and bracing against this.

Framing a gable overhang. Usually, the gable roof overhangs the end of the house. This is called an extended rake. It allows for shading and protects the upper ends of the house from rainwater.

If you want an extended rake, you must run the side plate logs out past the ends of the walls the distance necessary to support the overhanging roof.

Short gable overhangs, as above, can be framed by attaching flying rafters to the end of the ridge board and soffit boards with short blocking 2 × 4s between. Below, is a common method of supporting end rafters.

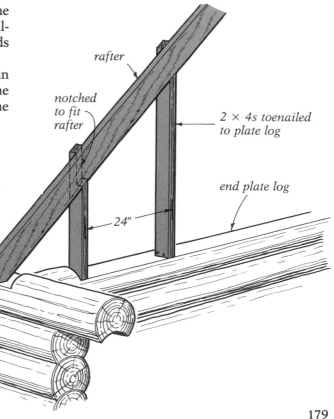

rafter

notched to fit rafter

2 × 4s toenailed to plate log

end plate log

plate log

24"

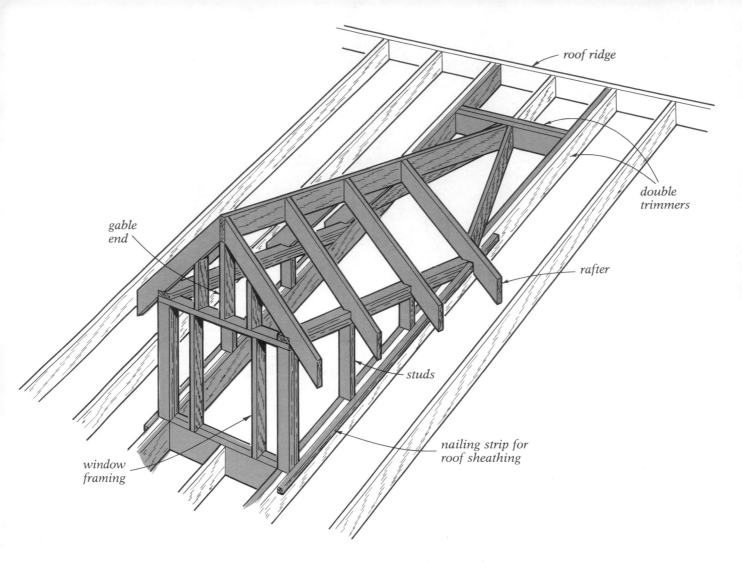

roof ridge

double trimmers

gable end

rafter

studs

window framing

nailing strip for roof sheathing

Gable dormers are framed as shown. Note the multiplicity of cuts.

Gable ends. If the gable end is made of dimension stock, and not logs, frame and cover it as shown on page 179.

Dormers are quite often used to add flair as well as space to a second floor or attic. (Photo courtesy Building with Logs Ltd.)

PART 3.   HOUSE RAISING AND FINISH WORK

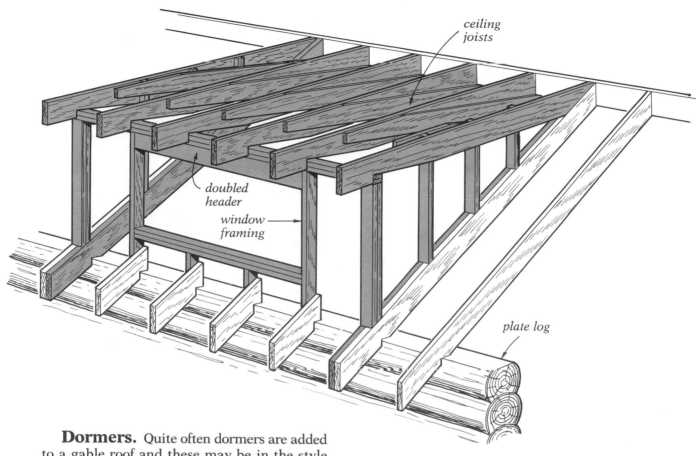

ceiling
joists

doubled
header

window
framing

plate log

Dormers. Quite often dormers are added to a gable roof and these may be in the style of gable, matching the shape of the main roof-line, or a shed design, as shown.

Another popular style is a shed dormer, which is framed in this manner.

When exposed sheathing is used on built-up log roofs, the sheathing is usually left exposed at the overhang and gable end.

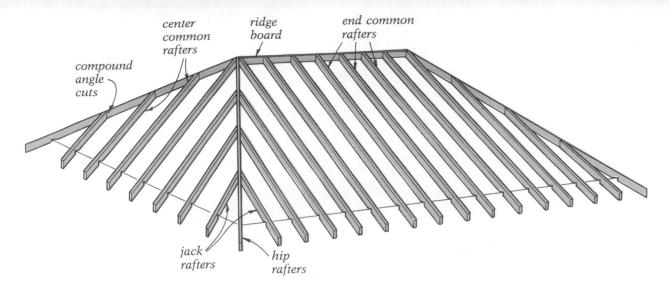

center common rafters

compound angle cuts

ridge board

end common rafters

jack rafters

hip rafters

This is typical framing for a hip roof. First frame the center common rafters. Then add the center-end common rafter and fit the hip rafters at each corner.

Framing for a hip roof.

A hip roof is framed in about the same way as a gable roof, except each end of the roof is angled down to the log plate. This eliminates the gable end of the building entirely. The hip portion of the roof is constructed after the center gable portion.

First erect and brace the center common rafters in position. Then measure, cut, and nail the end common rafters to the end of the ridge board and end plates. Then you cut hip rafters to run to each corner of the end wall. Finally, measure and cut the jack rafters to run from the end wall plate, joining the hip rafters. Carefully measure each of the jack rafters to fit. Precise cutting of the compound angle is important.

It's a good idea to cut the hip rafters a bit longer than necessary. Cut them to size after they've been installed, and before you nail up facia boards. Note that the upper ends of the hip rafters are cut with a compound angle on each side, forming a wedge-shaped end. All the jack rafters run parallel to the common rafters.

Valley rafters for L-shaped gable or hip roof.

Where two roof lines meet, you need a valley rafter. After the valley rafters have been installed, then valley jack rafters are installed between the valley rafter and the ridge board. Quite often valley and hip rafters are doubled for extra strength.

Although the various rafters seem confusing, you can simplify construction by starting with the basic common rafter and then adding in those that are needed for the roof line.

Hip rafters must be cut on a compound angle.

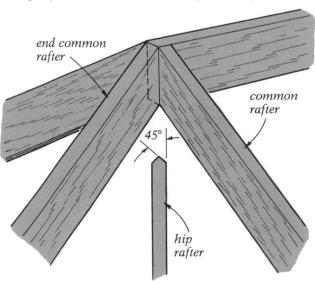

end common rafter

common rafter

45°

hip rafter

182

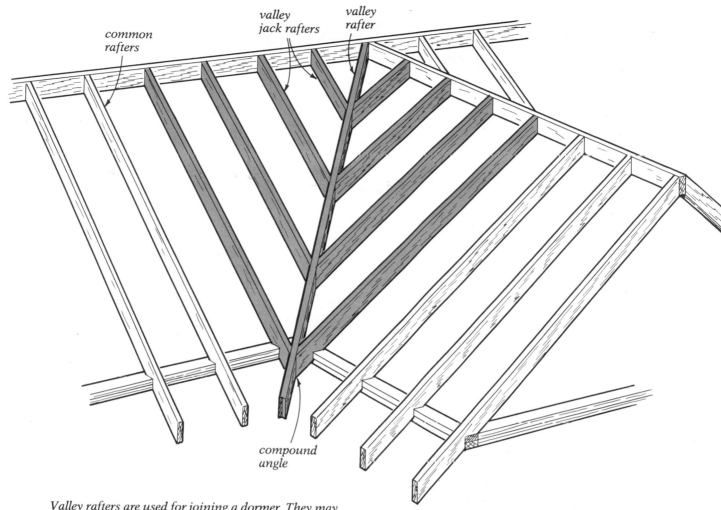

common
rafters

valley
jack rafters

valley
rafter

compound
angle

Valley rafters are used for joining a dormer. They may also appear at a roof line change.

To cut compound angles, first use a bevel gauge set for the first angle.

Set the circular saw blade at the second angle to complete the cut.

CHAPTER 10.   ROOF FRAMING

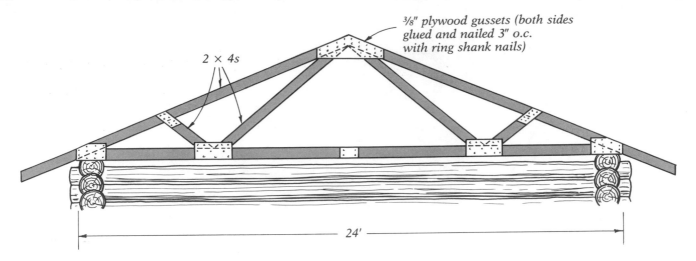

3/8" plywood gussets (both sides glued and nailed 3" o.c. with ring shank nails)

2 × 4s

24'

Roof trusses are a simple and easy way of erecting a roof. They are made up of a number of parts preassembled before installing on the walls.

Trusses. Roof trusses are another gable-roof construction form. They're actually a frame consisting of two rafters and a joist joined with braces between and held together with either metal or wood gussets. Because they can be assembled on the ground, you can build them quickly and easily. You can make up pattern pieces to cut from and then nail them together using a jig fastened to a smooth, flat surface. You can also have them ready-made to your specifications at many building supply companies.

There are several different kinds of trusses and they can span greater distances than traditional rafter and joist roof framing. But their main advantage is the speed with which they can be put up. Once they're assembled you can quickly lift them into place, bracing them temporarily until you get the sheathing installed.

Because trusses take a great deal of stress, you should make sure they're made of structurally sound materials. They must also be stored flat until put up, or they can twist and warp.

Naturally, because of the weight involved, trusses take more work to get them in position. It takes at least two people to handle the job, even for short-span trusses. Three workers are better, especially if you use larger trusses.

Trusses must first be lifted over the walls and placed inside the wall logs, with eaves extending as shown. Nail temporary blocks on the wall plate logs to prevent the ends from sliding. Then use a long push pole to swing the truss up into position. Hold the truss there until it can be fastened to the plate log and braced solidly. (Note: A swaying truss can be dangerous. Steady it with ropes.)

Plywood gussets, as shown, are used to hold truss units together. Metal gussets are also popular.

PART 3. HOUSE RAISING AND FINISH WORK

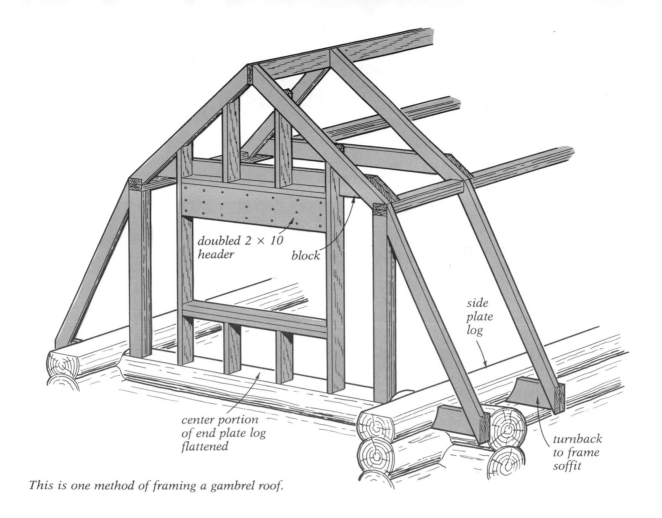

doubled 2 × 10 header

block

side plate log

center portion of end plate log flattened

turnback to frame soffit

This is one method of framing a gambrel roof.

Once a couple of trusses have been erected, nail up temporary—but sturdy—braces to steady them. If you must leave any kind of roof framing job before finishing it, make sure it's thoroughly braced so a strong wind won't blow it over while you are gone.

Gambrel roof. Gambrel roofs give you a lot of space in an attic and are quite popular with today's modern log home designs. Although they appear complicated, they are simply a combination of two common rafters (one on each side) making a double-angle roof line. The assembled rafters are strengthened with a cross bracing much like a flat truss.

Shown are the most common methods of framing a gambrel roof. Most often, the purlins at the rafter joints are supported by knee-wall studs, although there are other methods. Common, too, are short horizontal boards, called lookouts, running from the lower wall studs to the ends of the gambrel rafters. Collar beams may be used instead of the purlins.

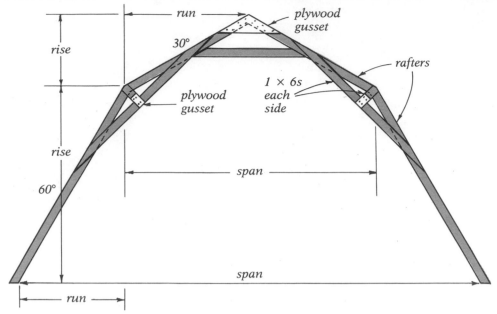

A gambrel truss system with short blocks between the trusses makes a sturdy roof.

This strong roof uses purlins over the trusses. You can also use tongue-and-groove sheathing if the goal is a built-up roof.

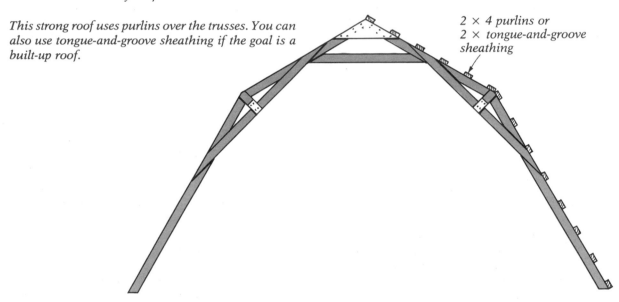

This is a typical framing job showing the gable end, gable overhang, L-gable for a room addition and shed roof to the side.

PART 3. HOUSE RAISING AND FINISH WORK

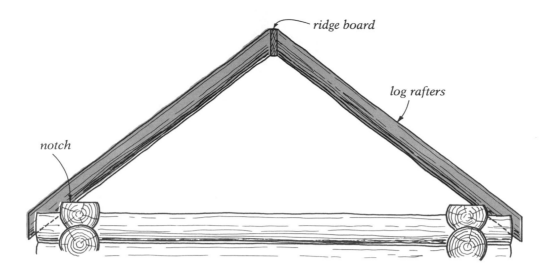

Principles for gable log framing are nearly the same as those for dimension lumber. Below ridge pole is commonly substituted for a ridge board.

Log roof framing

Logs can also be used for roof framing. The most common style, again, is a gable roof. Rafters are laid out in the same fashion as dimension materials, with or without a ridge board. The ridge board can be a 1×6 or 1×8 of dimension material, but is most commonly a true ridge pole instead. If a true ridge pole is used, make sure it juts well past the extended rake end. It can be cut to the desired length later. When using a true ridge pole, the rafters should be notched in place. The ends of the rafters can be seated using a standard bird's mouth on the top-plate log or by other methods (such as a double notch). Rafter logs should be no smaller than 6 inches in diameter. Larger rafters may be needed depending on their length.

The normal log rafter spacing is 24 inches, although it may be 30 inches if you use larger logs. You can hew, or flatten, the upper sides of the rafters to provide a more even surface for fastening the sheathing. If you intend to add a ceiling, you will also have to flatten the undersides.

Because log rafter framing is basically the same as dimension lumber framing, complicated roofs can be difficult to build—you're better off sticking with a simple gable roof, if possible.

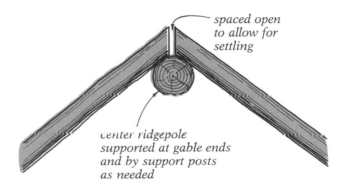

Rafters can be notched to fit over the plate log as with dimension lumber. A double notch is strong.

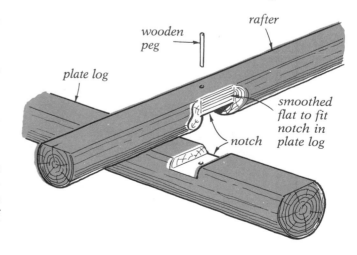

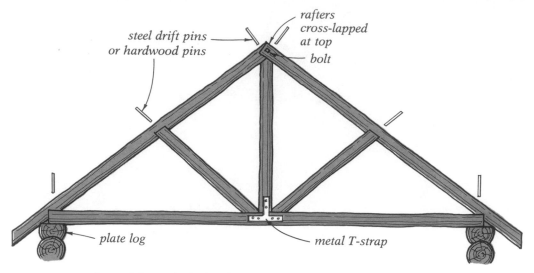

steel drift pins
or hardwood pins

rafters
cross-lapped
at top

bolt

plate log

metal T-strap

Log trusses are commonly used for cathedral and other open ceiling designs.

Here exposed tongue-and-groove decking is used with rafters and insulation, followed by top decking.

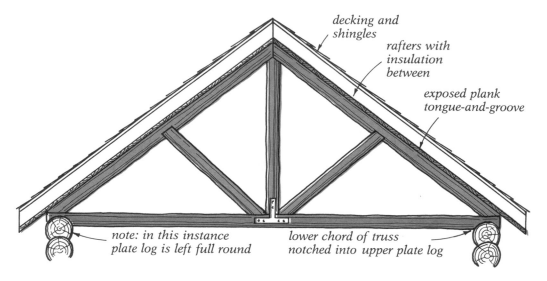

decking and
shingles

rafters with
insulation
between

exposed plank
tongue-and-groove

*note: in this instance
plate log is left full round*

*lower chord of truss
notched into upper plate log*

Log trusses. You can use log to build trusses—this is a traditional method of framing for post-and-beam construction. The system is primarily used in homes that have an open or cathedral ceiling over the first floor but serves well for an open second floor too.

Using special truss joints, the trusses can usually be spaced from 10 to 15 feet apart. Purlins are spiked to the trusses and sometimes the sheathing is fastened directly to the purlins. Sometimes rafters are fastened on top of the purlins and *then* the sheathing is attached. As you can imagine, roofs made with log trusses are extremely heavy. It takes a few healthy workers to get them up and secured in place.

Purlin log roof framing. Another traditional, and simple, method of log roof framing makes use of log purlins running the full length of the house, extending through the log gable ends. One purlin is usually placed halfway up the roof and another is used as a ridge pole. Wider roofs may require two to a side, spaced 3 to 4 feet apart. Spans of up to 20 feet can be done this way using 10-inch minimum diameter logs. If the span is longer, a support must be provided. This is usually a center chord plus additional upright chords to support each of the purlins. This provides an open log roof framework that is appealing. An alternative is to use a scissor truss joined in the center with a large bolt, shown above.

PART 3.   HOUSE RAISING AND FINISH WORK

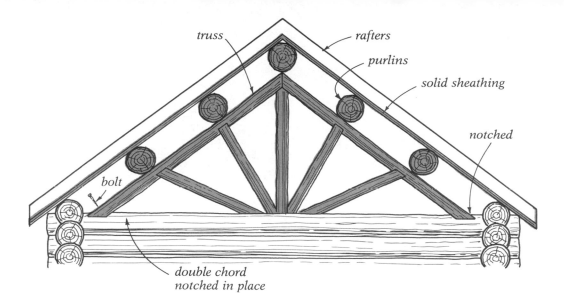

Log purlins may be placed on top of the trusses, followed with the sheathing and rafters. This provides an extremely strong, if not massive, roof. Note the use of doubled chords on the bottom for extra strength, excellent for a longer span.

One of the most common methods of log roof framing, especially in the North, is using purlins running the full length of the house (through the gable ends) and supporting the log rafter. These are then covered with exposed sheathing or tongue-and-groove decking. A built-up roof goes on top.

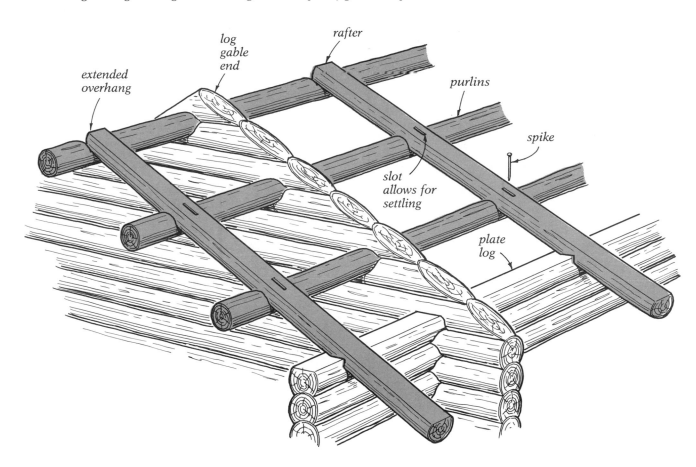

CHAPTER 10. ROOF FRAMING

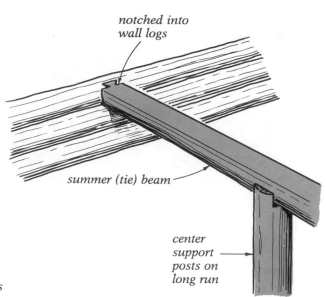

notched into
wall logs

summer (tie) beam

center
support
posts on
long run

Summer, or tie, beams must be notched into the walls to help hold them and prevent them from spreading.

Again, although some builders merely attach the sheathing directly to the horizontal purlins, you get a better job by first installing log or dimension rafters to the purlins. Log rafters are installed by cutting a slot at each spot the rafter joins a purlin and spiking them through the slot, allowing for settling. Join the rafters securely to the plate log with a double notch (page 189) and leave space at the top to allow for settling.

The top of the rafters should be flattened to attach the sheathing. If the planking or sheathing shows on the underside of the roof you should probably create a built-up roof, installing insulation above the inner layer of sheathing. Shown on previous pages are several different designs. Roofs can also be installed with rigid insulation; the roofing is nailed directly over the insulation.

Roof venting and circulation

Built-up roofs need built-in ventilation systems. *Any* closed-off attic system needs some method of air circulation and venting to release moisture and prevent condensation. The most common solution is to install purchased vents in the gable ends of the home. You can also make your own. The size of the vents should be approximately 1/300 of the square

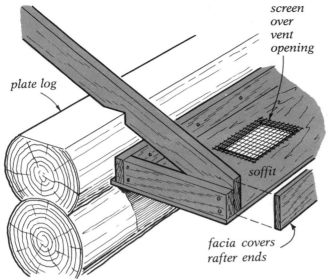

screen over vent opening

plate log

soffit

facia covers rafter ends

Soffit vents allow air circulation upward toward ridge vents. This circulation carries off water vapor generated within the home, which would otherwise condense on roof framing and boards to induce rot. Insulation of high R-value must be installed below the air channels. Screening over soffit vent openings is essential to ward off insects, birds, and rodents.

footage of the house ceiling. Adding vents in the soffit helps create air flow through the attic, too.

Soffits and cornices

On log roofs with exposed sheathing, the underside of the roof that extends past the wall logs is usually left open. The appearance of the log rafters and sheathing can add to the appeal of the house. Whether log or dimension lumber is used for rafters, snow stops or freize boards must be installed between the rafters to keep out the weather.

Skylights

Skylights and other roof openings are framed using the same techniques as you would for framing floor or ceiling openings. Double the framing members around the opening to provide more strength.

Insulating

The ceiling or the roof will have to be insulated depending on whether the house is open to the roof or has a ceiling and closed attic. See Chapter 11.

If you want to cut roofing costs on a small vacation or hunting lodge, use sawn native stock ripped into 1×6s, covered with hand-split wooden shakes.

PART 3.   HOUSE RAISING AND FINISH WORK

Chapter 11 ROOFING

Covering the top

There are many roofing materials that may be suitable for your log home. Your choice will depend on cost, a style to complement the design of your home, the availability of materials, and how much labor you want to put into this phase. You can make your own split or shake shingles if you have the materials. (But it takes a great deal of time unless you have a power tool, such as the band saw mill with shingle accessory or a good froe and lots of spare time.

On the other hand, you could purchase wooden shakes or shingles, which is an expensive proposition. Remember, there is some danger of fire from chimney sparks unless the shingles are treated with fire retardant. In fact, some localities may not allow wood shingles. Check the rules governing use of wooden shakes or shingles in your area.

The most common roofing material is asphalt and is often chosen by modern-day log home builders.

Decking

Regardless of the roof covering used, decking must first be laid down over the rafters or purlins. In the old days, when wood shingles were the only choice, strips of wood were simply nailed across the rafters and shingles nailed down over these. Because of the way the shingles were laid, they rarely let in rainwater except during heavy, blowing storms. However, unless you're building a simple hunting cabin in the back woods, solid decking should be used. Not only does it provide a more weatherproof roof, but it strengthens the roof and adds insulation as well.

Once the roof framing is in place you're ready to start closing the building in. First install the roof decking. There are several materials that can be used for decking: 1 × 12s are popular.

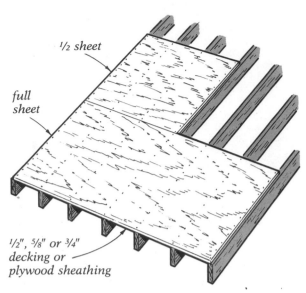

¹⁄₂ sheet

full sheet

¹⁄₂", ⁵⁄₈" or ³⁄₄" decking or plywood sheathing

Plywood is laid with the lengthwise measurement of the sheets (that is, the top grain) running at right angles to the rafters. Start at one end with a full sheet, then nail a half sheet above it to stagger the joints.

Several different materials can be used for decking. 1 × 12 decking is common and fairly economical. Run it across the rafters and extend it out past the eaves to support the hanging, or fly, rafters. In some parts of the country, this may be the most economical way to lay decking. One advantage of this type of decking is that one man can easily do the roof by himself; it may take two people to hoist and install heavy plywood sheets. Probably the most economical method for sheathing is to use 1 × 12s of native lumber sawed by a local sawmill. You could also saw it yourself with a portable sawmill. Remember, green wood shrinks and leaves gaps.

Decking for wooden shingles. In
areas with damp climates, the decking for wooden shingles must be spaced boards. (Wooden shingles in damp climates may need to be treated with a fungicide.) Usually these are 1 × 3s or 1 × 4s spaced to create proper nailing distances. This is economical if you can saw your own sheathing boards and split or saw your own shakes and shingles. The spacing distance of the board is determined by the weather exposure of the shingles. All end joints of the boards must be positioned over a rafter and joints should be staggered on the joists. Use two 8d ring-shank nails at each rafter. If

The most commonly-used decking for residential construction is plywood. Greater rafter spans require thicker decking. (Eureka)

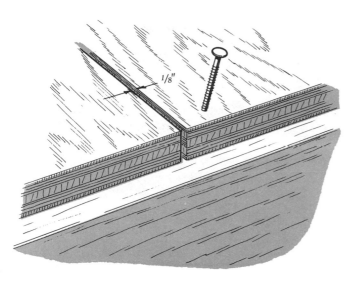

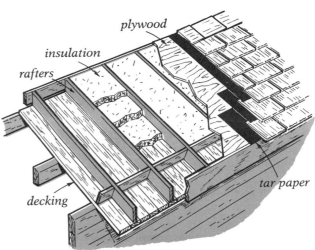

Use ring shank nails for plywood decking. Leave an ⅛-inch space between the edges of the sheets for expansion.

To make a built-up roof, nail the decking up, cover it with insulation, add spacers and rafters, then exterior plywood and shingles of your choice.

the soffits or underside of the roof ends are to be open, use solid boards in those areas to create a better appearance.

Tongue-and-groove decking.
If you plan to have an exposed-beam ceiling, use solid tongue-and-groove decking. This is available in 2-inch stock. Simply nail it in place, fitting the tongue of one piece into the groove of the next.

Plywood decking.
Probably the most commonly-used sheathing is plywood and, if you have a helper or two, the work goes very fast. Plywood is strong and has better insulation value than solid wood boards. It can be used with shake or shingle roofs and is commonly used under asphalt shingles.

Purchase sheathing grade plywood. The rafter spacing determines the thickness of the plywood: ⅝-inch may be used when rafters are spaced 16 inches on center, however, ⅜-inch or ½-inch is a better idea. Check the local building codes governing plywood decking thickness. One advantage of the extra thickness is that it provides better nail-holding power.

To install plywood sheathing, lay it so the grain runs at right angles to the rafters. It should also be staggered on the rafters. Start at one end with a full sheet (remember to extend the sheet for the hanging rafter) and then cut a sheet in half and nail it in place with the outside edge flush with the first sheet. (If the edges are exposed to the weather, use plywood made with exterior grade glue.) This creates staggered joints for all succeeding sheets in those two rows. Do the rest of the roof in the same manner. Leave ⅛-inch gaps between the pieces (in warm, damp climates, this spacing may have to be increased a bit).

Use 6d ring-shank nails for sheathing ½-inch thick and under, and 8d for ½-inch and thicker boards. Space nails about 5 inches apart on edges and about 10 inches apart on the center nailing.

Nail spaced boards on top of the plywood sheathing to provide ventilation under shakes. Use 1 × 2s for this instead of the wider stock. Special metal clips can be used to hold the edges of the plywood sheets that are not nailed.

All sheathing joints at valleys, chimney openings, and roof peaks must be a tight fit.

There are, of course, other materials that can be used for sheathing, including new paper-backed insulation boards. But plywood is still the choice in most areas of the country. It's the best material most often specified by local building codes.

Roof covering

Wood shakes or shingles. Commercial wooden shakes or shingles come in several different materials and styles. They're cut from redwood, cypress, or red cedar, with red cedar being the most common choice. Tapered shingles are sawed and may have plain butt ends or fancy butt ends.

Shakes, on the other hand, are split rather than sawed. Shakes may be split extra wide and taper sawed to produce two tapered shingles, each with a smooth surface for nailing and a rougher split surface for exposure. Shakes may also be split straight rather than tapered.

The most common shingle lengths are 16, 18, and 24 inches, although 30-inch shingles are available. Each length has a different exposed area. The correct length of the shingles and the amount of exposure it is to have is determined by the roof pitch.

Wood shakes or shingles are traditional log home coverings. Shingles are sawn. Shakes are split.

Step 1. *Photo right, you can split your own shakes, but it takes a lot of time to split enough for a large home. First select large-diameter logs of white oak, red cedar, spruce, fir, or pine. Cut them into the lengths you desire and split in half using a maul and wedge.*

Step 2. *Photo below, split large logs into quarters.*

Step 3. *Photo below, remove the heartwood from the split billets.*

Making shakes or shingles. Again,

the best choice of materials is red cedar. However, cypress can be used—if available—or spruce, pine, fir, or balsam. Pine has a tendency to rot fairly quickly. Hardwoods such as red or white oak can also be used. The biggest problem in using hardwoods is finding a clear, straight-grained trunk section big enough to cut shakes from. There can't be any knots in the log.

The first step is to saw the log into the proper lengths. The short log sections are called shake bolts. The logs should be at least 18 inches to 2 feet in diameter to produce 6- to 8-inch wide shakes. Shakes usually measure ⅝-inch at the thick end.

Next, use a splitting wedge and maul to split the bolt into quarters. A large log should be split further into eighths. Position a froe about ½ to ⅝ inch away from one edge of the end of the block, following the radial lines of the grain. Drive the sharpened edge of the froe into the end of the block, then turn and twist its handle to pry the shake away from the main block.

Occasionally a shake runs wider than you want. If this happens, split the shake again from the largest end. Once a shake has been split from the block, turn the block upside down and split another shake away. Work on the same face from which you cut the first shake.

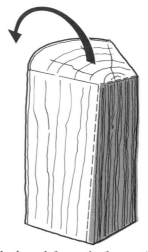

Turn the block end for end after each split.

Step 4. *Use a wooden mallet on a froe to split shakes to the thickness you desire.*

Step 5. *Once the shake starts to split, twist downward on the froe to force the split further.*

You can also split a one-eighth block in half and continue splitting until you get shakes at the desired thickness. (The shake is normally a bit larger on the outside.)

Another alternative is to merely split the log bolt in half and then cut off shakes following the grain pattern. This results in more even shingles, that is, not tapered edge-to-edge, though the shingles will have a tendency to cup or warp up on the edges.

Wood splits differently. Oak, for instance, must be quartered before splitting. Shakes from other woods, such as pine, cedar, or spruce, can be split off half blocks. Splitting takes skill—you'll soon learn that splits won't come off perfectly every time.

You can speed the process up by using a power shake maker, adapting a standard hydraulic cylinder from a firewood log splitter. You can also saw your own shingles using a portable sawmill.

To estimate how much you need, first figure the square footage of your roof, including eaves. Wooden shingles are sold in bundles and figured in squares. A square of shingles is 100 feet square. It takes four bundles of the shingles to make up a square. Add about 10 percent for waste.

After you split your first few shingles you will see that a couple of pickup truck loads of shake bolts won't go very far. It takes a great deal of material and effort to provide even enough shakes for a small to medium-sized home.

Installing shakes or shingles.

You can install wood shakes or shingles with a hammer, but a shingling hatchet will speed the job. It has a sharpened edge, a grooved head (for driving nails), and an adjustable guide, which is used to position shingles for correct exposure.

Wooden shingles are started at the bottom of the roof line with a double layer, as shown. Place roofing felt over the sheathing before installing shingles. The ends of the shingles should project past the end of the facia board by ½ to ¾ inches so that water runoff is directed into the gutter. You could nail a piece of beveled siding along the gable ends to direct water onto the roof surface, rather than allowing it to drip off the ends. Metal drip stops can

The Wood-Mizer bandsaw sawmill has a shingle-cutting accessory. (Laskowski Industries)

Basic installation methods are the same for shakes and shingles.

PART 3.   HOUSE RAISING AND FINISH WORK

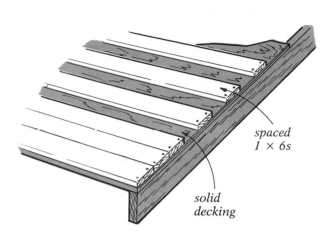

spaced 1 × 6s

solid decking

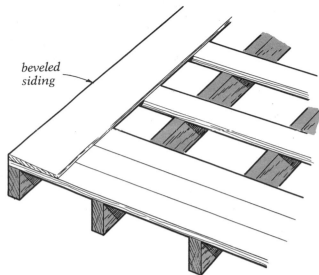

beveled siding

The roof decking for shakes and shingles may be either spaced or solid sheathing. In areas where wind-driven snow is encountered, solid sheathing is better. If solid sheathing is used, spacers 1-inch thick should be used over the sheathing. Spaced sheathing should be 1 × 6s.

Beveled siding on eave ends helps direct water away from the eaves.

also be used on both the gable ends and the eaves.

Maintain the proper exposure, or amount of overlap, of the shingles: Leave about ⅓ of the shingles exposed. This provides a triple layer of shingles covering the roof.

Make sure you get the first double layer of shingles straight along the bottom edge. Since the upper ends of the shingles may not all match, measure with the exposure guide on your shingling hatchet.

Place a 36-inch-wide strip of 15-pound building felt over the sheathing boards at the eave line. Place a doubled starter course of shingles over the felt, leaving about a half inch projecting below the facia board.

After the starter course is in place, put an 18-inch-wide strip of 15-pound building felt (minimum) over the top portion of the shakes. Extend it onto the sheathing with the bottom edge of the felt at a distance above the shake or shingle butt equal to twice the length of the weather exposure. For example, if 24-inch shakes are laid with a 10-inch exposure, the bottom edge of the felt should be applied 20 inches above the shake butts. The strip will cover the top 4 inches of shake and extend 14 inches onto sheathing.

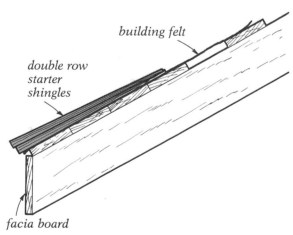

building felt

double row starter shingles

facia board

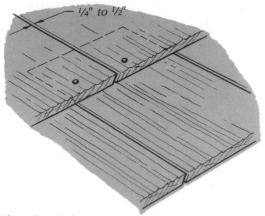

Place the shakes approximately ¼ to ½ inch apart to allow for possible expansion.

Alternate the layers of shingles and building felt until you reach the roof peak. Stagger the joints between the shingles so all cracks are covered. (Photos in this series courtesy of Red Cedar Shingle and Handsplit Shake Bureau.)

Use aluminum, hot-dipped galvanized, or zinc-coated steel nails for roofing. Use two nails in each shake, approximately one inch in from each side. Succeeding shakes should cover the nails.

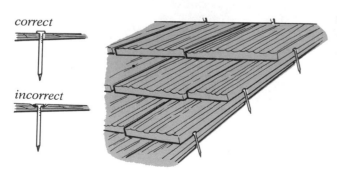

Each shingle layer should be nailed down with just two nails. The nails must be about ¾ to 1 inch from each edge and spaced so they will be ¾ to 1 inch under the next covering course of shingles. Use only aluminum, hot-dipped galvanized or zinc-coated steel nails.

The shakes will be of varying widths. You must randomly position them so that you have a pleasing pattern and so that they're properly covered by the next course.

Nail down the first layer of the bottom course, then nail the second layer of the bottom course over the top of the first, covering the cracks created by the first course. Leave a ¼-inch space between shingles. When installing shakes, the spacing may be as much as ⅜ inch.

The next course of shingles is then nailed down over the first. You can use a snapped chalkline as a guide, or nail a straight edge down to butt the shingles against. This is the easiest method and provides a clean-looking line to the exposed edge. However, make sure you keep measuring as you go—the exposure must be measured correctly so that you don't end up at the top of the roof with a wedge-shaped course of shingles. You must also keep the nail line correctly spaced so it will be covered by the next course.

Put a layer of 15-pound roofing felt under each succeeding course of shakes or shingles. The felt should be spaced about ⅓ of the way down from the upper end of the under layer of shingles.

Watch your selection of shingles so that you don't cover one course of narrow shingles with

You can use a temporary guide strip to align shingles. Or you can snap a chalk line.

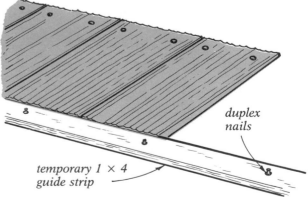

PART 3. HOUSE RAISING AND FINISH WORK

another. This would leave too much open spacing in the roof. Use combinations of wide and narrow pieces.

Roofs with valleys should be started at the valleys; alternate metal flashing between the layers of shingles as shown. The valley flashing must extend at least 10 inches on each side.

Conventional flashing is used for all other locations. Don't sheath the location of the chimney. Some builders merely cut away this hole later, but this usually leads to a messy job that causes leaking. Instead, install the chimney or vent first, then roof and flash around it.

The ridge line may be covered in any of several different ways. You could use a special ready-made cover. You can make your own, too, by beveling the edges of the shingles and overlapping them, as shown (next page). The bevels should alternate from side to side to avoid creating a single line of water entry.

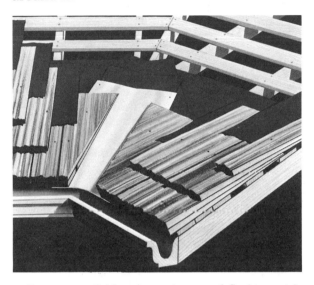

Valleys are roofed by alternating metal flashing with the shingle layers.

Add flashing to any areas where structures such as chimneys protrude through the roof line.

Chimneys should be constructed with masonry chimney flashing, which is interlaced with shingles.

Hips and roof peaks are finished off by laying shingles as shown. The courses are often doubled.

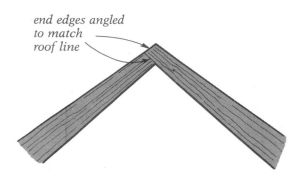

end edges angled
to match
roof line

The edges of the shakes or shingles at peaks must be cut at the roof angle to provide a finished appearance.

An easy, quick method of installing shingles is to use shingle panels consisting of shingles nailed to spacer boards. These panels are simply nailed at the proper spacing. (Photo courtesy Shakertown.)

Make sure you cut the angles on the valley shingles neatly—use wide shingles in this area. You should never end a course at a valley or gable end with a narrow shingle. Use it instead on an inside space, or cut down succeeding shingles to create an even shingle width across the area.

Wood shingles are also available in panel form; that is, a number of shingles fastened to a piece of plywood sheathing. To install, you merely nail the panels to the rafter. Nail the first course of shingle panels in place, butted against a special guide strip temporarily nailed across the rafters. This first course of shingles must end exactly on a rafter centerline. Succeeding courses can join between rafters if you use special metal clips for the plywood. Again, the main thing is to provide proper spacing for the shingle joints.

Asphalt shingles. Most asphalt shingles are easy to install and are available in a number of different colors and patterns. Some, in fact, are textured to resemble wooden shakes. Asphalt shingles are probably used on more than 95 percent of new homes. They're also fairly inexpensive in comparison to other roofing materials. An asphalt roof is rot and vermin proof.

There are many different installation methods, including the three-tab lock-down strip, individual lock-down, individual staple-down, T-lock, two-tab hexagon, three-tab hexagon, giant individual American shingle and giant individual Dutch-lap shingle. Specific information is provided on the shingle packages. Because the most common shingles are the three-tab strip shingles, those are discussed here.

Strip shingles are normally used on roof pitches ranging from 4 in 12 to 8 in 12. The self-sealing kind are most commonly used, but are also the most expensive. Shingles are sold in various weights—the heavy weight shingles have a longer life expectancy (and guarantee) than the lighter shingles. Lightweight shingles are usually guaranteed for 15 years, heavyweights up to 25 years. Heavier shingles last longer for the cost; their main disadvantage is their weight.

For a longer-lasting roof, choose a darker color. Why? The chips of stone gradually loosen

PART 3. HOUSE RAISING AND FINISH WORK

and are flushed away from the asphalt, leaving dark streaks or blotches. These are less apparent on the darker-colored shingles. Also, use a variegated pattern, if possible. And don't shingle on a hot day; you'll stick to the asphalt or slide on it, which damages it considerably.

Asphalt shingle needs. Asphalt shingles are sold in bundles or paper-wrapped packages. The number of packages or bundles needed to make up 100 square feet of roofing (a square) varies depending on the thickness, weight, and size of the shingles. Three-tab shingle strips are typically 12 by 36 inches. When installing, 5 inches of shingle is normally left exposed.

You must estimate correctly, because you can't return opened bundles. If you run short you may not be able to purchase shingles that perfectly match those already installed.

If you have the correct number of shingles on hand, get them all up on the roof and scatter the bundles over the sheathing before you start. It makes the job much easier. This often can be done by the supplier, if you make arrangements when you purchase the shingles.

A simple gable roof is easy to figure. Measure from eave to eave and rake to rake using a steel tape. Multiply the numbers and divide

by 100 to get the number of squares you need. Round off to the next number of squares if the number comes out uneven. Remember, the first course of shingles must be doubled, so add in that amount. The ridge also requires doubled shingles. Normally it takes one square of shingles for each 90 linear feet of ridge.

To figure a hip roof, measure and simply add the surfaces together, again allowing for the extra layer on the ridge and eaves.

Roofs and valleys generate quite a bit of waste because the shingles must be cut to fit. For these, multiply the valley length by 1 ½

Place bundles of asphalt shingles and other roofing materials on the roof in convenient locations.

Asphalt shingles are economical and easy to install. (Photo courtesy Wilderness Log Homes.)

The first step in installing asphalt shingle is to install metal drip caps at eaves.

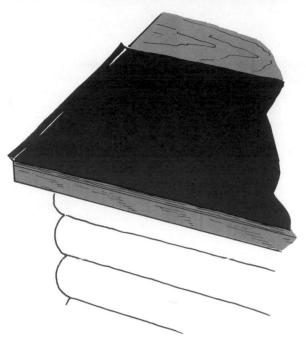

Tack a 36-inch-wide strip of roll building felt down before starting the first course of shingles.

to find the amount of additional material needed, and then add this number to the total area of the roof. You must also add in dormers (if any), including the ridge, eave, etc.

In addition to the shingles, you'll also need enough 15-pound roofing felt to cover the roof as an underlayment. This is usually over-lapped 2 inches. Figure by taking the total square feet number of roof and adding 15 per-cent for the overlap and waste. Most conven-tional rolls have 400 square feet (which also includes the two-inch overlap).

Fasten each shingle with four roofing nails. This normally works out to about 350 nails per square. The nail length must suit the thick-ness of the shingles to be applied; nails should enter into the decking at least ¾ inch.

The tools needed for asphalt roofing in-clude a hammer, rule, chalk line, and a carpet or hooked-bill knife. Use a pair of tin snips to cut the shingles.

Installing asphalt shingles. Roll felt may be stored on the roof, but it can roll off with disastrous results to anyone unfor-tunate enough to be below. Bring it up one roll at a time and install, or install it all before you start the shingles (on a small roof that you plan to do in one day). Leaving it overnight exposes it to moisture and the possibility of

a rainstorm, which can be devastating. Long exposure of the sun causes it to buckle.

Starting at one edge of the roof, position the roll flush with the bottom of the sheathing. The chalk line on the roofing felt should be facing up. Tack a nail or two in the corner to hold it in place, allowing the felt to hang over the eave about six inches. Now carefully roll towards the opposite end of the roof, making sure you keep the lower edge flush with the bottom of the sheathing. When you get about a foot from the opposite end, stop. Cut the felt with a hook knife, leaving about a foot to ex-tend out over the end. This is a bit tricky for the first course; it takes care to keep from drop-ping the roll. You can temporarily tack it with roofing nails as you go to prevent the material from sliding downward on the sheathing.

After cutting it off, temporarily block the roll so it can't fall from the roof. Now go back to the starting end and smooth out any bub-bles or bumps, and remove the temporary nails. With the entire strip positioned smoothly, nail it using short roofing nails spaced about 3 feet apart and about 8 inches from the eave edge. Use a couple of nails at each rake end and then trim away the excess felt. Install the second strip in the same manner, overlapping by 2 inches as indicated by the chalk line, or you can wait until you start the roof edge.

PART 3. HOUSE RAISING AND FINISH WORK

Start at an end, bottom corner of the roof and nail on a row (a half dozen or so) shingles placed upside down (with tabs pointing toward roof eave). Then place another row of shingles directly over this to create a doubled row of shingles. (Note: No building felt was used on this job, although it is recommended.)

Continue cutting the ends off the shingles until you get a stair-step effect up to a half-tab as shown. You can continue these courses completely across the roof if you desire.

Cut half a tab off the outside end of a shingle and install it in place with the proper exposure (usually just covering the stick-down strip).

If the felt is to go over a hip roof, roll it up over the edge, cut off about a foot, and start again. On valleys, cut the felt at the centerline and then start again. Always keep the lines and edge of the felt parallel to the roof eave. The parallel lines on the felt will help you judge the position of the shingles properly.

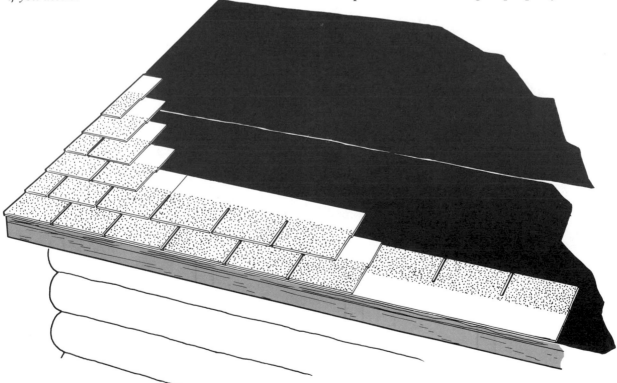

To cut a shingle, score across the back with a sharp utility knife using a carpenter's square as a guide.

After scoring the shingle, tear it apart.

Again, the normal amount of shingle exposed to the weather is 5 inches, but, to avoid ending with too small or too large a course at the ridge line, you may have to adjust this exposure. It can be narrowed or widened by merely sliding the courses up or down. The exposure, however, should not be more than 6 inches or you'll expose the dark, uncovered, part of the shingle. To determine this spacing, measure from the eave to the ridge then divide by five to see if you come out with whole numbers. If you don't, add ¼ inch at a time until you do (but no more than 6 inches). This gives you the exact number of full courses needed. The last course should extend past the ridge with ¼ of the shingle width projecting beyond the ridge edge.

Since the shingle courses are rarely seen close up, you can also adjust the last few rows. Nail with a 5-inch exposure until you get within a half dozen courses. Then space out a course of shingles, adjusting until you get the proper number of shingles needed to end up correctly. Measure the spacing, count the courses, and continue laying with the new spacing. This method reduces, rather than widens, the exposure. The angle from the ground makes it appear that the shingle courses get closer together at the top of the roof anyway.

It's a good idea to dry-lay a course of shingles to see how they'll fall in valleys. Avoid ending with a tiny piece of a tab. To solve the problem of a smaller-than-half-size tab, cut the next-to-last shingle as well, spacing them both to create the right space. It may be necessary to start from a centerline mark for the first course.

If a gutter is to be installed, fasten hanging straps before installing the shingles.

Start at one end, in the lower corner that is best for you. This depends on whether you want to work right- or left-handed. Although you may have to place the starting shingles from a ladder, you can do most of the shingling by resting on the previously installed courses and working uphill.

As with wooden shingles, always double the first, or bottom, course of shingles. With asphalt shingles, the under layer on the first course is installed with the bottom, or underside, up and the tabs facing towards the top. Install with ¼-inch extended out past the rake strip. Nail with four shingle nails spaced about an inch below, and in line with, each cut.

For the top layer of the first course, start with a full shingle. Position it (right side up) flush with the end and bottom edge of the upside-down shingle. Nail it with four nails spaced 1 inch above each slot, 1 inch from the inside end, and 3 inches from the rake end.

PART 3. HOUSE RAISING AND FINISH WORK

Shingle the entire roof in stair-step fashion to the eave. Do the opposite side in the same manner.

The roof peak is finished by cutting individual tabs from a shingle and overlapping them.

Then butt a second shingle next to the first, being sure that it's flush with the bottom edge of the under course. Nail it in place.

To assure a straight course, go to the opposite end of the building and temporarily fasten a full shingle, taking care that it's also positioned flush with the bottom edge of the under course. Snap a chalk line across the top edge of the two shingles. Now you can nail the first course straight. You can also make sure that the vertical slots line up exactly by placing a temporary shingle at the rake end and snapping a chalk line.

Start the second course on top of the first, spacing it with a 5-inch (or predetermined) exposure. Measure and mark. Cut half of the outside tab away on the first shingle. Position the outside (cut) end ¼ inch past the rake edge. If the bottom edge is positioned just above the cut slots of the undercourse, it will be approximately a 5-inch exposure. Ensure that slots line up with vertical guidelines.

Valley shingling can be done in two ways. A smooth-lined valley has flashing or building felt underneath.

A laced valley is a more complicated affair, with shingle courses from each side of the valley laced together.

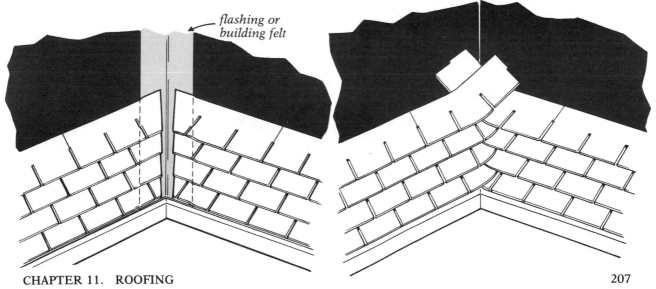

flashing or building felt

To start the third course, cut a full tab off the outside edge end of the shingle and position it on top of the second course. The beginning of the fourth course consists of a shingle cut in half; the fifth course, a single tab, and the sixth course, a tab cut in half. All should be nailed in place.

To assure perfectly straight courses of shingles, measure on the opposite end of the roof and snap chalk guidelines for each course. (You'll have to have two rows of roofing felt installed first.) You could, of course, install one course at a time all the way across the roof, but this means you have to go up and down, carrying shingles—a lot of work. With shingle bundles and nails positioned around you, you can do the starting course, then shingle as far as you can reach with six more, slide backwards—still sitting down—and continue across the roof, adding courses without getting up.

Don't discard the cut ends of the shingles, they can be used on the opposite end of the roof. The pattern shown will create a perfectly aligned, alternating pattern of slots.

Shingle one side of the roof, then go to the opposite side and finish it. Fold the upper end of the shingle over the roof ridge and nail it, as shown. Then do the opposite roof side.

Shingles can be cut with a large pair of tin snips, though it's hard on your fingers. It would be better to use a sharp knife. Turn the shingle over and score it from the back side, then break it apart. Lay another shingle over the first to create a guide for the knife blade.

To finish the ridge, cut the shingles into three separate tabs and then nail. A hip-roof ridge cap is done the same way, starting with the hip portions and ending with the center ridge line.

Valley shingling is the harder to do correctly—expect quite a bit of time and some waste of shingles. There are two ways to cover valleys: smooth-lined and laced. Smooth-lined valleys are made up of shingles cut on an angle to follow the valley line. Flashing or 90-pound building felt goes under the shingles. A better-looking valley, though more complicated, is the laced valley. The shingle courses are started at each end of the opposite valley-rake ends

Metal roofing is still a common material on many log homes. It's nailed down with special nails. Use special tin strips to seal off ridge and edges. (Photo courtesy Building with Logs Ltd.)

PART 3.   HOUSE RAISING AND FINISH WORK

and brought up to the valley, where they are laced (overlapped) as shown on page 207.

The hardest shingling job is a valley roof or dormer that is lower than the peak of the adjoining roof. The courses must be started to line up at the top of the valley.

Roll roofing. Small recreational cabins are often roofed over with a solid sheathing material covered with heavy roofing felt, tarred and nailed in place.

Metal roofing. Metal roofs are economical and easy to install. Simply nail panels to purlins or girts that you've nailed crosswise to the rafters. Special metal ridge strips seal off the ridges.

With metal roofs, you have to give up something of the appearance. The roof distracts from the beauty of the logs.

Flashing

Flashing must be installed at all junctions of the roof where a vertical surface meets the roofline. This includes chimneys, plumbing vents, electrical service entrances or where a dormer joins the roof.

You can use asphalt roofing material and roofing cement to create your own flashing, but metal flashing lasts longer and has a better appearance. Copper or aluminum are the materials most commonly used. Neither will shrink, crack, or pull away as asphalt can.

Plumbing vents. The easiest way to flash a plumbing vent or electrical-service entrance is to simply buy a plastic or metal collar that fits snugly around the pipe. You shingle over the top flange and seal around the pipe and collar with asphalt cement. You can make your own as shown. The shingles must be carefully cut and sealed firmly.

Flashing vertical surfaces. Where a dormer or other structure joins the roof, alternate the rough tabs of flashing with the shingles (page 201). Also use asphalt cement to seal and to prevent rainwater from blowing in.

Use metal flashing installed between shingles (as shown) for flashing a chimney or flue.

Fixtures such as this roof vent use special flashing collars that are interlaced with the shingles.

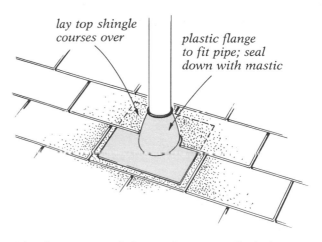

lay top shingle courses over

plastic flange to fit pipe; seal down with mastic

Plumbing vents and electrical masts are flashed using purchased or homemade collars.

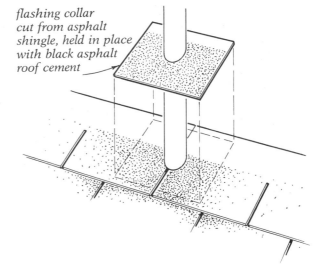

flashing collar cut from asphalt shingle, held in place with black asphalt roof cement

A proper roof drainage system can protect the soil surrounding the house from erosion and keep water from splashing up on logs.

Gutters

A roof should have a proper drainage system, not only to protect the roof, but to prevent drip water from ruining the fill around the house. This should be designed to allow for proper drainage of the water to downspouts, away from the foundation, or into a cistern. The number of downspouts needed varies with the size of the house. Although you can place one at almost any location, too many downspouts may detract from the appearance of the house. Design the installation with this in mind.

The gutter system should be designed so it properly drains into downspouts.

There are several different kinds of holding brackets and your choice depends on availability in your area, whether you already have the shingles on hand, or if you utilize a facia.

Chapter 12 DOORS AND WINDOWS

Opening on the world

When the pioneers wanted a cabin window, they had to make do with a tiny piece of scraped animal skin or oiled paper hung over an opening in the wall. Early homesteaders often carried single panes of glass across half a continent so that they could have one small window when they built their new homes. But today's log home builder has a wide variety of styles and sizes of windows from which to choose. And a full range of ready-made doors are also available. These fixtures range from a simple, one-piece nonmovable sash window to huge sliding patio doors of wood or aluminum. With the proper tools, windows and doors can even be made on site.

Selection of the windows and doors is largely a matter of choice. Early log homes traditionally had small windows, and this resulted in dark, dim interiors. Some log home builders use small windows today. They're more economical and easier to install than larger windows. But a picture window not only provides a good view, it also looks good with a larger home.

What is important is to find a style of windows and doors that suits your home design, is practical and aesthetically pleasing, and fits your life-style.

Door and window framing

Framing means creating a boxlike enclosure to finish off the ends of the log walls at the doorway or window opening. This provides a smooth surface for anchoring the door or window itself in place. Framing is the same

A window must be suitable for your climate and must fit in with the style of your home.

whether you use a purchased, fully-framed unit or a homemade window or door.

Window and door frames for conventional homes are simply nailed in place in the rough openings. But, because of the shrinkage and settling in log homes, special techniques must be used to install these frames.

The rough openings for the frames can be fashioned in one of three ways. The first is to simply build the log house walls with full-length logs; then cut out the rough opening with a chain saw. The second method—one that allows you to use shorter logs for less waste—is to cut rough logs to length to allow for the rough openings. Cut logs are held in place by attaching temporary wood straps to their sides, or by inserting steel reinforcing rods in holes drilled through them. The last way involves putting the frames in place, squared and temporarily nailed to the bottom log. Logs are then cut to fit as the walls are erected. *All frames for both windows and doors must be installed before the logs going over the top of them are installed.* Allow for settling with a slip joint, created between the frame header and the lower surface of the log above it. Space

Doors may include side-hung entry doors or sliding patio doors. (Photo by Louisiana-Pacific Corp.)

A heat-mirror door provides 65 percent better insulation than conventional doors or double glazed windows. The thin heat-mirror film allows light rays to pass through but reflects radiated heat. (Photo courtesy Louisiana-Pacific Corporation.)

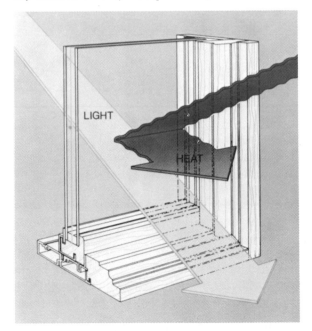

PART 3. HOUSE RAISING AND FINISH WORK

must also be left between wall logs and the side of the frame.

Preparing walls and frames. One way to prepare the rough opening for a door or window frame involves cutting a spline groove in the ends of the logs, as shown, after all logs for the opening have been put in place. You can do this with the tip of your chain saw if you're pretty handy with one, but *there is a danger of kickback with this technique.* Make sure the chain saw has a chain brake and that you have a tight grip on it, thumbs locked under the handles, left elbow locked. A jig for stopping the depth of the cut will help. It takes several passes for a smooth, straight groove. You can also use a heavy-duty router for this chore. Finish the groove at the bottom log with a chisel.

Another method: Bore a series of holes with a brace and bit, and then simply saw off the logs on the centerline of the bored holes. Finish with a chisel.

With the slot cut in the ends of the logs, you can fasten a strip to the outside of the frame sides, as shown, or use a spline in both. A variation, but one that requires a bit more chain-saw work, is to create tenons on the ends of the logs and a mortise slot in the frame. Another method is to simply bore holes with key-shaped slots, as shown. Nail the frame in place to the log ends and use stop molding to cover up the slots. This is the easiest, fastest, though least-effective method.

Most log home kits have a special T-spline arrangement coupled with a special foam insulation strip to prevent air infiltration.

Building the frame. The frames (also called bucks) for windows and doors of log homes are usually made of heavier material than standard construction framing, largely because the proportions are more in keeping with the massiveness of the log walls. Use at least 2-inch nominal-thickness material for exterior frames. In fact, 4- and 6-inch timbers in the openings can look good. The frame material should be free of knots, cracks, or blemishes and can be made in a shop or assembled on the site. Use a router or circular saw to cut the dado for the frame headers.

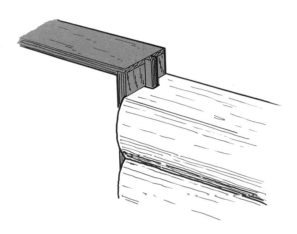

A splined slip joint is a common method to hold the bucks in place.

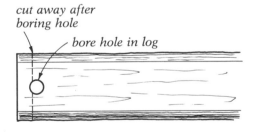

You can cut a spline by boring holes and sawing away the log ends.

Insert a spline in both the buck and wall as shown.

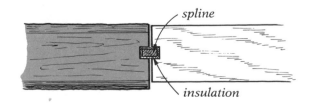

The rough frame or buck that holds the window or door may be included in a purchased window-frame unit. (Photo courtesy Arkansas Log Homes, Inc.)

You can make rough frames and slide the windows or doors in place.

The rough window bucks can be installed after the logs are erected. You'd then cut openings in the logs. (Photo courtesy Beaver Log Homes.)

PART 3.   HOUSE RAISING AND FINISH WORK

Inset photo left, you may install window frames first and then build around them. Photo below, always frame the bucks for stability.

The first step on either window or door frames is to fasten the bottom piece to the two side pieces with nails driven outside. Slide the top piece into the dadoes and fasten it with waterproof glue and ring-shanked nails. Use a carpenter's square to square the frame, then fasten a diagonal brace across the front and back of the frame to hold it until it's secured.

The spline groove can be cut in the wall logs with a chain saw, but it takes a good grip to prevent kickback. (Photo courtesy Beaver Log Homes.)

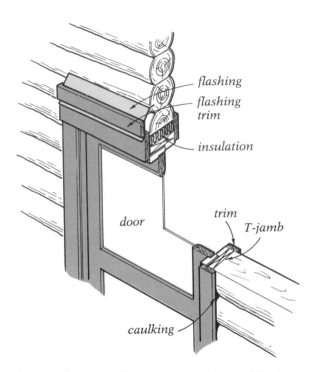

You can fit the log above the door with metal flashing or cut large log ends back at an angle to fit the window or door frame width.

Make sure bottom of door thresholds are shaped in the manner shown.

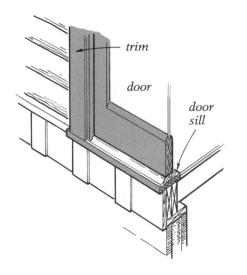

Installing the frame.

Slide the frame into place. Splines are much easier to install than mortise and tenon—if the wall logs have already been put in place. Make sure the frame is solidly in place, square and plumb in all directions, and then anchor the bottom board to the log beneath. If you have a concrete slab, use concrete screws and anchor mollies in the concrete to secure the bottom board.

Achieving perfectly square and plumb window and door frames is harder with log homes than with dimension construction. Because of this, window and door units should be somewhat smaller than the frame openings. Wedge them in place with shims. *Anchor them to the frame only, not into the log walls beyond.* Cover the outside edges with trim.

There must be a certain amount of space left between the top edge of the frame and the underside of the log above it for settling. For every foot of wall height, figure ¾ inch for most green logs and ⅜ inch for most dry logs. When the logs eventually settle, the space will be reduced to only a small crack.

Stuff insulation into the space between the frame header and the underside of the upper log. It shouldn't be crammed in place. Leave it loose and fluffy, because it will gradually be compressed as the logs settle and shrink.

There are a number of ways to trim around the upper part of the doors or windows to prevent air leaks and water infiltration. The simplest and fastest method is shown. But it's best to use metal flashing set in a slot in the underside of the log.

Cut the slot with a chain saw or circular saw, before final installation of the upper log. First, position the log, cut the notch, and then roll it back. Now cut the slot. Place a bead of caulking in the slot, push the metal into place, and use finishing nails driven through the log slot and metal to secure it. Then turn the log back into place over the frame.

Finishing log ends.

The easiest way to finish the log ends of the opening is to simply leave them sawed off square. A jig helps keep these cuts square. In most cases, however, the log ends will be larger in diameter than the width of the frame.

There are two ways you can finish these ends so they will not only look better, but will

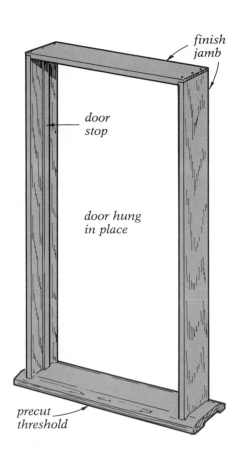

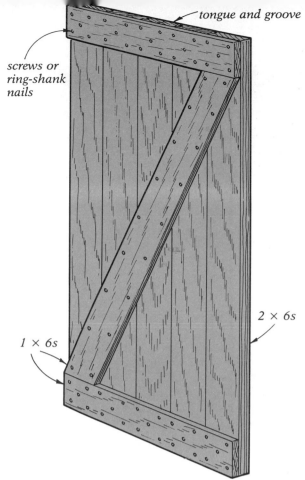

You can also make a preassembled door-and-frame unit yourself and slide it into place in the rough frame.

Plank and board doors are not difficult to fashion.

prevent air leaks too. The first is to angle their edges back. Start with the exact width of the frame. This evens up any variance in log sizes. Another method—one frequently used by kit log home builders—is to cut the ends of the logs to the same width of the frame, then angle the rest of the log back.

Bits and pieces of insulation can be stuffed in openings and cracks. Nail a wooden trim piece to the frame as shown (it must not be nailed to the logs). Caulking will seal up the joint. The joint will have to be recaulked periodically until the logs have stopped settling. Then caulking around the outside back edge will stay in place.

Thresholds. In some cases the frame may be the final finish frame. If so the bottom, or threshold (preferably oak), should be shaped as shown. Don't nail it to the bottom log; use lag screws instead. The area beneath the threshold must be sealed with caulking. (Use caulking beneath the window sills as well.)

Making doors

There are several different styles of doors, including plank (or board) doors, tongue-and-groove doors, and frame and panel doors.

Making a plank door. This type of door is the easiest to build. Exterior plank doors are traditionally constructed from 1½- to 2-inch-thick material. The door is usually made with tongue-and-groove planks, their edges beveled, although three different cross-lapped layers of ¾-inch stock could be used. Cross bracing is fastened to the inside surface of the door with lag bolts or large countersunk wood screws. In the past, builders used extra wide cross bracing to keep the door from sagging, but a diagonal brace run down from the inside top corner will do the job. The outside edges of the door should be beveled, both for appearances and to prevent splintering.

A window can be mounted in this type of door by simply cutting an opening. Rout a

With the right tools you can make your own doors, such as this Dutch door.

Step 1. *Custom-made doors are hung in the rough opening on a finish door frame. This may be the rough buck, but most often it's an inside frame squared and fastened in place with wooden shingle shims, as shown upper left, to hold it square.*

groove in the back of the door to hold a piece of glass. Use thin molding strips to secure the glass.

Dutch doors are made in the same way as plank doors. An overlapping strip covers the split between top and bottom halves to prevent drafts. In cold climates, however, dutch doors are not nearly as efficient as one-piece doors.

Making a frame and panel door. You can also make your own frame and panel doors. Special shaper cutters make this job easy.

Hanging custom-made or un-framed doors.

If you're hanging custom-made doors in a *rough frame*, you must first make absolutely sure that the frame is square and the sides are plumb.

Heavy-duty strap hinges are often used to hang bulky plank doors. Simply fasten the hinges to the back of the door and to the inside edge of the door frame. Note: A wide frame is

usually recommended for full T-strap hinges.

Most conventional doors are hung with butt hinges. Heavy exterior doors made of solid wood require three hinges. Mortise butt hinges to fit into the side of the doorjamb (or inside finish frame) and into the edge of the door as well. Steps for mortising and fitting the doors are shown on preceding pages.

An alternative, as shown earlier, is to make your own preassembled door and frame. Make it somewhat smaller than the original opening and position it with shims.

For a cabin in the woods, door pulls and a padlock and hasp may be the only door fittings needed. But most full-time log home owners prefer standard door locks. They're installed in the door and doorjamb using a special tool.

After the door has been hung properly, position the doorstops on the inside to provide a weather-tight closure.

Use the same techniques to construct and hang interior doors. Lighter-weight stock, such as 5/4-inch stock, is used most often, however.

218

PART 3. HOUSE RAISING AND FINISH WORK

Step 2. *Measure the door and cut it to fit the frame, making it about ¼ inch smaller all around than the frame.*

Steps 3 and 4. *Above, use a hand plane on the edges. Below, locate the position for the butt hinges.*

Step 5. *Cut the mortises for the butt hinges.*

Step 6. *Hang the door, fastening it solidly by the hinges. Make sure it swings freely; then fasten the door stop in place. (Continued next page)*

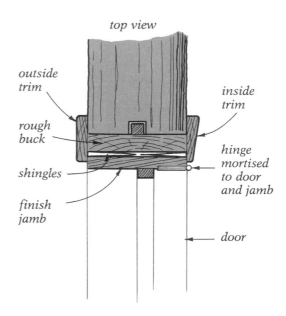

top view

outside trim

inside trim

rough buck

shingles

finish jamb

hinge mortised to door and jamb

door

Step 7. *Install the door knob, following the manufacturer's directions.*

Step 8. *Use hole saw to cut the door knob.*

Step 9. *Bore the side hole with a paddle bit.*

Step 10. *Then cut the mortise for the strike plate.*

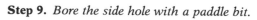

PART 3.   HOUSE RAISING AND FINISH WORK

Making windows

It is also possible to make windows. But window building is more complicated than nailing up doors and requires more in the way of tools and woodworking knowledge. That isn't to say that it can't be done by the average do-it-yourselfer, but a great deal more time and patience is required.

There are four basic window styles: fixed sash, swinging sash, sliding sash, and tilting sash. All consist of one or more wood frames enclosing a piece of glass.

The simplest window is a fixed sash. This type window may be nothing more than a piece of glass set in a rabbet that has been cut in the rough frame. Thin, wood molding strips, caulked and fastened from the inside, hold the glass in place in the frame. Or the window can be made of a purchased wooden sash, set in place with window stops on the inside or outside. A large plate glass window can also be handmade and installed in this manner.

If you were to hinge this sash on one side, you'd have a swinging sash window. This window will swing to the inside or outside, depending on how it is set up. If the swing is to the inside, it leaves space for a storm window or screen on the outside. But windows that swing inward can be a nuisance.

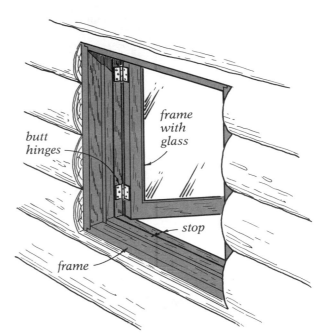

By hinging a sash you have a simple window that can be opened.

A sash made of several window panes, rather than one large one, looks best with log homes. A combination of a fixed and swinging windows can be made by hinging the sash to tilt outward.

You can make windows yourself, though it's complicated, with the possible exception of a fixed sash such as this picture window, which is simply a glass fastened in place, trimmed, and caulked well.

Allow for settling of the logs above the frames. Stuff the space with insulation and cover it with a trim board. (Photo courtesy Beaver Log Homes.)

The easiest method of window installation is to simply install prefabricated units that include the window and finished frame.

Stained glass is especially appropriate for a log cabin.

The most popular type of window is the double-hung sash. This can be made on the site using a pair of sash frames and stops, ripped to size and fastened to the finished jamb sides.

Installing prefabricated door and window units

Prefabricated window units are available in a large variety of sizes and styles, including sliding, casement, and awning. They consist of a window installed in a factory-made finish frame, or jamb. Just slide the unit in place in the rough window-frame opening. Shim it with wooden shingles and nail into the rough frame. It must not be nailed to the surrounding log ends.

Prehung interior doors are also available in many types. They are easy to install, especially on conventionally constructed partition walls.

For a personal touch, you may want to install stained glass in your home.

Shutters

Shutters can provide extra security for a log house that will not be lived in full time. A flush-mounted shutter system is good. Shutters also help with nighttime heat retention over large window or door spaces. Or you can use movable insulated panels to cut down on heat loss through these areas.

Interior shutters can be used to shut out the cold and retain heat during the night. If made of wood that matches the interior surfaces of the logs, they provide a compatible window treatment. (Photo courtesy Armstrong World Industries.)

Chapter 13 STAIRS

The right steps

Stairs that have been built properly are efficient, safe, and good-looking. On the other hand, poorly designed or constructed stairs detract from the appearance of a home and can be dangerous as well. There are a variety of stair shapes, sizes, and designs that can be used. They range from a simple wooden or concrete step to complicated spirals.

A staircase made by stacking sections of logs on a steel support pipe is easily done.

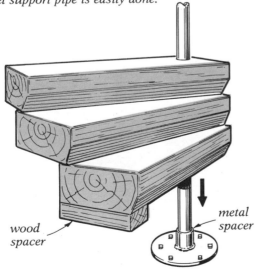

Stairs are an important part of the home, and unique stairs can be the focal point. (Photo courtesy Wilderness Log Homes.)

CHAPTER 13. STAIRS

223

Tread and Riser Relationships

Total rise	No. risers	Riser height	No. treads	Tread width
7'-8"	12	7²¹/₃₂"	11	9" to 9¾"
8'-0"	13	7⅜"	12	9½" to 10"
8'-4"	14	7⅛"	13	10" to 10½"
8'-9"	14	7½"	13	10⁵/₁₆"
9'-0"	15	7³/₁₆"	14	10" to 10½"

Almost any style construction can be used for stairs, so long as safe materials and designs are used. (Photo courtesy Wilderness Log Homes.)

Log shrinkage and settling must be allowed for when installing the stairs in log homes. This is done by anchoring the top of the stairs firmly and positioning the lower part on wooden wedges or shims, temporarily fastened. As the walls settle and the stairs move down and out, the shims can be removed to accommodate the shift. Cover the shims with a piece of wooden molding.

Make stairways from logs or dimension lumber. There are any number of ways to build stairs with logs, though the simplest design is a wooden post with heavy-duty pegs set in it. This was often the only type of stairway used in old-time cabins, and mainly provided access to the loft above.

To make a log stairway, first make a pair of stair horses from logs that are either left in the round, hewed, or sawed into timbers. The steps, which are usually half rounds, split logs, or thick slabs, are positioned in slots or notches cut into the sides of the stair horses. A sapling handrail will add to the rustic appearance of this stairway.

You can also fasten support blocks to the flat-hewed side of the log to create step supports, but this isn't quite as strong or as good looking as other designs.

Planning your stairway

The width of the step and the height of the risers are set by the stair angle and height. There are, however, some standard tread and riser dimension relationships, as shown in the chart. Use the chart as a rough guide. If your total rise is the same as any of those shown, it's a simple matter to adapt the tread and riser measurements. But you should create an exacting plan. Here are some general rules you can follow:

1. Twice the riser height plus the tread width should equal about 25 inches.

2. Riser height plus tread width should equal about 17 to 18 inches.

3. Tread width times riser height should equal about 75 inches.

You shouldn't end up with stair tread narrower than 10½ inches or risers higher than 6½ to 7¾ inches. All treads should be of the same size and all risers the same height.

A stairway should be wide enough that you can move up and down easily while carrying large pieces of furniture. It should not be narrower than 2½ feet (for utility stairs), though a 3-foot-wide main stairway is most common. Stairs can, of course, be wider—up to 4 feet or more, if you like. On wide stairs, you should add a middle stair horse to help carry the weight.

Stairs must not be so steep that they're hard to climb. On the other hand, an extremely shallow stairway takes up a lot of space. The larger the stairway, the larger the opening in the floor above must be. But a steep, narrow stairway can be extremely dangerous.

In addition, make sure there is enough headroom for clearance. Careful measurements will help you avoid skull crackers.

To find the total run, multiply the number of risers by the number of treads less one (there is always one less tread than riser). All this must be thought through before rough framing, and a careful design on paper can eliminate most construction problems. In fact, it's a good idea to rough out the stair supports at the same time you do floor or ceiling framing.

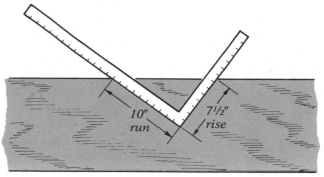

Use a framing or carpenter's square to lay out the cuts.

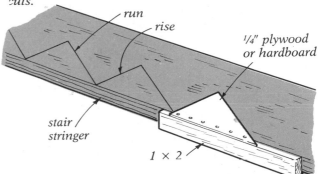

You can use a special jig to make cuts in the stringers, then cut the top and bottom to shape.

This is the way typical stairs should be framed. Enclosing the area under stairs gives you additional storage space.

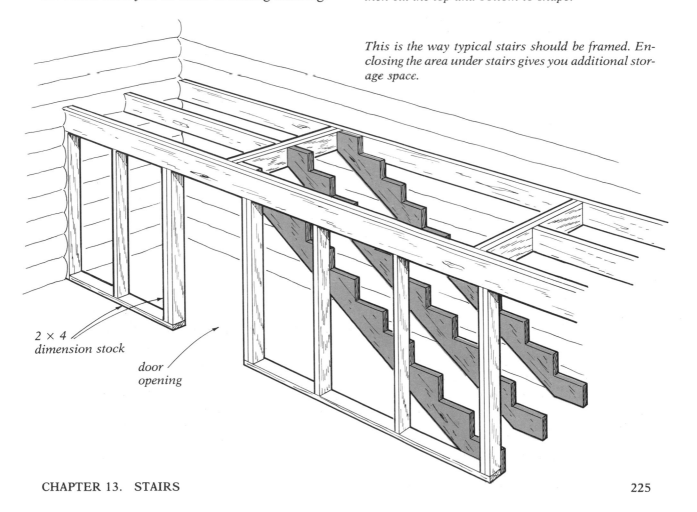

CHAPTER 13. STAIRS

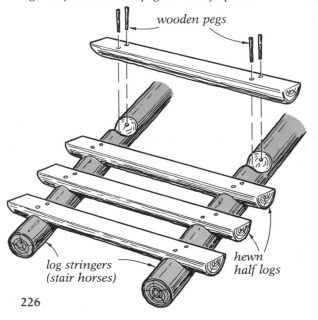

The problem of shrinkage and settling must be taken into account when constructing stairs. The top of the stairs can be anchored and the bottom placed on shims that can be removed as the stair settles.

top can be anchored
(for more flexibility
add heavy-duty hinges)

stair
horse

shims

Building the stairs

Stair horses. The basic purpose of stair horses (sometimes called stringers) is to create a stepped platform to support stair treads. Stair horses can be made of timbers or dimension lumber. Make sure you pick lumber that is free of knots, cracks, and other defects, especially if the stock is to show on an open stairway. Most stair horses are also constructed of 2× material with 2×12s the most common choice because this size allows for full cutting of the tread and risers without weakening the material. However, 2×10s are sometimes used.

The simplest way to find the length of material needed is to measure from the top edge of the stair landing to the floor at the end of the total run, and then add a foot or two extra to this measurement. Or you can simply make a full-size drawing of the tread and riser, measure the bridge dimension, and multiply this by the number of risers. Again, add a foot or two.

The cutting diagram of a typical stair horse is shown on page 225. To lay out the cutting diagram on the stock, use a square held with the tread and riser dimensions. Better yet, use a special jig that has been cut as shown. This helps make a more accurate layout. Then cut the bottom and top.

You can cut notches in a log using a chain

One of the simplest stairs uses log stairhorses. Split logs are fastened with pegs or heavy spikes.

wooden pegs

log stringers
(stair horses)

hewn
half logs

Cut the notches for the log steps with a chain saw.

PART 3. HOUSE RAISING AND FINISH WORK

saw, but notches in dimension lumber should be cut with a circular saw. Finish the inside of the cut with a handsaw. You can make the cuts entirely with a handsaw, too. You can also clamp a couple of boards together and cut them at the same time. It's quite a bit of work, however, to saw through 3½ inches of stock all at once, though in the end the cuts will be more accurately matched. Stair horses can also be built up with blocks, as shown below, instead of being cut.

Each tread can have a nose extending out past the riser, but it should not extend more than 1¾ inches. Purchased treads are mill shaped, but you can do the work yourself if you have a shaper or table saw equipped for routing.

The angle of the stair horse should not be more than 50 degrees or less than 20 degrees. A 30- to 35-degree angle is considered ideal.

Openings for the stairways are framed when the floor is framed. If possible, have the long dimension of the stairway run parallel or at right angles to the overhead floor joists. Anything else becomes complicated. A minimum rough opening is 3 by 10 feet. When possible, place the stairway from an upper floor over the basement stairway to conserve space. Shown are the steps required to lay out stairs, including the floor and ceiling cut. For a finished look, install the tread and risers with a glue block and screws, as shown.

Built-up block stringers can be used to support steps. A doubled stringer provides extra support.

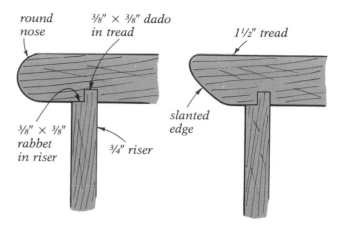

Stair nosings can be either round or slanted.

Glue blocks and screws strengthen the tread and risers.

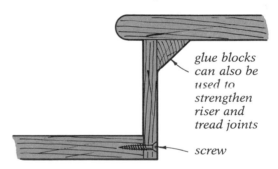

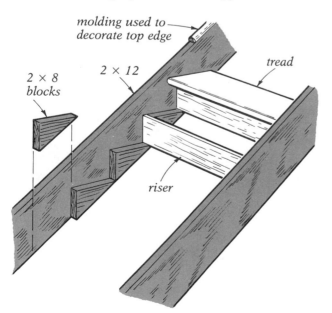

227

Milled slabs allow pegging of mortises and tenons, shown in these stairs by Building with Logs Ltd.

Metal kit stairs are attractive and easy to assemble. These are by Studio Stairs.

Open stairs. Stairs without an enclosing wall should have some kind of banister or handrail. Handrails should be of standard height (remember that odd heights may be uncomfortable to guests).

One advantage of an enclosed stairway is that the space under the stairs can be used for storage. Even when the space above the stairs is left open, the area under the stairs can be closed off for the additional storage space.

Steps and landings. In many cases, a simple straight stairway won't do and you'll need a landing. Long flights of stairs (over 15 or 16 steps) *should* have a landing. This can be nothing more than a wooden platform that divides the stairway into two straight sets of stairs; or the stairs can meet at a right angle, or turn in the opposite direction.

Stairs with landings are not hard to build if you think of them as two sets of straight stairs and a simple wooden platform. Make the landing at least the same width as the stairway (measured between railings).

Winding or curved stairs. You may also want to use curved stairs. These are complicated to build and, because the treads are narrower on the inside of the curve, can be dangerous. Make the narrowest portion as wide as possible.

Spiral stairways are built in much the same way as winding stairs. Actually, they are nothing more than an extension of a winding design.

Ready-made stairs. These come in any number of styles and shapes. Your building materials supplier will need to know the total rise, stair tread and rise measurement, headroom, and total run. Most stairways don't come as a kit, but the individual pieces are preshaped. You have to cut and fit to install them. Also, most ready-made stairways have only the starting pieces, and no stair rails.

PART 3.   HOUSE RAISING AND FINISH WORK

Chapter 14 **FINISHING THE INTERIOR**

Starting on the inside

Now that the house is completely enclosed, you can take a breather before starting the finishing and decorating work on the interior. After the hard work of erecting the structure, interior work will seem easy by comparison. But bear in mind that this can be the most discouraging part of the job of building a log house. It can take a lot longer and may, at times, seem to come to a complete halt. The time you spend planning this finishing work can help you avoid redoing jobs because of mistakes.

You will find a seemingly endless number of schemes and materials to use on the interior. The choice is yours. For a weekend hunting cabin, you probably wouldn't do much more than sand or smooth the interior logs and install a floor. A full-time home, however, requires much more work.

Finishing the logs

Exposed logs. Will the interior log surfaces be exposed or covered? In many homes some surfaces are left exposed while others, such as partition walls, are constructed of dimension lumber and covered with paneling and wallboard.

You *must* clean all log surfaces, even in cabins that are only to be used occasionally. If you peeled the bark away before construction, you won't need to do much. Use a stiff scrub brush and warm soapy water (with a bit of household laundry bleach or a mildewcide

Now the push is over and your house is enclosed. Of the many ways you can finish the inside of a log home, the most popular is to allow the surface of the logs to show. (Photo courtesy Lincoln Logs Ltd.)

added) to scrub away any debris, dirt, and bits of bark that may be left. Mix one cup of bleach in each two-gallon bucket of water. Remove protruding bits of bark, stubs of branches, or slivers of wood. Clean up, too, any excess runs of caulking or chinking material.

If the logs were properly peeled, a good scrubbing is all that is needed. However, if the logs were not properly peeled, or not peeled at all, a steel bristle brush may be in order. But this will leave scratch marks on most logs, making for an ugly appearance.

Once all logs have been thoroughly cleaned, allow them to dry for a couple of days. When they are completely dry, brush on a coat of boiled linseed oil (mixed three parts linseed oil to one part turpentine). You can also add in a bit of walnut oil stain if you want to darken the wood. But it will darken with age anyway.

This coat should be allowed to dry for about a week. In spots where it soaks in quickly, such as the exposed ends of logs, brush on more oil as necessary. Wipe off any excess gummy material with a soft cloth at the end of the week

Another wall covering that fits well in log homes is paneling, especially the rough-hewn styles. (Photo courtesy Masonite Corp.)

PART 3. HOUSE RAISING AND FINISH WORK

and apply a second, final coat. Wipe this coat smooth as it dries to prevent any excessively gummy areas. You can apply a coat of semi-gloss varnish to the surface after the oil has dried thoroughly.

The newer penetrating oil sealers are excellent alternatives to boiled linseed oil. Finishes such as those from Watco, Dennis, and Flecto are simply brushed on and allowed to dry. Then wipe and coat again. Wiping the entire surface down with fine steel wool and a bit of paste wax after the final coat is dry provides a long-lasting luster that shows off the beauty of the logs.

Surfaces such as exposed ceiling beams and decking should be given the same treatment. Houses that have square-cut log interiors may need nothing more than a good sanding to cut down on some of the rough saw marks and to bring out the beauty of the grain. Finish the logs with a satin-sheen varnish.

Covered walls.
You may want to cover walls with other materials. Although this may detract from the appearance of the interior, it does provide additional insulation. The walls can be covered with gypsum board, which can be painted or wallpapered. Other wall-covering materials include solid wood sheathing or paneling, plywood paneling, hardboard paneling, ceramic tile (in baths), or imitation brick and stone.

Regardless of the material used, you first have to fasten vertical furring strips to the logs to create a flat, flush, and plumb surface. On logs with a flattened inside surface, this isn't usually a problem. Round logs, particularly on walls where the logs are of different sizes, present an entirely different situation. You will have to shim out to compensate for the wide variations in the plumb line of the logs. To do this, start at the inner surface of the log that protrudes farthest into the room. Drop a plumb line to the floor from this point. Make a mark and, using a long straightedge, draw a line along the floor surface as a guide for the upright furring strips.

Regardless of how fussy you are, you'll probably end up with corners a bit out of square. Don't worry, it happens to professionals too. Shim out 1 × 2 furring strips as needed,

spacing them on 16- or 24-inch centers. You could create a false wall of 2 × 2s or 2 × 4s, as shown next page. Though this type of wall uses up space, it can serve as a run for electrical and plumbing lines. It can also be insulated, adding to the already high insulation factor of about R-1 for each inch of log.

Installing gypsum board.
Whether it's called gypsum board, plasterboard, wallboard, or Sheetrock, it goes up the same way—somewhat like paneling. Putting up gypsum board is hard and dusty work. It also takes time and skill to get a smooth, finished appearance. Again, you need a solid surface on which to fasten the material.

Gypsum board is available in 4 × 8 sheets and larger—up to 16-foot lengths. It is available in thicknesses of ¼ to ⅝ inches, with ½ inch being the most common. Ceilings are ordinarily covered with ⅜-inch material. Gypsum board can be installed horizontally on the walls instead of vertically—the work will go faster and there will be less waste. Longer sheets can be used horizontally, but it takes a couple of people to manhandle these big sheets.

In almost every case, ceiling coverings are installed first, followed by the walls. When the covering material is applied on a ceiling, it

Or you can install, tape, and finish gypsum board.

must run crosswise, or 90 degrees, to the ceiling joists. Again, this can be a physically demanding job. T-shaped props cut about 1 inch longer than the floor-to-ceiling measurement can be used to help brace a large sheet until you get it nailed. It takes two people to get the panels up and braced properly.

Once the sheet has been properly positioned, nail it with annular-threaded wallboard nails spaced about 6 to 8 inches apart. The trick is to drive these nails so they pull the panel up tightly against the framing. Then drive the nail just a bit deeper to dimple the surface of the material. You don't want to crack the paper covering, just make a slight dent. Using a special wallboard hammer, called a crown-head claw hammer, can make this chore easier. With the sheet nailed solidly in place, remove the wood props. Install the remainder of the sheets, abutting their edges solidly. Cut out light fixture openings in the ceiling using a wallboard or utility knife.

Whether the material is installed horizontally or vertically on walls, the vertical joints must fall on a vertical framing member (stud or furring strip). Of course, you start with the bottom panel when installing the panels horizontally. Then put in succeeding panels. There is no need to nail the overlap of outside corners; use metal corner strips instead.

To install paneling or gypsum board, below left, you can install furring strips over the walls. Logs with flattened inside surfaces pose little problem. Round logs, below middle, particularly those of different sizes, can pose problems of shimming and anchoring. Drop a plumb line from largest log to establish the starting point of the furring strips. Below right, you may prefer to create a false wall of 2 × 4s over round logs.

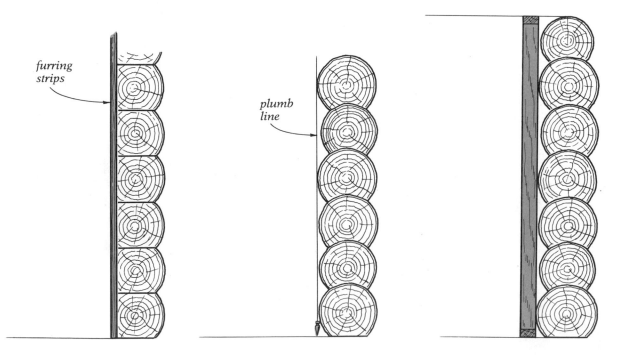

furring strips

plumb line

PART 3. HOUSE RAISING AND FINISH WORK

To cut gypsum board, use a utility knife and a metal square or, better yet, a large-wallboard T-square. Score the Sheetrock on one side, and then bend and snap it backward. Now cut along the crease in the paper on the opposite side. A keyhole saw can be used to cut holes for electrical fixtures, etc. Use a template to mark outlet holes. Make sure you measure carefully to avoid having to tape over large gaps.

Corners must be framed beforehand to create the proper nailing surface at each corner.

Wallboard can also be applied with a special adhesive, but some nailing will nevertheless be required.

After the wallboard has been installed, joints and small gaps must be taped over and finished to create a smooth surface. First, apply a coat of ready-mix plasterboard compound with a 4-inch joint-finishing knife. Then press paper tape into this, holding the knife at about a 45-degree angle. After this has been allowed to dry for 24 hours, apply a second coat. Let this dry and put on a third, final coat with a 10-inch knife. Feather the sides out to create a 10-inch wide area that is as smooth and flush with the surrounding surfaces as possible. Sand after the second and third coats.

The dimpled nail lines normally get three coats of compound. Sand between each coat.

Inside corners are taped and finished in the same way as the joint lines. A corner-taping tool helps with this chore. Don't apply too much compound in the corner crease—it will crack and fall out eventually.

Outside corners are finished by building up the corners with compound to create a smooth joint between the edge of the metal corner strip and the wall surface. It may take as many as two or three coats. Sand smooth. Remember the compound shrinks as it dries.

You can either tape the wall-to-ceiling joints or use wood molding.

Installing paneling.

Paneling, whether plywood, hardboard, or hardboard coated with plastic, is fairly easy to install. First figure the amount needed. Plywood paneling comes in 4 × 8 foot sheets. Merely measure the length of the wall in feet and divide by four to come up with a rough figure.

Decorative wood shingles add a unique touch to a home. (Photo courtesy Heatilator, Inc.)

Subtract a half panel for each door and fireplace and a quarter panel for each window.

Since plywood paneling runs from ¼ to as little as ³⁄₁₆-inch thick, the studs it's fastened to should be no farther apart than 16 inches on center. You may want to add a sheet of ³⁄₈-inch gypsum board to the wall first for more stability, sound deadening, and insulation. An additional measure to improve the appearance: Paint the backing material gypsum board furring strips, stud edges in the area where the paneling sheets are to join. That way the small crack between the joining edges won't show after the panels are installed. This is not necessary with sheets that have an overlap edge.

Measure the floor-to-ceiling height and cut the plywood as necessary. Position the first sheet in the starting corner and plumb it using a carpenter's square. Temporarily tack it into place. Check the corner joint where the sheet edge butts. If you're extremely lucky, the edge of the corner will fit perfectly.

However, if you're like most of us, the corner will bow in or out or be out of plumb, resulting in a gap along the edge of the plywood. If so, scribe the plywood and then cut it to fit using a saber saw. Refit it in the corner, make sure it's plumb, and nail—or secure solidly with panel adhesive. If you're nailing, start in the center of the panel and fasten it with nails colored to match the paneling or panel-

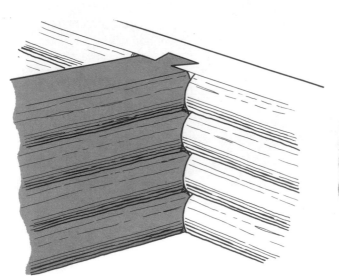

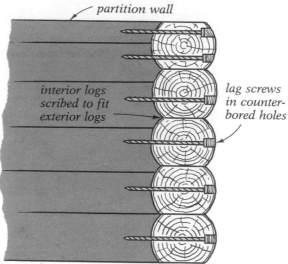

partition wall

interior logs scribed to fit exterior logs

lag screws in counter-bored holes

note: this works well when you don't have interior wall logs same size as exterior wall logs

In all but the smallest log homes there will be partition walls. These may be made of logs, and built at the same time as the exterior wall.

The interior log walls may be constructed after the exterior log walls have been finished. They may be fastened with long bolts through the exterior walls.

ing grooves. The nails should be spaced about 6 inches apart on the edges of the paneling and about 12 inches apart in the center. Once you have the first panel securely in place, butt the next one up against it, temporarily tack it, and check for plumb. If it is okay, nail it in place.

Ceiling coverings

You may want to leave the ceiling exposed with beams and decked roofing finished off to show the beauty of the wood. This is often done with cathedral ceilings or on single-story homes without attics. If the ceiling under a second story floor has log joists, you may want to cover the second floor decking and leave the joists exposed. Just fill the spaces between the log joists with gypsum board or ceiling tiles.

If you don't want to fully expose the log beams, or if they are round, so that it's almost impossible to get the material up between the joists, nail furring strips to the log sides and then attach a ceiling covering to the strips. This leaves an area for running electrical lines to overhead light fixtures.

Acoustical ceiling tile. Ceiling tile may be fastened to wooden furring strips across

the ceiling joists. Or you could use a new metal strip system. You can also fasten them directly to the underside of the floor decking between the log or beam ceiling joists. You can, of course, install a suspended ceiling if you prefer.

Partition walls

Room partitions can be constructed in either of two ways. You can use logs, but you usually must install them at the same time the joining wall logs are put in place. For partitions constructed after the log house is enclosed, it is easiest to use dimension lumber. Just stand partition frames up on the subfloor and fasten them in place.

Log walls look natural in a log home and they add strength to the structure. In fact, long walls need the support provided by a cross wall. For this reason, an L-shaped log house is much stronger than straight boxes.

The biggest problem with interior log walls is that more time is spent in construction. The massiveness of logs on interior walls not only makes the house a bit darker, but gives it more of a closed-in feeling. Walls of dimension lumber can be finished with paint or light wall-

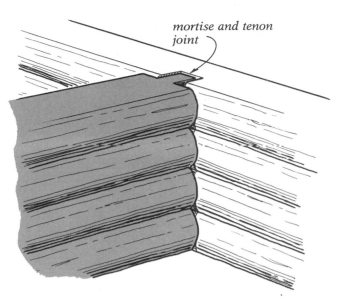

mortise and tenon joint

The best way to fasten log or dimension-lumber walls may be to notch the exterior wall and cut tenons on the interior wall. This makes a joint that will not cause problems when the logs shrink and settle.

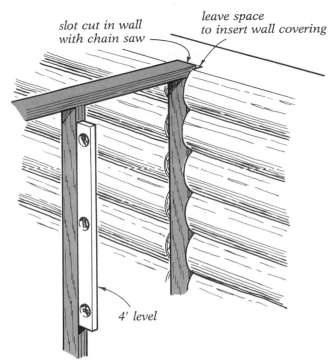

slot cut in wall with chain saw

leave space to insert wall covering

4' level

Dimension walls may be simply nailed together and slid into position in a notch in the log wall, before being plumbed, and then nailed to the subfloor.

paper and thereby lighten the atmosphere. Used in combination with the outside walls of logs, they make for a pleasing interior and provide runs for wiring and plumbing as well.

You can install a separate log partition by fastening it to the exterior log wall with lag bolts from the outside. Naturally, the logs used for the partitions must be the same size as the outside wall logs.

Another method for this type wall involves notching the exterior wall (floor-to-ceiling) and cutting tenons to fit into the notch on the ends of the partition-wall logs. The tenons should be tight, but do not jam them in place. With this method you can use smaller logs than those used for the exterior walls.

Dimension lumber walls must not be anchored in any way to the exterior log walls. Instead, cut shallow notches, including space for any wall covering on each side, and slip the wall into the notches. A snug, but not tight, fit makes a better, cleaner-looking joint. Wide molding can be used, if necessary, to help seal off the joint.

Regardless which method is used, any wall of logs should have slip joints at the top to allow for shrinkage and settling. Don't anchor them to the ceiling. Interior log partitions should have smooth corners.

Regardless of the wall system, all interior walls should have slip joints to allow for likely shrinkage of the exterior wall logs.

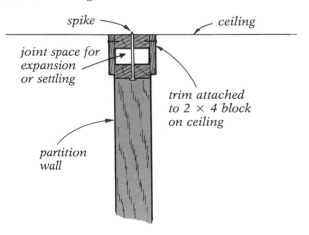

spike

ceiling

joint space for expansion or settling

trim attached to 2 × 4 block on ceiling

partition wall

CHAPTER 14. FINISHING THE INTERIOR

Finish flooring

The floor can be almost anything from tongue-and-groove planking to a poured concrete slab covered with inlaid sheet flooring or carpeting. The choice depends mostly on whether the house is to be used as a vacation cabin or year-round home. Regardless of the kind of finish flooring, a subflooring of ¾-inch plywood or ¾-inch planks is needed to cover the joist logs.

If the subfloor has been down since the early phases of construction, clean it thoroughly to remove building debris. Sweep and, if possible, damp mop the area to get rid of as much dust as possible. This is especially important when flooring is to be installed with an adhesive.

Wood flooring. Traditional finish flooring for log homes is wood. This can be tongue-and-groove planks or parquet blocks or strips. All are available in a variety of woods, finished or unfinished. Some are nailed down while others are installed with adhesive.

Traditional, nailed wood planks. Tongue-and-groove nailed down planks are available in oak, pine, and other woods. They require the most time to install, but last the longest. These planks are typically ¾-inch or more thick and are nailed to the subfloor as shown. A nail set is used to drive the nail head below the surface of the flooring so that the next strip will fit into place.

The starting layout of the strips is very important. If planks are to run throughout the house, they must all be parallel, regardless of room interior wall angles or room shapes. It may be best to lay the finish floor before installing partition walls; this cuts down on waste and time needed to cut around all the partitions.

Start your installation by using the longest pieces you have. Then use the short, cut-off ends to fill in small rooms such as bathrooms and closets.

Don't drive nails in too deep, which may split the wood. Also, check the subfloor to make sure all the nails are tight. Popped nails cause fitting problems. You should lay down a vapor

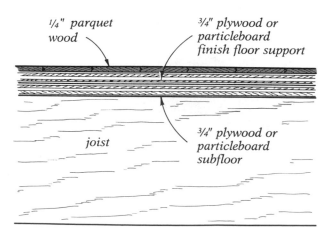

Tongue-and-groove hardwood planks are usually nailed down in the tongue, then finished with heavy duty floor sanders.

Parquet wood flooring is often simply glued down over a doubled wood floor, built up as shown.

nail set below surface with nailset

hardwood planks, tongue and groove

plywood subfloor

floor joists

¼" parquet wood

¾" plywood or particleboard finish floor support

joist

¾" plywood or particleboard subfloor

PART 3. HOUSE RAISING AND FINISH WORK

barrier of building paper or building felt over the subfloor before installing finish flooring.

If you like, make a dry run in a large room, laying out the room before nailing down the strips. All joints must be staggered. You may have to coax the strips into place with a scrap piece and a hammer.

Install the first starter strip at a long wall edge, but set ½-inch away from the wall to allow for warpage or shrinkage. Snap a chalk line to ensure that you get this starter strip installed as straight as possible. Then nail it through the top (the nail will be covered by the baseboard molding). Blind nailing the edge as well makes it more secure and prevents it from tipping upwards.

The planks are tongue-and-groove on the ends, too. You may have to nail them on the ends to drive them tightly in place. The most important thing is to make sure the strips are driven tightly together, without any open cracks showing.

Glued down wood floors.
A plank floor can be installed over concrete by first installing fake, or sleeper, joists. However the best approach is to use a glued down wooden floor. These are available in a number of different woods, styles, and thicknesses, including strips, planks, and even pegs to simulate a pegged floor. These are all installed with mastic; different mastics are needed depending on the surface the flooring will cover.

Most of these floors are thinner than ¾-inch nailed down flooring—some as thin as ¼-inch. To compensate, the subflooring must be thicker. Don't scrimp on subfloor thickness; that can only cause headaches later. You may also need to install a vapor barrier. There are big differences in the way various glued floorings are installed; so check the manufacturer's directions carefully.

Wood glued down strips or planks are started the same way nailed down strips are. But start wooden blocks in the center of the room. Measure from each side to establish a centerline and snap chalk lines. Position a row of loose tiles each way to check for fit. Spread mastic on a small area and lay the tiles block

fashion. You'll have to cut the edge tiles to bring them to the walls. But leave about ¼ inch of spacing all around, which will be covered by the baseboard. You could also lay the tiles diagonally.

Resilient floor tile.
This is an easy-to-lay flooring material for the do-it-yourselfer. Again, the proper underlayment must be in place, as specified by the manufacturer. Establish a centerline, spread the adhesive, and lay the tile in pyramid fashion, starting at the center of the room. The tiles should be positioned carefully by first butting the edge against the previously laid tile and then lowering the opposite edge down to the adhesive. Sliding the tiles in place pushes the adhesive up between the joints.

Cut tiles to fit around corners, etc. First scribe to fit and then cut with a pair of tin snips.

Self-sticking tiles are among the easiest to install. Simply peel off the paper backing and stick them down on a clean, dust-free subfloor.

Sheet vinyl.
One of the longest lasting and easiest to maintain surfaces, sheet vinyl is difficult for most do-it-yourselfers to install. Newer, more flexible materials developed in the past few years have made the job easier. Some styles require adhesive under the full sheet, while newer ones may be fastened in place with a border of adhesive or even staples, which are covered later with molding. The hardest part is getting the solid pieces in place, cut to fit around the room perimeter without unsightly gaps.

Carpeting.
This is excellent because of the warmth and comfort it offers, though it does need continued maintenance. Most carpeting jobs should be left to the pros, but carpet tiles can be used on small or informal rooms and are easy for the do-it-yourselfers to install. They are installed in the same way as resilient and wood tiles.

Ceramic tiles.
These are installed on floors, walls, countertops, or concrete tub forms. They are more expensive than other materials but are easier to maintain and last

longer than most. The same layout and starting system is used for ceramic tiles (including wall tiles) as for other tile. Many tiles come in pregrouted sheets.

To install tile, lay out the starter tiles, spread adhesive, and position the tiles. Allow the adhesive to set. Then apply grout, wash away the excess, and polish with a soft cloth.

Ceramic tile can be cut with abrasive-grit saw blades. But the usual way to cut them is to scribe a tile with a special tile cutter, which can be rented from most tile suppliers, and then snap it on the scored line. You can also use an ordinary glass cutter to score the tile. Then position the scored surface over a piece of wire, such as a coat hanger, on a flat surface. Push down on both sides of the tile sharply to snap the tile off. Use a pair of pliers to nibble away areas when you must tile around an outside corner or a pipe. Since tile is quite heavy, it takes a substantial subfloor to hold the weight; check the manufacturer's suggestions.

Other flooring materials include brick, flagstone, or imitation brick and stone.

Insulation

Floors that are directly over an unheated crawl space or basement must be insulated. The insulation should be placed between the floor joists and should create a minimum insulation value of R-19. This adds sound deadening as well.

The most common under-floor insulation is roll or batt fiberglass or mineral wool in standard widths to fit between joists. The insulation can be backed (foil or paper) or without backing. If backed insulation is used, the backing acts as a vapor barrier and should be placed to face the heated area. Insulation can sometimes be stuffed or stapled in place. A better and longer-lasting system is to use some sort of holding device—wood, metal strapping, or even chicken wire stapled to the bottom of the joists.

A well-heated basement requires sidewall insulation.

Insulation that covers the ceiling and attic is called cap insulation. It normally runs between ceiling joists from wall to wall. This insulation must be installed properly. The minimum insulation value should be R-19. You may need to double the thickness, in which case the top layer should not be backed.

To install, merely push the material between the joists with the backing facing the living area. The second layer should be at right angles to the first; no joints should be directly over one another. The big problem with batts is putting them in place at the house eaves or against snow stops to prevent air infiltration.

Insulating an attic is hot, hard, and uncomfortable work. Wear safety goggles to protect your eyes and a dust mask to avoid breathing the tiny insulation fibers that will fill the air. Wear old clothes and take a shower as soon as you get through with the job. [The following material is courtesy of Justus Log Homes.]

Fiberglass batt insulation. This material is intended for use in exterior frame walls on basement packages, attic areas for truss models, and in crawl-space floor areas if desired.

The insulation you will be using in standard construction walls will be 5½ inches thick with a foil face. Your first step will be to cut and fit insulation into all standard width stud cavities (16 inches o.c.). Measure the height between the top of the sole place and the top plate and add 2 inches, then roll insulation out on floor and cut across the foil face at the dimension you have determined. Measure and cut accurately so you get a snug fit in the wall cavity. A little trick that will save time stapling later on is to tear back the foil face about an inch at each end. This will then become a stapling flange like those on the sides of the insulation. You do not need to cut the insulation strips to width for standard stud cavities because it's already pre cut to size. Staple the insulation to the studs every 6 to 8 inches and the same at the top and bottom plates.

The next step is to cut the insulation to fit snugly into all of the nonstandard cavities. You may find that it is easier to strip off the foil face before pressing insulation into tight cavities. If you do, remember to later apply some type of vapor resistant cover over this area— use the foil face stripped off the insulation or 3- to 6-mil polyethylene sheeting. Use rust-re-

PART 3. HOUSE RAISING AND FINISH WORK

sistant fasteners. Note: This material *must* be protected against moisture when being stored or installed.

For attic installations with a truss roof, use either faced or unfaced insulation with a separate vapor-resistant barrier. Install with rust-resistant fasteners. The material supplied should fit snugly between the bottom cords of the trusses. If you choose to measure the area to be covered and cut to length before installation, allow for an extra 3½ inches on each end to fit up on top of the top plates of the walls. Stapling again is 6 to 8 inches on center at all edges. If insulation must be spliced, tear back the face to allow for overlap at the splice joint. If vent blocks are used above exterior walls between trusses, remember to not block the holes in the vent blocks with insulation. That will hinder air circulation.

A few other hints: When installing the insulation in any cavity, watch out for protruding nails. When working in attic spaces, make sure that you have adequate support when crawling over trusses. Remember to allow at least 3 inches of air space around electrical boxes that contain fans, lights or other heat generating electrical equipment. And check with fireplace manufacturers about requirements for installation around their equipment. A final caution: promptly cover (with whatever wall covering you are using) all insulation, as most of the materials used in the covering for the glass batt are combustible.

Rigid insulation. To install rigid insulation in rafter roofs, follow these procedures:

Install sheets at the outside walls first. Cut sheets to fit between the rafters. For 16-inch centers, cut sheets to 14⅝ inches to allow for a snug friction fit. That way the insulation sheets can be pushed in and will remain in place without nailing until the finish ceiling is installed. Cut insulation to fit the contour of the top plate. This allows insulation to seat more snugly at the outside wall, and prevents it from closing off the vent block holes.

For 24-inch center applications, cut sheets to 22⅝ inches. It's best to chalk a line on the insulation and cut carefully with circular saw or handsaw. When the ridge pieces are being fitted, they should also be cut to fit the contour

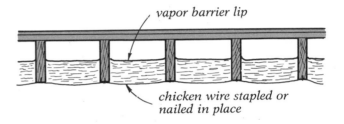

Chicken wire stapled to underside of floor joists can be used to hold insulation in place over crawl spaces.

of the cavity. The snug fit will increase insulation at this point.

For cavities other than standard widths, cut the insulation as close as possible and press it snugly in place.

A few notes of caution for handling and storage: The foil face of the insulation is easily torn, so exercise caution when storing or handling this material. An approved vapor resisting barrier must be applied on the heated side of the bottom edge of the rafters before the finished ceiling is installed. When applying vapor barriers, use rust-resistant fasteners.

This material is very lightweight and, if stored where it is exposed to wind, it should be well-stacked, covered and weighted down. Follow the same precautions set forth for fiberglass insulation when installing around heat-generating appliances.

Gloves and protective clothing are also recommended here.

Log home interiors can be left natural or decorated like those of conventional homes. (Photo by Lincoln Logs.)

PART 3.   HOUSE RAISING AND FINISH WORK

Chapter 15   CABINETMAKING AND MILLWORK

The new inside

The interior design of your log home can follow almost any style. In fact, the interior doesn't even have to suggest that it's part of a log home. But the beauty of polished and hand crafted logs on the interior is what endears log homes to many.

One of the minor benefits of a log interior is that almost anything can be hung on the walls by simply driving a nail. If you want to move the item, just pull out the nail and patch the hole. Most of the damage simply disappears into the rough-hewn look of the logs.

You will probably plan the room layouts well in advance of construction. Your plan should include the location of built-in items such as closets and kitchen or vanity cabinets. After the home has been roughed in, however, make a reevaluation. You may find things need to be changed around. Although changing a house plan at this time can be frustrating and expensive, it's still cheaper than doing it after the cabinets and closets have been installed.

Cabinets

One of the first steps is to build and install cabinets in the kitchen, pantry, washroom, and utility rooms. They are the same as those used in traditionally constructed homes. You may, however, lean toward a more rustic look, to match the wood used in this type of house. For instance, knotty pine or cedar is a dramatic cabinet wood often used in log homes. On the other hand, a set of cabinets complete with raised fronts and panel doors made of elm, pecan, or oak can give a touch of elegance to the warm, rustic appearance of a hand-polished log interior.

For a simple vacation lodge, you can get by with cabinets that are little more than a box with doors fastened to the walls and floor.

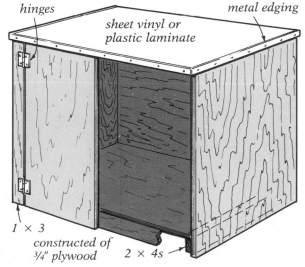

hinges   sheet vinyl or plastic laminate   metal edging

1 × 3

constructed of ¾" plywood   *2 × 4s*

Many folks who build their own log homes also like to finish the job by building their own cabinets. Cabinets can be built with simple hand tools. But stationary power tools make the job easier and faster. Here's an example of typical plans. Install the constructed boxes in place. The cabinets must be fastened to the walls in a way to allow for shrinkage and log settling, as indicated.

You have two choices: you can purchase preassembled sections of cabinets, which are simply joined together to make up the cabinet arrangement you desire; or you can make, or have made, custom cabinets to suit you. Manufacturers of preassembled cabinets are listed in the Appendix.

Naturally, if the building is a simple hunting and fishing lodge, you can furnish it economically. You need only a simple boxlike cabinet to hold the sink and a few other cabinets above it for dishes. Simple cabinets are fairly inexpensive and you can save time by simply nailing up a purchased unit.

Constructing cabinets. Cabinets built on site can be constructed of almost any material, including rough-sawed planks and 2× material. Unless well dried, however, the wood will shrink, twist, and warp. The resulting cracks are not only ugly but let in pests. For a wilderness cabinet, however, this may be the only choice.

Shop-built cabinets. In most instances, however, you will want to have better-looking and longer-lasting cabinets. Make the

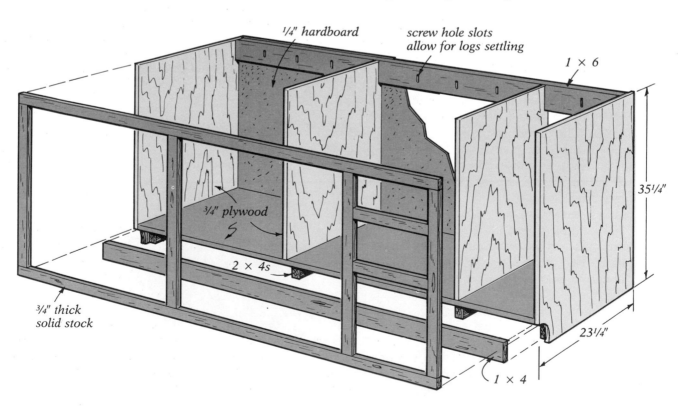

1/4" hardboard

screw hole slots allow for logs settling

1 × 6

35 1/4"

3/4" plywood

2 × 4s

3/4" thick solid stock

23 1/4"

1 × 4

PART 3. HOUSE RAISING AND FINISH WORK

cabinets completely self-enclosed boxes, constructing them in your shop or in the center of a large, unfinished room; then slide them against the wall and fasten them in place.

There are several advantages to this type of construction. First, the cabinets can be made completely mouse and pest proof. Second, they're separate from walls and won't be affected by the settling and shrinkage problems.

Cabinet construction can be broken down into three separate operations. First build the cabinet case. Fasten this to the log wall—shim, level, and plumb as necessary. Before installing the floor cabinets, holes must be cut in the bottom for the sink, dishwasher, garbage disposal, and supply lines. These are positioned first and the cabinet is slipped down over them.

Fasten the unit with large roundhead screws in slotted holes (to compensate for shrinkage and settling). Use wooden shingle shims to level and plumb the unit. Put a trim piece along the front edge and down to the floor to cover any gap left by the shims.

Scribe a thin piece of molding to fit the contour of the log wall and then nail it against the cabinet side. You may have to replace this piece as the logs shrink and settle. This should be done on any end of the cabinet joining the log wall. If the cabinets are placed against a standard dimension wall partition, you will have few fitting problems. Anchor to the wall using No. 8 cement-coated nails.

Wall cabinets are constructed the same way. Build an enclosed box, and fasten it to the walls, again using the key-shaped slots for the wood screws and the scribed molding pieces.

Often wall cabinets consist of two boxes, one on either side of a window. A shelf for an overhead fluorescent light can be covered with a false front and a decorative trim board can be suspended beneath to conceal the light fixture. One of the problems in fastening cabinets to log walls is getting the ends of the two cabinets the same distance from the wall so that the trim board will fit with a tight, neat joint. Homemade braces can be used to hold the wall cabinets in place until they are firmly anchored.

Some cabinetmakers prefer to build and install the wall cabinets (using high braces) before installing the floor cabinets. It's some-

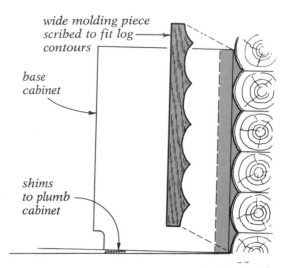

Another problem, especially with walls of round logs, is covering the edge between the cabinet and wall. This must be done with a wide molding scribed to fit.

what easier than reaching over the previously-installed floor cabinets.

Once these cases have been anchored, measure and construct the doors and drawers. This is where you can add a personal touch by designing your own door and drawer fronts. Drawer and door fronts are only installed after the cases have been positioned because the cabinet may twist during installation; then the doors wouldn't fit properly.

Install the countertop next. Countertops can be made of various materials, including plywood covered with plastic laminate. This is the most common, least expensive, and easiest to maintain. Or you could cover cabinets with ceramic tile, which lasts longer but is harder to install. You can also use solid wood. Strips of hardwood can be glued together with waterproof glue to create a butcher-block countertop. These match rustic-style cabinets and are extremely practical.

Purchased molded-plastic laminate can also be installed. First cut out the opening for the sink as desired, then fasten from the bottom with wood screws.

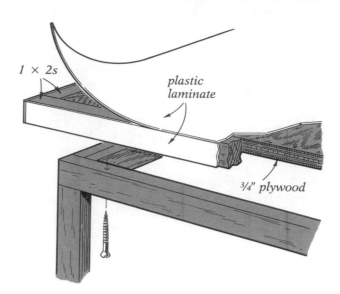

1 × 2s

plastic
laminate

3/4" plywood

With plastic laminate, the top is made and the laminate glued before the top is installed.

Installing plastic-laminate tops.

1. Cut plywood to the correct size, and then add an edging of 1 × 2 stock.

2. Cut a front piece of laminate to fit the edging with about 1/8-inch extra width. Spread contact cement on the back of the laminate strip and the front of the wood edging.

3. Allow the cement to become tacky, then press the pieces together making sure the strip aligns properly with the edges.

4. Sand with a belt sander to make the edge of the laminate strip flush with the plywood top. Remove any dirt or debris from the top.

5. Coat the underside of the laminate pieces and the top of the plywood with contact cement and allow it to become tacky.

6. Use wooden spacers to position the laminate without allowing the glue surfaces to touch. Remove the wooden spacer strips and seal the laminate in place with a heavy roller or block of wood and a hammer.

7. Use a router with a laminate trimmer or a laminate hand scorer to cut away excess.

8. Finish with a fine file and clean.

9. Measure the sink opening by first laying the sink rim in place and marking around it.

10. Bore a starting hole.

11. Cut out the opening with saber saw.

12. Install a back splash (if desired).

13. Fasten the top in place using wood screws driven up through the facing and back support from the bottom.

Install the countertops next. These may consist of a plastic laminate covering plywood as shown here. (Photo courtesy Nutone.)

If you cover a counter with ceramic tile, the plywood top must be installed first. The ceramic tile laid into a bed of mastic and then grouted. Then the sink installed. (Photo courtesy American-Olean.)

Installing ceramic tile.

1. Anchor the plywood top to the cabinet and cut out the hole for the sink with a saber saw.

2. Apply mastic to the plywood top (a little at a time) and install the ceramic tile in the mastic.

3. Treat the edge and the back splash, or area between the countertop and the upper wall cabinets, the same.

4. After the tile has had a chance to set up, apply grout and wipe the excess away with a squeegee. Clean away the remainder with a damp cloth.

5. Finally, give the material a buffing with a clean, soft cloth.

Building butcher block tops.

1. Cut wood strips to the proper width, then smear waterproof glue on their surfaces and clamp together.

2. Allow the glue to set overnight, then use a belt sander to remove glue lines and smooth the rough wood surface.

3. Round the outer edge with a router and apply a coat or two of olive oil. Other wood-finishing oils are poisonous.

4. Fasten the top in place with screws from the cabinet into the bottom.

After the tops are installed, position the sink and hook it to its waste and drain.

Closets

Closets are often the most overlooked rooms in a home, and they can cause the most frustration—there is never enough closet space. Usually they're so crammed with disorganized junk that you can't find anything you want without getting banged on the head by falling debris, or having to dig through musty piles of old clothes, shoes, and fishing gear.

The simplest closet is the storage wall in a master bedroom. Normally three existing walls are used. One wall in the center separates the his and her sections. A header in front hides the upper portion of the closet. Bifold doors are anchored to 2 × 4s at the extreme corners.

You could use a free-standing unit designed for the basement, attic, or garage. This is an excellent choice for a log home, because of the wall-settling problem. Start by making a foundation of 2 × 4 lumber nailed together on edge. To this nail, in order, the floor, side, back, and ceiling of ¾-inch exterior plywood. To support hollow-core doors, install a 2 × 4 at each side of the closet front. You can use plywood doors instead and eliminate front posts, but manufactured doors are less likely to warp.

Line the closet with aromatic red cedar, applying pieces in random lengths, horizontally. Before hanging doors, cover them with red cedar too. Use small nails and a cartridge-type adhesive because the surface of the hollow-core door is very thin.

Trimming around covered walls is a simple matter of plumbing and mitering.

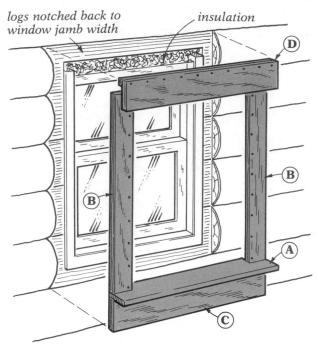

logs notched back to window jamb width

insulation

Trimming around exterior doors and windows must be done in special ways to deal with settling problems. Shown is typical window trim. Install the pieces in the alphabetical order shown. Nail only to the window jamb, except for the top piece; nail it with a spacer to the top log.

Finally, add a cedar shelf and hang the clothes rod centered between doors and back. Install magnetic catches to keep doors closed. Finish the doors and closet exterior, but not the interior.

Trimming out

Trimming out or applying finish trim and molding can be either hard or easy. If you want to take it easy, apply as little trim as possible. Instead, allow your craftsmanship to show where possible. Of course, you'll need to trim around dimension partition walls and ceiling joints.

You'll also have to trim around window and door units. This can be done in a variety of ways depending on how you finished the ends of the wall logs butting the window or door frame. If the logs butt tightly against a fairly thin stock, you won't be able to add trim. This doesn't look as good and doesn't offer much draft protection. Cutting back the log ends as shown allows for a better use of trim.

Before installing trim pieces, stuff all cracks with mineral wool or fiberglass insulation. Cut the appropriate trim pieces to size and shape. Nail them to the window frame, *not to the logs*, to allow for settling. The window sill (or stool) can be attached to both the logs and frame.

The open space above all windows and doors will also have to be covered with a trim piece, which must be scribed to fit the upper log and fastened to it (not the window frame). A wide baseboard molding leaves space to run electrical wires and water lines, although the latter are best run through a plumbing core in the center of the house. Baseboard molding also covers the gap between flooring materials and the irregular log walls. You can add insulation behind the baseboard and caulk to the top to prevent drafts.

You can tack and glue rope around joints for an unusual trim. Give it a coat of varnish or sealer.

Any trim placed between ceiling and walls must be of a slip-joint design so it won't be ruined by the settling of wall logs.

Chapter 16 DECKS, PORCHES, AND BALCONIES

Outside space

An extension such as a deck, porch, or greenhouse, along with a well thought out landscaping job, makes a log home more valuable, attractive, and livable. Decks at ground level or hanging from the second floor, sheltered by an overhanging gable or porch roof, provide a shady spot for family dining or just plain relaxing. Fit a deck with screens and you've added a summer room that can be used for dining or sleeping without the bother of insects. A porch or deck can also be made as an extension of a floor and covered by the roof of the house.

A front porch adds the equivalent of an extra room in the warmer seasons.

A long porch becomes an integral part of the design.

Decks and porches have been built simply with flat rocks for supports.

A deck can be used as a balcony if it extends over a lower floor. This home has a two-car garage in the basement. (Photo courtesy Bellaire Log Homes.)

Decks

A deck is probably the simplest outdoor structure to build. You can build the deck and later cover it with a roof, enclose a portion of it with a greenhouse, put in a hot tub, or completely enclose it to create a screened in porch.

Construct a deck with log framing and rough sawed lumber, of dimension lumber, or of a combination of the two. The deck support and framing can be made of logs, and dimension lumber can be used to both cover the decking and as handrails. A combination is popular because log framing blends well with the home, and the dimension lumber allows for easier construction of the deck—and it's a smoother flooring surface. Make sure that any exposed lumber is treated or that a preservative is used to add life to the deck. Redwood will probably last the longest. But pressure-treated wood can be long-lived, too.

Most kit log home companies offer decks as an accessory package. Many decks are included as an integral part of the home design, and are not merely tacked on.

All deck framing must be solid and well designed to hold not only the deck and the weight it must support, but snow loads as well. This means the foundations for the deck must be as solid as those for the rest of the house. Low decks may sit directly on piers, but higher

PART 3.   HOUSE RAISING AND FINISH WORK

decks must have wood support beams. These can be dimension lumber, logs, or sawed beams.

Deck building basics.

Log framing. Normally joist logs are set into notches cut in the house sill log. Use the same size logs and flatten them so the porch floor will be at the same height, or just a bit lower than, the house floor to allow a threshold to properly join the two. The thickness of the flooring material used for the decking must be taken into consideration. A sill log resting on concrete piers, or wooden beams supported by concrete piers, as shown, completes the initial framing. The outer sill log's top surface must be a bit lower than the house sill to slope the deck away from the house and provide proper drainage (this is normally 1 inch to every 6 feet). The end joists are treated as sill logs. The decking can be installed parallel to the house wall or at angles.

For decking that runs away from (at right angles to) the wall surface, you have to create a box sill of logs as shown. Use log joists as girders supported with center pieces. Or you can simply nail the joists down over the first logs (at right angles) to create the same thing. Box in the ends to finish it off. Narrow decks usually don't need center piers and girder support, but decks over 6 feet wide do.

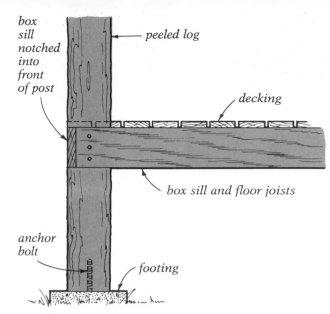

Peeled logs make excellent support posts.

Depending on the soil conditions, larger decks may require piers over footings.

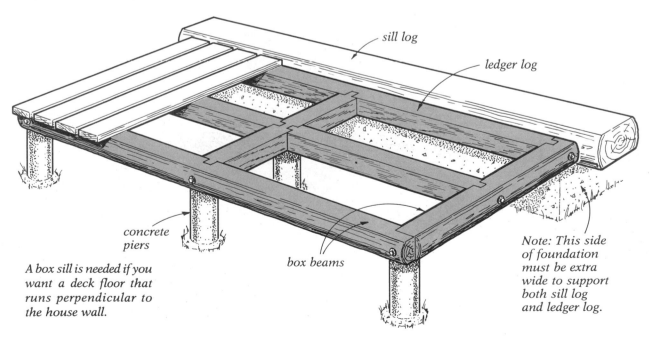

A box sill is needed if you want a deck floor that runs perpendicular to the house wall.

Note: This side of foundation must be extra wide to support both sill log and ledger log.

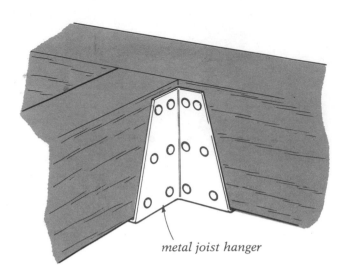

metal joist hanger

Use joists hangers to fasten deck joists.

This shows a typical framing method for a deck of dimension lumber.

If kiln-dried dimension stock is used for decking, it must be spaced about ⅛-inch apart to allow for water drainage. With green rough-sawed lumber, space as close together as possible and hope for the best. It may shrink enough to leave 1-inch cracks, depending on the type of wood and when it was cut.

Peeled, rough sawed, or hewed logs make good-looking support posts. Old barn beams make excellent posts for this application and blend in well.

Post logs must be treated with creosote or penta before application. Soaking their ends in a barrel for a few hours seems to give the best saturation.

Dimension framing. Framing a dimension stock deck is somewhat easier, but it probably will be more costly. Shown are framing methods for a dimension deck. A ledger is nailed to the sill log and the framing members fastened in place using joist hangers. The end supports are the same, using heavy poles or timbers for the uprights where necessary. You can also add extra bracing as shown.

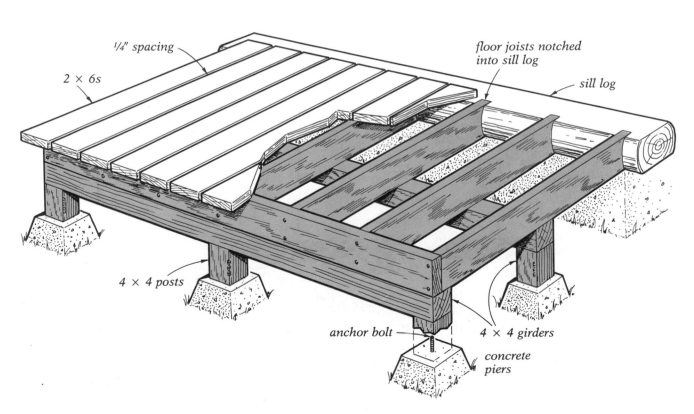

¼" spacing

2 × 6s

floor joists notched into sill log

sill log

4 × 4 posts

anchor bolt

4 × 4 girders

concrete piers

Balconies

A balcony is usually nothing more than a second-story porch. A cantilevered balcony is popular. The most common support for this type is an extension of the upper floor log joists through the wall logs (as shown). Heavy flooring material is then attached to the joists to complete the structure.

Again, combining log support with dimension stock can make this extremely attractive. It is even more pleasant if it's covered with extending gable or a wide eave.

Photo left, cantilevered decks serve well for contemporary log designs. Photo below left, cantilevered balconies have been traditional with Scandinavian log homes, and they are popular in Canada and the northern U.S. (Photo by Building with Logs, Ltd.). Drawing below, cantilevered decks look good.

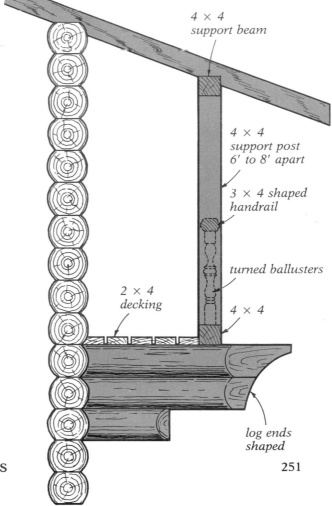

4 × 4 support beam

4 × 4 support post 6' to 8' apart

3 × 4 shaped handrail

turned ballusters

2 × 4 decking

4 × 4

log ends shaped

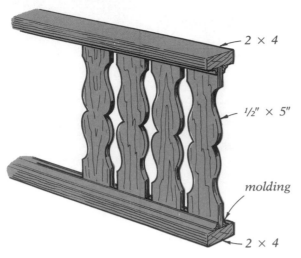

Fancy ballusters can be cut with a bandsaw.

Railings may be simply peeled logs, bolted to uprights.

Railings

All but the lowest ground-level decks should have railings of some sort. Railings can, of course, be constructed of peeled saplings that are bolted securely to peeled log uprights, as shown. However, unless allowed to cure first, the small-diameter logs often sag and split, creating unsightly and dangerous railing. They should be cut, peeled, and smoothed with a

Ensure that all railings are securely anchored.

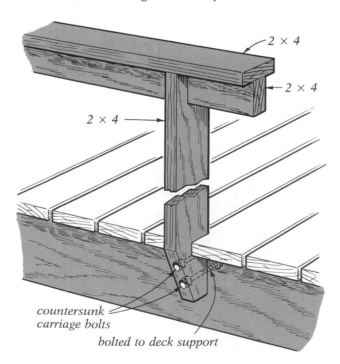

drawknife for the best appearance. Then stack and allow them to cure for a year.

A railing constructed with dimension lumber can complement almost any deck, regardless of whether it's made from logs or dimension stock. The railing must be sturdy and splinter free. One thing to keep in mind: Because of the massive appearance of log homes, materials used for such things as balcony railings should also be fairly heavy and massive—2 × 6s and even 2 × 8s don't look out of place.

Porches

Porches range from a simple walkway along the front of the house to fully enclosed rooms with space for dining and sleeping in the warmer seasons. Although a porch can be added on after the house is built, it's best to incorporate the porch into construction of the house. Anytime a roof is added to an existing building, there is a chance of water leakage.

The easiest way to build a porch on a log home is to simply extend the foundation (or piers) to the length of the intended porch, and then run the log purlins of the roof out. Set up long, peeled support poles as corner uprights, and install the flooring of the porch.

The gable end of the porch can be enclosed, but you may want to leave it open so the log purlins show.

252

A porch is simply a deck with a roof over it.

You can double your outdoor living space with a balcony above a ground-level porch. Usually if the overhang is 5 feet or less you won't need support posts, but anything wider needs support.

Porches can be enclosed with screening to provide a breezeway or pleasant summer room. (Photo courtesy New England Log Homes, Inc.)

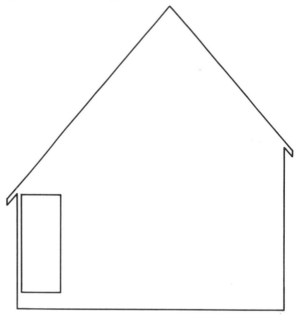

There are numerous roof styles for porches. The simplest and most integrated is the continuous eave.

If the house roof is steep, the continuous eave creates a "cat slide" as mountain folks referred to it.

An L-gable roof is often used when the porch is at right angles to the house roof line. The end can be a gable or hip style.

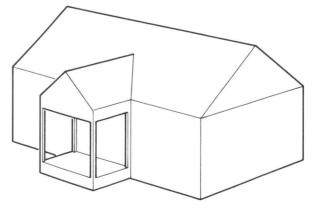

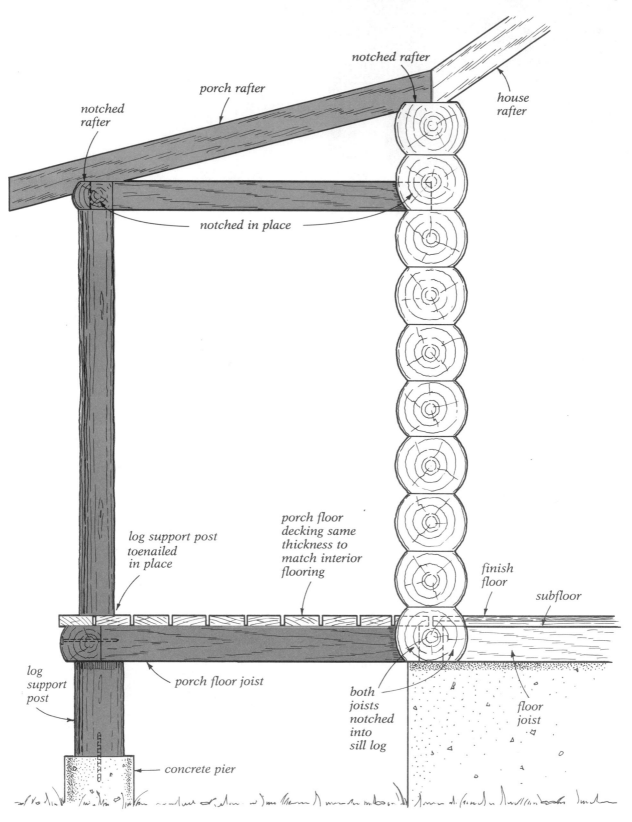

This shows basic framing of a log porch and decking.

notched rafter

porch rafter

notched rafter

house rafter

notched in place

log support post toenailed in place

porch floor decking same thickness to match interior flooring

finish floor

subfloor

log support post

porch floor joist

both joists notched into sill log

floor joist

concrete pier

254   PART 3.   HOUSE RAISING AND FINISH WORK

Continuous-eave porch. There are various porch roofs. The continuous eave is popular on low, flat homes, where the porch roof is merely an extension of the main roof. This can be used effectively on houses with a relatively low roof pitch and for narrow porches. However, a steep-roofed house can create a design called a "cat slide" by the old-time mountain builders—a narrow porch that is uncomfortable.

You can enclose a porch with screen panels that can be exchanged with airtight fiberglass panels for the colder seasons.

This is a simple roof over a concrete patio at the rear of a contemporary house.

Another style of roof is set in at the eave, but at a shallower angle than the house roof pitch. If this is to be waterproof, the porch must be constructed at the same time as the house and care must be taken to assure a solid nailing joint. Shown are construction details of the overlapping joinery of the porch and house rafters for this type of roof. The advantage here is that it produces a wider, larger porch area because of the break in the roofline.

This is a typical roof joinery for a porch roof.

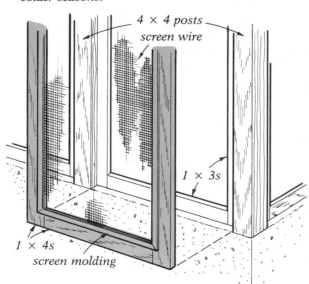

4 × 4 posts
screen wire

1 × 3s

1 × 4s
screen molding

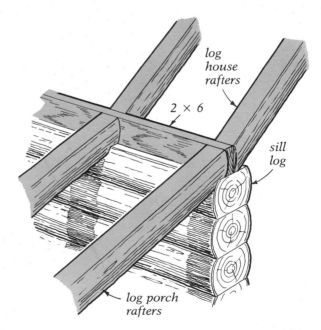

log house rafters

2 × 6

sill log

log porch rafters

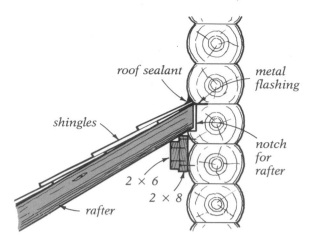

A lean-to roof can be used, but it tends to develop leaks along the joint.

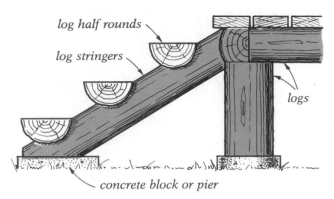

Log stairs with notched stringers may be made to match interior stairs.

Lean-to porch roof. The third porch roof style is the joined or lean-to. This kind of porch roof is joined to the side of the house and is not a continuation of the main roofline. The advantages are that the roofline can be entirely different from the house, allowing you to make the porch as large as you want. This style of roofline is commonly used when an addition is put on later. The main problem is that it's hard to create a watertight joint, particularly on a log wall. For that reason it's not recommended for log houses.

Hip roof. Another style is the hip roof. With this one, the porch is at a right angle to the main house, and the porch roof joins the house roof at right angles. The end of the porch can be finished with a gable or hip roof. This roof accommodates almost any size porch. Constructing the roof is a bit more complicated than with the other porches, and the porch must be constructed at the same time as the house roof. But when it is done properly it blends in with the rest of the house and has a professional appearance.

You can, of course, enclose the porch, using changeable panels of fiberglass and screening to create a sunroom in winter and a screened porch in summer. If you use this idea, enclose the bottom 12 inches or so of the porch walls to prevent the screens or fiberglass panels from being kicked or knocked out by the furniture legs.

Steps and stairs

You make steps and stairs to your porch the same way you would the inside stairs. You will probably want open stairs—without risers—to give an airy feeling. Again, massive materials should be used to blend in with the rest of the exterior. Steps to small decks can be made of poured concrete. But for an even better appearance, use railroad ties or old barn beams for the steps and on the ground leading up to the deck.

Steps can be split logs on posts sunk in the ground.

PART 3.   HOUSE RAISING AND FINISH WORK

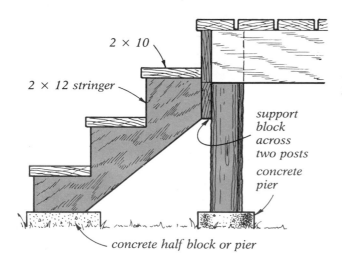

These are typical details for steps of lumber.

Poured concrete steps require a form that is almost as complex as wood steps themselves.

Landscaping

Blending your log home into the landscape is easy and, in fact, is one of the reasons many folks choose log homes in the first place. Because it lacks the stark formal lines of most houses, a log home is good-looking with even the most casual landscaping—little more than clearing away enough trees for an entryway. This doesn't mean that extensive landscaping will be out of place. But try to keep the rustic, informal setting. Odd pieces of cutoff logs and small saplings peeled and positioned creatively can be used to make such structures as fences, swing sets, sand boxes, garden shelters, and bridges.

To look natural, a log home should be landscaped to fit its setting. Here hand-split rail fence adds class.

Part 4

EXTRAORDINARY LOG STYLES

HEWED AND SQUARE-MILLED LOG

Yesterday and today

This chapter covers two separate methods of log home construction. The first, building with hewed logs, deals with the traditional method of construction. The second, building with square-milled logs, is a somewhat similar technique used by many of today's log home builders and several kit home manufacturers.

Hewed log homes

Although hewed log homes are still popular in the eastern mountain country of the United States, they had their origin in the Scandinavian countries. The number of old log buildings still standing is an indication of the long-lasting qualities of this kind of construction. Corner-notch construction literally locks the walls together so that nothing short of a tornado or other disaster can destroy the house. The logs used are massive, usually of hardwood hewed down to shape. Because most of the sapwood is removed, logs don't rot or deteriorate quickly. The biggest problem many of the older houses had is that they were constructed on weak or inadequate foundations; they've shifted or settled to one side as a result (with the locked corners still holding).

Hewed log homes with their dovetail corner notches are of centuries-old Scandinavian origin. They require skillful hewing and notching.

The main disadvantage of building a hewed log house is the work involved. It takes a tremendous effort to hew all the logs to the shape needed for a traditional home. In addition, cutting dovetail corner notches requires concentration and effort. To many purists, however, a hewed log home is the only type worth building.

Materials. Logs used for hewed construction are the same kind used for round-log construction. In the eastern and southern highlands, opt for white oak if possible. Or use other similar hardwoods. Use stone or stone-faced foundations to give the home a traditional look.

Hewing creates a log with two to four sides squared. It's anywhere from 5 to 8 inches thick.

Above, many fine examples of this hewed log style are scattered across North America. Below, the dogtrot log home was once common. This consisted of two small log rooms joined by a breezeway. (Photo courtesy Historical Society of Missouri.)

If constructed properly and chinked well, hewn logs provide a tight, good-looking home. Softwoods are more common in the North. Deciduous species, such as oak, are commonly used in the eastern highlands.

PART 4.   EXTRAORDINARY LOG STYLES

This cuts away almost all of the sapwood, leaving the heartwood. Where speed is important, only two (inner and outer) sides are hewed. This causes problems in cutting the notches on the ends, but it requires less effort to prepare the logs. The chinking covers the rounded area anyway. If the upper and lower sides of the log are not hewed, they should be at least debarked. Make sure you hew the logs while they are still green, then stack them carefully to prevent them from sagging and warping.

Construction. The first step is to cut the sill logs for front and back to length. Prop the logs on short log pieces and cut notches in the end, making sure the notches are on the same angle at each end.

Hewed log homes can have different types of notches. The most common (and strongest) is the half-dovetail, as shown. You have to start at the sill logs. The notches can be flush cut, as shown, or protruding. Though harder to make, they provide a more finished look. To get a uniform notch each time, follow the same angle of cut and cut the notches to leave the same amount of wood. Using a dovetail gauge to mark for the notches saves a lot of time. Cut the notches with a chain saw if you're expert.

Or make the downward vertical cut with a one-man crosscut saw, and then follow with an axe or large chisel to make the angled cut.

Smooth any imperfections in the cut with a large chisel and bore holes in the sill logs for anchor bolts. Position the sill logs, using sill seal or other insulation material laid in a line directly below the center of each log and on the foundation. Bolt the logs securely to the foundation.

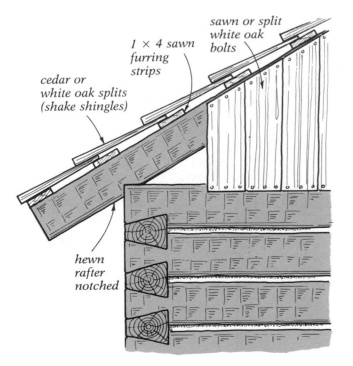

cedar or white oak splits (shake shingles)

1 × 4 sawn furring strips

sawn or split white oak bolts

hewn rafter notched

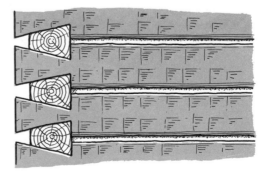

Left, the most popular notch is the dovetail.

The log ends can be made to protrude simply by cutting the notch further into the log length.

How to cut compound dovetails

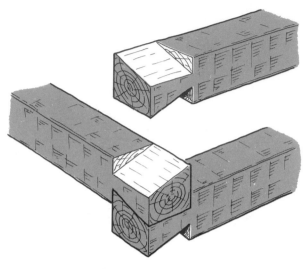

Above, a compound dovetail can hold a log home tightly together and provides a decorative and strong joint.

Step 1. To cut a compound joint, set a bevel gauge to 75 degrees on a long-wall sill log and mark the diagonal cut on the end.

Step 2. Use a small hand square to mark the matching lengthwise cut.

Step 3. Measure the width of the adjoining sill log and mark the width of the notch.

Step 4. *Saw straight down to the guide lines using a hand buck saw, a bowsaw or a chain saw.*

Step 5. *Use a large chisel to create the notch, patiently cutting away small layers.*

Step 6. *Position and secure the long-wall sill log. (Continued on next page.)*

Cut the first end logs to length, mark for the proper cuts on both the top and bottom of the ends, and cut the notches (or dovetail ends) as before. Make sure you keep the end notches aligned with each other. Fit them down over the side (or long sill) logs, carefully cutting and fitting to create a tight-fitting joint. Because of the nature of the notch, you won't be creating a half-log-high raised end on the foundation. The opening will be filled with chinking along with the rest of the spaces between the logs.

It's easy to cut away too much wood, so until you get the hang of cutting and fitting the notches, be careful. If you do cut away too much and logs rest on each other with a crack showing in the notch, you can hew off the bottom of the log to make it settle in place, but the log will be smaller than the others. As with the round-log construction, if the logs are hewed on only two sides, you will have to alternate large and small ends.

With the logs in place, there should be about 1½ to 2 inches left between them for chinking.

CHAPTER 17.   HEWED AND SQUARE-MILLED LOG

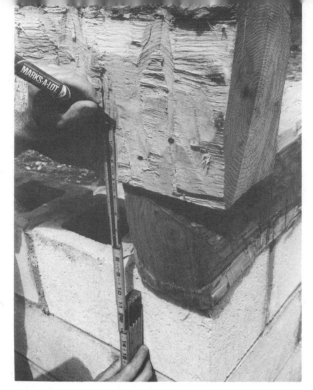

Step 7. *Position the overlapping short-wall sill log, after placing and notching the opposite-wall long-wall sill log. The two long-wall sill logs support the short-wall sill logs in a level position.*

Step 8. *Mark the distance using a straight edge.*

Step 9. *Mark the bevel, again using the bevel gauge set at the same angle as the lower notch.*

Step 10. *Cut notch and secure the log in place.*

PART 4.   EXTRAORDINARY LOG STYLES

Step 11. *The next wall log has the notch perpendicular to the first. Again use the bevel gauge.*

Step 12. *Continue the rest of the marking to match and cut.*

Step 13. *Position the next log and match the previously marked notch to the bottom of it.*

Step 14. *Cut and mount the next log, showing a completed series of compound dovetail notches.*

CHAPTER 17.   HEWED AND SQUARE-MILLED LOG

An A-and-V notch is fairly common.

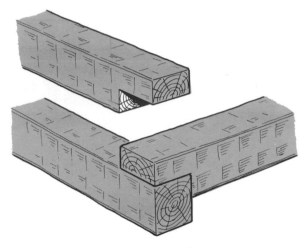

Logs can be simply half-notched.

An overlapping butt notch can be strengthened by adding a dovetail.

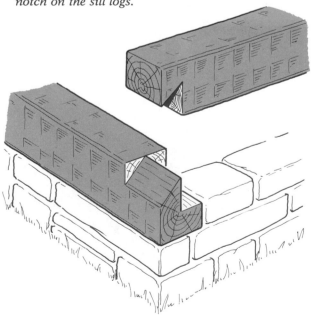

An overlapping butt notch is commonly used on hand-hewed and sawn logs.

For extra strength, some builders create a shouldered notch on the sill logs.

268

Most builders bore anchor bolt holes before installing the sill logs.

Joists. Hewed joists are installed the same way as you install round log joists. For the sake of appearances, you'll probably want log joists. If you decide on using them you will have a traditionally constructed hewed log home.

Once the sill logs are installed, the floor joists are also installed. Typically, these are hewed logs as well. Note the traditional puncheon floor.

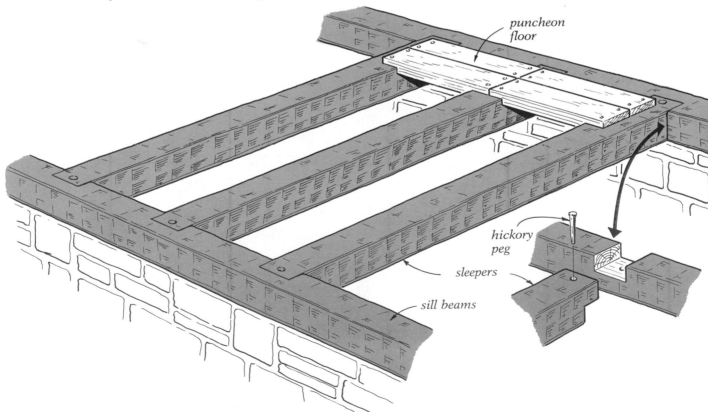

puncheon floor

hickory peg

sleepers

sill beams

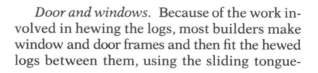

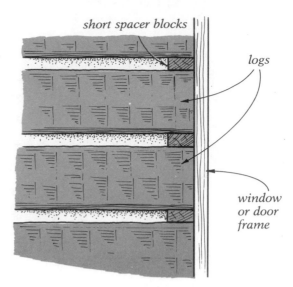

Log ends that join windows and doors must be supported with wood blocks until they are anchored.

You can cut the notches for the floor joists before installing the sill log.

Door and windows. Because of the work involved in hewing the logs, most builders make window and door frames and then fit the hewed logs between them, using the sliding tongue-

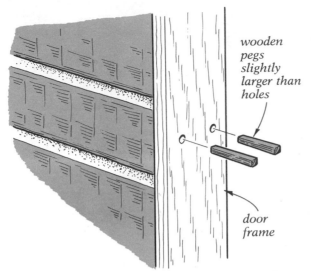

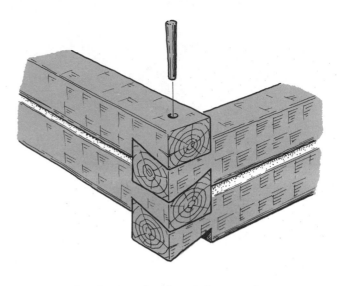

Old-timers pegged the door frames with wooden pegs. For this, the logs must be thoroughly cured.

The top plate log can be pinned down at the corners for more strength.

and-groove method of joining the frames to the log ends. The log ends joining the window and door frames have to be spaced and supported by wooden wedges or chips to hold the ends level. One method used by the old-timers was to bore holes through the facings and peg them in place (as shown). Spacers are needed until the log ends are thoroughly supported.

Probably the biggest headache in building a hewed log home is that logs have to be hoisted into place—they can't be rolled up on a ramp the way round logs can.

Flooring installation, wiring, plumbing runs, windows and doors, and ceiling joists are installed the same way you'd do the jobs in other types of log homes.

The top-plate log is often pinned down through the upper two logs at each corner joint to prevent the walls from being pushed outward by the force of the rafters.

Again, it's extremely important to create an exactly-straight roofline. There are two methods for doing this. The first is to make sure the top of the plate log is absolutely smooth, straight, and level, and that all rafters are notched the same. With the second method, you can use a plate that has bumps or irregularities in it. Snap a chalk line from end to end, after making sure those points are level. Then notch the rafters individually to fit the plate line (as shown).

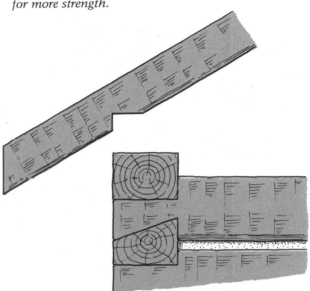

Hewed rafters are notched to fit onto the plate log.

Traditional hewed rafters were half-lapped and pegged at the top.

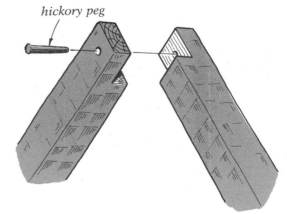

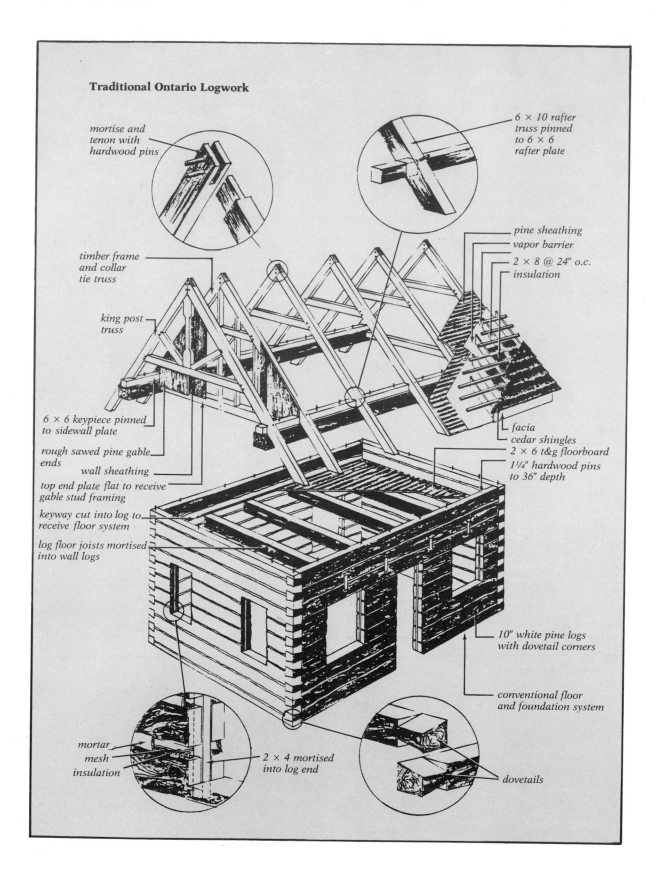

Traditional Ontario Logwork

mortise and tenon with hardwood pins

6 × 10 rafter truss pinned to 6 × 6 rafter plate

pine sheathing
vapor barrier
2 × 8 @ 24" o.c. insulation

timber frame and collar tie truss

king post truss

6 × 6 keypiece pinned to sidewall plate

rough sawed pine gable ends

wall sheathing

top end plate flat to receive gable stud framing

keyway cut into log to receive floor system

log floor joists mortised into wall logs

facia
cedar shingles

2 × 6 t&g floorboard

1¼" hardwood pins to 36" depth

10" white pine logs with dovetail corners

conventional floor and foundation system

mortar
mesh
insulation

2 × 4 mortised into log end

dovetails

Left, this is an exploded view of typical hewed-log home construction. (Drawing courtesy of Building with Logs Limited.)

Traditional hewed houses use hewed rafters, as shown. These are often held at the top and bottom with wooden pegs. There can be an overhang, but in many cases the rafters are cut flush with the sides. This, however, creates problems with rainwater. The wider overhang of recent designs lasts longer and requires less upkeep.

Gable ends. In most cases, the gable ends are covered with sawed planks. But you can also easily construct gable ends by running purlins for each log, as shown. Dovetailing their ends into the gable logs creates an extremely strong roof system.

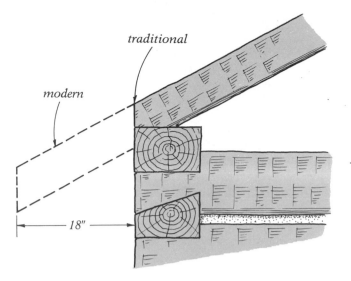

Traditional designs often called for a flush roof. But modern designs with a wide overhang protect the walls better from the elements.

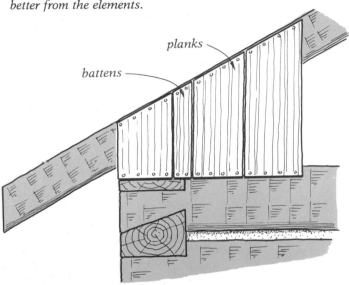

Photo left and drawing above, gable ends are generally covered with planks and battens or wooden shingles.

Gable ends could be purlins and logs.

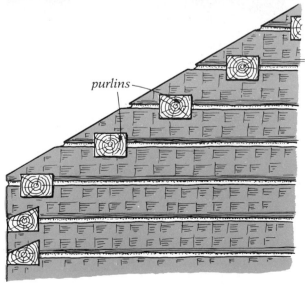

Chinking. The early hewed log cabins were chinked with whatever material was on hand, including mud, clay, grasses, and chunks of wood. Wood chinking is still used and can be quite decorative. There is, however, a tendency for the wood pieces to fall out of the logs. In the old days, chinking was a continuous job. Often old log homes were covered on the outside with plank and batten or clapboard siding; the inside walls were plastered over.

The materials used in chinking today are more sophisticated and can create a tight, weather- and wind-resistant house without the need for a lot of maintenance. Modern chinking consists of pieces of expanded metal wire, lathe, or screen wire stapled in place between the logs—both on the inside and outside of the log joint. Strips of fiberglass insulation torn from batting can be stuffed between the two pieces as shown, then a masonry chinking is applied over the screen or metal lath (masonry chinking is just mortar mix).

Splits combined with modern mortar provide a decorative and strong chinking.

Photo right, today, most log homes are chinked with mortar.

Step 1. *For modern mortar chinking, fill the space between the logs with fiberglass.*

Step 3. *Apply the mortar through and onto the mesh.*

Step 2. *Small mesh hardware cloth or screen serves to hold the insulation in place.*

Step 4. *Trowel the mortar to finish the job.*

Square-milled logs

Using square-milled logs is also popular with many builders today. This log construction method melds some of each technique mentioned for round log and hewed log construction. The logs are generally milled with all four sides square. Sometimes only three sides are milled, the fourth side being debarked and left round. The logs can also have splines or grooves cut into them to create better-fitting joints.

Photo left, square-milled logs are typically milled on three sides—the outside surface round. In this example, red cedar was used and the bark was left on. Photo below right, the interior of a square-mill home has a flat, smooth surface that can be finished in a natural color or covered with any type of paneling. Bottom photo, many log home builders today use square-milled logs.

Logs are joined with dovetail corners, modified dovetails, or end dovetails as shown earlier. Construction of the walls is similar to that described for round logs.

On most square-milled logs, the bark is peeled.

Three cuts are required to create the timbers.

Here is a simple butt joint.

The second course overlaps and butts in the opposite direction. All logs are anchored with spikes.

Short logs can often be joined end-to-end as shown.

Chapter 18 OTHER LOG STYLES

Many choices

You don't have to stick with traditional horizontal round or square-hewed log styles. There are many unusual log building styles that reflect the ingenuity and creativeness of log home builders.

Vertical log walls or stockade

Several log home kit manufacturers offer structures with this style of construction. It is fairly simple to build and can be done as you get the time. It's also a good way to make use of shorter logs, if you don't have access to the long logs necessary for horizontal log construction.

The principal drawback is that shrinkage and unevenness of round logs can cause air infiltration problems. This is solved in kit log homes by using cured and milled logs. Splines and caulking make the house waterproof and windproof. When building from scratch, you use a portable sawmill for the milling operation.

To build a vertical log house, place a flattened sill log on the foundation and anchor solidly. Note: The sill logs have half-lap joints

at the corners so that the top surfaces will be even. Cut the corner logs as needed and erect them at each corner. Make sure they're plumb and braced solidly. Cut the plate logs and in-

You don't have to stick with traditional building styles to build with logs, as this piece-en-piece A-frame attests. (Photo courtesy Boyne Falls Co.)

Vertical, or stockade, type construction is offered by some kit log home companies. (Photo courtesy Bellaire Log Homes.)

Post-and-beam construction creates an open framework of timbers that can be filled with anything from stones to firewood-length cordwood. (Cordwood photo courtesy Robert L. Roy, Earthwood Building School.)

stall them over the corner logs. Anchor them to the corner logs with mortise and tenon joints or heavy spikes. Use half-lap joints for the attaching ends. Measure diagonally from corner to corner at the top of the corner logs to be sure that the building is square. Cut the upright filler logs and install them. Alternate the tapers of the logs so the walls will be even in appearance. Fasten each log to the sill and upper plate by toenailing with spikes. Install door and window framing. Note: If you don't use a spline between upright logs, you'll have to continually recaulk and reseal the vertical logs as they cure and shrink.

Cured, milled logs are best for vertical walls. Splines and caulking provide the weatherproofing. And interior panels offer eye relief from logs.

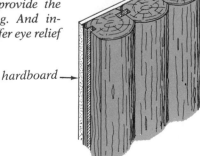

hardboard →

Post and beam

Post and beam, or timber-frame, construction, is not a technique for purists. It *is* used as a framework for various log styles such as *piece-en-piece*, slab wall, and cordwood or stackwall. Actually, once the posts and beams are installed, many different filler materials can be used between the framing members, including mortar and stones, mortar and logs, and horizontal (or vertical) filler logs.

Timber framing is an ancient art and a traditional building method in Europe. It was brought to America with the colonists and was popular until the "easier" method of stick construction, or balloon framing, developed. It is, however, regaining popularity.

There are some advantages to timber framing, particularly if you have trees on your property and have a way to saw them into timbers. Typically, timber-frame houses are constructed of hardwoods such as oak or walnut. But some softwoods, such as spruce and hemlock, are popular in New England states. The timbers can be sawed, hand hewed, or even planed.

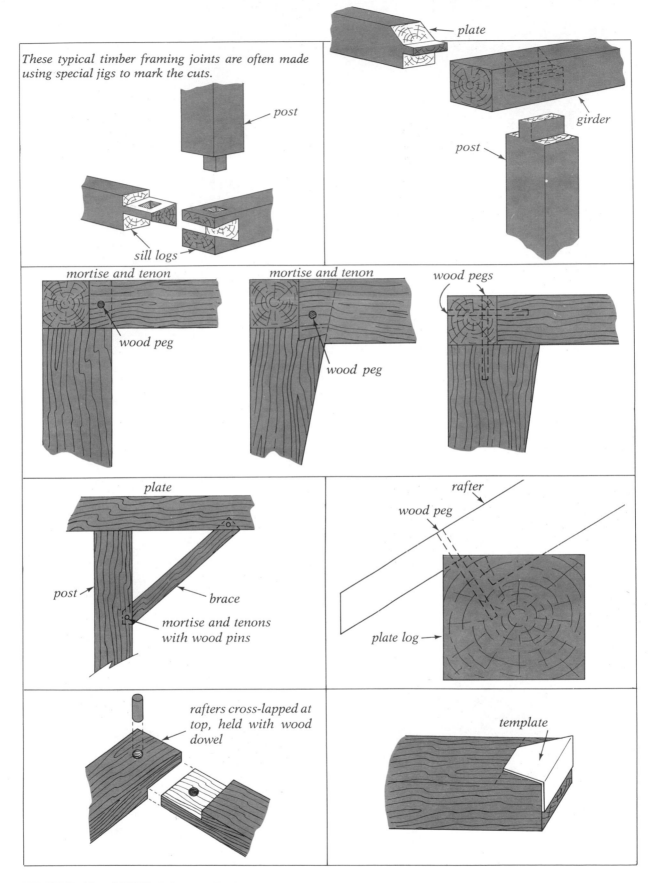

These typical timber framing joints are often made using special jigs to mark the cuts.

plate

post

girder

post

sill logs

mortise and tenon

wood peg

mortise and tenon

wood peg

wood pegs

plate

post

brace

mortise and tenons with wood pins

rafter

wood peg

plate log

rafters cross-lapped at top, held with wood dowel

template

Handsaws are used to make the precision cuts.

Large chisels remove the wood between the cuts.

Timber framing is really only a method of framing a house with large timbers, instead of small members such as 2×4s. The technique requires fewer pieces than standard construction and results in a long-lasting, beautiful structure that has its own ageless character. But the work is hard and slow. Timber framing purists insist on using elaborate mortise and tenon joints rather than simply nailing the pieces together.

Timber-frame builders, of course, can use modern tools. But purists insist on using as many of the old tools as possible, including various large chisels, corner chisels, large hammers, and even hand-turned boring machines. They also make up their own marking gauges.

Piece-en-piece

This venerable style of construction can still be seen in structures that were built over a century and a half ago in Canada. It was also popular with the original American colonists. Its main advantage is that you can use small, short logs. The main disadvantage is that the house can settle unevenly and usually doesn't have as neat an appearance as a standard log home.

In piece-en-piece timber framing, short horizontal logs fill between the vertical supports.

horizontal
filler logs

Mortises are cut using large chisels and a large brace and bit. Clean out the mortises with a good chisel.

Piece-en-piece is an old log home building style that dates back a century and a half. It's still popular today. (Photo courtesy Boyne Falls Log Homes.)

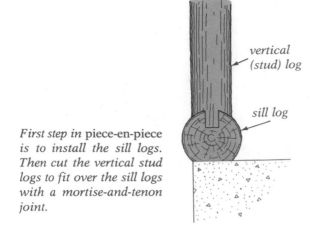

vertical
(stud) log

sill log

First step in piece-en-piece is to install the sill logs. Then cut the vertical stud logs to fit over the sill logs with a mortise-and-tenon joint.

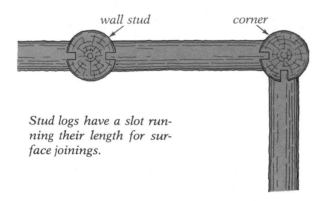

wall stud

corner

Stud logs have a slot running their length for surface joinings.

To mark stud tenons, mark quarter sections. Then measure from the center and snap chalk line.

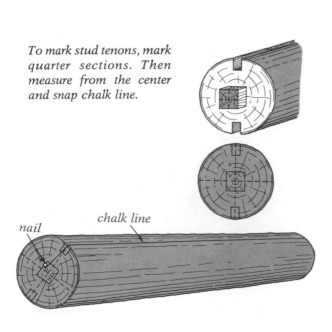

nail

chalk line

Piece-en-piece is actually a variation of timber-frame or post and beam construction. Square or round vertical members stand at each corner of the building, at doors, windows, and spaced along the walls. Long plate and sill beams tie vertical members together. Each of the vertical members is slotted and tongues are cut on short wall logs, which slide down in place between the vertical members.

One advantage of this type of construction is that because you work with smaller logs, it's a one- or two-person job. Another advantage is that by simply cutting a slot in a vertical member, you can add a wall or change its direction easily. The job is fairly easy to do piecemeal. Interior walls are easily attached, again by simply adding a notch. One disadvantage is that the large number of joints means there is more chance for air infiltration. Extra care must be taken to ensure that all joints are tightly constructed.

As in standard log construction, the first step is to build the foundation and install the sill logs. Then, cut vertical stud logs to the shape shown. They fit down over the sill log—a tenon fits in a mortise cut in the sill log. Check to see that the mortise and tenon joints fit properly, then take the studs down and cut the slots for holding filler logs.

One of the biggest problems of positioning tenons is finding the exact center of the log. By quartering it with chalk lines, as shown, this can be simplified. You can also use a jig. Once you have the vertical logs cut, position them on the sill log and brace them. Be sure they're plumb.

Cut the filler logs to length and shape their ends. Shown are various jigs for ensuring correct cuts. Also shown are various methods of joining the filler logs to the vertical logs.

When all the logs are properly cut, lower the filler logs between the verticals, making sure the joints are snug, but not so tight that they push the vertical logs out of alignment. Use a heavy hammer as needed to drive them firmly in place. The more time and effort spent in getting tight joints, the better the finished house will appear, and the more waterproof it will be. As you install the filler logs, alternate the tapers end to end.

Using sawed or hewed logs makes this kind of construction much easier. You can also cup

PART 4. EXTRAORDINARY LOG STYLES

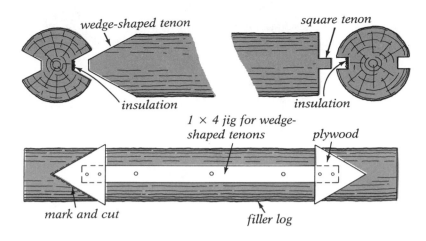

wedge-shaped tenon

square tenon

insulation

insulation

1 × 4 jig for wedge-shaped tenons

plywood

mark and cut

filler log

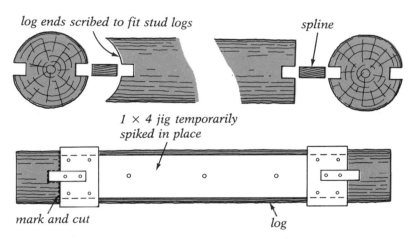

log ends scribed to fit stud logs

spline

1 × 4 jig temporarily spiked in place

mark and cut

log

the horizontal logs to provide tighter fitting joints, or use tongue-and-groove or spline fits. Caulk and insulate between the log joints as necessary. At the top of the center portion of the wall, you can add a cross-log support (as shown). This is notched and mortised to fit the top of the vertical logs.

Above, the filler logs are cut to length. Then jigs, like the two shown, are used to mark the tenons.

Below left, the filler logs can be cupped to provide a highly weathertight joint, or you can use splines.

A cross support is usually notched into the top of the vertical logs.

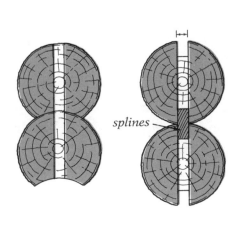

splines

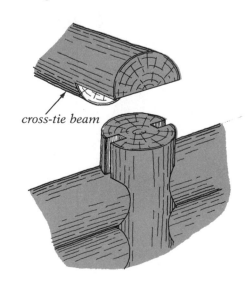

cross-tie beam

With the last filler log in place, you're ready to install the plate logs. These must be absolutely level to ensure that the rafters are level. Position these temporarily and raise or scribe to fit, particularly around the various cross logs.

Because the filler logs shrink and settle, there will be a gradually increasing gap between the top edge of the uppermost filler logs and the bottom of the plate logs. Cut grooves in the top filler logs and the bottom of the plate logs. Then you can fit a wide spline into the grooves, as shown. Hold this spline in place with nails. As the filler log settles, it will provide a weather stop.

You can use more than one plate log if necessary, but they must be joined with cross laps and pegged or spiked together solidly.

Slab walls

Timber-frame walls or those based on a variation of conventional construction can be covered with slabs. The slabs may be split logs or waste slabs from a sawmill. The structure is fast and economical to build, if you have a source of slabs. It isn't as sound nor as long

plate log

2 × 6
or 2 × 8
wide
spline

*gap allows
for settling*

top horizontal filler log

Above, the top plate log is fitted with a wide spline to allow for settling and shrinkage. Below, the plate logs must be notched properly before being installed.

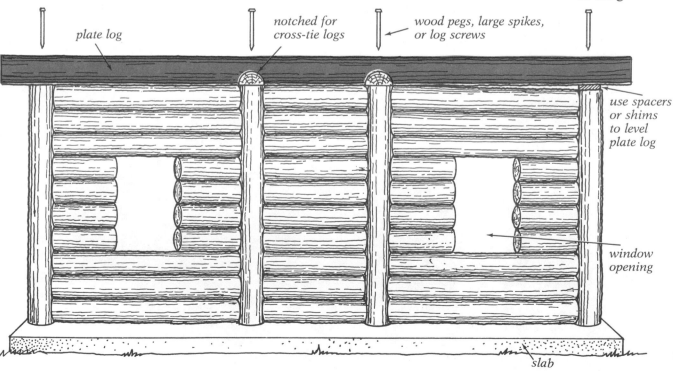

plate log

*notched for
cross-tie logs*

*wood pegs, large spikes,
or log screws*

*use spacers
or shims
to level
plate log*

*window
opening*

slab

PART 4. EXTRAORDINARY LOG STYLES

lasting as other log house designs and is not recommended unless you are building a simple hunting cabin in the woods.

Cordwood

There are several things that are appealing about this kind of construction. The two most inviting aspects are: It looks easy enough for anyone to do (it is); and it's inexpensive. You can build a 750-square foot log home for under $8,000, using only five to seven cords of wood. In addition, it may take only eight to 10 weekends to finish. You can simply use firewood-size pieces of wood—there's no hassle of finding, purchasing, or handling long, heavy logs. There are practically no design limits on this style of construction, either. You can build from standard house designs.

Stackwall, or cordwood, construction involves laying stove-wood size sticks or logs in a bed of mortar. Post and beam framing serves as the main support element, or the house can simply be freeform without additional framing, placing the masonry and wood upright timbers.

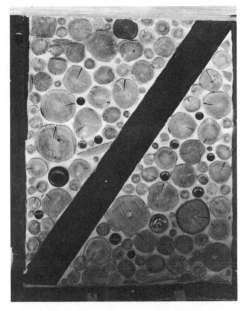

Building with cordwood is one of the most fascinating and unusual of log home construction techniques. It employs a combination of cordwood (firewood) logs and mortar, as well as mineral wool insulation.

The Log End Cave, built by Rob and Jaki Roy, shows how cordwood can be used to create the open end of an underground home. (Photo courtesy Earthwood Building School.)

Although the term cordwood implies a wooden wall, it is actually two thin masonry walls with an insulating gap between them. The blocks of wood, or bolts as they are called, do nothing more than set the overall width of the wall and stabilize the two masonry portions during the curing stage. In a typical 16-inch-thick wall, the width of the mortar webs is 4 inches. This provides a center space that is filled with insulating material of sawdust buffered with hydrated lime and strips of fiberglass cut from rolls or batts.

The double wall and heavy mass of cordwood construction has a unique way of storing energy and releasing it at night. Its insulation value can be equivalent to R-24. During the winter, the heating system of the house warms the interior of the structure. The inside masonry web absorbs the room heat and (because of the insulated gap in the center of the wall) stores it. When the temperature of the room drops, the stored energy radiates back into the room. Because very little thermal energy escapes to the outside, the structure is inexpensive to heat.

In the summer, the outer masonry web absorbs the exterior heat and then radiates it to the cooler night air, thus keeping the interior of the structure relatively cool.

The bolts of wood in the wall are flexible enough to allow for expansion differentials between the warm and the cool side of the wall. This prevents cracking, which can occur in a solid masonry wall. Probably the real beauty of this type of construction, though, is the way the walls can follow almost any line, giving you freedom to create your living space in almost any shape you want.

As mentioned, there are two other advantages to this type of construction. First, of course, is the availability of building materials. Second, and perhaps even more important to the average home-builder, is the relative lack of physical effort required. Lifting a 16-inch block of wood and a little mortar is a lot easier than hefting a 20-foot log around.

One problem faced by cordwood builders is building codes. Because the technique is not well known, you may have difficulty getting building permits in some areas.

Cordwood construction. The basic preparations are the same for cordwood housing as for conventional construction. The house

The novelty of building with cordwood is that you can escape the straight wall. Shown is the Earthwood Building School under construction.

PART 4.   EXTRAORDINARY LOG STYLES

Use jigs to mark tenons for cutting.

Step 1. *For cordwood construction, first position a row of mortar along with insulation strip.*

Step 2. *Bed the short logs across the mortar.*

Step 3. *Place more mortar and insulation around the logs as you go.*

can be built on a slab or over a crawl space but, because of the thick wall, the foundation and footing has to be that much wider and thicker.

Tools. Tools are few and simple. You'll need a means of mixing the mortar, either by hand in a wheelbarrow or mortar trough, or with a mixer. You will also need a bucket or mortarboard for carrying the mortar and a small and large mason's trowel. You should have a sanding block for rounding edges of the logs. Make a pointing tool from the end of a ½-inch bolt, or use an old kitchen knife. You'll also need a chain saw, wedges, and mauls for cutting and splitting the wood. You'll definitely need a good pair of rubber gloves to protect your hands as you work with the mortar.

Materials. Wood must be dried to 15 to 20 percent moisture content. Wood dried to that percentage is no longer green; it'll pick up some moisture during extremely wet weather, but dries back down to the 20 percent range during normal conditions. Green wood simply shrinks in size, leaving openings around it in the mortar, resulting in a drafty wall. This is an important thing to remember—a house constructed of green wood will become almost unlivable as the wood dries and shrinks. You can easily check the percentage of moisture in the wood with a small moisture meter.

Another advantage of cordwood construction is that there are several sources for wood. Almost any kind can be used, however, long-lasting woods such as cedar and oak are best.

Step 4. *After the mortar has somewhat set, it's tuck-pointed, or smoothed back, around the log ends.*

Students at the Earthwood Building School here construct an in-the-round building.

Cordwood can be stacked in place between post and beam construction. (Photo courtesy Earthwood Building School.)

You often find standing deadwood trees that are usable, but first determine if they're rotted. Even those that are completely bare of bark should be checked with the moisture meter and allowed to season properly. (When felling standing dead timber, take precautions against limbs falling on you.)

You can also recycle wood, such as old discarded utility poles, split rails, or even an old stack of firewood. Even logging slash can be used. Just cut the tops into the lengths you need for your wall.

You may have to cut your cordwood from green wood and cure it yourself. This means logging the wood, hauling it to the site, removing the bark, cutting it to the correct lengths, and splitting it. Then it should be stacked to be allowed to cure, which can take from one to as many as three years.

After debarking, the wood must be cut into exact lengths. Using a buzz saw powered by a tractor is the easiest method, but you can also do it with a chain saw. Use a small jig to gauge the lengths.

You should also split the larger pieces. There's an asthetic reason for this, but it mainly speeds the drying process. The varied shapes provide a more even mortar joint, as shown.

Naturally, you'll want to ensure that you have enough cordwood on hand to construct the building. If you run out, you'll have to wait for more logs to season. First determine the building perimeter, plus any interior walls if they're also to be constructed of cordwood. A cord of wood, which is $4 \times 4 \times 8$ feet long, will make up 96 square feet of wall space in a 16-inch-thick wall. It'll make up approximately 128 feet in a 12-inch-thick wall.

Mortar. This is basically standard masonry mortar mix. Most cordwood builders suggest that sawdust, such as that from a sawmill or chain saw, be added to the mortar mix. This prevents fast drying of the mortar. Use three parts sand, four parts sawdust, one part portland cement, and one part hydrated lime. If the mix is to be used in a load-bearing wall, use only three parts sawdust.

Construction. There are basically three different ways to use cordwood masonry: load-supporting curved walls; between post and

PART 4. EXTRAORDINARY LOG STYLES

beam framework; and between built-up corners of log ends.

Post and beam. This is the complicated, expensive, and time-consuming method, because you must first assemble the large beams. Then it's a matter of filling between the beams with the appropriate cordwood pieces and mortar. It has a traditional appearance and is probably the strongest of the construction types.

Built-up corners. This utilizes cordwood laid crosswise, much the same way you'd stack a firewood pile to create corners. Door and window frames are installed in place and the rest of the house wall is stacked and mortared.

Load-supporting curved walls. Merely stack the cordwood and masonry in a circle, placing door and window frames where needed in the masonry.

You could use strips of fiberglass insulation material, cut from batts, between the inner and outer webs of mortar, running it over, around, and through the logs as shown. Or put in insulation made from a mixture of hydrated lime and sawdust in an 8-inch-thick band, as shown.

One of the most important steps is pointing the mortar. This is done for several reasons. By pointing, or removing a bit of the mortar, you make the log ends protrude slightly. This also compacts the mortar joints between the logs and cuts down on the chances of mortar cracks. Of course, it makes a bit more decorative joint as well. You should keep the wall wet during the curing process to prevent excessive drying of the mortar.

Schools. Cordwood building is especially popular with first-time builders, and there are now two schools devoted to teaching the art. They are: The Indigenous Material Housing Institute, Upper Gagetown, N.B. Canada E0G 3E0 (home of Jack Henstridge, author of *Building the Cordwood Home*); and the Earthwood Building School, RR 1, Box 105, West Chazy, NY 12992. Earthwood is run by Rob and Jaki Roy. Rob Roy is the publisher of *Cordwood Masonry Houses*.

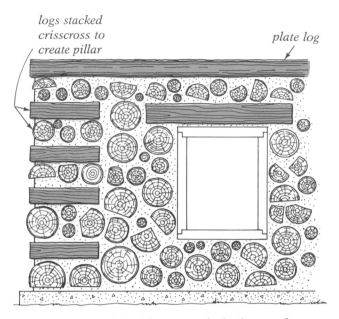

Corners in a cordwood house can be built up to function like pillars.

Some builders use sawdust for insulation. (Drawing by Indigenous Material Housing Institute.)

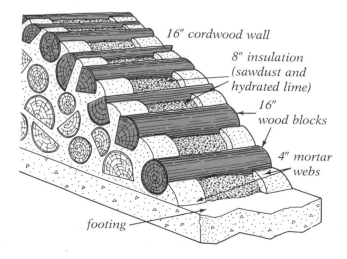

Part 5

HEAT AND UTILITIES

Chapter 19 **SOLAR HEATED LOG HOUSES**

Sun houses

Solar heating and log homes go hand in hand. Solar technology blended with the insulating potential of log construction creates an energy-saving combination. Almost any house can make use of solar energy, especially if it is sited properly and constructed to take advantage of the heat from the sun. However, the massiveness of log construction is perfect for effective trapping of energy from the sun.

Solar heating is a natural complement to a log home. Massive walls provide a natural heat sink that releases warmth after sundown. (Photo courtesy Justus Homes, Inc.)

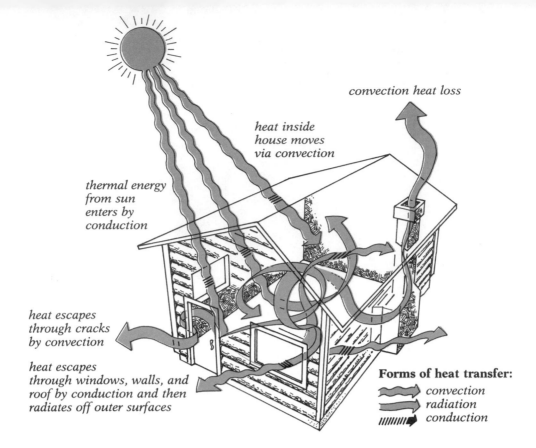

thermal energy from sun enters by conduction

heat inside house moves via convection

convection heat loss

heat escapes through cracks by convection

heat escapes through windows, walls, and roof by conduction and then radiates off outer surfaces

Forms of heat transfer:
convection
radiation
conduction

With an understanding of how heat is collected, stored, and released in a home, you can design a home to take advantage of passive solar principles.

Some designs provide more efficient use of energy, and because of the popularity of solar heating, most kit-built log home manufacturers offer solar home designs.

There are two different kinds of solar heating: passive and active. Passive solar heating can be built into the home and if done correctly it can supply an average of a third or more of your heating needs, depending on your latitude, the size of the house, the type of active heating system, and your life style. Real Log Homes, one of the leading kit manufacturers, conducted tests to determine the amount of energy savings and firewood needed to heat their log homes in various locations. Their homes are designed for wood heating and passive solar. They found in a Boston-area simulation that solar energy provided 31 percent of the season's heat with 2½ cords of wood doing the rest for a home of 1,875 square feet. Farther north, in McCloud, Minnesota, solar energy provided 22 percent of the season's heating needs and had to be supplemented by just 4½ cords of wood. Other heat loss calculations of log home performance at different

sites throughout the U.S. showed that 22 to 55 percent of heating needs could be met by passive solar design.

Passive solar

To understand how passive solar designs work you must first understand how heat is collected, stored, and moved through your home. Most matter on the earth such as rock, wood, and soil collects and then gives off heat from the sun. The walls and floors of your home accept heat in the form of sunshine and in turn radiate heat into a room. All solid materials allow internal heat movement (conduction) from molecule to molecule within the material. Naturally the denser the material, the faster the heat travels through it. Heat moves through concrete, for example, a lot faster than it does through wood. And it moves through denser woods much faster than through lighter woods.

Air carries heat by convection. As the air in a room warms, it expands, becoming lighter,

This is a typical passive solar style. Large windows face south, and a steep roof with few windows face north. (Photo courtesy Lincoln Logs Ltd.)

and so rises. Then, as the air gives off heat to surrounding cooler objects, it cools, contracts, and descends again. This forms convection current that helps move heat from room to room, within wall cavities, around wall studs, and between floors.

A home can be built to take advantage of these principles. Any passive solar design contains three elements: collection, storage, and distribution of heat.

One common idea is a two-story solarium with a huge stone fireplace at the back. (Wilderness Log Homes.)

CHAPTER 19. SOLAR HEATED LOG HOUSES

A passive solar design involves much more than just extra windows on the south side of a home. The collection portion of the system may consist of large south-facing windows, skylights, and sliding glass doors. Glazing should be insulated. Window space should be minimized on the usually sunless north side of the home, and to a lesser extent, on the east and west sides. The south side of the home should face within 30 degrees of true south to derive full solar benefit. From 10 a.m. to 2 p.m. the south side should be clear of obstructions rising more than 22 feet above the horizon.

Windbreaks can also make a big difference. An unobstructed north wind can have the same cooling effect on a building as someone blowing on a bowl of soup.

The storage system may consist of interior masses and/or slabs. Since the best heat-collecting mass is a concrete slab, foundation design is important. To have a concrete slab at ground level, you may have to forego having a basement. Instead, build an additional closet and storage space on the perimeter of main living floors. These spaces can replace lost basement space and can serve as air chambers or buffers between stored heat in the central part of the home and the cold outdoors. Closets and storage spaces, even stairways, on the out-

There are many active solar-heating designs that can be added on. (Photo courtesy Eureka Log Homes, Inc.)

PART 5. HEAT AND UTILITIES

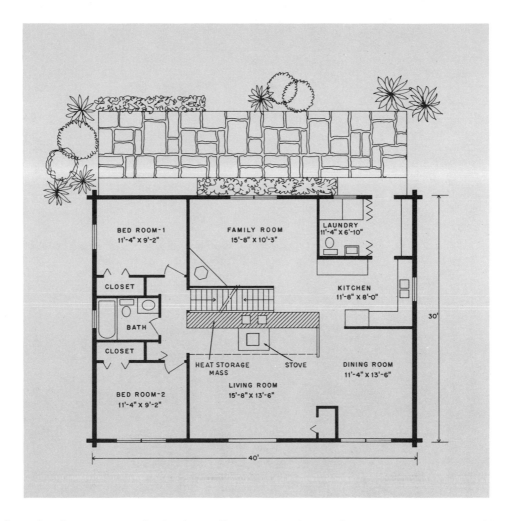

A typical floor plan for a passive solar log home illustrates the cluster of rooms around the central heat-storage mass backing the fireplace. (Photo courtesy Lincoln Logs Ltd.)

side perimeter of the living quarters are not traditional of course, but are worth getting used to. Then at night or during sunless periods, the storage masses reradiate the heat into the living spaces.

Other design differences? You'll want airlock entries that trap air between two doors and prevent heat loss when the doors are used. And you'll have no carpeting in the solar storage area. (The flooring in these areas must be a hard, conductive surface of masonry or tile. Carpets prevent heat from being stored.)

To get maximum solar heating advantages, there must be some fluctuation in the temperature of the home. To remove heat out of storage, room temperature must first drop, since the air temperature has to be lower than the temperature of the storage mass to allow the heat to escape. This can mean air temper-

atures as high as 76°F. during the day and as low as 62 at night. This may seem like a lot of fluctuation and tempt a family to cut the solar input during the day or go to nonsolar heat at night. However, this normally isn't necessary, since in a radiant heat distribution system, the cooler temperatures seem more comfortable than in homes without it.

The large south-facing windows lead to more sun glare than many families are used to and cause some families to pull the drapes, thereby stopping heat gain. Sun exposure means, too, that you'll need fade-resistant furniture fabrics.

Solar heated homes should have overhangs to shade windows from high-angle summer sun and insulating shades on windows and skylights. The overhangs should allow low-angle winter sun to enter.

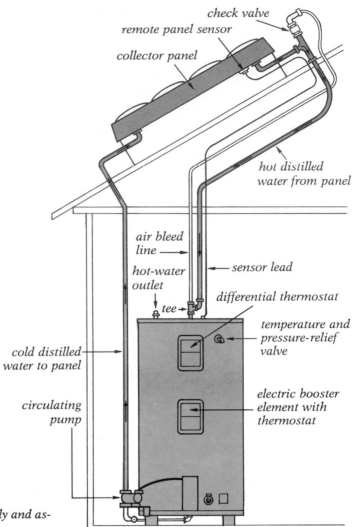

check valve

remote panel sensor

collector panel

hot distilled
water from panel

air bleed
line

sensor lead

hot-water
outlet

tee

differential thermostat

temperature and
pressure-relief
valve

cold distilled
water to panel

electric booster
element with
thermostat

circulating
pump

You can buy collector components separately and assemble your own system.

Active solar systems

Passive solar systems are fairly simple, but active solar heating and air conditioning systems can be complex and expensive to install, depending on the extent of the systems.

Hot water systems. Although a hot-water system can be complicated, the principle is simple. Water circulating between a hot water storage tank and collectors is heated to a high temperature by the sun. An electric heating element in the tank provides backup energy in times of heavy hot-water demand or during sunless periods. A heat pump can be installed to make use of the energy stored in the heated water. The heat is transmitted into the rooms through baseboard hot-water heating units.

There are numerous manufacturers of hot-water systems. In this chapter you'll see drawings of typical hot-water systems as well as one collector you can make on your own using components available from various sources.

PART 5. HEAT AND UTILITIES

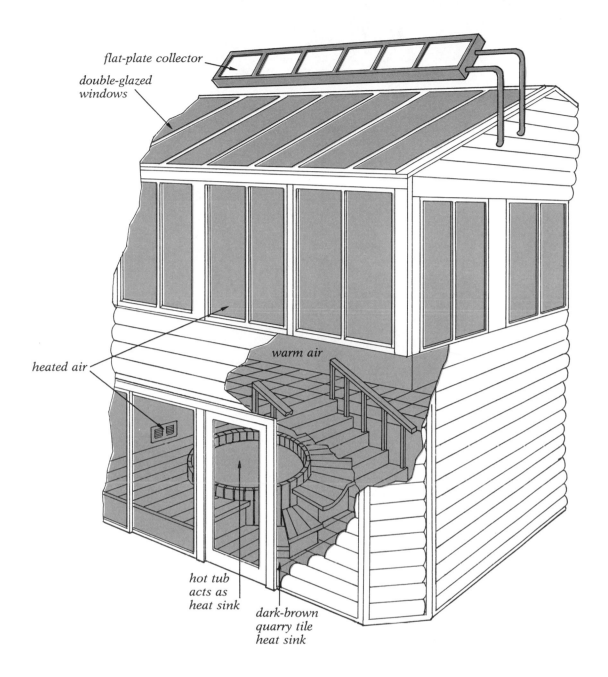

flat-plate collector

double-glazed windows

heated air

warm air

hot tub acts as heat sink

dark-brown quarry tile heat sink

More information, including sizing your system to your needs, as well as installation information, is available by writing to the sources mentioned in the Appendix.

Active air systems. An air solar system works on principles similar to that of a water-heated system. An air system has collectors on the roof that heat air. Air from the collectors is then brought down to a storage system, usually in the basement and consisting of a huge insulated box filled with rocks.

A larger greenhouse can house a hot tub year-round.

CHAPTER 19. SOLAR HEATED LOG HOUSES

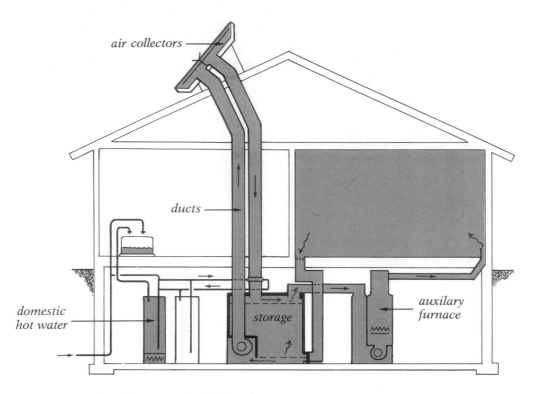

air collectors

ducts

domestic
hot water

storage

auxilary
furnace

*In many ways, an air solar system is similar to a
liquid system, employing fans rather than pumps.*

The air is forced by fans through the building,
and then recirculates through the collectors.
An auxiliary heating system such as a wood
stove or a furnace provides heat during sunless
periods. A heat pump can also be connected
to make further use of the heat and can power
a domestic hot-water system as well as provide hot-water heat for other areas of the house.
Additional information on various systems is
available from the sources listed in the Appendix.

Greenhouses

Greenhouses can be separate buildings or,
better yet, a portion of the house living space,
increasing the living space and adding passive
heating as well.

Greenhouses can be live-in sun rooms, fully
operating greenhouses, or a combination of the
two. By adding a water container in the greenhouse you can increase the heat retention of
the room. This can be done simply with water-
filled barrels painted black to absorb the heat,
or decoratively, with a fish tank, or with a
whirlpool spa.

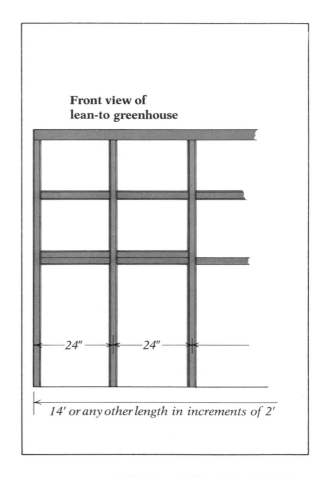

**Front view of
lean-to greenhouse**

24"   24"

14' or any other length in increments of 2'

These plans show how greenhouses can be made with dimension lumber and glass or plastic panels.

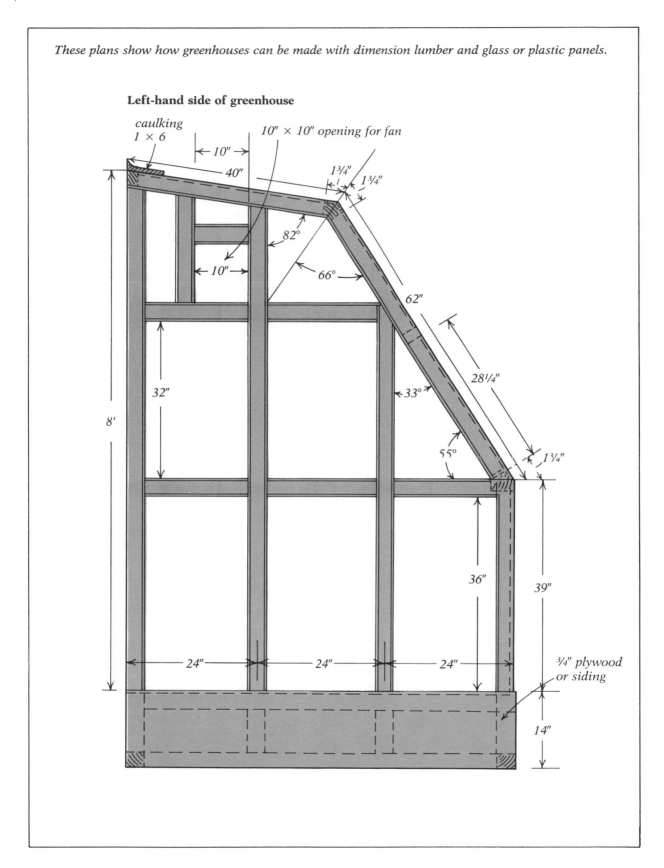

Left-hand side of greenhouse

caulking
1 × 6

10"

40"

10" × 10" opening for fan

1¾"

1¾"

82°

10"

66°

62"

33°

28¼"

55°

1¾"

32"

8'

36"

39"

¾" plywood
or siding

24"

24"

24"

14"

(Continued from page 301.)

Right-hand side of greenhouse

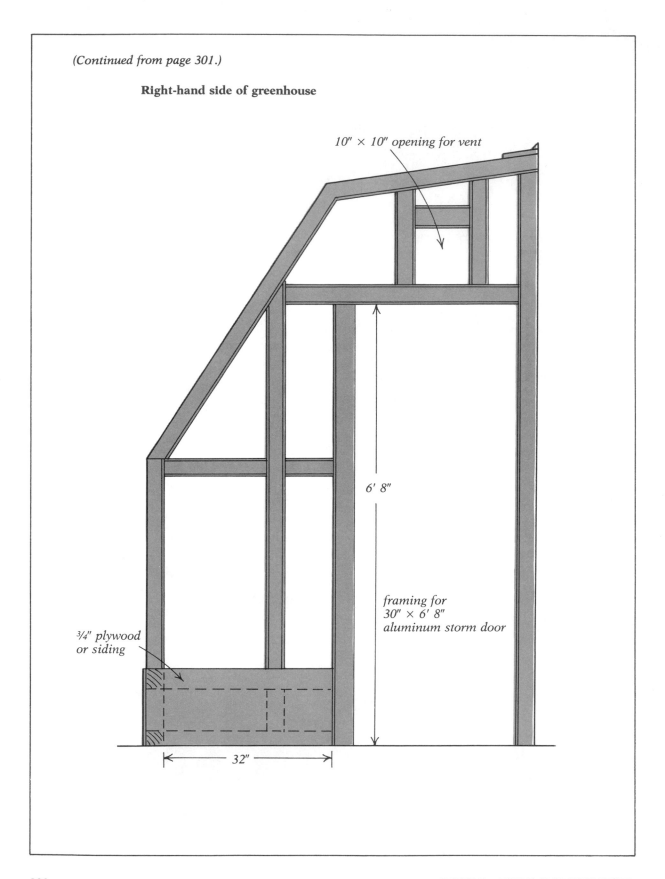

10″ × 10″ opening for vent

6′ 8″

*framing for
30″ × 6′ 8″
aluminum storm door*

*¾″ plywood
or siding*

32″

PART 5. HEAT AND UTILITIES

Chapter 20 WATER AND SEPTIC SYSTEMS

Pure water

An adequate supply of clean, safe water is as important today as it was to the first log home builders. Acquiring it, however, is quite a bit more complicated. Early settlers didn't have the worry about as many kinds of water pollution that plague both today's city and country dwellers. Today's homesteader must also take precautions against adding to the pollution problem with his own wastes. Urban or suburban dwellers, naturally, don't have much choice in these matters. They merely hook into the existing water and waste lines supplied by the municipality.

Today's rural and wilderness homesteaders have waste volume problems that early settlers didn't. We use much more water, mainly because of the huge water volume needed to flush wastes away—3½ to 5 gallons per flush, seven times a day per person.

Contractor-dug wells

The simplest and easiest, but most expensive, method of acquiring water is to have a well drilled by a professional. Using huge machines, these contractors can bore some wells in a matter of hours.

Before you hire a well-drilling contractor, check with your local agricultural extension office or Soil Conservation Service office to ascertain normal well depths, types of water, possible water contamination, and probable flow rates for the water table in your area. Although it's simple to have a well drilled,

Dug wells are still common in some parts of the country and may be feasible in your area. However, they're dangerous to dig and shore up. These shallow wells were quite often fitted with a simple hand pump.

you're not assured of obtaining a clean, healthful, and plentiful supply of water. Most fresh groundwater is located less than 200 foot deep. In fact, the average water-table depth in the U.S. is 50 feet, but that's average. You may have to drill several hundred feet. Although they supply a plentiful amount of water, deep wells are often contaminated with sulfur.

Again, county or local authorities can advise you on the feasibility of well drilling, its cost, and the possibility of an alternate water source. They may also be able to suggest reliable drilling contractors. Well-drilling rigs are monstrous machines. They need plenty of space for setup, and they can tear up a lot of ground if the soil is soft and wet. The sludge used for drilling the well must have a place to run off, too.

The possible depth of your new well will be of prime concern, because you'll be paying by the foot. Also the well must be cased with pipe to prevent it from caving in and to keep surface contamination out. Casing is sold by the installed foot. There are various kinds of casing. The amount needed for each well depends on local soil type and depth of bedrock. Make sure you allot plenty of money for the well, and make sure you have an adequate flow of water before the contractor quits. Having a contractor come back to dig a well deeper is extremely costly—many contractors won't even attempt it.

Many homeowners fail to give adequate consideration to the placement of deep wells. Water deep in the earth comes from a number of veins rather than from ground surface water soaking into the earth. Even so, the well must not be placed below a septic or sewage system or below any animal feed lots. It should be located at least 100 feet away and uphill from any possible contamination source because contaminants, including toxic chemicals, can sometimes seep into a well.

If the cost of drilling the well runs $10 per foot, a 250 foot well would cost $2,500 before you even install the casing, pump, and lines. Thus, a drilled well can be extremely expensive.

Advantages of a deep well? A deep well often provides a large flow rate and more storage depth, which means it usually can't be pumped dry as quickly as a shallow well. This may be

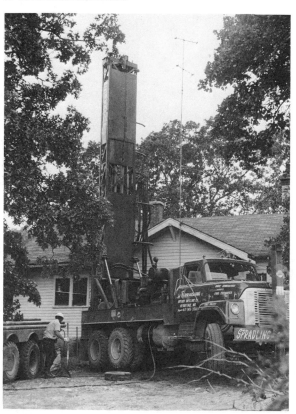

To early settlers, a water supply was little more than a sparkling spring. Today's log home owners living in rural areas usually depend on a well for their water. The simplest means of obtaining a well is to have one drilled by a contractor. The trucks used by well-drilling contractors must travel over access roads large enough to accommodate them.

304

important if you need large amounts of water for animals or irrigation.

Disadvantage of deep wells? One drawback is that most deep wells supply hard water and may be mineral laden, which can cause problems inside piping and plumbing. So a deep well may require that you add water softener to the total cost of the well.

Pumps

There are basically two kinds of pumps for deep wells. The choice depends on the depth of the water-entry point. Jet pumps at ground surface can lift water from depths of about 100 feet, but they're more effective with lesser lifts. With a jet pump, only the pipes are submerged in the well, not the pump itself.

Submersible pumps, which are more expensive than jet pumps, are installed at the bottom of the well, and can be used in wells of almost any depth. The size and price of the pump depends on the depth and gallons-per-minute requirement.

Another consideration is that the water must be brought into the house below frostline and into a storage tank. The top of the well is covered with a protective metal cap. You may want to build a well house over the top to protect the cap.

This drawing shows a drilled well—simple, but expensive. Jet pumps can be used on wells less than 100 feet deep.

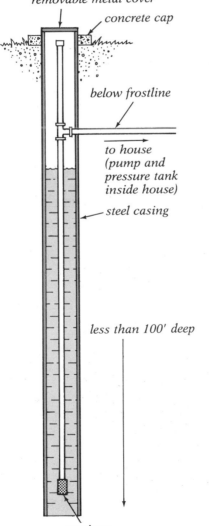

Submersible deep-well pumps are used on wells deeper than 100 feet.

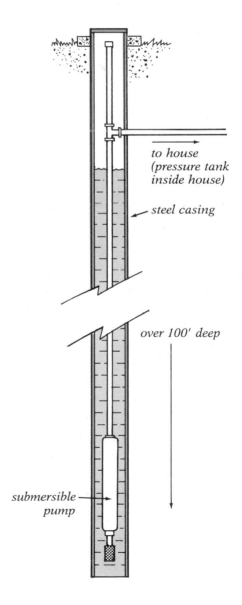

Driven wells

To drive a well, a heavy-duty pipe with a special point fastened to it is driven—by means of heavy weights—through the ground into sand veins bearing water. Naturally, this can't be done in areas of shallow bedrock. This is a fairly economical method of acquiring a well, but the depth of the well may be quite limited.

Wells can be driven as deep as 100 feet using a heavy hammer, or better yet a pile-driven weight, if there are no rocks in the soil. Most driven wells, however, can't be driven any deeper than 20 or 25 feet and then only if there are no rocks. As you go deeper, heavy-duty pipe lengths are screwed in place with special couplings. Before driving, the bottom length of pipe is fitted with a sharp-pointed end with screens in it through which water can enter.

In another method of driving a well an open-end pipe, much like a small well casing, is employed. In fact, this was the most common method of driving deep wells 20 years ago. A fairly large casing is driven by heavy weights

You might be able to drill your own well using special do-it-yourself drilling rigs like this one from Deeprock Manufacturing Co.

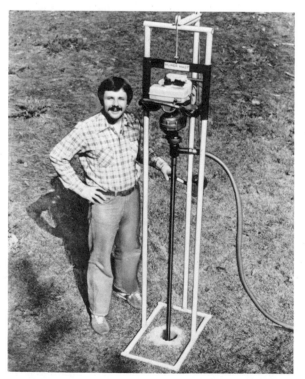

that are repeatedly lifted and dropped onto it. The soil forced up into the pipe is flushed out with water to create an open well.

Dug wells

Another alternative, though not a very appealing one for most people, is a hand-dug well. If you're building on an old farmstead, there may be an existing hand-dug well that is still usable. In almost all instances, hand-dug wells need to be cleaned out and checked for contamination. Anyway they're usually not consistent producers. Cleaning them out is extremely dangerous because they are normally laid up with rock or brick—no mortar—and cave-ins are common. Because dug wells are normally shallow and supply surface water, they can be contaminated easily.

It's still possible to dig wells by hand. After all, most early settlers dug them. The job, however, is hard and extremely dangerous. With care, a dug well could provide small amounts of water. But most won't keep up with today's water demand from washers, showers, and flush toilets. Another disadvantage in undertaking to dig a well is that there is no guarantee how deep you will have to dig before you reach a water supply.

Never enter any kind of well or cistern to clean it without first lowering a candle into it. If the candle goes out from lack of oxygen, open the top of the well or cistern to allow fresh air to enter fully before you enter. Have someone on hand at all times because there may still be dangerous fumes or an oxygen shortage.

Drilling your own well

In some parts of the country it's feasible to drill your own well with do-it-yourself equipment. Again, local soil experts can give you an indication of the practicality of do-it-yourself drilling in your area. Do-it-yourself can save you money over having a well-drilling contractor do the job for you. Once you've purchased the equipment you may decide to further offset costs by moonlighting for neighbors.

Cisterns

Cisterns are simply catchments for rainwater. They may range from a simple water barrel at the corner of the porch to an elaborate underground or aboveground storage tank connected to roof gutters. There are several forms of cisterns, but the most common is simply a buried underground tank. They're made by excavating to the size needed, lining with bricks, and then placing a concrete cover on top to provide a completely enclosed shell. The concrete cover usually has a manhole lid, and both are usually protected with a wooden cover.

Cisterns catch and hold rainwater. The most common cisterns use an underground concrete- or brick-lined storage tank. This is connected to a roof guttering system. A charcoal-filter system cleans water coming from the roof.

Some springs may be used for a water source, if they have been okayed by your state health department.

Cisterns are popular because they trap soft rainwater. In addition to providing excellent soft water, if fitted with an old-fashioned hand pump, they can also provide domestic water in the event of a power failure. Some employ electric pumps.

The roof gutters can be used to collect rainwater, which should run through a charcoal-filled filtering pipe before entering the cistern. The downspout may be fitted with a valve that can be used to direct rainwater into the cistern or to a diversion pipe that carries the rainwater away if the cistern is full. Because the first bit of rainwater from roof gutters includes dirt, leaves, debris, and bird droppings, most people allow the rain to wash the roof and flush the gutters before they go outside to open the downspout valve that allows water into the cistern.

Although cisterns don't allow debris and small critters to enter until the cisterns get older and develop cracks, they do need occasional cleaning, just like wells.

Another form of cistern is actually a water storage tank into which water flows from an uphill spring or is pumped by windmill from a spring below the house. Such a cistern can either be underground and made of concrete or aboveground and made of redwood.

Well house

If a portion of the well is exposed aboveground, build a well house over it. This can be constructed easily from cut-off ends from your log home or from extra concrete blocks.

Springs

Springs have been a common source of water for centuries. In some remote, back-country areas springs may still be useful. But don't count on finding a usable spring. A beautiful bubbling spring may hide several surprises. It may be a wet-weather spring, drying up completely during the summer months. Or it may have a generally inadequate flow rate. A spring must supply at least four to six gallons of water a minute to meet the needs of most homesteads. However, a storage tank or cistern can be constructed to help handle peak demands.

The biggest concern with springs, however, is pollution. This is especially likely in areas underlain with limestone, a common geological formation that creates springs. The sparkling-clear spring water bubbling out from under a pristine limestone bluff on your property may be connected to a sinkhole used as a garbage dump many miles away. Scientists have poured harmless dye into sinkholes and discovered the same dye emitted from home faucets at goodly distances away. Remember, for generations the prime dumping grounds for rural folks have been deep ravines, or in mountainous country, the prevalent sinkholes. Many industrial and agricultural firms have used sinkholes for burial of hazardous wastes

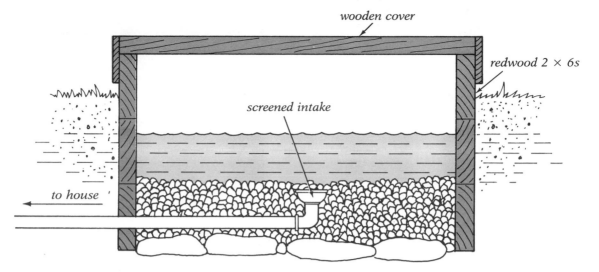

wooden cover

redwood 2 × 6s

screened intake

to house

A spring that seeps over a wide area should be enclosed in a large box.

and farmers have used them as collection areas for pesticide containers.

Of course, the contamination hazard has grown along with the expanding rural population. Here surface runoff gets into underground water sources and doesn't have a chance to purify naturally, as happens with a stream or even large lake. Instead the contamination may steadily increase.

In short, before considering any spring as a water source, have the water thoroughly tested.

Testing your water source

The need to have a water source tested is just as critical, whether you plan to tap a new source or use an existing one. A test should be performed on the water from a drilled well, too, every few years. A recent study in Iowa indicated, after a test of 18 percent of the rural farm wells, that over half were contaminated, usually with nitrates or bacteria. The people who'd been using the water for years all assumed that the water was just fine. Many mysterious health problems can be traced to contaminated well water, including "blue babies" or babies that develop cyanosis, a form of anemia. In these instances nitrite replaces oxygen in the blood. Also, coliform bacteria that cause flue-like infections are borne in animal wastes and are quite commonly found in

shallow dug wells. A common tip-off to the presence of coliform bacteria is that people who use the water continuously develop an immunity, but visitors usually become ill.

Check with your local county extension or Soil Conservation Service office. They can direct you to a water testing laboratory in your area. To ensure that the water you collect for testing is not contaminated by outside sources as you gather it, carefully follow the instructions that accompany the sample container supplied by the testing lab.

Developing a spring

The ideal spot for a spring is high above the location of your house, and nearby houses. This allows gravity flow of water into your house and positions your waste disposal systems downhill, some distance from the spring itself. If the gravity flow of water is constant, you can use a simple piping system. However, if the flow is small, you'll have to bury the pipeline from the spring below frost line to prevent freeze-ups in winter.

Ideally the storage tank should be above the house, between the house and spring. If it's 65 to 100 feet higher than the house, it'll provide enough head pressure at the faucets so no pump will be required. Wooden storage tanks can be used, but they tend to transmit

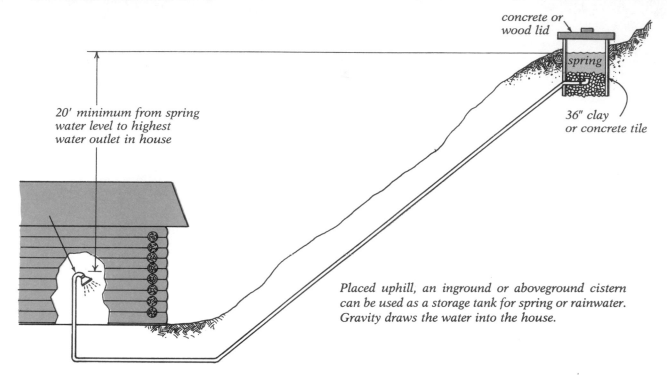

20' minimum from spring water level to highest water outlet in house

concrete or wood lid

spring

36" clay or concrete tile

Placed uphill, an inground or aboveground cistern can be used as a storage tank for spring or rainwater. Gravity draws the water into the house.

the sun's heat to the water. A buried concrete tank provides cooler water, but burial may not allow placement at the height needed for adequate head pressure.

If the spring is located below your house, you'll need some method of pumping the spring water uphill. Water can be pumped a short distance with a simple well pump. This can also be done with a wind-powered pump, or with a water ram if the spring has a good downhill flow at the spring source. However, pumping water any distance uphill from a spring can become expensive. The advantage of the windmill and water ram is that no electricity is required.

Regardless of which method you use, you'll have to close off the spring to prevent rainwater pollution and to prevent debris and small critters from getting in. You'll also have to cap it off and provide a filter inlet for the water that is to be pumped out. If the ground is soft, dig down around the spring area for several feet and then sink a couple of lengths of large concrete pipe. Cap the top and provide an outlet pipe. The cap should be constructed so you can lift it off as necessary for cleaning. The inlet for the pipe should be covered with a screen to prevent sand and debris from entering. You'll occasionally have to clean the screen.

If the spring seeps out over a wide area,

you can enclose it with a wooden box made of redwood 2 × 6s. Fill this with gravel and place a tight-fitting cover over it.

Sometimes a spring located on a hillside seeps from several different places. Join these sources together to acquire a better water flow. This can be done by digging ditches between the seeps and covering the ditches with concrete or wood covers.

If the spring seeps from solid rock there's not much you can do at the spring source. However, a collecting tank can be used. If you tamper with the rock you may inadvertently divert the spring water or stop its flow altogether.

A spring house

Old-timers took advantage of the cooling effects of clear, cold running water from a spring by building a structure over it to provide a place for cooling produce such as cheese and milk.

Using stream, lake, or pond water

In some parts of the country lakes, streams, and even man-made ponds can be used as water

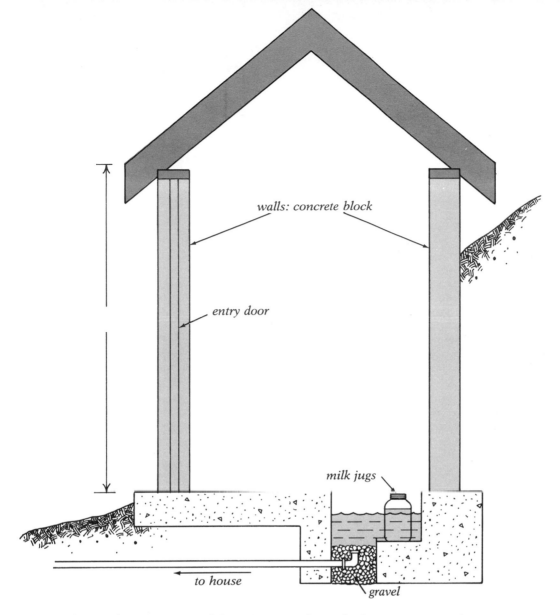

walls: concrete block

entry door

milk jugs

to house

gravel

In a spring house, the temperature of the spring water keeps the house interior cool.

sources. But the water should be treated and, in almost all cases, a home purifying system must be used. Purifiers are available from plumbing supply houses but are somewhat expensive and require a lot of maintenance.

Water disposal

Proper rural sewage disposal is becoming increasingly important. Many a fishing or hunting shack merely runs solid waste out onto the back hillside, but that shouldn't be condoned in even the most remote wilderness area. Waste disposal is governed by numerous state,

local, and municipal laws and regulations. Before you consider the kind of waste disposal system to use, check with local and state authorities as to what is allowed in your area and what permits are required. You may be required to pass inspection at various stages of construction, showing that the proper materials and methods are being used.

There are several waste disposal systems suitable for rural homes, including septic tank, sewage lagoon, or the new dry waste-disposal systems. Each has its advantages and disadvantages of cost, ease of installation, and ease of operation. Some may be limited by the geological formations and pollution in your area.

Septic tanks

A septic tank with distribution field is the most common means of sewage disposal in rural areas. This consists of a waste line running from the house to a tank buried underground. From this, a waste line runs to a series of drain tiles or pipes buried underground and covered with gravel or permeable material. Bacteria breaks down the solid wastes collected in the tank. The effluent runs into the distribution field where it percolates slowly into the soil.

To have a properly working septic system, you must have soil that readily absorbs the waste that leaches out through the effluent field. The best soil is a sandy loam. The worst kind is clay soil in which the wastes seal off the soil and so won't be absorbed. This causes buildups necessitating frequent cleaning of the tank and system. Without cleaning, the waste will accumulate until it's eventually forced to the surface, contaminating surrounding groundwater sources.

Soil that has chert streams is also hazard-

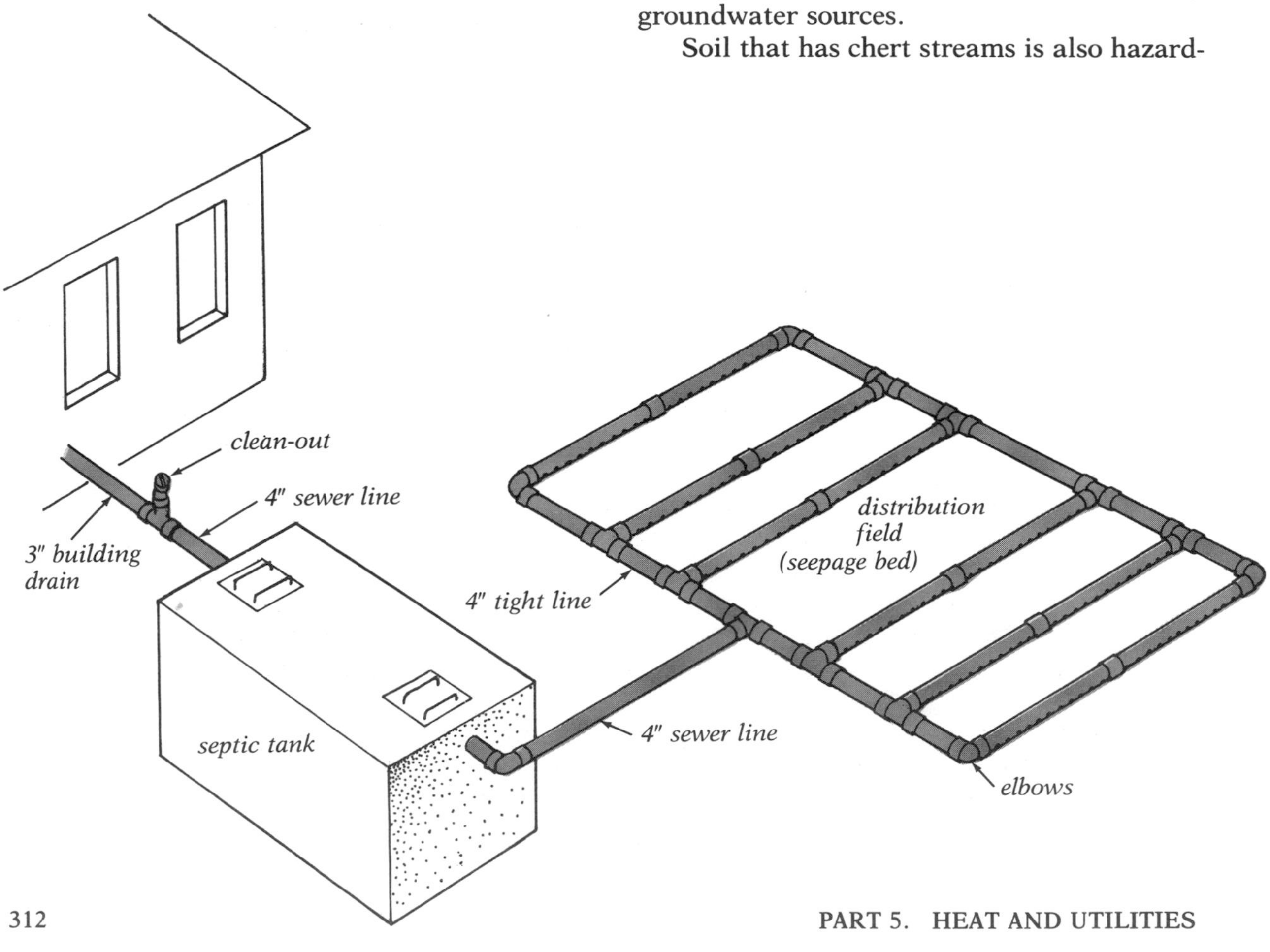

Of equal importance to a good supply of water is the proper disposal of wastes. A suburban log homeowner can simply hook into the existing sewer. But a rural builder has to create a proper disposal system according to local building codes, the kind of soil in his area, and other limiting factors. One of the most common waste disposal systems is the septic tank. This consists of a line running from the house to an underground tank. The tank collects the wastes and breaks down the solids through anaerobic action. Then the liquid effluent runs into a distribution field.

clean-out

4" sewer line

3" building drain

distribution field (seepage bed)

4" tight line

septic tank

4" sewer line

elbows

ous because the waste follows a chert stream to an underground water source. (Chert is a rock.) A serious hazard can result in areas where the water table is high enough to reach the effluent.

In planning your system, make a sketch, to scale, on your plot plan. Also make a sketch of the elevation to get an idea of the location of each element of the system in relation to one another. The septic tank should be at least 100 feet away from and somewhat lower than the water supply. Normally the tank is placed 12 to 15 feet from the house to make it easy to connect it to the house drain and sewer line. If the house has a basement, extending the distance to 20 feet helps alleviate the possibility of sewage seeping into the basement.

You may want a separate drain for the basement that does not have a bathroom. In fact, many builders like to keep the kitchen and other gray-water drains separate, filtering these for use in gardens. Storm drains can be discharged on the ground some distance from the house. But all toilet sewage must go through the septic tank to help ensure gradual decomposition to harmless matter.

In the past, all waste lines were made of cast iron or clay tile. Today most are made of easy-to-use plastic piping. Four-inch plastic pipe is adequate for most dwellings. It should be laid with a uniform slope of ¼-inch per foot. If there is a considerable difference in elevation, a steeper slope should be used at the start of the line and then shifted to a ¼-inch slope within 10 feet of the tank entrance to prevent the effluent from entering the tank at a high velocity, which can disturb the working action of bacteria.

A septic system is fairly easy to install. You can actually build the tank yourself. First, figure out what size will be needed. A 500 gallon tank is adequate for families of five to seven people. The tank size should be increased by 70 gallons for each additional person. A 500 gallon tank would normally be about 6 feet long by 3 feet wide and 5 feet deep. You can purchase a tank made of preformed concrete, metal, or even fiberglass. All you have to do then is dig the hole and bury the tank. In most instances, the septic tank top is about a foot below ground to facilitate construction as well as maintenance.

Here are details for a two-compartment, 100-gallon septic tank made of concrete.

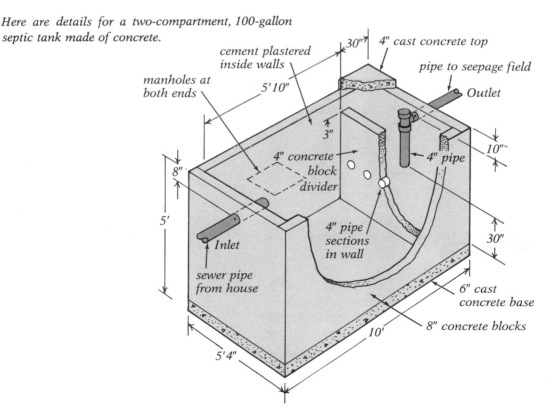

You can also pour a concrete septic tank. This is done using wooden forms, much as you'd pour a miniature basement. These forms can be constructed or sometimes rented. Achieving a waterproof concrete pour is extremely important when pouring a holding tank such as this. For a 6-foot tank, you'll need 2⅛ cubic yards of concrete. Make sure the ready mix has at least six sacks of cement per cubic yard of concrete. If you're mixing the concrete yourself, you will need 13½ sacks of cement, 1⅛ cubic yards of sand and 1½ cubic yards of gravel. Make sure you use an appropriate amount of water: no more than five gallons per sack of cement with average damp sand.

Constructing the disposal field.

Ceramic sewer tile has given way to perforated plastic pipe. The four-inch plastic pipe is easy to install. The pipes are fastened together using plastic cement and laid in trenches at least 18 inches wide and 24 inches deep. The pipe

should be laid on an even, smooth grade of four inches per 100 feet. Use a grade board to assure an even slope. If you are installing on a steep hillside, follow the contours of the hill. There are usually two or more laterals in the disposal field, and they are usually about 100-feet long. The laterals are joined by a distribution box.

To determine how large a distribution field you need, you should first take an absorption test. This is done by digging a hole 8 inches across and 18 to 24 inches deep in the area where you plan to locate the absorption system. That is, the hole depth should be about the same as the depth of the proposed piping. Wet down the sides of the hole, then fill it with about a foot of water. Allow the water to fall 6 inches and then measure the time required for the water to fall an additional six inches. Determine the average time needed for the water to fall one inch. This is done by dividing the total time by the number of inches the water level dropped. The average time needed for one inch of water to fall determines the

This is a form plan for a poured tank.

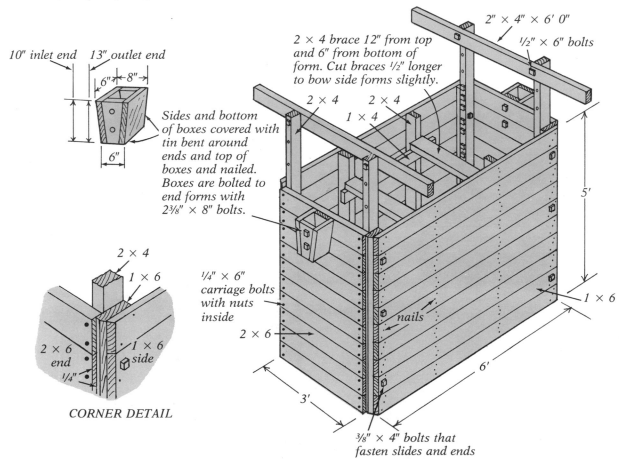

PART 5. HEAT AND UTILITIES

total feet needed for your disposal system.

After digging the trenches, set grade stakes and fill with crushed rock or gravel. After installing the plastic pipe, cover with black roofing paper and backfill with coarse gravel or stone, followed by an earth fill. (Note: If the soil is tight in your area, you can try to solve the problem by placing the absorption system on a sand bed.)

If your proposed drain field is exceptionally rocky, necessitating blasting, you might not be able to use septic-tank system at all.

Lagoon

If you have exceptionally tight subsoil and also sufficient land area and ground slope, you may be able to use an oxidation lagoon instead of a septic-tank system. Properly sited and constructed, a lagoon can be less costly than a septic system. A lagoon is simply a small pond with a uniform depth of three feet. The size of the pond should be determined by the amount of sewage that will enter it, though the lagoon should not have less than 900 square feet of surface. Of course, a lagoon must be located downhill from the home and in an inconspicuous place that, to prevent noticeable odors, is at least 100 feet from the dwelling. Since there will be overflow from the lagoon, plan so that overflow causes the least nuisance. Consider, too, the odor carrying effects of a prevailing wind.

Sewage is received into the lagoon through sewer pipe directly from the house and against the bottom center of the lagoon. Bacteria and oxygen break down the waste. The solids settle to the bottom and the effluent flows out.

The best equipment for lagoon construction is a bulldozer. However, a tractor with a bucket or scoop also works. It's important to create a bowl shape with a berm extending

The disposal field is as important as the tank. It's commonly constructed of perforated plastic pipe in a gravel bed. The pipe must be laid on a proper grade, without dips or sags. Wooden grade stakes ensure this.

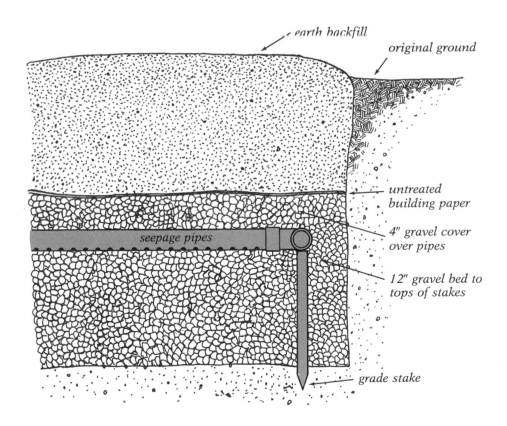

earth backfill

original ground

untreated building paper

seepage pipes

4" gravel cover over pipes

12" gravel bed to tops of stakes

grade stake

above surrounding ground surfaces so that surface water can't enter the lagoon and flush it out. The berm should be sloped gently and grassed-in to prevent erosion. And it should be wide enough for easy mowing. Here again, four-inch plastic pipe with solid solvent-sealed joints is the best choice for waste piping. But ensure there is no opening between the joints because tree roots are drawn to leakages and will grow into the sewer line, necessitating pipe removal and cleaning. Allow a ¼-inch slope per foot. A cleanout located about six inches above the water line helps in eventual maintenance. Anchor the outlet line to the bottom of the lagoon with a concrete slab. (Note: Before construction of a lagoon you must contact the state health board or clean water commission and ask for a permit.)

Privy

The privy, or outhouse, has been replaced by the flush toilet, even in rural areas. But it is still a common "facility" at vacation homes and during construction of log homes.

Local zoning and health departments have jurisdiction over privy construction and use. But these guidelines should be useful:

1. Privies should be at least 100 feet away and down grade from any water supply, although this may still allow seepage into the water supply.

2. Privies should be insect tight, employing screen wire at openings. Flies, mosquitoes, and other pests breed on waste and can carry many diseases.

3. On the other hand, privies should be well ventilated to dissipate odors. A cupful of wood ash or lime sprinkled over fresh stools helps prevent odors and break down the accumulations.

4. The seat holes should be lidded.

5. The privy and pit area should be sprayed with insecticide about once a month because privies are favored homes for spiders and thus were once a chief hazard area for spider bites.

6. Garbage or other waste should not be dumped into the privy.

7. Privies should be moved when the waste builds up to within 2 feet of the ground surface. Then fill clean soil over the waste.

Many folks can do with an old-fashioned privy. It does the job if you have no running water. These plans are for a two-holer.

Privy construction. The privy shown is a copy of a campground model. It rests on a poured reinforced concrete pad constructed in ring fashion, with a hole in the middle. Anchor bolts in the concrete ring allow removal of the privy, and the ring can be moved for re-use too.

Framing is 2 × 4s. First step is to lay out the two uprights and each side sill plate and nail them. Cut the tops of the uprights to the angle shown. Cut the angled top pieces now as well and anchor them in place either with metal plates or by toenailing. The sheathing will help hold them securely. Before cutting and fitting the 2 × 4 cross braces, ensure that the sides are square. Hold the cross braces with wooden clamps and mark where they cross. Then cut a cross-lap joint.

Once the side frames are assembled, stand them in position and cut the bottom sill plates, front and back, and fasten them to the side sill plates with anchor plates. Nail the top plates across to tie the two sides together. Cut and nail the center upright for the front as well as the two braces; then cut and nail the back diagonal bracing. Note: Install center 2 × 4 below the seat front and the edge of the rear portion of the floor. Then frame-in the seat support.

For the seat board, enlarge the squared drawing shown and cut to size. Or you can use a lidded commercial toilet seat. Fit the seat board before marking cutouts for side braces. Cut a hole for the vent pipe. Then install the seat front, flooring, and seat board.

Cut and install the rafters, toenailing them into the two top plates. Note: The outside rafters fit flush with the outside framing. Note: For ventilation and light, leave areas between the rafters open, front and back. Nail the facia boards and sheathing in place. If you use asphalt shingles or asphalt paper for roofing, employ ⅝- or ¾-inch exterior plywood sheathing. Or use corrugated reinforced fiberglass panels, which provide a great deal more light. In this case, nail 1 × 4 sheathing boards across the rafters to provide a nailing surface. Then seal all edges with special corrugated closures.

PART 5. HEAT AND UTILITIES

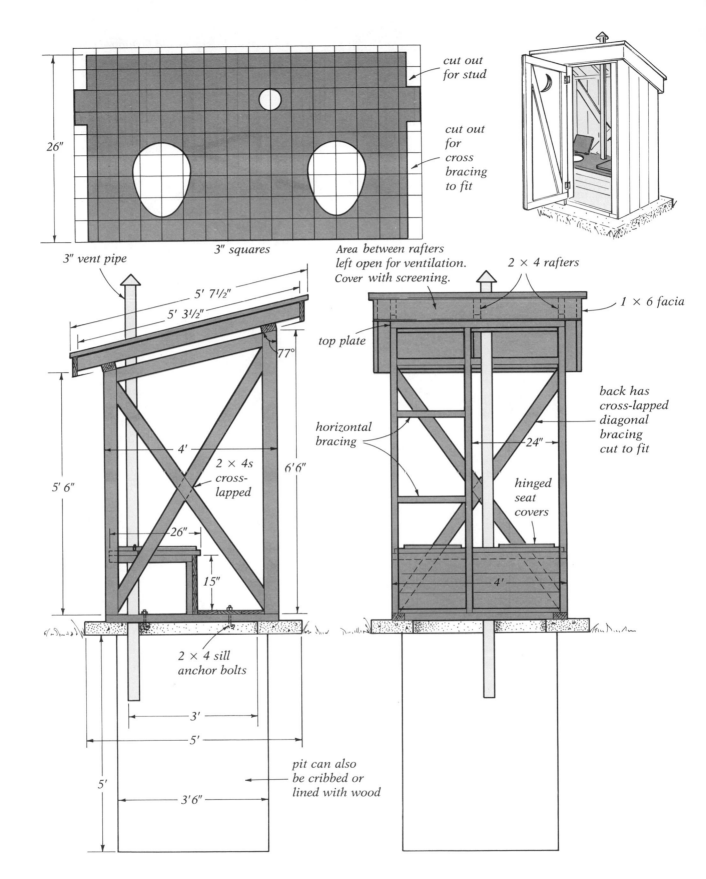

cut out for stud

cut out for cross bracing to fit

26"

3" squares

3" vent pipe

5' 7½"

5' 3½"

Area between rafters left open for ventilation. Cover with screening.

2 × 4 rafters

1 × 6 facia

top plate

77°

4'

2 × 4s cross-lapped

6'6"

5' 6"

horizontal bracing

back has cross-lapped diagonal bracing cut to fit

24"

26"

15"

hinged seat covers

4'

2 × 4 sill anchor bolts

3'

5'

pit can also be cribbed or lined with wood

5'

3'6"

Composting (waterless) toilets are also an alternative method of waste disposal. They're a completely self-contained toilet system that needs no water, chemicals, or plumbing for year-round family use. There are several styles and models of composters, ranging from small units that can be used for vacation homes to large-family units. (Drawing courtesy of Clivus Multrum USA, Inc.)

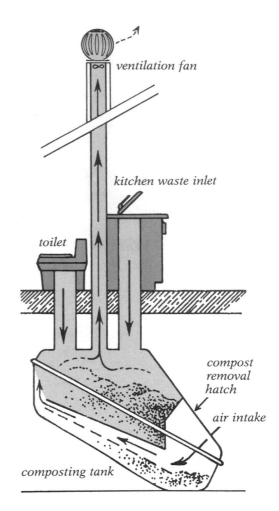

The vent pipe can be tin or plastic. Caulk it well where it protrudes through the roof.

For the inside of the door, use 1 × 4 framing. Of course, you will want to install a lock inside as well as a latch outside. A screen door spring will keep the door closed.

Then position the concrete ring over the pit. Bore holes in sill plates to fit over the pad's anchor bolts. Then install the privy over the bolts and fasten with washers and nuts.

Now, for the last item: Where did you put the last Montgomery Ward catalog?

Composting toilets

In recent years technology has made composting toilets practical alternatives to water-powered waste-disposal systems. There are several kinds on the market. All work on the principle of composting by evaporation of liquids and bacterial breakdown of wastes at warm temperatures. Solid wastes are composted into humus which can then be used as a soil conditioner.

Small composting-toilet units require a heater to speed up the composting and these units must be emptied fairly frequently. Larger units have large basement composting bins and need to be emptied less often.

Regardless of size, composting toilets can be good-looking home additions that are completely self-contained and emit no odors inside the house. They use no chemicals and do not discharge pollutants, and they can save over 40,000 gallons of water a year in the average

home. Anything organic from human wastes to grass clippings, laundry lint to paper towels, can be converted to fertile soil in these units. As the waste decomposes, it is reduced in volume by 90 percent. The principal by-products of the composting system—water vapor and carbon dioxide—are usually drawn through ventilation systems out through roof stacks.

The frequency of removal of composted materials depends on the size of the unit. The larger, in-basement units, work for several years before removal of compost is necessary. Then the unit delivers about 1½ cubic feet of compost per person per year. The only disadvantage to these units is their initial cost, but compared to a complete septic system, plus the continued cost of water to run it, they can soon more than pay for themselves. With these systems, most homes can make use of a separate gray-water system for the kitchen, bath water, and laundry.

Chapter 21 **PLUMBING**

Plumbing systems for a log home are not much different from those for a house of dimensioned lumber. But there are two important differences. The first is that the pipes must be installed so that settling and shrinkage of the logs does not cause damage to the piping. The second is, because it's difficult to run piping through log walls, other routing must be provided—such as through floors, ceilings, and interior walls. One solution is to incorporate as much of the plumbing as possible in a central core. This may mean locating the bathroom and kitchen so that they are backed against one another with a small framed-in service closet between. On a two-story house this design would be continued overhead to the upstairs bathroom. Likewise, a house with a basement should have the water supply, drain waste, and water heater close to this central core to cut down on pipe.

Codes

A plumbing system, in concept, is simple: It's a means of piping water to and through the house and of removing waste from the house. Most handy people could install a plumbing system. But even with its simplicity, a plumbing system can become a hazard if improperly installed or if employing the wrong types and sizes of hardware. For this reason plumbing installation and materials are tightly regulated. In almost all instances (except for some wilderness areas) you will need a plumbing permit before you begin installing the system. In some areas only licensed technicians are allowed to do plumbing work. Check with your local housing or building authorities about permits and inspections. Rules and regulations vary considerably from one area to another, and the red tape in some areas can be frustrating.

Planning

Draw a working diagram of your intended plumbing layout. Be sure to show all appliances that will be connected to the system so you can determine exactly where any openings must be cut in the walls, floors, or ceilings for pipes or drains. If you work from a published blueprint, or if you are buying a kit log home, you should have a working diagram for your plumbing installation. Follow it for the steps, locations, materials, and procedures suggested. If you're building your log home from scratch, make up your own plumbing floor plan and elevation sketch. This can help you develop a supply list with the number of elbows, length of various pipes, fittings, etc.

The best plumbing design for a log home locates most piping in a central core, with the bathroom and kitchen backed up against each other. A small, framed-in service closet should go between them. Five principal options are shown here.

If you're building your log home from scratch, you can make your own plumbing floor plans like those below.

A. Bath and kitchen back to back

exterior log wall

1½" waste branches
3" soil vent
lav
sink
tub
toilet
automatic washer
SIDE VIEW

bathroom group	6
kitchen sink	2
auto. washer	2
fixture units	10

B. Bath with kitchen remoted

exterior log wall

3" roof increaser
1½" waste branches
3" soil vent
lav
sink
tub
toilet
1½" waste & vent

waste vent hole cut in log wall

bathroom group	6
kitchen sink	2
fixture units	8

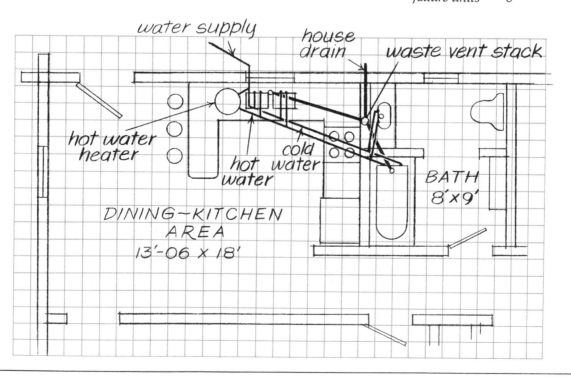

water supply
house drain
waste vent stack
hot water heater
hot water
cold water
BATH 8'x9'
DINING~KITCHEN AREA 13'-06 X 18'

C. Half bath with kitchen remoted

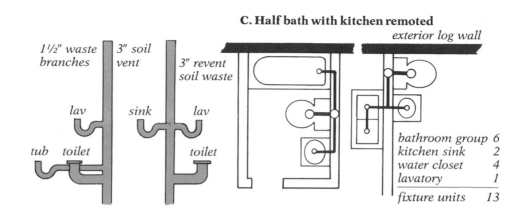

1½" waste branches   3" soil vent   3" revent soil waste

lav   sink   lav

tub   toilet   toilet

exterior log wall

bathroom group	6
kitchen sink	2
water closet	4
lavatory	1
fixture units	13

D. Bath up and down

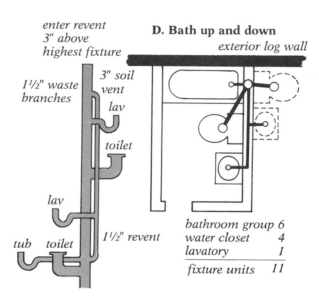

enter revent 3" above highest fixture

1½" waste branches

3" soil vent

lav

toilet

lav

tub   toilet   1½" revent

exterior log wall

bathroom group	6
water closet	4
lavatory	1
fixture units	11

E. Slab job

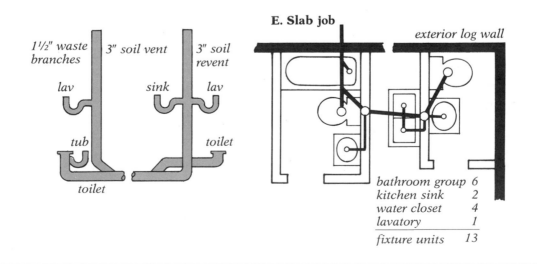

1½" waste branches   3" soil vent   3" soil revent

lav   sink   lav

tub   toilet

toilet

exterior log wall

bathroom group	6
kitchen sink	2
water closet	4
lavatory	1
fixture units	13

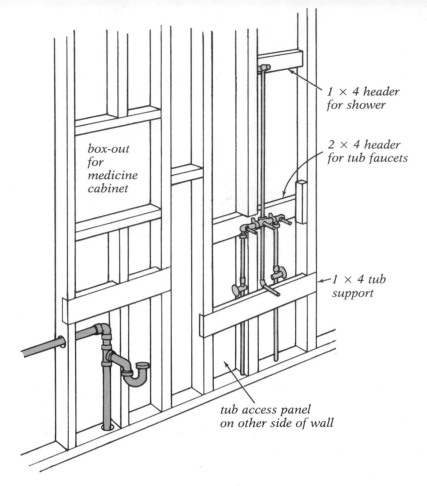

This is a typical rough-in plan for a bathroom fixture.

box-out
for
medicine
cabinet

1 × 4 header
for shower

2 × 4 header
for tub faucets

1 × 4 tub
support

tub access panel
on other side of wall

Do the plumbing in two stages, including rough-in during house construction, followed by a second stage: finishing, with installation of fixtures. (Photo courtesy Genova, Inc.)

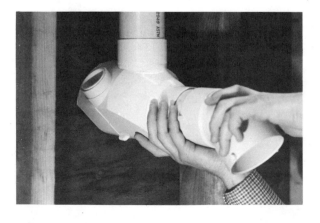

In most instances, plumbing installations take place in two distinct phases: (1) rough-in, or installation of the plumbing through the floors and walls, and (2) finish, which includes installation of fixtures, after wall and floor coverings are installed and after the interior is finished. In the central-core scheme of log home construction, these stages have a tendency to run together, more than for a house of dimensioned lumber. However, there still is a waiting period for the installation of tubs and other fixtures. For this reason, open pipes must absolutely be closed off temporarily during construction to keep dirt and debris out.

The plumbing system should be laid out as a whole. This is done during the early stages of rough construction. Using a felt-tipped marker or a crayon on floors and walls, mark the exact location of the hot and cold supply lines for all fixtures. Also mark the drain and vent hole locations. Locate the hot-water tank as close to the supply main as possible. Then measure and make a list of the number, size, and lengths of pipes necessary, as well as fittings needed.

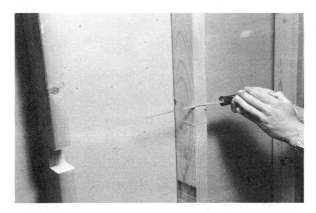

A good plumbing job has neat workmanship in the places not easily seen. Carefully cut studs for horizontal runs. (Photo courtesy Genova, Inc.)

After sawing the stud, chisel out the notch. (Photo courtesy Genova, Inc.)

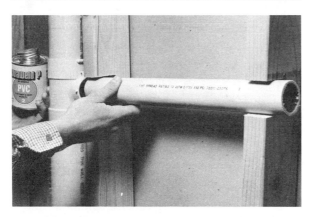

Remove just enough material to allow space for the plumbing, not so much that it weakens or damages the stud. (Photo courtesy Genova, Inc.)

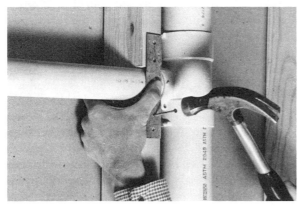

Use metal strapping to secure the plumbing and to help prevent someone's accidentally driving a nail into the pipe after the wall is closed in. (Photo courtesy Genova, Inc.)

CHAPTER 21. PLUMBING

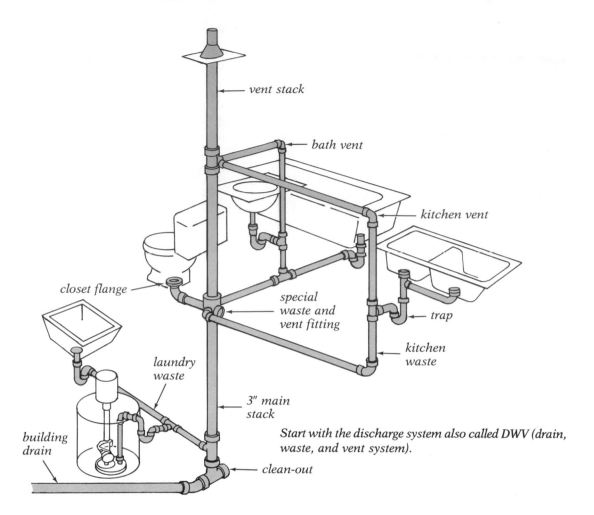

vent stack

bath vent

kitchen vent

closet flange

special
waste and
vent fitting

trap

kitchen
waste

laundry
waste

3" main
stack

building
drain

*Start with the discharge system also called DWV (drain,
waste, and vent system).*

clean-out

Discharge systems

Since the drainage system is somewhat more complicated and not as adaptable as the supply system, it's usually laid out and roughed-in first. Then the supply system is installed to accommodate the drainage system locations.

Good design and proper materials are extremely important in a waste discharge system. The system must discharge wastes properly to prevent noxious and dangerous fumes from coming back into the house. The system consists of a central drain into which various branch drains run. Since the system works on gravity alone, all pipes must be as vertical as possible or with an adequate downward pitch. Waste pipes are also larger than those used for supply lines. The system must have proper air outlets to vent waste gases and proper traps to prevent odors and gases from backing up into the house.

Before attempting to do any plumbing yourself, you should read the code that applies in your area and obtain some complete do-it-yourself plumbing guidebooks.

Materials

There are several materials used for waste drainage systems. When you purchase materials for these systems, specify that they will be used for a waste discharge system. Plastic, copper, and cast iron are the materials commonly used. Cast iron was the most widely used material until recently. Plastic pipe for waste discharge has been increasingly popular. Copper is expensive because of the large-diameter pipes needed. Also, copper must be soldered. Cast iron, although quite common because it is more economical, is complicated to assemble. And large, expensive tools are needed. Rigid plastic pipe is so popular that

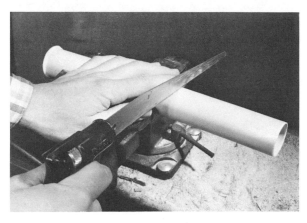

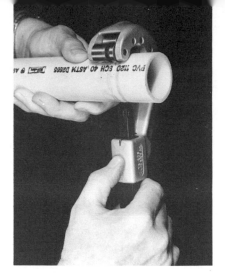

Plastic is easy to use. First measure length and then cut with a hacksaw. (Photo courtesy Genova, Inc.)

Rigid plastic pipes may be cut with a large plastic-cutting wheel in an ordinary pipe cutter. (Photo courtesy Genova, Inc.)

Remove burrs on the end of pipe with a file or knife, or with sandpaper. Lightly touch up the outside edge.

Check the fit before you weld. Mark both fitting and pipe so you can align them properly.

Wipe pipe with clean rag and cleaner. Follow immediately with solvent cement liberally on pipe and sparingly on socket. Push pipe into socket with slight twisting motion.

even mail-order catalogs carry complete selections. All you need do is determine the lengths of pipe needed. But the real reason for the popularity of plastic is probably the ease with which it can be installed. Almost anyone with a hacksaw, file, and bottle of adhesive can install a plastic waste discharge system.

Wipe the pipe with a clean rag and cleaner, then follow immediately with solvent cement. Apply cement liberally on the pipe and sparingly on the socket.

Quickly push the pipe into the socket with a slight twisting motion until it bottoms. Adjust the alignment of the fitting immediately—before the solvent sets up.

CHAPTER 21. PLUMBING

325

All drain pipes, including the house sewer, need clean-outs. This one is made from a 4-inch, long-sweep PVC sewer Y adapted to the 3-inch house drainage system 5 feet beyond the foundation. (Photo by Genova, Inc.)

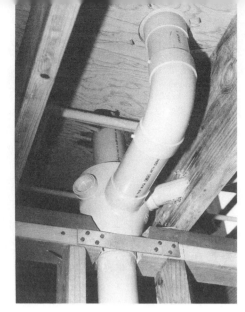

Anchor the soil stack in place. (Photo courtesy Genova, Inc.)

Sizes

Again, codes stringently regulate the sizes of the pipe that can be used. Listed below are the common plastic pipe sizes for homes:

House drain	3 to 4 inches
Soil stack	3 to 4 inches
Kitchen drains	2 inches
Toilet	3 to 4 inches
Bathtubs, showers, sinks	1½ inches

Regardless of the materials you use, the basic steps are the same. Determine the position of each fixture and mark locations of the waste and supply lines following manufacturer directions. Mark these carefully using a felt-tipped pen or a large crayon. Carefully cut the holes for the fixtures, ensuring that you don't weaken any bracing, floors, or walls excessively or unnecessarily. Keep all holes as neat and small as possible to prevent rodents from entering. With the system laid out and holes cut, you can then measure exactly the amount of materials you will need.

The installation of the waste system starts with the building drain. As shown, there are various ways of installing this building drain. From the top bathroom (second floor, if a two story house) make a closet and soil-stack connection as shown, fitting it properly. Drop a plumb bob from the center of the soil stack opening directly to the basement through the lower floors. Then run piping between the house sewer and building to this location, and complete the lower soil stack building-drain connection as shown. Include the cleanout. Connect to the underground building drain, and anchor this assembly in place with pipe strapping.

It's a good idea to assemble as much of the section as you can before permanent installation, making a dry-run fitting to be sure all pipes are of the correct length and at the right angle, and that you have the fittings turned properly. Assemble the section on the floor and position it, anchoring with braces and pipe strapping. The building drain, or that portion that runs from the bottom of the soil stack to the house sewer, must have at least a ¼-inch-per-foot slope. There must also be a Y-branch with a sanitary cleanout plug installed at the bottom of the soil stack as well. The soil stack should also be straight up and down. You can add the basement drain at this time. If you have a crawl space, run the soil stack from the sanitary Y to the house sewer as shown, anchoring the run with pipe hangers to the floor above.

Continue up with the soil stack until you reach the location of the first venting pipes. Join these to the soil stack using a sanitary Tee. Place this Tee on the soil stack, and then add additional lengths of soil stack to connect to the sanitary Tee for the toilet of the upper or second floor. Provide connections for other branch lines.

PART 5.   HEAT AND UTILITIES

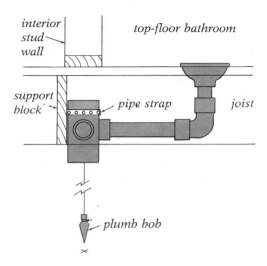

interior stud wall

top-floor bathroom

support block

pipe strap

joist

plumb bob

Starting at the top bathroom, make up a closet and soil stack connection. Drop a plumb bob from the center of the soil stack down through the floors to mark the building drain connection.

These drawings show building drain systems for basements and crawl spaces.

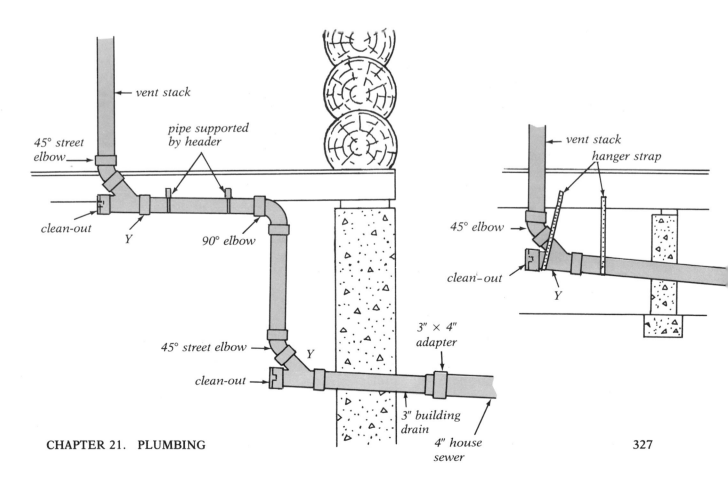

vent stack

pipe supported by header

45° street elbow

clean-out

Y

90° elbow

45° street elbow

clean-out

Y

3" × 4" adapter

3" building drain

4" house sewer

vent stack

hanger strap

45° elbow

clean-out

Y

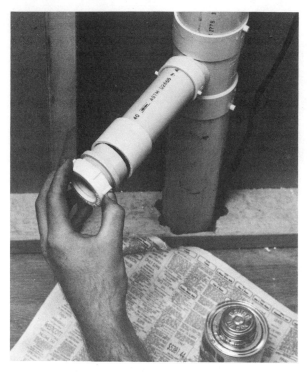

Join other branch lines to the soil stack. (Photo courtesy Genova, Inc.)

Extend the soil stack through the roof. Leave a height of at least a foot when you cut it off. Photo inset, fit purchased flashing into shingles. Make sure there are no gaps. (Photo courtesy Genova, Inc.)

Once you have reached the upper end of the last branch or vent lines, continue the soil stack up to the roof. The pipe should extend at least six inches above the roof and be fitted with flashing and shingled. A tighter fit can be made if the rough-in plumbing is done before the roof is shingled.

Once the soil-stack assembly is in place, measure the branch lines, then cut and fit. Fit them between the fixture drains and the sanitary openings in the soil stack. Run these as necessary under floors, between floors, or inside walls, but avoid sharp bends and be sure you maintain the necessary ¼-inch-per-foot drop from the fixture drain to the soil-stack joint. Of course, each fixture should be fitted with a trap.

You may also need to supply a second, or waste stack, in addition to the soil stack, especially if some fixtures such as a dishwasher or extra shower are too far away from the soil stack to allow for easy routing of the branch lines.

The waste discharge system must be fitted with a proper venting system to prevent siphoning. The branch waste line slopes from the fixture down towards the soil pipe, but the end of the branch line at the fixture must always be higher than the end of the fixture trap and connected to a vent line (at that location) that is pitched up at an angle to connect into the soil stack above any drain lines on the same branch. There are several methods of doing this, and in some instances you may also have to include a horizontal vent line into which the various fixture vents connect before it connects higher up on the soil stack.

You must then run a vent riser from the branch drain line of any fixture and connect it to the soil stack. Or if you prefer, run it through the roof separately.

After completion of the rough-in of the waste discharge system, block off openings to prevent debris from getting into the pipes and to prevent noxious sewer gases from getting into the house before the fixtures can be installed. You may prefer not to connect to the sewer until the system is completed.

Installing the pressure-system water supply

After the waste system is installed and the holes are cut for the supply lines, it's fairly easy to install the supply system, matching it to the waste system. Start with either a water main and meter, if you are located in a municipality, or with a supply pipe from a well.

The materials used for supply pipe range from galvanized or plain steel to wrought iron, copper, and plastic. The choice will depend on code rulings, availability, and cost. Galvanized steel or iron pipe is normally used to bring the water into the house and is still used in some areas for the house plumbing systems. It's long lasting, but does have several disadvantages, particularly for the do-it-yourselfer. It requires a lot of work and special, expensive tools to cut and install. You can, in some instances, measure the amounts of pipe needed and pay to have the pieces cut and threaded to fit at a plumbing supply store. But this will be expensive and you'll have a pile of pipes to puzzle out the pipe network at home. Most do-it-yourself builders choose either copper or plastic piping.

Copper pipe is one of the easiest-to-use plumbing materials and it is one of the most common. It's available in either rigid or flexible types and can be joined by soldered or flare fittings. The flare fittings and flexible copper piping are easier for the do-it-yourselfer to use, though a bit more expensive. The tools needed for copper pipe installation are not particularly expensive, and with proper attention to details, even a first-timer can install a good system.

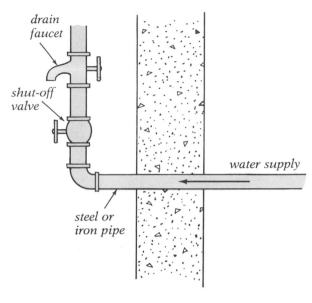

A water supply system must have a shut-off valve and a drain at the point of entry.

Steel plumbing can be installed using precut and threaded pieces, but steel requires hard and cumbersome work.

To assemble a steel system, you must first cut the pipe using a pipe cutter, then thread it with special threading tools. Next apply compound or tape to the threads and tighten the fitting with heavy wrenches. (Photo courtesy Genova, Inc.)

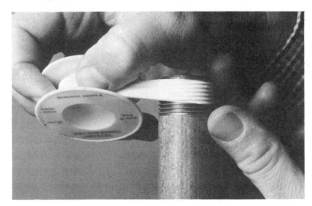

Plastic supply systems can be installed with a handful of tools you probably already have on hand. CPVC (chlorinated polyvinyl chloride) and PB (polybutylene) are the two basic hot and cold water piping thermoplastics. CPVC is a rigid material used for the production of straight lengths of ½- and ¾-inch tubing as well as a variety of fittings and valves.

A rigid copper system is assembled by sweat soldering the fittings to the pipe.

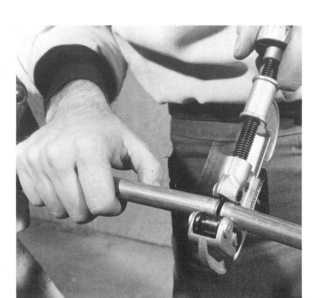

Step 1. *Copper tubing is easily cut with a special pipe-cutting tool.*

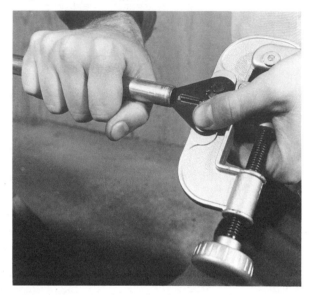

Step 2. *Remove burrs on the inside of the cut ends of copper tubing.*

Step 3. *A flaring tool readies flexible tubing for fitting. Note: The fitting's flare nut must be installed first.*

Step 4. *The handle of the flaring tool is turned to create the flared end on the tubing.*

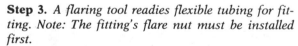

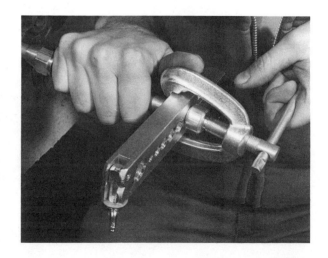

It's easily joined by solvent welding. PB is a flexible thermoplastic material, generally available as coils of flexible tubing. PB cannot be solvent welded but is easily joined mechanically. Both CPVC and PB tubing are designed to withstand continuous operating pressures of 100 psi at water temperatures of 180 degrees.

Both CPVC and PB are impervious to corrosion and mineral buildup within pipes. Plastic pipe can also save energy by retarding heat loss in hot-water supply lines. (Note: Some authorities are worried about the outgassing degradation of plastic over the years and so caution that plastic pipe may eventually be proven ill-advised for use with drinking water.)

Plastic pipe is easy to cut. Almost any fine-toothed saw can be used. (Photo courtesy Genova, Inc.)

Both CPVC and PB plastic pipe come in copper-tubing sizes and can be flared to adapt standard flare fittings. This can enable easy connection at faucets, other fixtures, and appliances. (Photo courtesy Genova, Inc.)

To flare plastic pipe, use a standard flaring tool. Make sure the end to be flared is squarely and cleanly cut. Warm it in boiling water first to prevent cracking. Successful flares have clean edges without cracks where the tube was expanded. Don't forget to install the flare nut before flaring. (Photo courtesy Genova, Inc.)

Step 5. *This is what proper flaring looks like.*

Step 6. *The pipe is joined with the flare fittings. Don't overtighten.*

To bend flexible tubing without kinking, you must use a special bending tool.

There are stringent regulations in local codes governing the sizes of pipes, but the most common are these: main supply (1 inch), hot and cold mains (¾ to 1 inch), branch lines (¾ to ½ inch), fixture branches (½ to ⅜ inch), depending on fixture.

Most municipalities supply water at an average pressure of about 50 psi. With this pressure, the above pipe sizes suffice. If you have less pressure, increase the pipe size a bit.

Fittings

If you use rigid piping you will need a fitting for each direction change. If you use flexible copper or plastic tubing, it can be snaked around to fit most contours, eliminating the cost of fittings and saving the time needed to install them. Reducing the number of fittings also reduces the chances for leaks, which can occur at any fitting.

Several materials that can be used for waste discharge systems including plastic, copper, and cast iron. Fittings are available in each material.

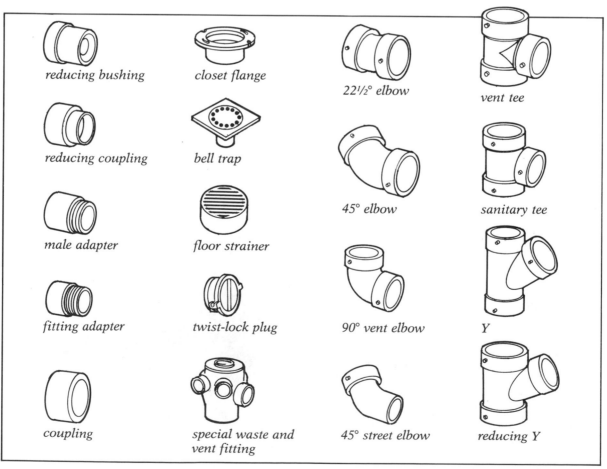

reducing bushing

closet flange

22½° elbow

vent tee

reducing coupling

bell trap

45° elbow

sanitary tee

male adapter

floor strainer

90° vent elbow

Y

fitting adapter

twist-lock plug

coupling

special waste and vent fitting

45° street elbow

reducing Y

The water supply line from the well or water main should have already been installed through the basement wall below the frost line. In a crawl space, the water line must be well insulated to prevent freezing. Install a shutoff valve at the point of entry, and a faucet above it as shown earlier. This allows you to completely shut off the water and drain it from the lines when you need to work on them. If you're connecting to a water main, this is about all that is necessary, although you may be required to leave space for the meter. (In some locales this connection may have to be made by a licensed plumber.)

If you use a well, connect the water supply to the pressure tank (in some cases the pump may be installed first). The rest of the installation is exactly like that of a city-water supply. Make sure any opening in the wall through which the supply line is run is caulked. The next step is to position the hot-water heater near the location of the water entry.

This is a typical pressure water-supply system.

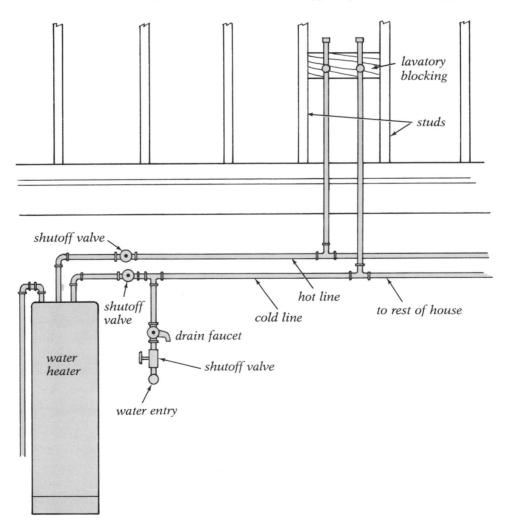

333

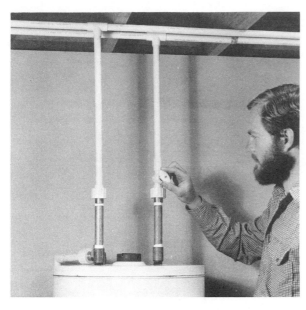

Photo above, the water heater should be next to the water entry point. Continue the entry run to the water heater as shown. Below, install a temperature and relief valve on your water heater. (Photo courtesy Genova, Inc.)

Photo above, with flexible materials, you merely run lines to the various fixture locations. Below, make sure all lines are anchored and supported well. (Photo courtesy Genova, Inc.)

Continue the pipe run to the water heater and provide a Tee—one leg runs to the water heater and the other to the main cold-water supply. Connect a shutoff valve on the hot-water supply side so you can turn the water off to the water heater when you work on it. Install a temperature and relief valve on your water heater (if it doesn't already have one). *This is extremely important.* This safety valve has a pipe that runs down to the floor. It allows steam released to be directed safely away. Join the hot-water outlet pipe to the water heater with a union, and you're ready to make the runs of the hot-water and cold-water supply lines. At this point you can decide to change pipe materials.

With flexible copper, it's merely a matter of snaking the lines along the shortest route possible, yet having them properly concealed and supported in walls and ceilings. Leave plenty of tubing for connections. If you're installing rigid piping, the system is basically the same except it takes more time to cut and join parts to make up the runs.

A good plumbing installation is neat and tidy with no more cutting of the wood structure than necessary. The supply lines are usually installed about eight inches apart; the hot water is on the left-hand side. Provide a shutoff valve at each fixture. This makes it easy to service the fixture. Make sure pipes are pitched downwards towards stop and waste valves in

PART 5. HEAT AND UTILITIES

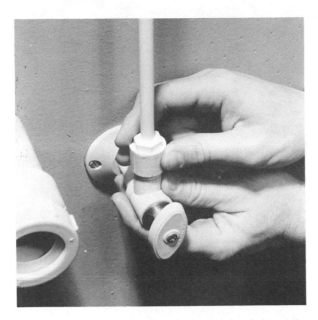

Photo left, finishing may start with the water closets. First install the water-supply lines. Below left, screw the closet flange to the floor. The flange shown has a temporary seal that can be knocked out just before closet installation. Below right, the closet hold-down bolts are positioned in the flange. (Photo courtesy Genova, Inc.)

Below, a wax toilet gasket installed around the outlet horn of the toilet bowl seals the connection between the toilet bowl and the discharge system. (Photo courtesy Genova, Inc.)

Below, lower the prepared bowl squarely onto the toilet flange so that the bolts enter matching holes in the bowl's base. The bowl should contact the floor so that it's square with the wall and centered on the flange. (Photo courtesy Genova, Inc.)

the system. With copper tubing, make sure the tubing doesn't sag. This allows you to completely drain the system.

You must install air chambers on each supply pipe to prevent water hammer. Check and recheck all joints to ensure they're smooth and don't leak. Use freeze-proof faucets for outdoor outlets.

Finishing

The timing of finishing, or installation of the fixtures, varies from job to job. But this is commonly done after the house itself is almost finished. Finish plumbing is not a particularly

hard job, but you should pay attention to the manufacturer's directions to ensure that fixtures are installed properly and that no warranties are violated during installation.

Water closets

These usually consist of a separate tank and bowl. The first step is to install the bowl according to the manufacturer's directions. This means putting a watertight seal between the bottom of the bowl and the floor. You then turn the bowl up onto this seal and fasten it with special floor anchors. The tank is next, and finally the supply line as shown.

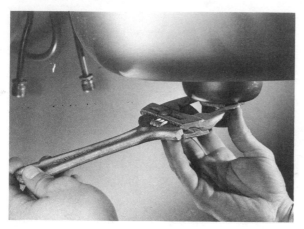

Step 1. *A sink or lavatory connection starts with installation of the sink's basket drains with rings of plumber's putty applied topside. Tighten from below, with washer and gasket in place. A fixture wrench is handy for this job. (Photos courtesy Genova, Inc.)*

Step 2. *Install a continuous drain tee to the sink's tailpiece using a slip jam nut. The best continuous wastes come as units for a center or side opening.*

Step 3. *Next install the connecting drain between sink bowls. Make it watertight with slip jam nuts.*

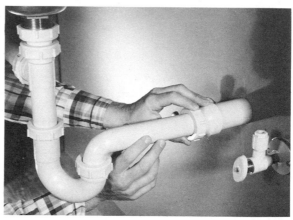

Step 4. *The P-trap can be installed from the outlet of the continuous waste to the waste opening in the wall. Use slip jam nuts.*

Step 5. *Flexible plastic risers with shutoff valves are used to connect to the sink faucet.*

Sinks and lavatories

Sinks that are not on a pedestal or are not supported by a lavatory are anchored to the wall using a special bracket. In most instances, the sink is supported. Lavatories are constructed much as cabinets are, with openings cut in them for the waste and supply lines. The sink is installed in the lavatory and connected to the waste and supply lines.

PART 5. HEAT AND UTILITIES

These are typical sink supplies.

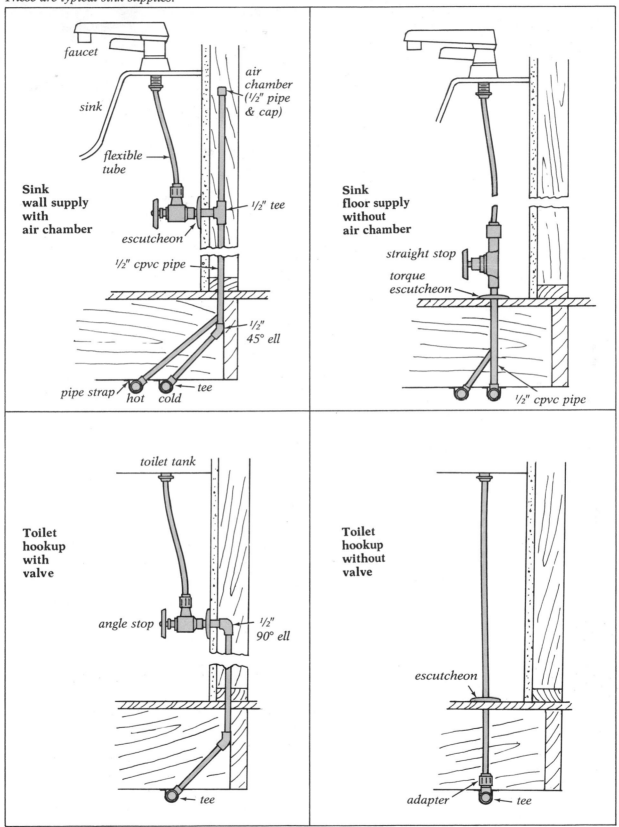

Sink wall supply with air chamber

faucet

sink

air chamber (½" pipe & cap)

flexible tube

½" tee

escutcheon

½" cpvc pipe

½" 45° ell

pipe strap   hot   cold   tee

Sink floor supply without air chamber

straight stop

torque escutcheon

½" cpvc pipe

Toilet hookup with valve

toilet tank

angle stop   ½" 90° ell

tee

Toilet hookup without valve

escutcheon

adapter   tee

Tubs

Manufacturer's directions should be followed for each tub. Often tubs are installed and connected as shown. If there is a shower, install it in accord with tub work. If there is a separate shower unit, you might install it as shown.

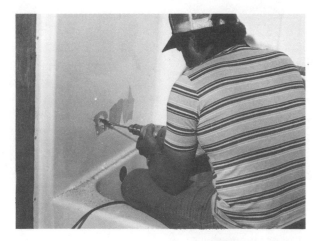

Step 1. *Installation of the tub hookup starts with the boring of holes in wall for faucet locations. (Photo courtesy Genova, Inc.)*

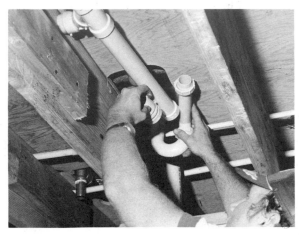

Step 2. *Left, waste runs and vents for a bathtub are connected beneath the floor, under the tub. (Photo courtesy Genova, Inc.)*

Step 4. *A transition union is used to plumb the water to a tub-shower mixing valve. Transition unions compensate for different amounts of thermal expansion/contraction between the metal and plastic. (Photo courtesy Genova, Inc.)*

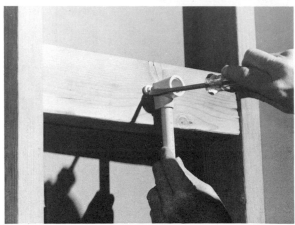

Step 3. *Shower arm plumbing is firmly attached to a crosspiece anchored between studs. (Photo courtesy Genova, Inc.)*

Step 5. *The shower's waste pipe drops through the floor using 2-inch pipe and connects to a 2-inch P-trap. (Photo courtesy Genova, Inc.)*

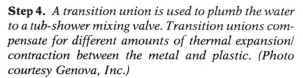

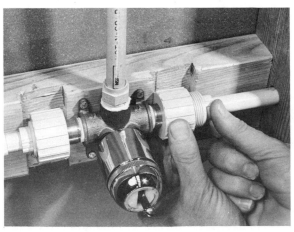

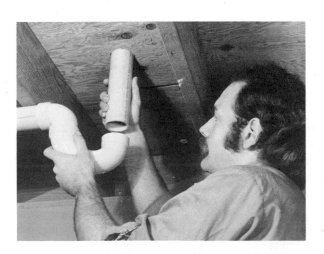

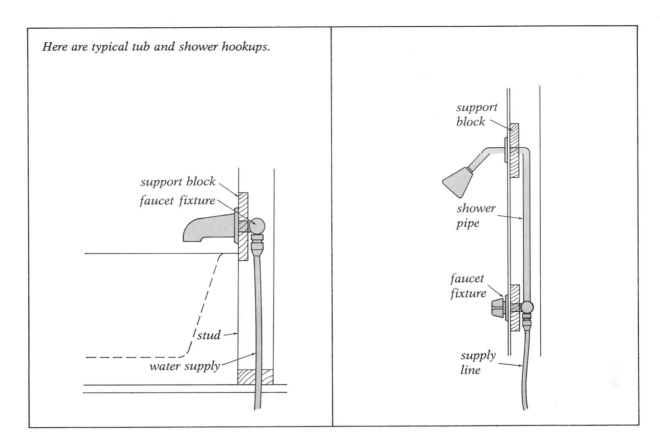

Here are typical tub and shower hookups.

support block
faucet fixture
stud
water supply

support block
shower pipe
faucet fixture
supply line

Insulating the pipes

Any pipes that run through unheated areas should be insulated. You may also insulate hot-water pipes to cut down on heat loss and, thus, energy costs.

For an exterior faucet, drill the log so that the supply pipe drains toward the source. Provide a shutoff inside the house so you can turn off the faucet during freezing weather.

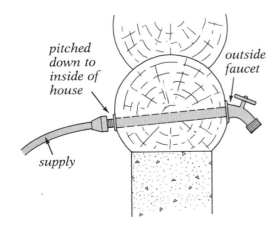

pitched down to inside of house

outside faucet

supply

Chapter 22

WIRING AND LIGHTING

Turning on the power

A dwelling in the wilderness, far from the nearest utility pole and used only infrequently, may need little or no electricity. Here the electricity occasionally needed can be supplied by a gasoline generator. However, people who live in a log home year-round usually insist on having electricity.

Provided you follow safety rules and pay careful attention to every job detail, the wiring of most homes is not particularly strenuous or complicated. However, log homes present special challenges in wiring. Here fixtures and wiring should be positioned and protected from being crushed during settling and shrinkage of the log walls and roof. Also, because log walls are solid, there are no convenient wall openings for wiring runs, fixture outlets, and switch boxes. Two approaches help greatly. The first is to incorporate as much of the wiring as possible in the central core of the house. The second is to make runs and place light switches and outlets in hollow interior stud walls.

Of course, a lot of the wiring can be run through the attic or the basement. Or, you can do as most kit log home suppliers do: Run electrical lines through a recess in the bottom log at the floor. This recess can be covered with a piece of fake log. Or you can cover the recess with a decorative baseboard molding. The recess also allows you to easily install baseboard receptacles or electric baseboard heating.

It's best to do wiring much like plumbing: in two stages. First, rough-in the wiring as the construction progresses. In other words, run all the wires, but don't install fixtures. To provide a light switch at the doorway of an outside log wall, you can bore a hole there in each log as it's installed and then notch the log for the switch box. If you have the wiring well

It's not hard to wire a log home, but you must follow all code and safety rules.

planned, you can thread the wire through as the logs are going up, saving the time and hassle of trying to push the wire through after the wall is finished.

Again, the finishing stage consists of installation of lights and fixtures.

Understanding electricity

You can make electricity a compliant slave in your home. But to do that you must have an understanding of basic electrical principles that result in a safe, efficient job. The high voltage supplied by the utility company is converted either to 120 or 240 volts and comes into your house through the service entrance. This consists of a service panel inside the house that routes power into a number of branch circuits. A meter connected to the service entrance measures the amount of electricity used. The service entrance is fitted with either fuses or circuit breakers to stop the flow of electricity in the event a circuit is overloaded or you want to work on the circuit. Thus, the fuses or circuit breakers allow you to manually cut off electricity to a branch at the service box.

The black and red wires coming in from the service entrance are called *hot* wires and the white wire is called *neutral*. The white wire is always on the return side of the circuit, but current flows through the white wire just as it flows through the other two wires.

Even if you shut off power at the service entrance panel by turning off the main circuit breaker or pulling the main fuse, electricity still comes into the panel on the service entrance side of the fuse or breakers. *So those wires will still be hot.*

There are two basic safety rules governing electrical work: Shut off current to any part of an electrical system before working on it. And be certain you shut off the correct circuit. To ensure that you've shut off the correct circuit, you should perform a simple test using a small tester, even if you are reasonably sure that the circuit is dead. To be doubly sure you can also shut off the power to the entire house by pulling the main fuse or circuit breaker. Even so, test the circuit before working on it.

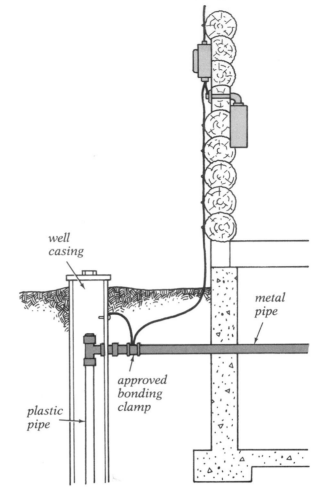

The electrical system must be properly grounded, starting at the service box. As the drawings on these two pages indicate, the ground connects either to an appropriate water supply pipe or to a properly installed metal rod placed deep in the earth outside.

Another important rule is that wires of the same color are to be connected together. Thus you must always connect the black wire to another black wire and the white wire to another white wire. Never break a white wire for a connection, because it must be continuous to provide the ground. This rule can only be broken in certain circuits and must be marked each time it's done.

Wires coming into the service entrance panel normally include a red insulated wire and a black insulated wire, plus a neutral ground wire, which is either white or a twisted uncovered wire. By connecting the black wire and one neutral wire to a branch, you have a 120-volt circuit. However, if you connect the black and red wire to a branch, you have a 240-volt circuit.

342

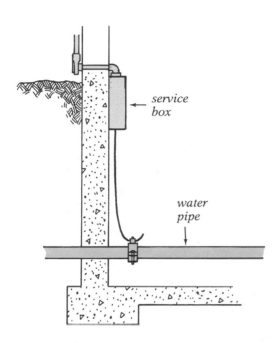

service
box

water
pipe

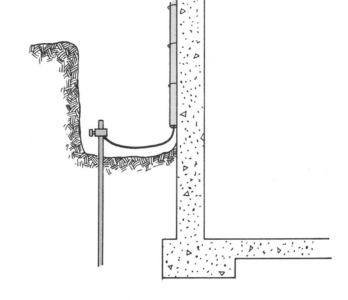

Grounding and safety

The entire electrical system must be properly grounded, starting at the service box. This can be done in several ways. The ground wire, which runs to a metal rod outside in the earth, or to an appropriate water-supply pipe, must be attached to the neutral busbar of the service box. The neutral busbar must be grounded to the service box according to manufacturer's directions.

The rest of your electrical system must also be grounded. The methods for doing this are called *system ground* and *equipment ground*.

Equipment ground. Here, all metal parts of the system are grounded. In raceways of metal, such as conduit, the metal is used as the ground. If you use nonmetallic plastic-sheathed cable, only the system is grounded. However, you must then ground each box, fixture, and receptacle.

System ground. Here, all neutral incoming wire is grounded, and all neutral wires of a circuit are grounded. If you use three-wire conductor with a ground cable and ground all boxes, you have both a system and equipment ground circuit.

Grounding is actually a deliberate connection of the system to the earth, thus *ground*, and is a safety device designed to help prevent shocks and fire. Bathroom, outdoor, or other receptacles that may be subject to moisture should be equipped with a ground-fault circuit interrupter (GFCI). This is a simple device that immediately shuts off the electricity should there be a fault in the ground to the fixture.

The code

All electrical system designs, materials, and working techniques are governed by rules and regulations. Each local area may have its own code rulings and regulations governing elec-

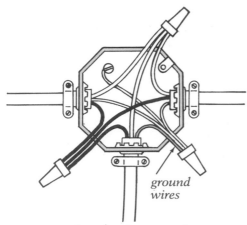

ground
wires

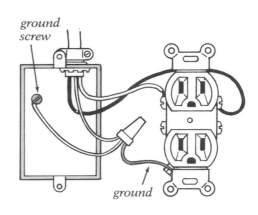

ground
screw

ground

There are several materials to use for wiring runs. Local codes specify which are allowed. As shown, any location where electrical wires must be spliced (joined), or connected to a terminal, electrical fixture, or switch must be enclosed in a box.

The rest of the system must be properly grounded using either a system ground, an equipment ground, or a combination of the two.

trical materials and how they may be used in that area. *The National Electrical Code* book, which is periodically revised to include the latest in materials and information can be obtained at libraries or obtained from the National Fire Protection Association, Batterymarch Park, Quincy, MA 02269. The *Code* provides the information you need to assure a safe, efficient electrical system. Although rules and regulations can be a great help, you'll also need an illustrated guide for do-it-yourselfers, such as my *Basic House Wiring*, available by order through bookstores.

The local codes may also govern what wiring you are allowed to do yourself and what only a licensed electrician may do. In some rural areas, you are allowed to do the entire job yourself. In many municipalities, however, you may not even be allowed to do part of the job. Check with local authorities for information and to obtain necessary permits.

Materials

Wiring. The most common material used for wiring today is nonmetallic-sheathed plastic cable. It may contain two or more plastic-covered copper wires. The sizes most commonly used in house wiring are No. 12 and No. 14. The cable is classified according to the

number of wires in it. For instance, a cable with three No. 14 size wires is called 14–3. A No. 12 wire with two wires plus a ground is called 12–2 with ground.

There are basically two types of plastic-covered cable: NM and NMC. NM may be used only in dry locations and consists of individual wires covered with insulation. Each wire is also spirally wrapped with paper. The entire bundle of wires is wrapped in a fibrous material that is enclosed in a plastic sheath. Type NMC cable is a dual-purpose (wet/dry) cable and so can be used in all types of wiring. It normally consists of individual wires covered with plastic, embedded in a solid-plastic cable. Make sure that the cable you use for wet applications is stamped NMC.

In addition, there is armored cable, which has a spirally-wound steel cable sheathing the wires. Or some locales may specify that wires be run in metal piping called conduit. There are also other kinds of wire for low-voltage and other jobs around the home.

Boxes. The *Code* requires that boxes be used wherever wires are spliced, connected, or attached to electrical equipment. Boxes come in many styles, sizes, and kinds. They may be metal or plastic. The choice depends on local code. Boxes must be securely anchored. The number of wires that can be run into a box is limited by the box design and size, according to code. Your local electrical supplier will be

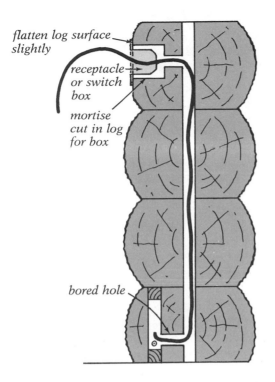

flatten log surface
slightly

receptacle
or switch
box

mortise
cut in log
for box

bored hole

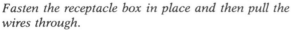

Fasten the receptacle box in place and then pull the wires through.

This is a typical receptacle. It must be grounded.

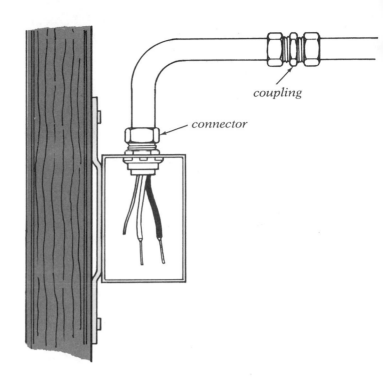

coupling

connector

Conduit should be fed through a connector. Be sure to use conduit that is large enough for the wire.

This is wiring for a typical switch.

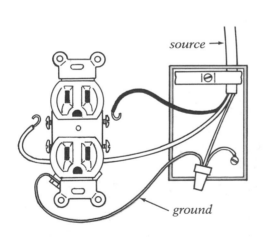

source →

ground

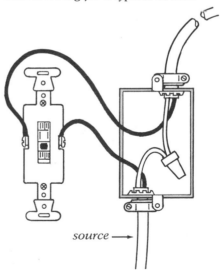

source →

able to help you determine the box sizes you'll need at each location.

Receptacles. These come in different kinds, colors, and styles. But code requires that all receptacles be grounded and that all receptacles have a silver-colored and a brass-

colored terminal, plus a green (or similar) grounding terminal.

Switches and fixtures. Switch types and styles vary greatly. And, of course, the styles of lighting fixtures are almost limitless. Consult your local supplier.

Planning

The first step in planning is to determine your electrical needs. Start with a room-by-room list of services you'll want your electrical system to perform. You can then determine how many outlets you'll need and the amount of other hardware necessary. This is important for several reasons. The first, of course, is convenience. But even more important, later, an overloaded wiring system can be the cause of fires.

Determine the service size necessary by adding up the square feet in your house. It's suggested that there be at least a 20-amp general-purpose circuit for each 500 square feet. In addition, the kitchen and laundry areas should have two separate 20-amp circuits. This is a minimum figure. In most instances, a 100-amp service entrance panel is suggested as a minimum. If you have a full shop or heat your home with electricity, you may need 150- to 200-amp service.

You must have an adequate number of circuits. In almost all cases, it's better to have too many circuits than not enough. Avoid putting all lights in the house on the same circuit. Shown is a typical system of house wiring circuits.

For ease of use and for safety, wall outlets should be spaced no farther than six feet apart (measured horizontally) along walls, dividers, or sliding panels. Floor receptacles can be counted in this six-foot requirement if they are located close to the wall. Counter space in the kitchen and dining room must also have a receptacle, and the wall by the bathroom wash basin must have one. Each family dwelling must also have at least one outdoor receptacle.

In addition to the proper number of outlets and service requirements, you must use the proper size and type of wiring. The minimum wire size by most codes is No. 12 for branch circuits. However, No. 14 may be accepted by some codes. Larger appliances and heating units require larger, heavy-duty wire.

After making up a list of your needs, convert the list into an electrical wiring diagram on the floor plan of your house. Although this diagram doesn't have to be as precise and com-

This floor plan for house wiring could be used as a working drawing for the local inspector.

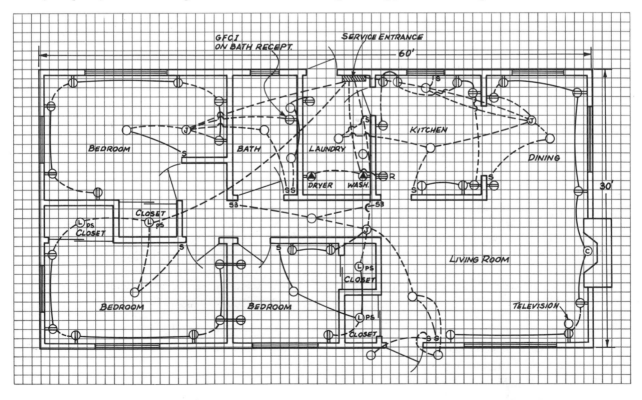

PART 5. HEAT AND UTILITIES

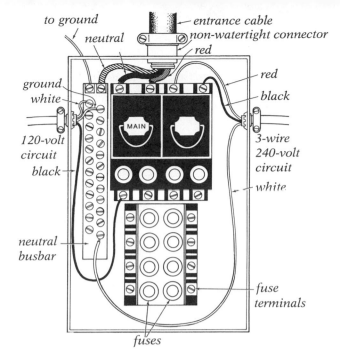
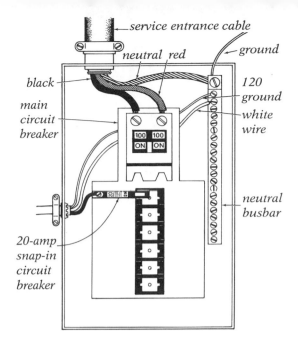

The service panel may be either a fuse box or a circuit-breaker panel.

plicated as the professional plan shown, it should indicate the locations of all switches, receptacles and light fixtures, as well as the routing of the various wires. This can save you a lot on material costs. Also, the diagram gives you an idea of the best method of routing your wires, as well as a preview of any construction problems you might face.

Installation

If you already have temporary power into the home, you can start at the service entrance panel to install the entire system. Individual wires are run for the individual circuits. The boxes are installed. And the inside finish work is done. You can run wires at the time of construction to simplify things, merely running them into the general location of the service entrance and leaving plenty of wire for hookups later. After the inside wall finishing is complete, the fixtures, switches and receptacles are connected to the previously run wires, the individual circuits connected to the service panel, and a test made of the system to make sure it's been installed properly.

Finally, the entrance cable wires are brought in, the meter is installed, and the system is connected. Or you may wish to completely finish the service entrance, except for

the final connections by the utility company outside the house.

Service entrance. The service entrance consists of six major components:

1. The service wire from the utility company to the building or service-entrance pole.

2. The service entrance cable or mast, with individual service entrance wires.

3. The meter socket.

4. A complete disconnect, which allows you to disconnect all power coming in from the utility wire.

5. Overcurrent protection in the form of fuses or circuit breakers.

6. The ground.

There are several methods of installing a service entrance. These are fairly well regulated by local code. There are four main types of installation:

1. Conduit.

2. Mast.

3. Service entrance cable.

4. Underground cable.

After the service entrance has been installed, the entrance panel (service box) is installed. Again, this can be a fuse box or circuit breaker panel. It's firmly anchored in an easily accessible place in the home. The service wires are installed as shown.

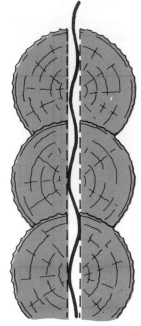

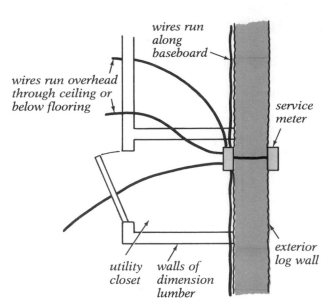

Wiring log homes presents challenges not faced in dimension-lumber homes. All wiring, for instance, must be protected from settling or shrinkage caused by the drying of the logs. You must ensure that wire has an ample channel should walls settle and shrink.

Because log walls are solid, it's impossible to easily make wiring runs. One solution is to incorporate as much of the wiring as possible in a central core.

Ground. The entire system is grounded. The most common method of ground, and the safest, is to run the ground wire to a pipe of an underground cold-water supply system. If at all possible, make the connection on the street side of the water meter so if the meter is removed for repair, the ground remains connected. If this can't be done, install a jumper on the system. The ground should run the shortest distance to the nearest water pipe. The wire should be no smaller than No. 8 and should be securely fastened.

In rural areas or places where a pipe ground is not possible, an alternative is to create a *made ground* by driving a copper rod at least ½ inch in diameter and eight feet long into the ground. Check local codes on this. A wire no larger than No. 6 is clamped to the rod with a copper clamp. It's a good idea to check the ground installation to make sure the ground's resistance does not exceed 25 ohms.

Running the wire. As mentioned before, the running of wires according to your wiring floor plan is merely a matter of threading the wires from the various fixture, receptacle, and switch locations, making sure they

are not pinched in any way. Then fasten the receptacle or switch fixture boxes securely and pull the wires into the boxes, leaving extra length for connection. Of course, make sure all power to any electrical circuits or systems you intend to work on is shut off.

Cable may be threaded through holes bored in a standard stud wall, anchored in place, or routed through holes bored in joists. Ensure, however, you don't weaken any structural members of the house. Cable should be firmly anchored at least every four feet to prevent its sagging.

Pull at least eight inches of extra wire into the boxes at the various locations and bend it over so it can't be pulled out. Make sure you also have enough material for proper connection at the service box. In most cases the wires will have to be turned and threaded considerably inside the service box, so leave extra.

Wiring in conduit is somewhat trickier because you have to make adjustments for the less flexible nature of conduit.

For a simple hunting lodge, you may decide to use exposed wiring. Exposed wiring is simple and fast to install. But it is unsightly and of course is exposed to abuse.

Finishing

After roughing-in the wiring, the next step is to finish the walls and ceilings. You then install the various switches, fixtures, and receptacles and fasten them to their boxes.

Circuit examples. There are many combinations that can be used to wire various circuits. You may want to draw up a "spider legs" diagram to help envision the systems.

After all connections are complete, the circuits are connected into the service entrance panel, shown earlier, *without the service entrance panel connected.* This is done by waiting until all wiring is done, then wiring-in the service entrance panel, or connecting the outside wires of the service utility wires to the service entrance wires. If you already had this done, the main house fuse or circuit breaker can be thrown. The panel entrance wires are hot and you must carefully avoid them.

Heavy-duty wiring. Heavy-duty wiring, such as for an electric range or water heater is installed only by carefully following all manufacturer's instructions.

Testing

Because an improperly-installed electrical system can be dangerous, check your system thoroughly before covering up any portion and turning it on. Make tests to determine that you have the system properly installed. The easiest test uses a couple of dry cell batteries and a door bell wired as shown. You can buy testers that will also do the job. The incoming current from the service panel must be turned off, or it must not be connected.

Lighting

Adequate lighting is very important. Consider room needs before starting your wiring to determine location and number of lights needed for each room. In most instances, every room in the house should have a ceiling light (except for the living room, which is usually lighted by lamps). You may add track lighting

One energy saving step you can take is installation of point-of-use water heaters. These units, often no larger than a desk telephone, heat water on demand.

for more versatility. Make sure there is plenty of light in hallways, basements, closets, and stairs.

Pay particular attention to the lighting in work areas such as kitchens. There should be plenty of light from a good ceiling fixture as well as over the stove, countertop, and sink areas. All lighting in wet areas near kitchen sinks and bathrooms should be properly protected with a ground-fault circuit interrupter (GFCI).

Point-of-use water heaters

Instead of huge water-heating storage tanks hidden in the attic or basement, there are now tankless heaters that can be installed almost anywhere. The units, often no larger than a desk telephone, respond to the demand for hot water placed on the system, rather than on storage of hot water. In other words, these heaters produce hot water only on demand and do not store heated water. The tankless system eliminates stand-by loss and so offers energy savings of up to 50 percent or more.

Chapter 23 **BE YOUR OWN POWER COMPANY**

On your own

Building a log home yourself may be only part of your expression of self-sufficiency. The expression may also include production of your own heat and power. Methods can range from a simple solar-designed log home, to using a solar water heater, to building a photovoltaic system, to damming a small stream for hydroelectric power. Because of the technical complexity of such projects, we can't discuss them in depth here. You'll find sources for more information in the Appendix. Here perhaps a brief survey on the main options will help you decide whether to pursue a subject further.

Generators

The simplest way of creating electrical power is with a gasoline-powered generator. Many hunting and fishing camps use this source of power. Of course, there are several drawbacks, particularly if power must be generated over long periods. The first drawback is the cost and inconvenience of carting gasoline for the generator. The second is the noise, odor, and nuisance that intrude on the quiet and beauty of the backcountry.

The smallest generators are simple hand-carried models that generate AC power for a few lights, a refrigerator, or a rechargeable vehicle battery. Large generators must be trailer-carried; these can meet a houseful of electrical needs.

The simplest way to power a small hunting lodge is to use a portable gasoline-powered generator. (Photo courtesy McCulloch Corp.)

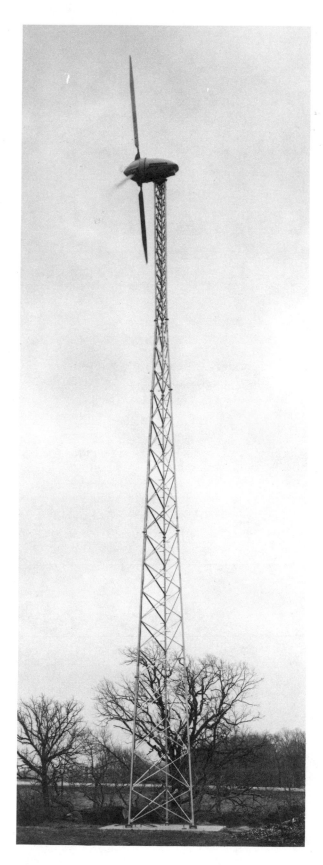

Today's technology provides small, inexpensive wind turbines that can be installed at a vacation home and sophisticated models that can power small homes. (Photo courtesy Windwork, Inc.)

Wind power

For ages man has used wind to produce power. In many parts of the country, windmills still pump water from wells. Many of these old-timers are crude compared to today's wind machines, but they can still pump enough water to keep livestock watertanks filled.

Wind-power technology is advancing rapidly. And wind power is now feasible for creation of electricity for domestic use.

To harness the wind for electricity, you must live in an area that has enough wind to power a generator. You can obtain a rough estimation by writing to the Environmental Data Service, National Climatic Center, Federal Building, Asheville, NC, 28801. For $6 the Service will send their 80-page *Climatic Atlas of the U.S.*, which gives information on wind speeds and prevailing wind directions throughout the U.S.

As a rule, you must have an average wind speed of at least 10 mph to make wind-generated power feasible. However, wind speeds are often localized. That is, your mountaintop location might have plenty of wind, but a nearby valley may get little of it. You can check the average windspeed at your site using a small hand-held measuring device. These range in price from $10 to $30 from Solar Wind Division of Enertech, P.O. Box 420, Norwich, VT 05055.

Probably the biggest disadvantage to wind power is its cost. A lot of sophisticated equipment makes up a wind-powered generating plant, including propeller and generator, tower, lead-acid storage batteries, power conversion unit, and a backup generator to provide power when the batteries are low. Add the cost of labor to install the system and you can end up with an investment of well over $15,000. But if you're more than 2,000 feet from the nearest utility pole and have to pay to bring the electricity line in, the wind-generating plant may actually cost less.

There are some advantages to a wind-powered system. It's quiet and efficient compared to a smelly, noisy gas-powered or diesel-powered generator, and it costs little to operate. Also, it's a nonpolluting source of energy. That can be mighty important when you have fought to buy land in undeveloped backcountry, far from the inroads of civilization. Wind-generating plants can pay for themselves in around four years. Also you can build your own wind-powered plant if you're industrious. This can be done from scratch or from kits. For more information, write the manufacturers listed in the Appendix.

Water power

A lot of work and not a little engineering go into building a safe, efficient hydroelectric plant. There are thousands of small streams across the country that can be harnessed for hydroelectricity.

Advantages? The source of power is normally dependable and constant. Most hydroelectric plants don't require storage capacity.

They are a nonpolluting, efficient source of electricity. And once the initial setup has been made, they're cheap to run. However, installation of a plant large enough to produce electricity for an average home can cost over $15,000, even if you do most of the work yourself. Once the plant is operating, you won't have to pay for electricity from a power company, and you may have extra capacity to sell electricity back to the utility.

Check with local authorities to determine if you can legally dam a small stream on your own property. Then you will probably have to follow strict regulations for construction of the system.

The first step: Determine the water flow and the correct-size turbine to use for the optimum amount of electrical power. You'll be limited in size by the water flow you can create. Larger generators, naturally, generate more electricity. The amount of power you can generate from your stream depends on two things: The volume of water flowing plus the distance the water falls, or the *head*. High flow with a small head and low flow with a high head can give the same amount of power.

Another way to generate power is with water. Small streams can be harnessed to generate power for home use.

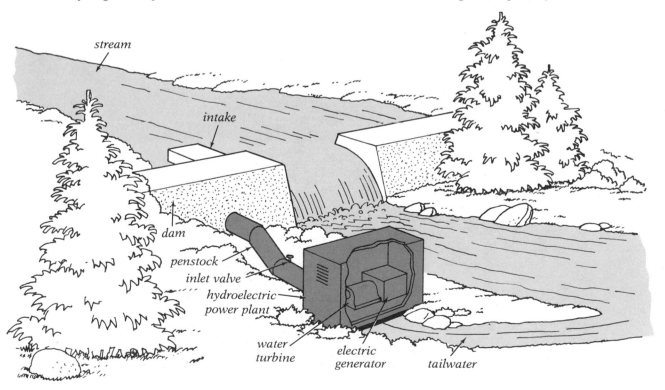

Measure the flow of the stream in early spring when the stream is swollen and during the drier, summer months as well. To measure the average depth and width of the stream, partially fill a bottle with water and allow it to float downstream. Measure the distance it has floated in one minute. Then multiply the average depth by the average width and that product by the distance the bottle travels. Multiply this by the constant 0.8. This gives you an approximation of the cubic feet of flow per minute.

If you aren't lucky enough to have a waterfall on your property, you may have to create more head, which makes the cost higher, by damming the stream to raise the water level. Use a surveyor's transit to determine the head or measure it as shown.

After determining the capacity of your stream and determining that there are no legal impediments for your own hydroelectric plant, the next step is to write the manufacturers of hydroelectric equipment for catalogs and other information. Listed in the Appendix, these companies can provide engineering information that will help you design your system.

Hydraulic ram

Hydraulic rams are almost perpetual energy sources and can be used in areas where stream flow is not strong enough for a hydroelectric plant. You can make your own ram from scratch, or purchase the parts in kit form or already assembled. (Makers are listed in the Appendix.) To help you determine the feasibility of your using a hydraulic ram, manufacturers will need your water-flow data.

Hydraulic rams are fairly easy to install and more economical buy than a hydroelectric plant because they don't use expensive hardware needed for a dam and the plant itself.

DC current

DC (Direct current) is easier and less expensive to produce than AC (alternating current) both in wind-generated electric and hydroelectric plants. However, in almost all instances, you'll probably want to convert the DC power to AC because AC is much more practical. AC is also more economical to trans-

This is a simple way to measure the head.

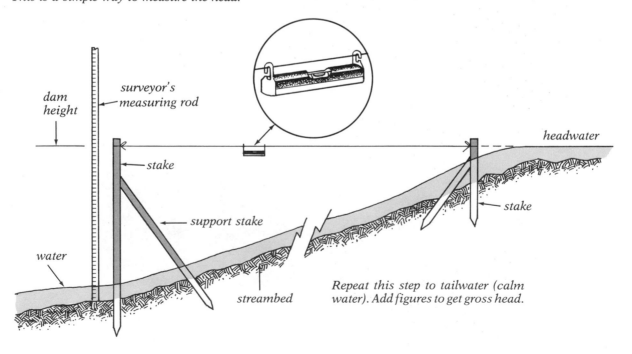

dam height

surveyor's measuring rod

headwater

stake

water

support stake

stake

streambed

Repeat this step to tailwater (calm water). Add figures to get gross head.

mit over long distances. However, the main advantage of AC is that almost all appliances, TVs, lighting, and electrical motors are designed for AC. Rewiring the appliances ordinarily is either too expensive or just not possible.

Solar hot water heating

One of the most feasible and least expensive ways of jumping into alternative energy is to make your own solar water-heating system. This can be anything from a simple coil of black water hose for a shower used at a summer home to a complete year-round hot-water system. For more on solar possibilities, see Chapter 19.

If you have a fairly good flow of water you can also use the water's own pressure to pump water uphill to your home using a venerable and highly efficient, hydraulic ram, shown in the photo below, courtesy Rife Hydraulic Engine Manufacturing Company. The drawing below shows a typical ram installation.

A solar water heater can be simply a coil of black hose used to create a solar hot-water shower or a sophisticated system for year-round use.

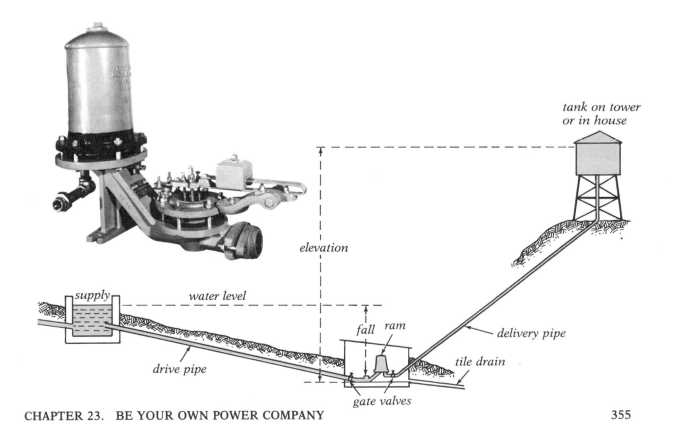

Chapter 24 HEATING WITH WOOD

Home and hearth

A roaring, crackling fire in a huge stone fireplace and the reflective fire glow from interior log walls create an atmosphere that log homes are famous for. Wood heat is a natural way of heating your log home, whether in a fireplace, wood stove, or wood-burning furnace.

Wood as fuel makes sense for several reasons. For one thing, it's a renewable resource. And for many people with a free wood supply, wood greatly helps reduce heating bills. Even if you have to purchase wood, today's efficient fireplaces, stoves, or furnaces, can still save you money.

Make a wood survey of your lot and mark diseased, dead, insect infested, brushy, crooked, or broken hardwood trees. Include wolf trees, that is, large trees with spreading tops that shade a great deal of the understory and so prevent young trees from growing. Little needed, undesirable species, or weed trees can be cut, allowing reducing competition for more desirable species. You should, however, leave a few dead or hollow trees on your woodlot as homes for cavity-nesting wildlife such as squirrels, woodpeckers, and owls.

Other sources of firewood include slash left over from logging operations. Slash can be the tops from trees cut for your log home or left from commercial logging operations on or near your property. Make sure you have permission to cut or remove trees from property other than your own. You may be able to pick up slash and pruned limbs from refuse areas. Sawmills are another good source. They often sell slabs and other waste wood at low cost.

Airtight wood-burning stoves make far more efficient use of fuel wood than stoves of yesteryear.

Also, check with power companies. They may sell the prunings they periodically make near their powerlines.

Firewood may also be available from nearby national or state forests. Check with your local forest officers for guidance and permits.

Which woods to use

Softwoods (conifers), such as pine, fir, or spruce, are easy to ignite. They burn quickly with a hot fire. However, the speed with which they burn and their comparatively lower density and, therefore, lesser mass for combustion make them less desirable than hardwoods (deciduous trees). With softwoods, a fire needs frequent wood replenishment. On the other hand, a softwood fire can be the perfect answer when you want a quick fire to remove the chill from the air. Avoid using scrap lumber and refuse in a fireplace. These materials, especially when dry, produce sparks, which escape up the flue, causing a fire hazard.

Dry wood provides more heat than green, unseasoned wood. There are advantages to drying firewood to a 20 percent moisture content. Stack wood properly and leave it to dry for a year if possible. Warm weather promotes the quickest drying. Most wood of more than four-inch diameter should be split. It should then be stacked so as much of its surface as possible has air flowing around it to draw off moisture bound in the wood. Cover the wood only on the top to keep rain and snow from rewetting it.

The best fire, that is, a fire that is longer-burning, is produced from denser hardwoods such as oak, hickory, locust, maple, birch, or ash. In fireplaces, these species burn unspectacularly and with a short flame, but in stoves they're the best. By combining both softwoods and hardwoods you can regulate the rate of burn.

One cord of hardwood such as ash provides the fuel equivalent of 168 gallons of oil. Dense hardwoods such as white oak can produce the equivalent of 192 gallons of oil. If you want to add aroma to a fireplace fire, add woods from fruit and nut trees. Apple, cherry, hickory, and pecan, for instance, all emit pleasant fruity fragrances.

If you have your own wood lot you can grow and cut a perpetual supply of firewood. Cutting firewood is easy for a log home builder since the tools needed for building, such as a chain saw, can also be used for firewood cutting. (Photo courtesy McCulloch Corp.)

358

Most wood species will not burn well when wet or green. Many swamp grown woods are nearly impossible to ignite unless they have been split and air-dried a good while. For this reason, it's wise to try to cut each year's supply the year before, stacking it to cure for the coming winter. There is roughly an eight percent (by volume) difference between green and seasoned wood.

In the past, firewood was sold by the cord, however, today a lot of it is sold by the bundle at supermarkets or by weight or truckload by commercial dealers. A standard cord of wood measures 4 × 4 × 8 feet; which equals 128 cubic feet, of which only about 80 cubic feet will be solid wood, owing to air space. Wood is often sold by the rick or even by the pile, which can consist of considerably less than a cord.

A face cord is 4 × 8 feet whatever the length of the logs. Most states require the seller to furnish a bill of sale showing the name and address of the purchaser and seller and how many full cords or fractions of cord are involved in the sale. A cord of wood sells for anywhere from $50 to $150 depending on locale, wood species, degree of seasoning, and general availability of firewood in the vicinity.

Cutting, splitting, and seasoning firewood

Wood that is split ignites and burns with a more even heat than logs that are left whole, mainly because it has seasoned properly. Rather than using an axe, split wood with a splitting maul or on stubborn wood with maul and wedges, or with a power splitter. The wood should be split soon after it has been cut. Green wood and frozen wood split much easier than dried wood. If you have a choice for splitting, pick only straight pieces of wood without knots. You can split knotty pieces and those with large crotch sections, but this takes greater effort.

Log splitting by hand may look difficult. But it can be pleasant work. Experienced splitters use a maul of about eight pounds and develop a firm but easy-going rhythm with a balanced stance—feet well apart. With a bit of experience, and after strengthening your hands and forearms and letting your back tone-

up for the constant stooping and lifting, you can split more wood by hand in less time than it takes to set up a splitting machine and load the logs onto the splitter.

To split by hand, stand the log on end, and examine the medullary rays radiating from the center of the log. Also look for splits that air-drying has started. On small diameter logs, strike right in the center, directly over the rays. On larger pieces, if you want to split the log into quarters, strike the back side of the block, then the near side and if the bolt hasn't split, then the center. As soon as the log starts to split, move yourself a quarter circle around the log, or turn it, and strike the near side perpendicular to the first split. Then strike the far side. Often the entire block simply falls into four pieces like a quartered pie. You must have a good splitting maul for this chore. Wrap the

Hand splitting firewood with a maul requires effort all right. A maul with a heavy head allows easier down swings. The hardest parts of the work, though, are the bending and lifting for logs. (Photo courtesy Sotz-Corp.)

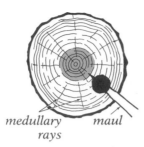

medullary maul
rays

Careful examination of the log end before striking it with the maul can reveal checks, usually along medullary rays, that indicate weakness.

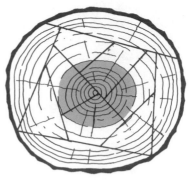

Large logs can often be slabbed, as shown, as you work around the perimeter of the log.

handle near the head with duct tape to help prevent split shards from nicking it up if they scrape the handle while it descends into the split.

There are some tough pieces to split, such as crotch and knot sections. Elm wood, though not very dense, has interlocked fibers that make it extremely difficult to split by hand. These

If you have a lot of firewood to split, you can rent or purchase a power wood splitter (Photo courtesy McCulloch Corp.)

are often best split by a wedge and maul. You may need two wedges if the first wedge becomes pinched in place. The second wedge can be used to open the split further. Switch the two wedges until the log splits. (Always wear safety glasses when striking wedges.)

On large-diameter logs it's usually best to split off side slabs first and then address the center section. Shown in the drawings are some of the tougher splitting problems and how to solve them.

Once you have the wood split, proper stacking will promote rapid air-drying. Small amounts of wood may simply be stacked chimney fashion to allow maximum air circulation. Or you may prefer to stack wood up in ricks. The top should be covered with a tarp or plastic to run off rainwater. If you want to speed up the drying time, you could build a solar dryer.

Wood stoves

Wood stoves can provide an efficient and economical method of heating and cooking. Unless properly installed and operated, however, a wood stove can be a fire hazard. There are hundreds of different styles and sizes, ranging from modern-looking metal designs to ornately-cast models with a 19th century look. Some stoves even have soft soapstone set in their sides to absorb heat and reradiate it slowly, resulting in a more even heat output as the fire dies down.

PART 5. HEAT AND UTILITIES

Wood stoves come in many styles.

By Sotz Corporation

By Atlanta Stove Works, Inc.

By Atlanta Stove Works, Inc.

By Atlanta Stove Works, Inc.

By Atlanta Stove Works, Inc.

By Webster Stove Foundry

By Monarch Appliance Div. Malleable Iron Range Co.

By Atlanta Stove Works, Inc.

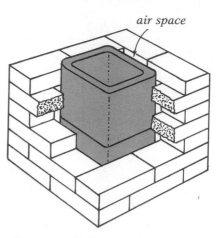

air space

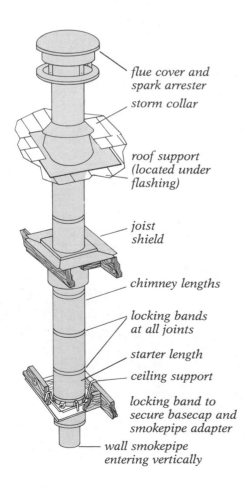

Below, safe operation of a wood stove depends on good stove construction as well as a safe and proper flue. Flues can be either of masonry (right) with flue liner, or a double-insulated metal (below), which is often sold in kit form and is easy to assemble. (Metal-chimney drawing courtesy of Selkirk Metalbestos.)

flue cover and
spark arrester

storm collar

roof support
(located under
flashing)

joist
shield

chimney lengths

locking bands
at all joints

starter length

ceiling support

locking band to
secure basecap and
smokepipe adapter

wall smokepipe
entering vertically

The first installation task is the flue. This can be one of two types: a constructed masonry flue with clay liners or a purchased double-wall, insulated metal flue, usually of stainless steel to retard deterioration. A masonry flue takes more time to install and is harder to keep clean, but is less expensive than the metal, especially stainless steel. A stainless-steel flue, on the other hand, is a safer system because it is less prone to deterioration. Double-wall metal flues have an inner liner and an outer casting, both constructed of high-quality stainless steel with more than two inches of inert mineral fiber insulation. Once installed, flexible retainers at the ends of the chimney sections allow the insulation to form a continuous column of protection. This eliminates hot spots and leaks at the joints, a major cause of chimney fires. Metal flues are sold in kit form by hardware stores and by alternative-energy and building-supply houses. The kits are easy to install.

Stove installation. Select a location out of room traffic patterns and near a door through which you'll bring wood and carry out ashes. The distance of a wood heater from combustible materials can vary, depending on insulating layers. Check the instructions that come with the appliance before positioning it. Where your chimney passes through walls, ceilings, or roofs, use UL-listed insulating materials. Do not use a gas vent (type B) flue with a wood-burning fireplace, even if you plan to install a gas log burner. The chimney diameter should be the same size as, or larger than, the appliance smoke outlet, regardless of the fuel used.

Once you've positioned your appliance, cut through the ceiling, side wall, or cathedral ceiling for the chimney. It's very important to maintain the proper clearances. An insulated chimney can be installed in the open, or enclosed in wooden paneling with just two inches of clearance to combustibles. (Check the manufacturer's specifications before you install.) It's not necessary to enclose the section of insulated chimney pipe that runs from the appliance to the ceiling. Most building codes, however, require that all parts of your insulated chimney running from floor to ceiling must be enclosed. This protects the chimney assembly from impacts. There are no general enclosure requirements for attic and crawl spaces or garages. An attic insulation shield should be used to keep blown or layered insulation away from the chimney. Framing of the chimney passages through walls, the ceiling above the support, and the roof structures must allow two inches of clear space between the insulated stovepipe and the framing material. Use special accessories to hold the chimney in a fixed position and ensure that the required clearance is maintained.

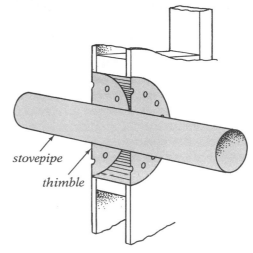

As an alternative to brick, where stovepipe penetrates a wall, ceiling, or floor, you can use a UL listed ventilated, insulated thimble. (Courtesy Woodstock Soapstone Co. Inc.)

Position your stove the proper distance from combustibles. The manufacturer should provide directions. These shown are typical for radiant heaters (those without a separate metal jacket around them). Brick (18-inch radius) around the flue penetration of the wall provides insulation and firestop. (Courtesy Woodstock Soapstone Co. Inc.)

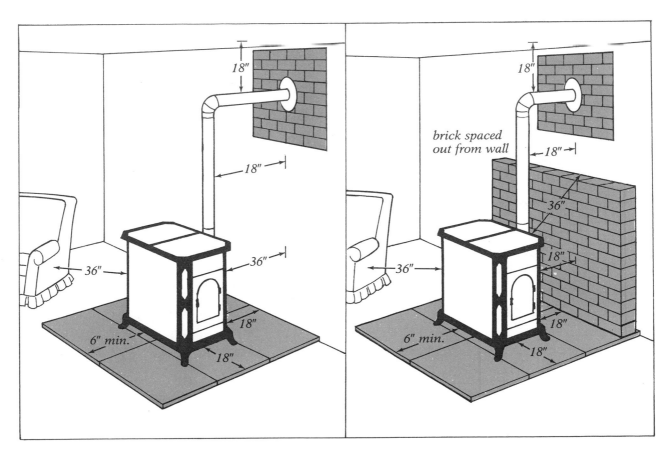

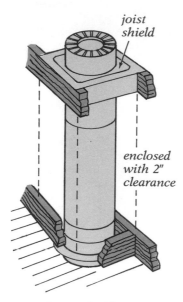

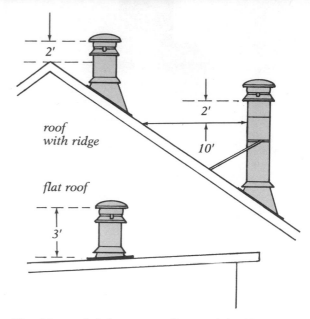

Use an attic insulation shield or joist shield to keep insulation away from the chimney pipe.

The chimney height must conform with building code requirements. Check with local authorities.

Roof flashing must fit the pitch of your roof. By using two rules and a level you can determine the roof pitch. Hold a foot-long ruler level with one end against the roof and measure the number of inches from the other end down to the roof. This gives you the rise per 12 inches of run. Select the appropriate fittings.

Before installation of the chimney, be sure that the height of the chimney is enough to conform to building codes. A chimney must extend at least three feet above the roof, where it passes through the roof, and at least two feet higher than any part of the building within 10 feet.

An improperly installed heating system can void your fire insurance. Look for a metal plate or label attached to the heater that bears the mark or seal of a well-known safety testing laboratory or approval organization. Don't buy a heater that is bigger than you need. If you buy too large a heater, you'll have to burn it slowly. Low fires contribute to the formation of creosote. A moderate fire in a small stove, causes fewer such problems. Look for a heater that has a *heat output in BTUs per hour* rating label which shows that the rating has been established by test. Smaller stoves usually have about a 15,000 Btu rating. Larger stoves may be 50,000.

Consult your appliance installation booklet for placement guides and required distances between the unit and surrounding combusti-

ble materials. The distance can range from zero to 36 inches, depending on design and operation. *Be sure you know the proper clearance for your heating unit before you install it.* If no information is available on clearance, maintain at least 36 inches from walls, woodwork, and furnishings.

Each wood-burning stove, heater, or fireplace should have its *own* chimney. Don't connect other appliances if the stove is designed for open-front use (so you can view the fire) because such a heater functions like a fireplace and needs all the draft possible to prevent smoking. Connecting an airtight, or controlled-draft, wood stove to a chimney that is used for a gas furnace may plug up the chimney with creosote. This could cause carbon monoxide poisoning when the gas furnace is fired. In short, a wood-burning appliance sharing a flue with another appliance can result in big trouble.

The first installation step: Unpack all parts and carefully read instructions on assembly and installation. Count for the presence of all parts. Assemble the appliance according to instructions and then place a trouble light inside it in a darkened room to check for leaks or air holes. Seal any leaks with stove cement. Position the stove on a noncombustible or prepared surface such as bricks or cement patio blocks. It's a good idea to seat the supporting surface on a sheet of asbestos. Fill in joints

PART 5. HEAT AND UTILITIES

Stoves and fireplaces must stand on a hearth of solid brick, stone, or masonry. They should never be placed directly on combustible materials. A special fire-rated stove pad consisting of approved fire resistant material can be used in some instances. (Photo courtesy Preway Inc.)

with mortar. No sparks should be able to find their way down to combustible surfaces. Connect the appliance to the flue using stovepipe sections. You'll usually need one elbow and a damper to complete the installation. The more elbows, the greater the accumulation of ash and creosote at the elbows. Follow manufacturer's directions for assembly, installation, and clearance. You can purchase pipe sections with a damper already installed or buy a damper and bore holes in the metal to install it yourself. The damper should be positioned within a few feet of the stove. Pitch horizontal pipe upward about ¼ inch for each foot of run. Apply stove cement to each joint and fasten each securely with sheet-metal screws. A special heavy-duty metal connector is used to connect the stovepipe to the flue, as shown. If you have high or long runs of horizontal pipe, anchor the pipe to the ceiling with screws and wire wrapped tightly around it. Stovepipe must be at least 18 inches from combustible surfaces.

Fireplaces

To many people, a log home wouldn't be authentic without a fireplace. But old-fashioned fireplaces are only about 10 percent efficient, with almost 90 percent of the potential fuel energy going up the chimney. Today's

modern fireplaces are tremendously more efficient and easier to use.

There are three basic fireplace styles. The first is the masonry fireplace, which the builder constructs from bricks or stone using firebrick to line the entire inner surface. This fireplace continues up with a full masonry chimney and flue. But the building of such a fireplace requires a great deal of masonry expertise and a thorough understanding of fireplace design. It can cause trouble for a first-time builder. If the fireplace isn't designed properly it'll smoke, or not draw properly.

In the past, fireplace flues were little more than mud and stones.

A competent mason with a knowledge of fireplace design can construct a full masonry fireplace. It's not a job for the average do-it-yourselfer.

A tremendous pile of stones goes into the construction of a fireplace and flue.

The second type of fireplace is the masonry fireplace, using an interior metal liner. The liner forms the inside of the fireplace and allows even a first-timer to construct a good fireplace. Such setups can be fitted with ductwork that makes the fireplace function almost like a circulating furnace. It can provide as much as four times the heat output of a same-size conventional fireplace. There are many fireplace manufacturers noted in the Appendix.

The third type of fireplace is the ready-to-install metal firebox ahd chimney. These allow you to build a working fireplace in almost any room without using masonry. In a typical installation, wood framing supports a metal firebox, complete with firescreen. A lined,

Metal forms provide a heat circulating system (photo below and drawing next page) that draws room air into a heat exchange chamber surrounding the firebox and directs it into the room. (Photo courtesy Heatilator Inc.)

PART 5.   HEAT AND UTILITIES

Zero-clearance fireplaces consist of a manufactured fireplace, which usually also has a heat circulating feature and a metal chimney system. (Photos courtesy Superior Fireplace Co. and Preway Inc.)

You can build a masonry fireplace form and insert a steel box into the opening. This firebox has an auxiliary fan to circulate heated air into the room. (Photo courtesy Atlanta Stove Works, Inc.)

insulated metal flue completes the assembly. The framing is then covered with plywood or particle board, which serves as a base for a decorative covering. The rugged, warm appearance of brick and stone can be simulated with prefabricated fireplaces. All you need is a nonceramic decorative brick or fieldstone such as Z-brick.

Most prefabricated fireplaces are called *zero clearance fireplaces* because their insulating layers allow them to be installed next to woodwork. Before installation, check with your local building inspector. Then follow instructions for installation that comc with the fireplace.

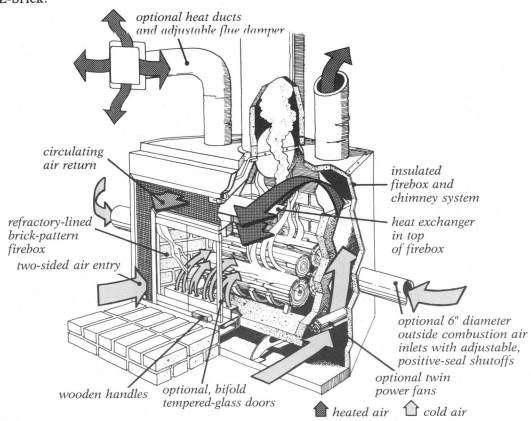

optional heat ducts and adjustable flue damper

circulating air return

insulated firebox and chimney system

refractory-lined brick-pattern firebox

heat exchanger in top of firebox

two-sided air entry

optional 6" diameter outside combustion air inlets with adjustable, positive-seal shutoffs

wooden handles

optional, bifold tempered-glass doors

optional twin power fans

heated air   cold air

Fireplace inserts

Inserts are designed mainly to improve heating efficiency of traditional fireplaces. As the name indicates, they are simply inserted partway or all the way into the fireplace opening and connected to the chimney flue.

The easiest fireplaces to install are insulated, zero-clearance models. They can be installed in almost any spot in the home without the hassle of heavy masonry work. (Photo courtesy Heatilator Inc.)

368

Heating and heat storage apparatus (HAHSA)

There are disadvantages to heating your home with wood-burning stoves and fireplaces. Smoke, wood debris, ashes, and even insects invade the home. And there's always the possibility that a poor installation will lead to a house fire. An alternative is the HAHSA, which stands for Heating and Heat Storage Apparatus. It's a wood-burning furnace that supplies home heat and domestic hot water from outside the home itself. Since the entire unit is outside, away from the house, the house stays cleaner and remains free of wood-burning fire hazards.

The HAHSA is a well-insulated 8 × 10-foot block structure with an airtight fire chamber and two heat exchangers contained in sand. The sand stores heat, so the HAHSA needs to be fired less often. Well-insulated underground pipes carry water to and from the HAHSA. For the manufacturer's address, consult the Appendix.

Coal

Many wood stoves and furnaces can be adapted to burn coal. However, coal is sooty to handle indoors and tends to create extra housecleaning chores. Coal may be cheaper than wood in some areas, but coal is a big emitter of sulphur oxides that react with water vapor to form acid rain.

Wood and multi-fuel furnaces

Wood-burning furnaces and multi-fuel furnaces are growing in popularity. In multi-fuel furnaces the wood-burning and coal firebox is separate from the gas or oil burner, but uses the same flue system. Better multi-fuel furnaces can burn the fuels separately or simultaneously. Installation of these is best left to the pros.

One alternative that many are considering these days is a HAHSA, (heating and heat storage apparatus), which is a furnace hut that sends heated air into your home. (Photo courtesy HAHSA Co.)

Multi-fuel furnaces burn wood, coal, and either oil or gas. Installation should be left to pros. (Photo by Monarch Appliance Division, Malleable Iron Range Co.)

Part 6

LOG HOME KITS
AND SCHOOLS

Chapter 25 KIT-BUILT HOUSES

Right from the box

Cost savings for log houses in precut kits have enabled many folks to afford a home who wouldn't otherwise have been able to. Assembling a kit is one of the fastest and most hassle-free methods of building a home. If you already have the land, all that's necessary is to pick out a home style you desire from the many offered by the kit log home manufacturer. The manufacturer may even help arrange financing. You order your home package and, while waiting for delivery, prepare the site and construct the foundation. Within a matter of weeks, the kit arrives on flatbed trailer trucks. A quality kit can be erected in a matter of days, surely within a month, even by inexperienced builders.

Kit homes allow you to save up to 30 percent of the cost of a contractor-built conventional home. A small one-story, two-bedroom log home package can cost about $10,000, while a large four-bedroom, two-story home may run about $30,000. The cost of a conventional home may cost from $35 to $50 per square foot, and a log home may cost only $25 to $35 per square foot. The cost savings is not in labor alone but in materials as well. For instance, a spacious 4,177 square foot home by Heritage Log Homes, including four bedrooms, four full baths, din-

ing room, den, country kitchen, large master bedroom, loft, family room, and a two-car garage with laundry and shop might go for around $22,000.

Even a contractor-built log home can cost less than a conventional home, mostly because of the speed with which the home can be erected. The total cost of a do-it-yourself log home may amount to 3½ times the package price, compared to 5 times the package price for contractor-built homes.

Precut kits have allowed many people to build their own home who wouldn't have attempted building from scratch. (Photo by New England Log Homes, Inc.)

In addition to the initial cost savings and the reward of building your own home, the low maintenance of a log home contributes to its low cost in the long run. And, of course, the insulating value of logs adds energy efficiency.

Although kit homes are easier to build than from-scratch homes, they still require extensive planning. There are hundreds of kit log home manufacturers. Most are reliable and offer a good product. But as in all of life, usually there are bad apples in the barrel. Shop around when considering a home package. A life savings invested in a house of poor materials or of poor design or shoddy joinery can create big disappointments. Consult several log home companies. Ask about modifying standard plans to suit your life-style. Most companies are willing to make substantial changes to suit individual requirements. In fact, you may be able to send your own design for appraisal and quotation.

You should have little trouble finding log

There are hundreds of designs, sizes, and styles of log homes to choose from, as the home (directly below) from Lincoln Logs Ltd. attests. Bottom, the shaped log home by Alta Industries features a byway to the garage on the right.

Photo next page, kits work well deep in the woods, no matter the style. (Photo: Boyne Falls Log Homes.)

PART 6.   LOG HOME KITS AND SCHOOLS

home manufacturers or log home dealers. Look in the Yellow Pages or watch the home pages of Sunday newspapers. Listed in the Appendix are a number of log home manufacturers. Each has many different styles, sizes, and types of log homes, and each is glad to send you literature.

Purchasing a log home is relatively easy. After the initial planning stages, the next step is financing. Most companies are happy to help you get the financing you need. Although they won't finance the project themselves, they can help provide a financing plan that can be presented to your banker.

There are several types of log home kits: log only kits, complete kits, do-it-yourself kits, fully contractor-built kits, and dozens of variations in between. The log-only kit is exactly that—a package of preshaped logs that can be used to construct the walls. You provide all other materials, including windows, doors, floor, roof framing, and decking (if not of logs).

A complete kit, on the other hand, normally includes doors, windows, floor beams, and roof framing materials. Depending on the manufacturer, it may also include such items as pressure-treated mudsills to seal the building to the foundation, log walls up to eight feet, 12-inch spikes to erect walls, polyfoam insulating sealer, caulking, trusses, and truss studding for roofs. Some manufacturers may throw in gable siding, finishing nails, plywood roof decking, felt paper, asphalt roofing shingles, snowblocks and louvers, a ridge vent, insulated windows, and all doors. All materials for log porches and balconies should be included if they are in the plans of the home. Models with cathedral ceilings should have cathedral-ceiling rafters and collar ties. Accessory materials such as shingles, wiring, plumbing, and interior partitions can usually be purchased locally at a lower cost than if they have to be shipped—and locally you can select the grade and type of material.

Top photo, many home manufacturers sell traditional North American homes in other countries. This Wilderness Log Home stands in Ashikaga, Japan.

Photo second from top, kits may be designed to bring out the beauty of vertical logs. (Photo courtesy Alta Industries Ltd.)

Photo directly below, expansive kit homes can grace any neighborhood (photo courtesy New England Log Homes, Inc.). Bottom photo, kits save you the hassle of finding and shaping logs. All you have to do is follow instructions and stack up the logs. (Photo courtesy Authentic Log Homes Corp.)

PART 6. LOG HOME KITS AND SCHOOLS

Wood

Depending on the manufacturer, logs may be of pine, cedar, spruce, oak, aspen, larch, or cypress. Pine is used in about 80 percent of the log home kits. It's easy to work and has a pleasant odor. Cedar is another excellent log. Some cedar systems, though, use four- to five-inch thick logs, which in a colder climate may mean you'll need double walls for sufficient insulation.

Spruce is also popular. Spruce logs are often cut from standing dead timber, which reduces drying time and shrinkage problems. Spruce, however, is subject to severe cracking and checking. Although some of this is cosmetic, some cracks run entirely through the log, particularly if the log is milled to shape.

Larch, aspen, and cypress are used to lesser

After deciding on the type of home and how much you want included in the kit, the next step is the choice of wood. Pine is popular with many kit manufacturers. It is easy to care for and easy to work with. (Photo courtesy Eureka Log Homes, Inc.)

degrees. Oak is used in some areas but the odor, weight, high value of oak for other purposes limits its use for log homes, although oak is commonly used for hewed-log homes. Oak checks severely, pine not as much, and cedar negligibly. In better-quality kits, all of the bark is removed.

Whole logs or cut logs?

Individual logs for homes may represent whole trees, or several logs may be cut from larger logs. A whole log, with the full heart of the tree, offers the best durability. If the entire heart is in the log, it won't check through in seasoning and it will be more rot-resistant. Cut logs can check entirely through the log. This is less common with cedar but very common with pine, oak, and spruce.

Regardless of the wood, the bark must be removed. This is the hand-peeling process at a New England Log Home plant. (Photo courtesy New England Log Homes, Inc.)

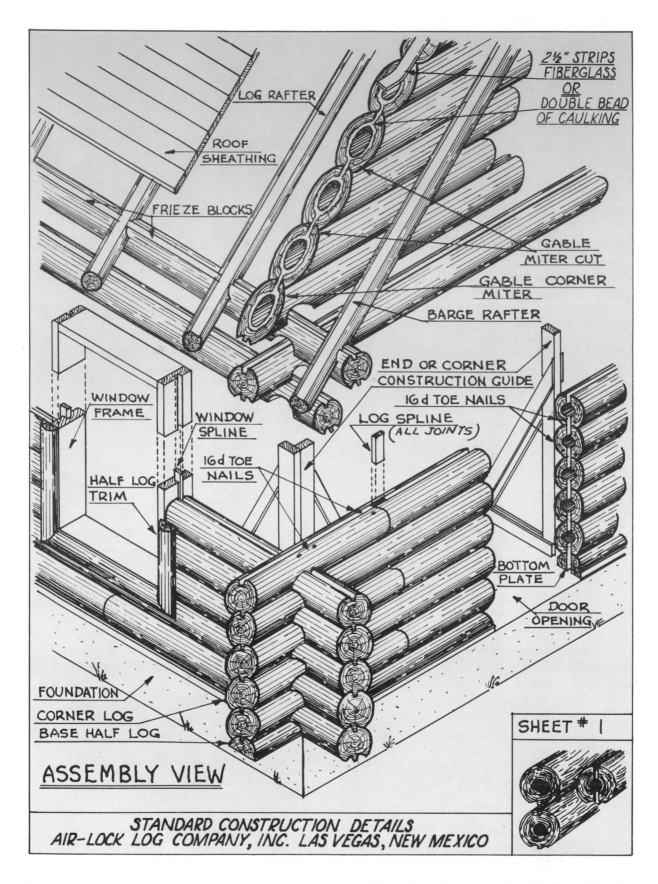

2½" STRIPS
FIBERGLASS
OR
DOUBLE BEAD
OF CAULKING

LOG RAFTER

ROOF
SHEATHING

FRIEZE BLOCKS

GABLE
MITER CUT

GABLE CORNER
MITER

BARGE RAFTER

END OR CORNER
CONSTRUCTION GUIDE

16d TOE NAILS

LOG SPLINE
(ALL JOINTS)

WINDOW
FRAME

WINDOW
SPLINE

16d TOE
NAILS

HALF LOG
TRIM

BOTTOM
PLATE

DOOR
OPENING

FOUNDATION

CORNER LOG

BASE HALF LOG

ASSEMBLY VIEW

SHEET #1

STANDARD CONSTRUCTION DETAILS
AIR-LOCK LOG COMPANY, INC. LAS VEGAS, NEW MEXICO

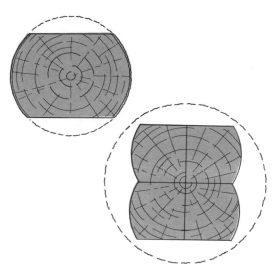

This is a single log cut from a whole tree and four quarters cut from a larger tree.

Logs may be shaped on two, three, or all four sides.

Most kit log homes are made with shaped logs. There are many possible cross-sectional configurations. (Photo courtesy Lok-n-Logs, Inc.)

Justus Homes uses a series of double tongue and grooves in solid red cedar.

Log shapes

Kits with uniform-size logs are more expensive because it takes more effort to mill the logs to the same shape and size. There are definite advantages to uniform-size logs, though. The first is that there are no shelves formed on the inside or outside of the house to catch rainwater or dust and dirt. Using uniform logs saves construction time, and makes installation of interior woodwork much easier.

Kit logs are milled in various cross sections. These are the basic shapes: two-sided, three-sided, four-sided, and completely turned or shaped. A two-sided log has two parallel sides and is normally cut whole from one tree with the heart of the tree left in. These are

Drawing at left, in addition to typical construction styles, kit suppliers offer other wrinkles including this hollow-log design from Air-Lock Log Company, Inc.

usually cut from a tree larger than eight inches in diameter.

Three-sided logs may or may not be cut from a whole tree. In most instances they are not. These logs are usually cut from large trees 24 inches or larger in diameter. All timbers are cut to a uniform size. A four-sided log is usually cut from a larger log, but sometimes a whole tree is used. Turned logs are normally cut from a whole tree, using giant lathes to turn the log to a uniform diameter. These logs range from 6 to 12 inches in diameter. A shaped log is usually four-sided. Three sides are cut flat and the fourth shaped to one of several different designs.

What about the surface-to-surface configuration of logs? In many cases this is simply a flat area with the logs spiked together and a bit of sealant between. Flat log surfaces can use splines or a tongue-and-groove system as shown.

Passive solar collection, wood heat, and fan circulated air system make the Franklin Energy Series an attractive option from Wilderness Log Homes.

Corner joints

The most commonly used corner system is butt-and-lap. With this, one log is butted into another. The next course laps over the first course in a stair step effect as shown earlier. In addition, these corners may be further tightened by a mortise-and-tenon joint. A tongue is provided in the end to fit into the mortise in the opposite log. This makes a strong, weatherproof joint. There are several variations on this joint.

The Justus cedar system uses a vertical dovetail to make up the corner, which provides a totally tight and easy-to-construct system. These homes have red cedar kiln-dried 4 × 8 timbers milled to a double tongue-and-groove shape. They are precision cut and machined to zero tolerance so they lock together sturdily.

There are several other wall systems, including hollow logs, log siding, and double walls. In most instances, the log courses are joined together with spikes every two feet, or there may be a continuous bolt from top to bottom log.

Several manufacturers offer vertical log-construction kits. These are easy to erect, cost less, and have a long life. Splitting is not ordinarily a problem either. They're made of split logs with a flat surface and spline.

Solar

Almost all kit manufacturers offer at least one passive solar home. These homes are engineered to gain a maximum of the sun's heat in winter, while losing a minimum of heat. These same homes are designed to gain a minimum of heat in the summer. As with most direct-gain solar homes, heat collection takes place in a large-glass-enclosed sun room. This heat is absorbed and stored in walls, stone, or other heat sinks. The heat is then transferred to the main living area by natural convection during winter (or ventilated outdoors in summer). Most of these houses feature large south windows with few, if any, windows on the north side. Large southern overhangs are also the norm. Porch roofs block the sun's rays in the summer but, due to the sun's lower arc in winter, act to direct solar rays into the house during the cold months.

Types of home packages

Kit log homes may come as complete turn-key packages, in which you purchase a home from a dealer and he constructs it right down to final details such as carpeting and draper-

PART 6.   LOG HOME KITS AND SCHOOLS

The sun space shown can be sealed off from the rest of the house at night and opened by day for solar collection. (Courtesy New England Log Homes.)

ies. This is the most expensive way to build a log home. Other packages consist of shells constructed by the dealer or a contractor working for the dealer. Here the builder erects a log shell and encloses the house. You do all the finish work such as wiring, plumbing, interior finishing, trimming, and, in some cases, roof shingling. This is an excellent way to get started if you don't have previous house-building experience or the time to construct the shell.

This Custom Greenbrier model is built with square timbers. (Photo courtesy Alta Industries Ltd.)

CHAPTER 25. KIT-BUILT HOUSES

Some do-it-yourselfers prefer the opposite approach: constructing the house shell, then subcontracting other chores. Of course, the more you can do yourself, the greater the saving.

A closed shell usually consists of girders, floor joists, floor insulation, subflooring, perimeter log walls, caulking, windows with screens, exterior doors, roof support systems, roof insulation, roof sheathing, and shingles—plus porches and decks, if included in the plans. In essence, this is everything needed to lock up your home and keep its interior weather resistant.

A complete package generally also includes everything inside the shell, plus interior walls and paneling, trim, doors, door hardware, and hardwood flooring—even the closet rods. A comprehensive package may exclude masonry, plumbing, wiring, heating, and kitchen cabinets.

Kit log homes are delivered to the site on large, 40-foot trailer trucks. So your site must be able to accommodate a truck of this size with enough room to properly unload the materials. Usually, you must have a crew on hand to unload the truck when it arrives because drivers may refuse to be unloaders.

Kit garages are available from Northern Products Log Homes, Inc.

Most home manufacturers offer accessory packages, including decks, as shown.

PART 6.   LOG HOME KITS AND SCHOOLS

Chapter 26 **BUILDING A KIT HOME**

Starting out

You've decided on a kit log home and purchased the package. You have the blueprints and construction manual on hand. Now you can go ahead with site preparation while awaiting delivery. Make sure you have on hand the tools and extra materials you need, as suggested by the construction manual. The house must be laid out and the foundation constructed, again following the manual. Most kit log homes can be built on virtually any conventional kind of foundation. Local building codes and your geographical location dictate what you can use.

Shown on upcoming pages are the typical foundations. The single most important factor in creating the foundation is to make it square, exactly the size indicated by the floor plans or blueprints. One common mistake is to confuse the outside log dimensions of the floor plans with the foundation dimensions. Make sure you understand the exact outside foundation size before beginning.

Taking delivery

You'll need a clear, level area to unload the logs. If the ground is muddy, it's a good idea to place straw over it to protect the logs. Not only must you have a road for the trailer truck to travel over to your site, but you must also have enough room to allow him to turn around and get out. There must also be plenty of space to store the logs. Big trucks are not off-road vehicles. They can get stuck easily. Having a trailer truck pulled out, at your expense, can be quite costly.

Generally, windows and doors are unloaded first. Make sure they are closed and locked before you start moving them. Unload

Many people find that assembling a kit is one of the most economical and practical methods of building a home. (Courtesy of Arkansas Log Homes.)

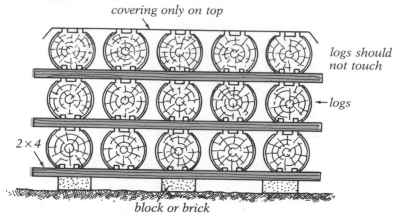

covering only on top

logs should not touch

← logs

2 × 4

block or brick

If the logs will not be used immediately, they must be properly stored, with spacers between them, on blocks or bricks to keep them off the ground. Also, protect the logs from the weather.

them and stand them upright on boards away from the unloading area. They should be protected from weather. Make sure all other breakable items are unloaded before you start with the logs.

The logs are usually tied in bundles that weigh between 3,000 to 6,000 pounds each. Though these bundles can be broken and the logs handed down by hand on log ramps, it's much easier to hire a forklift or a heavy-duty front-end loader for the job. The bundles can be lifted down and set across heavy timbers to keep them level, off the ground. Keep an eye out for loose logs, such as rafters, placed between bundles. Be especially careful when unloading rafters that have birdmouth notches because the ends can be snapped off easily. The carrier generally allows a couple of hours for you to unload the truck. After that you may be charged hourly, depending on the carrier. If you plan your unloading carefully and have help and equipment on hand, the chore shouldn't take more than a couple of hours.

Watch carefully for any damaged materials, especially the more fragile pieces such as windows and doors. If you see damage before unloading, make sure you note it on the freight bill or bill of lading.

Once you have your home on the ground and the truck is pulling out of the driveway, then comes the chore of sorting and identifying all the parts to ensure that you have everything. Along with the log package, you should get an elevation chart identifying each log by course and other components such as windows and doors. Logs and pieces should be sorted into piles. Place the logs around the founda-

tion so you won't have to move them again. Logs should not be piled on floor decks. Make sure the labels on the end of the logs face up. As you sort the logs, check each item off the inventory list or elevation drawing. Watch for areas where more than one log is joined to make up a course. Make sure you have all the logs for that course in place. Logs are seldom broken or damaged to the extent they can't be used, but misfortune does occur. If it happens during unloading, you're responsible. If the logs were damaged before unloading, make sure you note it.

Proper storage of the millwork is important. Because wood swells when wet and shrinks when dry, you should seal all windows and doors as soon as possible after delivery. A good grade of exterior primer followed by at least two coats of exterior oil or latex base paint should suffice. If water-base paint is used, an oil-base primer must be applied first. Or when using a transparent stain, use a semi-transparent stain or clear undercoat exterior, followed by at least two coats of clear sealant such as polyurethane.

You'd probably like to start on your home as soon as possible. If you are delayed, the logs must be properly stored. Stack them on lath strips and allow for ventilation between them and the ground. Cover them well using an opaque tarp with spacers between it and the logs (to allow for air circulation). Store them inside if possible. Storing them in an old building such as a barn, though, can lead to insect infestations.

The logs will probably be fairly clean when they arrive at your site, and with proper un-

PART 6. LOG HOME KITS AND SCHOOLS

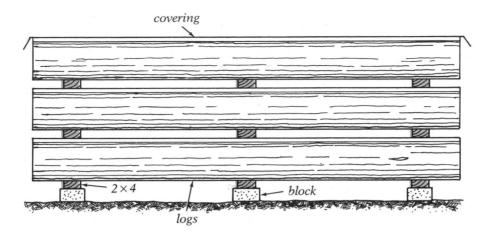

covering

2 × 4   block

logs

loading and handling, they should stay that way. It's a lot easier to keep them clean than try to clean them after they're installed. Trying to wash off a pair of boot tracks from ceiling joists can be quite a hassle.

Technical assistance

Log home manufacturers generally have representatives that can give assistance. This is handled in different ways. Some companies allot a set number of hours of assistance. They may come when you start laying the logs and again when you start putting up rafters. Incidentally, for the first few days, or at least until you really get started, it's easy to get too much help. A couple of helpers will be enough.

One special piece of equipment that may be needed on the job site is a high-sensitivity nail detector. This allows a building inspector to check the location of the building spikes after the walls have been erected. Check with the local building officials to see if a detector is needed. These devices are available from sources listed in the Appendix.

In some cases, construction consists simply of stacking and fastening the logs in place and leaving openings for the windows and doors. (Courtesy of Alta Industries.)

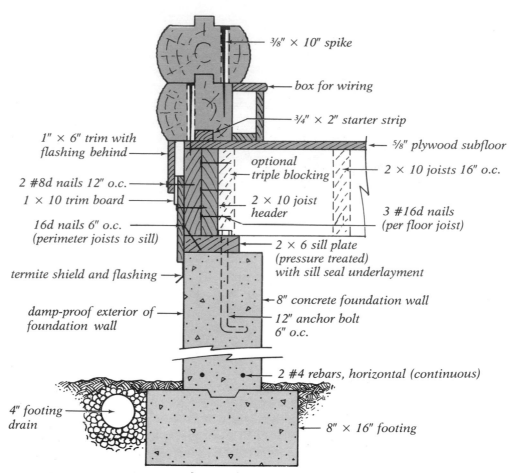

- 3/8" × 10" spike
- box for wiring
- 3/4" × 2" starter strip
- 1" × 6" trim with flashing behind
- 5/8" plywood subfloor
- optional triple blocking
- 2 × 10 joists 16" o.c.
- 2 #8d nails 12" o.c.
- 1 × 10 trim board
- 2 × 10 joist header
- 3 #16d nails (per floor joist)
- 16d nails 6" o.c. (perimeter joists to sill)
- 2 × 6 sill plate (pressure treated) with sill seal underlayment
- termite shield and flashing
- 8" concrete foundation wall
- damp-proof exterior of foundation wall
- 12" anchor bolt 6" o.c.
- 2 #4 rebars, horizontal (continuous)
- 4" footing drain
- 8" × 16" footing

Almost all kit log homes are placed on a box sill on the foundation, unless the foundation is a slab. Alternative foundations are shown in Chapter 6.

Getting started with the walls

If you plan box-sill floor joists and subflooring, you may prefer to wait until the delivery of the logs, to start. Before positioning any logs, take a final check of the foundation or deck, including a diagonal measurement to see how square the construction platform is. Very rarely is a foundation constructed perfectly square and to exact dimensions. The starting sill logs must be positioned square, however, and with the exact dimensions shown on the house blueprints. Do this by laying (but not anchoring) the first sill logs, and then measure the inside dimensions between logs. Shift the logs back and forth to ensure they're square.

Once the exact location of the starting logs is determined, you're ready to install them. There are a number of ways of starting. Some kits have a half-log for the sill. In others, a wooden spline must first be anchored to the deck or foundation, onto which the starting log—with a slot in its bottom—fits. Termite protection and drip-shield flashing are installed at the same time, as well as rubber gasket material or insulation and caulking to seal out water. Make absolutely sure you have the corners square. The starting logs will be the guide for the rest of the house. Starting logs are anchored with spikes or bolts. After the first half-log courses are set, two whole-log courses are installed.

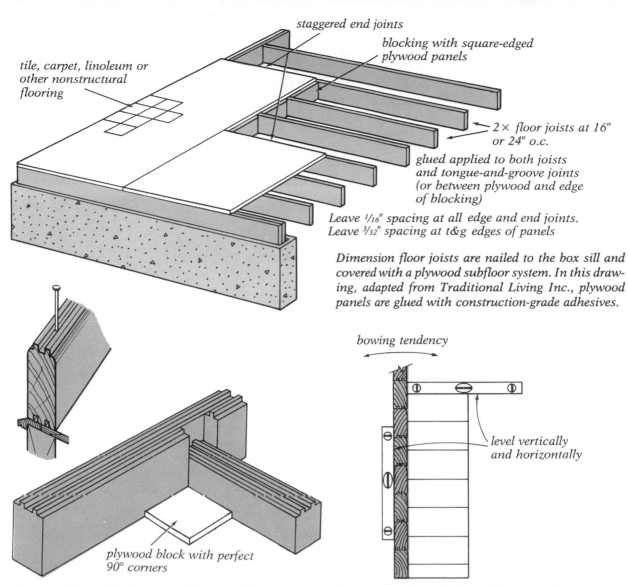

tile, carpet, linoleum or other nonstructural flooring

staggered end joints

blocking with square-edged plywood panels

2× floor joists at 16" or 24" o.c.

glued applied to both joists and tongue-and-groove joints (or between plywood and edge of blocking)

Leave ¹/₁₆" spacing at all edge and end joints. Leave ³/₃₂" spacing at t&g edges of panels

Dimension floor joists are nailed to the box sill and covered with a plywood subfloor system. In this drawing, adapted from Traditional Living Inc., plywood panels are glued with construction-grade adhesives.

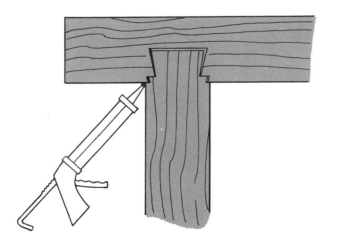

plywood block with perfect 90° corners

Square or flat-surfaced logs are often placed flush with the outside edge of the foundation, on a decorative splash shield or trim piece. And a simple plywood block or carpenter's square can be used on logs with flat inside surfaces to make sure corners are square.

When caulk is used, it's normally applied only on the outside edge of the house corner.

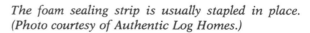
bowing tendency

level vertically and horizontally

Continually check the house for square by measuring diagonally. Check the wall for plumb as each log course is installed.

The foam sealing strip is usually stapled in place. (Photo courtesy of Authentic Log Homes.)

387

PLYWOOD FLOOR SYSTEMS

APA STURD-I-FLOOR

Span Index[1] (maximum joist spacing in inches)	Panel thickness (inches)	Nail size and type	Fastening: Glue-nailed[3] Spacing (inches)		Fastening: Nailed only[3] Spacing (inches)	
			Panel edges	Intermediate	Panel edges	Intermediate
16	5/8	6d deformed shank[2]	12	12	6	10
24	3/4	6d deformed shank[2]	12	12	6	10

[1] Special conditions may impose concentrated loads that require construction in excess of the material shown.
[2] 8d common nails may be substituted.
[3] Use only adhesives conforming to APA Specification AFG-01 applied in accordance with the manufacturers' recommendations.

PLYWOOD UNDERLAYMENT

Plywood Grades and Species Group	Application	Minimum Plywood thickness (inches)	Fastener size and type (set nails 1/16")	Fastener Spacing (inches)	
				panel edges	intermediate
Groups 1, 2, 3, 4, 5 UNDERLAYMENT INT-APA (with interior or exterior glue)	Over plywood subfloor	1/4	18 Ga. staples or 3d ring-shank nails	3	6 each way
UNDERLAYMENT C-C Plugged EXT-APA	Over lumber subfloor or other uneven surfaces	3/8	18 Ga. staples 3d ring-shank nails	3 6	6 each way 8 each way
Same grades as above, but Group 1 only	Over lumber floor up to 4" wide. Face grain must be perpendicular to boards	1/4	18 Ga. staples or 3d ring-shank nails	3	6 each way

GLUED & NAILED PLYWOOD FLOORING

Joist Spacing (inches)	Flooring Type	Plywood Grade and Index	Thickness (inches)
16	Resilient Flooring	Sturd-I-Floor 16" o/c	5/8
	Separate underlayment or structural finish flooring	C-D 32/16, 48/24	1/2, 5/8, 3/4
24	Resilient Flooring	Sturd-I-Floor 24" o/c	3/4, 7/8
	Separate underlayment or structural finish flooring	C-D 48/24	3/4

PLYWOOD SUBFLOORING

Panel Index[1]	Plywood Thickness (inches)	Nail size and type	Nail Spacing (inches)	
			Panel edges	Intermediate
32/16	1/2, 5/8	8d common	6	10
48/24	3/4, 7/8	8d common	6	10

[1] Special conditions may impose concentrated loads that require construction in excess of the material shown.

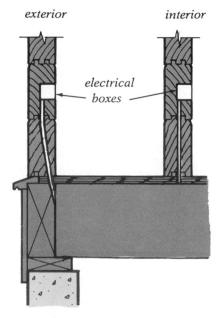

exterior   interior

electrical boxes

All electrical runs must be started with the first perimeter timber log. Bore these holes as soon as the logs are in place and secured, then continue boring on successive logs until you reach the box locations.

Electrical considerations

All electrical wiring that is to be run through the logs must be started now. Using your electrical plans, mark the locations of boxes and runs on the plywood subflooring with a crayon. Measure for each receptacle, and mark that location. Continue to bore the holes and cut the box locations as each log is installed.

Porch joists must also be installed as the first sill logs are installed, and this may take some special notching and on-the-job fitting.

Windows and doors

Once the starting logs are anchored, the doors and (sometimes) windows are located. This usually means the rough frame or the

The chart (left) of plywood floor systems shows recommendations of Traditional Living, Inc.

complete door frame and door unit are positioned, nailed to the decking, plumbed, and then propped sturdily in place. Use a pair of 2 × 4s or 2 × 6s to ensure that the doors or windows are braced properly and don't tilt out of alignment. Make absolutely sure the window and door units are plumb and square. If open bucks or frames are being used, make sure they're square and braced until they're finally locked in place. Note: In some cases the window and door openings are left and the frames merely slid in place after the entire house is roughed in.

Once the doors and windows have been properly located, stack the numbered logs in place. Make sure all log courses are laid up straight and square. Continually check both diagonally for squareness and with a four-foot level for plumb. Put the logs between the window or door units first. Where a complete window unit or open frame is used, the construction generally consists of spline interlocks. If so, drop the logs between windows and frames, fitting them to the spline carefully. Do not use a come-along during this process because you may pull the windows out of alignment or possibly crush or break them.

The foam sealer may run into the corner joint. (Beaver Log Homes)

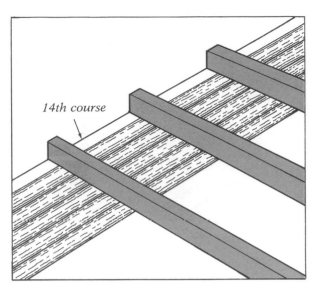

After reaching ceiling height in a home that will have a cathedral ceiling, tie girders go in.

Work on the center section of the wall. Then finish at the corners.

In cases where more than one log is joined, make sure logs are butted together, pulled tightly in place, and nailed securely. In some instances a come-along is needed to pull them together.

During construction, make sure you check the tops and bottoms of each log to ensure that the area where the logs are to be joined doesn't have debris, chips of wood, gravel, or mud that will keep the logs from abutting properly.

If you will have a fireplace, mark its location on the floor decking. In most cases the opening is cut after the walls are erected. Don't install spikes that can inadvertently be cut with a chain saw.

Many manufacturers supply insulation and sealant materials to be placed between log courses. Make sure they are properly installed according to the manufacturer's directions. Make sure all logs are securely spiked or bolted in place as directed.

There may be an inverted top half-log that fits over the ends. This provides a flat and level surface to which dimension gable ends can be fastened.

Predrilling the logs for the spikes can cut down on a lot of labor once installation is started. Make sure you keep the holes staggered from course to course.

As you place logs over the tops of the windows and doors, make sure they are properly fitted with window and door flashing and that the insulation filler is installed properly to allow for settling of the logs and yet keep out weather.

As the log walls go higher, you'll need to use sawhorses with walkboards, a step ladder, or, in some cases, scaffolding. If you must climb on the walls to work, make sure your shoes or boots are clean.

After the walls are completed, start the second floor joists and rafters. It usually takes 13 to 14 log courses to complete a single-story building. If there is to be a loft or second floor, the joists are often logs. These are fitted into notches in the side walls as shown. They must also be supported by support beams as dictated by your blueprints.

This may complete your log kit. You must then purchase rafter framing and decking to complete the home. In other cases, the entire roof framing system may be included, especially if the roof rafters are to be of logs. However, precut dimension rafters may be included with a purchased kit.

Once the beams for the ceiling joists are

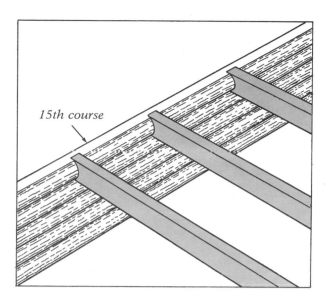

In a single-story home, the tie girders also serve as ceiling joists.

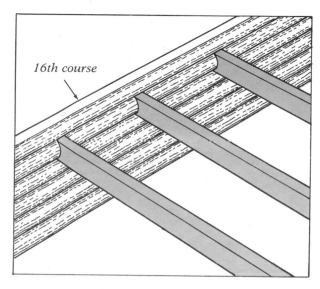

For two-stories, the girders serve as first-floor ceiling joists and second-floor floor joists.

Roof framing may be of logs or dimension lumber. (Photo courtesy of Arkansas Log Homes, Inc. & Traditional Living Inc.)

installed, then the decking is nailed down. Wiring is run to the second story. If the gable ends are to be of logs, they are erected at this time. However, if they're to be of dimension material to match dimension rafters, they're usually erected at the same time the rafters are installed.

This is also a good time to build stairs (usually you must supply them yourself).

Once the floor joists are in place, install the second floor, subfloor and loft decking.

The roof

Before installing the rafters, the second floor joists (or any collar beams or girders that hold the walls together) must be spiked. Otherwise the weight of the rafters will spread the upper walls apart. The porch roofs are constructed so their roofs can be properly tied in with the rest of the house roof. Erect the house rafters in pairs, placing the ridge board or ridge beam between them. In some instances log purlins must first be installed between the gable ends. This is a job that is handled best by more than one person. Install the rafters and nail securely in place. If you're erecting them over a cathedral ceiling, you will need scaffolding.

These are typical methods
of roof framing and adding
porch rafters.

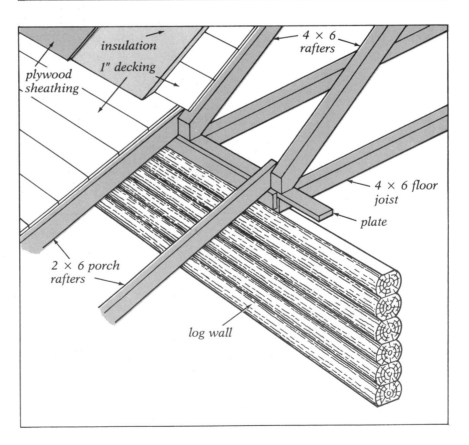

insulation

1" decking

plywood
sheathing

4 × 6
rafters

2 × 6 porch
rafters

log wall

insulation

1" decking

plywood
sheathing

4 × 6
rafters

4 × 6 floor
joist

plate

2 × 6 porch
rafters

log wall

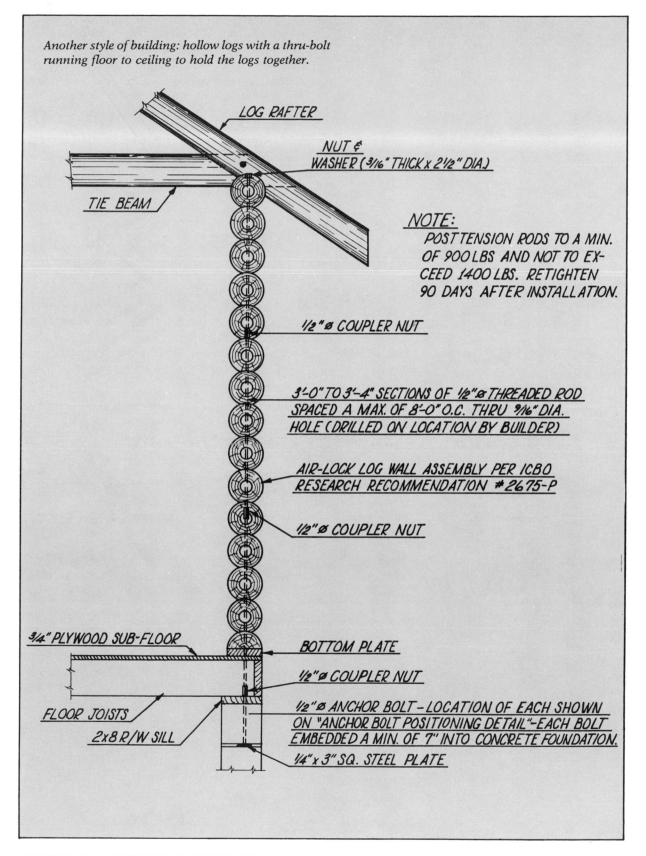

Another style of building: hollow logs with a thru-bolt running floor to ceiling to hold the logs together.

LOG RAFTER

NUT & WASHER (3/16" THICK x 2 1/2" DIA.)

TIE BEAM

NOTE:
POST TENSION RODS TO A MIN. OF 900 LBS AND NOT TO EXCEED 1400 LBS. RETIGHTEN 90 DAYS AFTER INSTALLATION.

1/2"ø COUPLER NUT

3'-0" TO 3'-4" SECTIONS OF 1/2"ø THREADED ROD SPACED A MAX. OF 8'-0" O.C. THRU 9/16" DIA. HOLE (DRILLED ON LOCATION BY BUILDER)

AIR-LOCK LOG WALL ASSEMBLY PER ICBO RESEARCH RECOMMENDATION #2675-P

1/2"ø COUPLER NUT

3/4" PLYWOOD SUB-FLOOR

BOTTOM PLATE

1/2"ø COUPLER NUT

FLOOR JOISTS

2x8 R/W SILL

1/2"ø ANCHOR BOLT-LOCATION OF EACH SHOWN ON "ANCHOR BOLT POSITIONING DETAIL"-EACH BOLT EMBEDDED A MIN. OF 7" INTO CONCRETE FOUNDATION.

1/4" x 3" SQ. STEEL PLATE

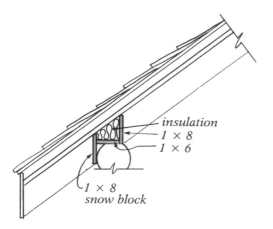

Roof decking, insulation, and roof covering are installed over purlins.

Here log rafters are being installed on a vertical log home. Note the windows have frames but no glass, which will be installed later. (Bellaire Log Homes)

After all rafters are in place, add the snow blocking, or short filler blocks, between them, nailing securely onto the plate log. If the roof overhang is to be left open, not covered with a soffit, snow blocks will usually be short pieces of log to match the rest of the wall logs. These blocks must be sealed in place with caulking.

Constructing the gable ends. From this point on, roof construction is the same as conventional housing, including the addition of the proper decking and insulation.

Interior and finishing

With the house closed in you can take a breather before tackling the next big chore, finishing the interior. In most instances this includes installation of interior partitions, completing the wiring and plumbing, installing trim, applying finish to the logs, and so on. Most interior framing is of dimension material.

Chapter 27 LOG HOME BUILDING SCHOOLS

Open classrooms

Prime evidence of the popularity of log building is the number of log building schools throughout much of the northwestern and northeastern parts of the United States and in Canada. These schools all work from much the same premise: teaching the building of chinkless, round-log style homes. There are some that offer courses on hewed, notched logs as well as *piece-en-piece* and timber framing. There are also schools that specialize in stackwall or cordwood house building.

The schools offer hands-on and classroom instruction in log building. Each of the schools offers a variety of courses, ranging from the basics of log home building to advanced log home design, foundation preparation, roofing, and so forth. Most classes consist of from 7 to 24 students who may range from young couples, to Fortune 500 executives, to grandmothers. The schools accept both men and women. About a third of the students at most schools are women. Beginners learn from hands-on experience how to operate log scribes, which gives the log builder the critical cut lines he or she must follow in shaping a log for a perfect fit. Students also become adept notch cutters. All students work on the construction of buildings.

The students may live on site in tents or in pleasant log homes in parklike settings. Most schools have access to motels in nearby towns. An increasing amount of interest from urban dwellers suggests that more and more log homes will be showing up in city settings.

Most of the courses last from 7 to 10 days, and courses are offered throughout the summer months, or during periods when outside work is feasible. Some schools operate throughout the winter.

One of the best ways to get hands-on log home building experience is to attend a log home building school. (Photo courtesy Minnesota Trailbound School of Log Building.)

The following course schedule from the Minnesota Trailbound School of Log Building indicates the detailed instruction available from the schools:

The ten-day basic log building course (100-plus hours) includes the following:

1. Site preparation, simple foundation work, squaring and leveling.

2. Tree felling with axe and saw, and safety procedures.

3. A thorough acquaintance with all hand tools used in this course, including sharpening techniques.

You'll get instruction in handling power tools such as chain saws. (Photo: Legendary Log Home School.)

Hand tools such as chisels and axes are classroom mainstays. (Photo courtesy Minnesota Trailbound School of Log Building.)

Most instruction is on the scribed, chinkless, long-log style of building. (Photo courtesy Minnesota Trailbound School of Log Building.)

There are also schools specializing in such techniques as cordwood (stackwall) construction. (Photo courtesy Earthwood Building School.)

PART 6. LOG HOME KITS AND SCHOOLS

4. Power saw maintenance, cleaning, sharpening, and how to purchase a new or used saw with all safety features.

5. Demonstrations of several skidding, hauling, and carrying methods.

6. Peeling bark from logs with drawknives and spuds.

7. How to properly construct floors.

8. Experience in full-scribing round logs with double-level log scribers.

9. Removal of channels and notches for a clean "chinkless" fit, using adz, axe, chain saw and various wood chisels.

10. Preparing for and installing doors and windows with regard to log settling and other factors.

11. Fastening logs with handmade pegs in auger-driven holes, and with metal spikes.

12. Notching-in tie beams and second floor structure. Ways to get what you need from the upstairs.

13. Gable log roofs and components: plates, purlins, rafters, ridgepole, various roof support systems.

14. Evening lecture on log building history and techniques.

In addition to basic log-building instruction, such advanced techniques as high log moving is taught. (Photo courtesy Minnesota Trailbound School of Log Building.)

Here is a typical class of log building students and their class project. (Photo courtesy Minnesota Trailbound School of Log Building.)

Most schools teach teamwork and have an old-fashioned barn-raising atmosphere that educates, while offering a relaxing vacation as well. (Photo courtesy Minnesota Trailbound School of Log Building.)

Students add the last log to an 1800-square-foot house in Canada. (Photo: Pat Wolfe Log Building Courses.)

This is a student-built house at Pat Wolfe Log Building Courses.

15. Several field trips to unique log buildings in the Ely-Isabella area.

16. Discussions of wood characteristics such as R-factors, shrinkage, weights, decay resistance, strengths of various tree species.

17. Field trip for tree identification and to clarify above discussion of characteristics.

18. Preservatives and coatings: varnish, linseed oil, chlorine bleach, penta, creosote, etc., with emphasis on hazards versus possible benefits.

19. Various chinking and caulking materials: mosses, clay, cement, oakum, fiberglass.

20. Floor and roof insulation techniques.

21. Demonstration of how porches and additions are attached originally or later.

22. Shingle making and laying.

23. Log lifting systems that can be used by one or two persons—rope and skids, skyline, and knuckleboom hydraulic loader.

If there is extra time, we may do some of the following:

1. Hewing logs flat with broad axe and notching for a full or half dovetail.

2. Exercises in model building and design.

3. Discussion on fireplaces and stoves, homemade and store-bought.

4. Making simple log furniture: tables, benches, shelves, coat racks, etc.

5. Discussion of a simple wind generator that powers one cabin at the camp.

6. Spring courses may spend a few hours planting tree seedlings in the local area to replace fivefold the number of trees annually cut for building on the courses.

If you want to build your own log home, but feel you need some hands-on experience before you jump into it, attend one of the schools. For course schedules, details and fees, contact the schools listed in the Appendix.

APPENDIX: SOURCES FOR MATERIALS AND INFORMATION

TOOLS

Foley Belsaw
(sawmills, wood planers, saw sharpeners)
6301 Equitable Road, Box 593
Kansas City, MO 64141

Hurdle Machine Works
(sawmill)
Hwy 57
Moscow, TN 38057

Laskowski Enterprises, Inc.
(sawmills and power tools)
4004 West 10th Street
Indianapolis, IN 46222

Mobile Mfg. Co.
(sawmill)
P. O. Box 258
Troutdale, OR 97060

Meadows Mill Company
(sawmill)
P. O. Box 1288
North Wilkesboro, NC 28659

Morbark Industries, Inc.
(logging equipment)
Box 1000
Winn, MI 48896

The Ross Bandmill
(sawmill)
W. K. Ross, Inc.
Main Street
West Hampstead, NH 03841

The Peavey Manufacturing Co.
(logging equipment)
Box 371
Brewer, ME 04412

Woodcraft Supply Corp.
(log home building tools)
P. O. Box 4000
Woburn, MA 01888

DeepRock Mfg. Co.
(do-it-yourself well-drilling equipment)
2200 Anderson Road
Opelika, AL 36802

Shopsmith Inc.
(multi-purpose shop tool)
750 Center Dr.
Vandalia, OH 45377

Toolmart Corp.
(lathe duplicator)
6840 Shingle Creek Pkwy.
Minneapolis, MN 55430

DOORS AND WINDOWS

Andersen Corp.
Bayport, MN 55003

Hurd Millwork Co.
520 S. Whelen Ave.
Medford, WI 54451

Louisiana Pacific Building Products
324 Wooster Rd. North
Barberton, OH 44203

Norandex Aluminum Building Products
7120 Krick Road
Cleveland, OH 44146

Pella Windows and Doors
102 Main St.
Pella, IA 50219

INTERIOR FINISHING PRODUCTS

American Olean Tile Company
1000 Cannon Avenue
Lansdale, PA 19446

Azrock Floor Products
San Antonio, TX 78206

The Iron Shop
(spiral stair kits)
P. O. Box 128
Broomall, PA 19008

American General Products
(studio stair)
1735 Holmes Road
Ypsilanti, MI 48197

Sykes Flooring Products
Div. Masonite Corporation
29 North Wacker Drive
Chicago, IL 60606

Tile Council of America
(do-it-yourself tile info)
P. O. Box 503
Mahwah, NJ 07430

Woodbridge Ornamental Iron Co.
(staircase)
2715 Clybourn Avenue
Chicago, IL 60614

Zar Finishes
Div. United Gilsonite Labs
P. O. Box 1422
Visalia, CA 93277

PREFABRICATED KITCHEN CABINET AND VANITY UNITS

Belwood Cabinets
Div. U. S. Industry
Hwy. 16 South
Ackerman, MS 39735

Boise Cascade Kitchen Cabinets
P. O. Box 514
Berryville, VA 22611

Haas Cabinet Co.
625 W. Utica St.
Sellersburg, IN 47172

Hager Mfg. Co.
P. O. Box 1117
Mankato, MN 56001

Kitchen Kompact Inc.
KK Plaza
Jeffersonville, IN 47130

Medallion Kitchens Inc.
810 1st Street South
Hopkins, MN 55343

Merillat Industries, Inc.
2075 W. Beecher Rd.
Adrian, MI 49221

Nutone Cabinets
Div. Scovill Mfg. Co.
Madison & Red Bank Rds.
Cincinnati, OH 45227

Quaker Maid Kitchen Cabinets
Div. Tappan Corp.
Route 61
Leesport, PA 19533

Rutt Custom Cabinets
Div. Leigh Products, Inc.
Route 53
Goodville, PA 17528

Style-Line Mfg. Co.
2081 S. 56th St.
West Allis, WI 53219

VT Industries Inc.
1000 Industrial Park
Holstein, IA 51025

Williams Vanity Cabinets
Div. Leigh Products, Inc.
1536 Grant St.
Elkhart, IN 46514

PLUMBING

Clivus Multrum USA, Inc.
(composting toilet)
14A Eliot Street
Cambridge, MA 02138

Enviroscope Corp.
(composting toilet)
711 West 17th Street, #F-8
Costa Mesa, CA 92627

Genova, Inc.
(plastic pipe, fittings, guttering)
7034 East Court Street, Box 308
Davison, MI 48423-0309

Humus 80
(composting toilet)
The Energy Alternative
P. O. Box 15 Downtown
Mongo, IN 46771

Tankless Heater Corp.
Melrose Square
Greenwich, CT 06830

HEATING AND COOLING

Atlanta Stove Works, Inc.
P. O. Box 5254
Atlanta, GA 30307

Catalytic Damper Corporation
Front and Prairie Streets
Conway, AR 72032

Ceramic Radiant Heat
Pleasant Drive
Lochmere, NH 03252

Chromalox Comfort Conditioning Div.
Emerson Electric Co.
8100 W. Florissant
St. Louis, MO 63136

HAHSA Co.
Falls, PA 18615

Hearthstone
RFD #1
Morrisville, VT 05661

Heatilator, Inc.
Mount Pleasant, IA 52641

Kingwood Furnaces
Basic Energy Systems, Inc.
P. O. Box 48
Des Moines, IA 50301

Majestic Company
245 Erie Street
Huntington, IN 46750

Monarch Ranges and Heaters
Malleable Iron Range Co.
Beaver Dam, WI 53916

Pacific Lamp & Stove Co.
Box 30610
Seattle, WA 98103

Preway, Inc.
1430 Second St. North
Wisconsin Rapids, WI 54494

Selkirk Metalbestos
(flue pipe)
Wallace Murray Corp.
P. O. Box 372
Nampa, ID 83651

Sotz Corporation
13600 N. Station Road
Columbia Station, OH 44028

Superior Fireplaces
Div. of Mobex Corp.
4325 Artesia Ave.
Fullerton, CA 92633

Thermograte Enterprises, Inc.
51 Iona Lane
St. Paul, MN 55117

U. S. Stove Co.
P. O. Box 151
S. Pittsburgh, TN 37380

Webster Stove Foundry
1827 S. Kingshighway
St. Louis, MO 63110

Woodstock Soapstone Co. Inc.
Route 4, Box 223
Woodstock, VT 05091

ALTERNATE ENERGY

Windmills, wind generators, inverters & supplies

Dempster Industries Inc.
Box 848
Beatrice, NB 68301

Windworks, Inc.
Route 3, Box 44A
Mukwonago, WI 53149

Thermax Corporation
One Mill Street
Burlington, VT 05401

Surplus Center
1000 W. O Street
P. O. Box 82209
Lincoln, NB 68501

Hydraulic rams

Rife Hydraulic Engine Mfg. Co.
Box 367
Millburn, NJ 07041

Solar

Heliotrope General
3733 Kenora Drive
Spring Valley, CA 92077

Hinds International, Inc.
P. O. Box 4327
Portland, OR 97208

Lieffring Sunrooms
7 West 62nd Terrace
Kansas City, MO 64113

National Solar Heating and Cooling
Information Center
Box 1607
Rockville, MD 20850

Raypak, Inc.
31111 Agoura Road
Westlake Village, CA 91361

Sunscreen
Phifer Wire Products, Inc.
P. O. Box 1700
Tuscaloosa, AL 35403-1700

LOG HOME KITS, PLANS AND BLUEPRINTS

Air-Lock Log Company, Inc.
P. O. Box 2506
Las Vegas, NM 87791

Alta Industries Ltd.
Box 88
Halcottsville, NY 12438

American Log Homes, Inc.
Box 535
Bourbon, MO 65441

Authentic Log Homes Corp.
P. O. Box 1288
Laramie, WY 82070

Beaver Log Homes
P. O. Box 1145
Claremore, OK 74017

Bellaire Log Homes
Box 322
Bellaire, MI 49615

Boyne Falls Log Homes
Hwy 131
Boyne Falls, MI 49173

Building With Logs, Ltd.
Box 158
Barrie, Ontario Canada L4M 4T2

Cabin Log Company of America, Inc.
2809 Hwy 167 North
Lafayette, LA 70507

Colorado Log Homes
5295 West 48th Avenue
Denver, CO 80212

Eureka Log Homes, Inc.
Commercial Avenue, Industrial Park
Berryville, AR 72616

Gastineau Log Homes, Inc.
Hwy 54
New Bloomfield, MO 65063

Green Mountain Cabins, Inc.
Box 190
Chester, VT 05143

Heritage Log Homes, Inc.
P. O. Box 610
Gatlinburg, TN 37738

Justus Log Homes, Inc.
P. O. Box 24426
Seattle, WA 98124

Lincoln Logs Ltd.
Gristmill Road
Chestertown, NY 12817

Lodge Log
3200 Gowen Road
Boise, ID 83705

Lok-n-Logs, Inc.
Route 80, RD No. 2, Box 212
Sherburne, NY 13460

Lumber Enterprises, Inc.
75777 Gallatin Road
Bozeman, MT 59715

National Log Construction Co.
P. O. Box 68
Thompson Falls, MT 59873

New England Log Homes, Inc.
2301 State Street
Hamden, CT 06518

New Homestead Log Co.
Industrial Park
Payette, ID 83661

Northeastern Log Homes, Inc.
P. O. Box 46
Kenduskeag, ME 04450

Northern Products Log Homes, Inc.
P. O. Box 616, Bomarc Road
Bangor, ME 04401

R & L Log Building Inc.
Mt. Upton, NY 13809

Rocky Mountain Log Homes
3353 Highway 93 South
Hamilton, MT 59840

Rustic Log Homes, Inc.
1207 Grover Road
Kings Mountain, NC 28086

Rustics of Lindbergh Lake, Inc.
Condon, MT 59826

Traditional Management Company, Inc.
P. O. Box 972
Hanover, NH 03755
   Traditional Log Homes, Inc.
   Vermont Log Buildings, Inc.
   Carolina Log Buildings, Inc.
   Arkansas Log Homes, Inc.
   Real Log Homes, Inc.
   Sierra Log Homes, Inc.

Ward Cabin Company
P. O. Box 72
Houlton, ME 04730

Western Valley Log Homes
P. O. Box D
Hamilton, MT 59840

Wilderness Log Homes
Rt. 2
Plymouth, WI 53073

Association

Log Homes Council
National Association of Homes
  Manufacturers
6521 Arlington Boulevard
Falls Church, VA 22042

LOG BUILDING SCHOOLS

Cornerstones
54 Cumberland Street
Brunswick, ME 04011

Earthwood Building School
Robert L. Roy, Director
RR 1, Box 105
West Chazy, NY 12992

Heartwood Owner-Builder School
Johnson Road
Washington, MA 01235

Indigenous Material Housing Institute
Upper Gagetown,
N. B., Canada EOG 3EO

Legendary Log Home School
P. O. Box 1150
Sisters, OR 97759

B. Allan Mackie
School of Log Building and
  Environmental Center
P. O. Box 1205, Prince George,
British Columbia, Canada V2L 4V3

Minnesota Trailbound School of Log
  Building
3544½ Grand Avenue
Minneapolis, MN 55408

Owner Builder Center
1824 4th Street
Berkeley, CA 94710
  (wood frame building—no log)

Shelter Institute
38 Center Street
Bath, ME 04530

Pat Wolfe Log Building Courses
RR #1
McDonalds Corners, Ontario
Canada KOG 1MO

INDEX